W9-AFE-253

LABOR *and the* NEW DEAL

A Da Capo Press Reprint Series

FRANKLIN D. ROOSEVELT AND THE ERA OF THE NEW DEAL

General Editor: Frank Freidel
Harvard University

LABOR *and the* NEW DEAL

EDITED BY

Milton Derber *and* Edwin Young

DA CAPO PRESS • NEW YORK • 1972

Library of Congress Cataloging in Publication Data

Derber, Milton, ed.
Labor and the New Deal.
(Franklin D. Roosevelt and the era of the New Deal)
Reprint of the 1957 ed.
Bibliography: p.
1. Trade-unions–U. S. 2. Labor and laboring classes–U. S.–1914- I. Young, Edwin, joint ed. II. Title. III. Series.
HD6508.D44 1972 331.88'0973 70-169656
ISBN 0-306-70364-5

This Da Capo Press edition of *Labor and the New Deal* is an unabridged republication of the first edition published in Madison, Wisconsin, in 1957. It is reprinted by special arrangement with the University of Wisconsin Press.

Published by Da Capo Press, Inc.
A Subsidiary of Plenum Publishing Corporation
227 West 17th Street, New York, New York 10011

Manufactured in the United States of America

LABOR *and the* NEW DEAL

ESSAYS BY

Elizabeth Brandeis
Milton Derber
Murray Edelman
R. W. Fleming
Phillips L. Garman
Bernard Karsh
Selig Perlman
Doris E. Pullman
L. Reed Tripp
Richard C. Wilcock
Edwin E. Witte
Edwin Young

A joint project of various members of the Department of Economics, University of Wisconsin, and the Institute of Labor and Industrial Relations, University of Illinois

LABOR *and the* NEW DEAL

EDITED BY

Milton Derber *and* Edwin Young

The University of Wisconsin Press

Madison, 1957

PUBLISHED BY THE
University of Wisconsin Press, Madison

Library of Congress Catalog Card Number 57-9813

Foreword

ALMOST a quarter of a century has elapsed since the dramatic "100 days" which launched Franklin D. Roosevelt's "New Deal." Although the depression decade left a permanent impress on the segment of our population now over the age of thirty-five, for the younger millions who are pouring through our colleges and into our factories and offices the New Deal is little more than a historical name. Yet there is hardly an aspect of current economic life which has not been profoundly influenced by the events of the 1930's, and none perhaps as profoundly as the labor movement and labor relations.

This volume is an endeavor to bring to college students, recent graduates, and other young men and women a realization of what present-day labor institutions owe to developments in the New Deal period. For the older generation as well as for foreign observers of the American labor scene it may also throw these developments into new or clearer perspective.

As the form of the volume indicates, we are not presenting a detailed and all-inclusive historical treatise. Instead, this is a collection of more or less independently written essays designed to analyze and interpret selected aspects of labor relations and the labor movement during the New Deal years and their implications for the present. The topics selected for discussion were those which appealed to the authors as of major significance, but a number of other important topics have been omitted because of the desire to prevent the volume from becoming too large.

Although a considerable amount of documentary study has gone into the volume, the emphasis is less on the uncovering of new facts than on interpretation of available materials. Several of the authors have also been able to present personal experiences and observations not previously in print.

Chapter 1 analyzes the unprecedented growth of organized labor in both industrial and geographical terms and demonstrates that the continued growth after 1939 was largely within the framework of New Deal developments. Chapter 2 traces the forces which created the split in the American Federation of Labor, appraises the favorable and adverse effects of this split for the union movement, and indicates why reunification was finally achieved twenty years later.

Since depression years are invariably a time of increased radical activity, Chapter 3 explores the substantial influence achieved by various radical groups among organizations of unemployed workers and later among the newly formed unions in the mass production industries. It also attempts to assess the long-run impact of the leftists upon the labor movement in the light of their decline after World War II.

One of the major factors in the expansion of organized labor was undoubtedly the encouragement given to unions by the federal government. Chapter 4 analyzes the impact of the Wagner Act in this respect, and also suggests that the Act has had some effects unforeseen and unintended by its authors. Chapter 5 traces the pressures and interests which influenced government labor action during the New Deal and indicates that the labor organizations themselves were a relatively unimportant source of pressure for policy changes. Chapter 6 elaborates this thesis with respect to protective labor legislation and Chapter 7 with respect to social security legislation. Both note, however, the growing interest and influence of the unions in these areas after 1939.

The New Deal period, of course, had a profound effect upon management labor relations policies. Chapter 8 traces important aspects of this impact but also suggests that management itself positively influenced the character of labor relations. Chapter 9 develops the significant changes which occurred in the structure and content of collective bargaining.

In concentrating on a particular period of time, it is easy to forget that the events of that period are the product of past decades. The New Deal period is especially conducive to this failure in perspective. Chapter 10 is designed to demonstrate that the events of the 1930's, despite their dramatic and far-reaching character, are understandable only in the light of the full stream of American labor history.

Foreword

One of the common difficulties of a collection of essays by different authors is that they often vary in basic assumptions, definitions, and concepts, thereby confusing the reader by their apparent inconsistencies and contradictions. We believe that this limitation has been held to a minimum here by the fact that the authors agreed to the following set of basic assumptions:

1. The history of labor during the 1929–39 decade must be regarded as a continuation of its experience in the American environment since the earliest days of the nation.

2. This history is essentially the result of labor's pragmatic trial-and-error adjustments to the changing American environment in the search for "a better deal" in industry and the community, rather than a doctrinaire or ideological struggle for a "new society." This is not to deny that social ideas influenced this development, but these ideas were constantly tested against experience and the doctrinaires never dominated the main current.

3. The labor movement is not a monolithic, homogeneous mass, but an institution comprised of numerous components, many of which have different or even opposing goals and methods.

4. Outstanding personalities (like Gompers, Lewis, and Roosevelt) have unquestionably affected particular events and developments, but the major trends have transcended personalities and have been the product of broad economic, social, and political forces such as the growth of population and markets, the fluctuations of the business cycle, war, and scientific and industrial innovations.

5. Since the eighteenth century (if not earlier) the general course of American history has favored the expansion and deepening of worker rights and dignity.

6. The New Deal was a typical American reaction to the catastrophe of the 1929 depression—pragmatic, nonphilosophical, experimental. But it was a great crystallization, a "social revolution" in keeping with the magnitude of the problems with which it had to deal.

7. The period between 1929 and 1939 saw a quickening of the process of governmental growth, but it was a growth protecting and strengthening democratic capitalism (quite in keeping with past trends) rather than a move in the direction of Communist or fascist totalitarianism.

The writing of the essays was preceded by several group discussions of the objectives and underlying assumptions. Each essay was submitted in draft form to the other members of the team for criticisms and suggestions. However, it should be emphasized that the final responsibility for each essay rests with the individual author.

The authors are collectively indebted to a great many individuals who have read various chapters and made significant criticisms and suggestions for change: Professor Irving Bernstein of the University of California at Los Angeles; Harry M. Douty and Nelson M. Bortz of the Division of Wages and Industrial Relations, U.S. Bureau of Labor Statistics; Professor Arthur H. Cole of the Research Center in Entrepreneurial History at Harvard University; Hiram S. Hall, management consultant; Francis Henson of the International Association of Machinists; Howard S. Kaltenborn of Industrial Relations Counselors Service, Inc.; Sidney Lens of Building Service Employees International Union; Frank Marquart of the United Automobile Workers; Professor Douglass C. North of the University of Washington; Professor Earl G. Planty of the University of Illinois; Frank Rising, management consultant; David J. Saposs, research associate at Harvard University; Professor Joel Seidman of the University of Chicago; and Professor Philip Taft of Brown University. Permission to use published material was granted by *The Annals of the American Academy of Political and Social Science* and The Twentieth Century Fund.

We also wish to express our appreciation to two of our former graduate assistants who helped in the gathering of the data: Frank Delauretis in respect to Chapter 1 and Milferd Lieberthal in respect to Chapter 3. Barbara Dennis, editor of the Illinois Institute of Labor and Industrial Relations, contributed significantly to the editing of the volume.

MILTON DERBER
EDWIN YOUNG

September, 1956

Contents

Tables and Charts

Growth and Expansion

MILTON DERBER

PERHAPS the most significant aspect of the labor movement in the New Deal period was its growth and expansion. At the height of national prosperity in 1929, union membership was estimated at only about 3.4 million. This represented an estimated decline of about 1.7 million from the post–World War I peak, and was the first extended period in which union membership had failed to advance during a time of general economic prosperity. With the onset of the Great Depression, union membership fell further, to a point below 3 million in 1933. By 1939, however, the membership was estimated at over 8 million, and the stage was set for a doubling of this figure in the sixteen war and postwar years which followed.[1]

This general picture of union growth is, of course, well-known. The detailed character of the development is less fully appreciated. If we look at the nation not as a single unit but rather as a collectivity of many separate geographical and industrial parts, we find exceedingly interesting and significant variations which enable us to interpret more intelligently what happened during the New Deal period and the years thereafter. The objective of this essay is to delineate some of these varying strands, to note similarities and differences, and to offer some explanations for them.

Difficulties in Estimating Union Membership

The task we have undertaken is a rather formidable one for two reasons. First, union membership is a tricky subject conceptually and available membership figures do not always mean what they imply. Ordinarily, a union member is defined as one who has paid his dues and other fees and adhered to various other rules in accordance with the constitution and bylaws of his organization. However, there are circumstances in which payment of dues is not necessarily a valid test, and a count of dues-paying members only may seriously underestimate the number of persons actually attached to the labor movement. On the other hand, some union membership claims are unduly loose. During organizing drives, for example, it is common for unions to count as members many who have done no more than sign membership application cards, and dues payment is often not expected until a collective bargaining agreement has been signed. In times of mass unemployment, the names of members are often permitted to remain on the books long after they have ceased dues payment. This is usually given official sanction by change or suspension of the rules. Thus, in a period of dramatic and volatile change, such as characterized the 1930's, a count of union members is likely to involve a hodgepodge of definitions (not to mention deficiencies in record-keeping), and it is difficult to be sure exactly what the statistics mean.[2]

The most reliable indexes of union membership on a large scale are usually to be found in financial reports of separate international unions to their general conventions. These reports reveal per capita tax receipts paid by local unions and ordinarily reflect fairly closely the average monthly or annual membership affiliated with the locals. In general, however, they lead to an underestimate of the number of union members because they do not give proper weight to members who, for a variety of reasons, are partially or completely delinquent but retain a loyalty to the union. Unfortunately, many of the internationals have kept their financial reports confidential, and a complete picture of union membership throughout the country cannot therefore be compiled from them.

The most commonly used statistics, because they are most accessible, are those based upon per capita tax payments to the American Federation of Labor or to its state and city central bodies. The national figures are generally the more satisfactory because they cover all the national and international unions affiliated with the Federation, but they throw little light on the geographical distribution of union members. The state and local statistics are better from a geographical point of view but suffer because they rarely cover all AFL affiliates and frequently omit sizable groups. All of the membership estimates based upon per capita tax payments are further limited by the fact that some unions pay more than their actual membership warrants to increase their voice in the organization or for public relations or other purposes, while many unions understate their membership in order to reduce their financial obligations. The situation is further complicated because unions change their policies in these respects over time. These figures should not be used for year-to-year comparisons; for longer periods they may be more reliable.

The dynamics of the New Deal period magnify the estimation problems. Until 1936 the AFL represented the great body of organized labor, the only major exception being the railroad brotherhoods. But with the rise of the CIO a very considerable proportion of union members was no longer represented in AFL statistics. For the most part, CIO membership statistics are less reliable than those of the AFL, especially for the early years when relatively few contracts had been signed and many union members did not pay dues. The separate unions rarely issued financial reports prior to World War II, and the CIO itself did not report membership data or per capita tax receipts on an individual union basis after its first convention.

In the light of this discussion, it is clear that any analysis of the growth of the labor movement in the New Deal period cannot be based on a strong statistical foundation. The most reliable data will be fragmentary. Much of the trend analysis will be qualitative rather than quantitative in character. It will be necessary to piece together materials from different sources, using different methods of estimation and interpretation. Nevertheless, the fragments are revealing and some valuable insights are feasible.

Extent of Distribution of Union Members in 1929

In 1929 the main concentrations of the estimated 3.4 million members of the American labor movement were found in a relatively small number of industries and areas—the anthracite mines of Pennsylvania; the clothing markets of New York, Chicago, and a few other large cities; the shoe towns of Massachusetts; the major railroad centers; and the building construction and printing industries of some of the large metropolitan areas. At the same time, sprinklings of union groups existed in a vast number of smaller cities and towns throughout the nation. Most of these were small craft or occupational groups—building tradesmen, printers, barbers, musicians, postal employees, firemen, and the like. For the most part they exercised little influence outside of their immediate sphere of activity and often little within it. Collectively, however, they represented a substantial proportion of the total union membership.

Unionism was virtually nonexistent in the large-scale manufacturing sector of the economy. The gains achieved during World War I in meat-packing and the metal industries were almost entirely wiped out after the war as a result of the failure of the steel strike in 1919 and a widespread employer counterattack. In bituminous coal mining and ladies' garments, once-powerful organizations were in distressed positions for reasons to be noted later.

No statistical count is available of the number of communities with labor unions in 1929. Nevertheless, some indication of their spread may be obtained by an examination of locals affiliated with various state federations and city centrals. In Illinois, for example, of the nine cities with populations in excess of 50,000, seven had locals affiliated with the State Federation of Labor; of the fifteen cities with populations between 25,000 and 50,000, twelve had affiliated locals; of the thirty-four cities with populations between 10,000 and 25,000, twenty-one had affiliated locals; and of the 134 communities between 2,500 and 10,000, forty-two had affiliated locals. It is probably safe to conclude that unionism existed in practically every city in excess of 25,000 population, in a substantial majority of the cities between 10,000 and 25,000, and in nearly a third of the cities between 2,500 and 10,000.

Illinois has long been one of the major centers of unionization in the nation. But even less well organized states provide evidence of the widespread character of the labor movement. For example, the Minnesota State Federation had affiliated locals not only in the three major cities of the state but also in five of the eleven cities with populations of between 10,000 and 25,000 and in two of the fifty-nine cities of between 2,500 and 10,000. Similarly, the Texas State Federation had affiliates in all ten cities with over 50,000 population, in five of six cities over 25,000, and in seven of twenty cities over 10,000. Only two of the 123 communities between 2,500 and 10,000 had affiliated locals, however. The picture in California is almost identical. Even in the weakly unionized state of Virginia, central labor bodies existed in eight cities. In virtually every part of the country, except the smaller towns and rural areas, there was some sign of unionism, although it was often extremely limited in size and scope.

Impact of the Great Depression

In the depression years of 1930, 1931, and 1932, the labor movement continued the downward trend of the previous prosperity decade. Dues-paying membership fell precipitously as numerous unionized jobs vanished. The building unions, one of the few groups to grow during the 1920's because of the construction boom, were the greatest sufferers at this time. Nonetheless, the unions managed to "carry" the bulk of their members, and per capita payments to the AFL registered a decline of only about 400,000—a surprising figure in the light of the unemployment situation. In its major centers, union nuclei remained and were ready to take advantage of conditions as soon as they became favorable.

Another major consequence of the depression was the loss of prestige suffered by employers generally and particularly by the large industrialists who had successfully defeated the mass production unions of the World War I period and repelled efforts at new unionization through a combination of power tactics and welfare capitalism. Factory workers throughout the country were embittered and aggrieved. Like the union nuclei, they were ripe for organization when the economic upturn came.

Initial Aspects of the New Deal

Had the economic upturn of 1933 come without the New Deal, there is every reason to believe that unionism would have made some recovery—almost certainly in the old union centers of mining, garment manufacturing, and construction, possibly in new areas as well. But it probably would not have been substantial because the economic advances of 1933 and 1934 were quite limited. For example, the Federal Reserve Board index of industrial production (1935–39 = 100) rose from 57 in 1932 only to 68 in 1933 and to 74 in 1934, virtually the same level as in 1931 and considerably below the 90 of 1930 and the 110 of 1929. The gross national product as estimated by the United States Department of Commerce was lower in 1933 than in 1932, and the 1931 figure of 75.9 billion dollars was not exceeded until 1936. Nonfarm employees in 1933 numbered on the average only a fraction more than in 1932, and the 1934 level was only about 10 per cent higher, in part because of a shorter work week. A significant level of economic recovery was not actually achieved until the middle of 1935.

Labor and the New Deal

The New Deal, however, added to the limited economic recovery a powerful psychological spark of confidence and optimism. To unionism it gave a significant legal support, initially in Section 7(a) of the NIRA and later in the Wagner Act. The result was a boom in unionism which was destined to surpass in both scope and strength all previous union booms including the rise of the Knights of Labor in 1885–86, the first major AFL expansion between 1897 and 1904, and the World War I upsurge in 1916–20. In two years, 1933–34, unionism recovered all the ground lost since about 1923.

The first significant feature of the 1933 union boom was that the immediately effective growth came in the centers where union nuclei were engrained—most notably the bituminous coal mines and the large garment centers. Here was to be a key link between the past and the future. The story in West Virginia is illuminating.[3] Unionism was well established in West Virginia coal mines prior to World War I. It flourished until the mid-twenties when the ill-fated Jacksonville agreement was broken. From 1927 on, the United Mine Workers Union struggled to maintain itself and to regain its strength. A turning point came in 1931 when 12,000 miners in the northern coal fields of the state conducted a successful strike. In January, 1932, the UMW claimed 6,000 members under contract and 12,000 more on strike. The Miners were thus ready to take full advantage of the New Deal. Within nine months of the inauguration of President Roosevelt, practically all mines in the state were operating under union contract. In January, 1936, the UMW claimed 650 locals with 105,000 members in West Virginia. This development was duplicated, with variations, in the other coal fields of the Central States area—Pennsylvania, Ohio, Indiana, and Illinois. Nationwide, according to union reports received by Wolman, the total paid-up and exonerated membership of the UMW rose from 297,769 in 1933 to 528,685 in July, 1934.

The story of the International Ladies Garment Workers Union first in New York and the other major garment centers and then in the smaller communities is equally dramatic. During the late 1920's the ILGWU had been torn apart by the battle between its Socialist and Communist wings, particularly in New York and Chicago. The defeat of the Communists in 1927 and 1928 was achieved at great cost to the union in terms of both members and finance. In 1929 the union made a substantial recovery, but the Great Depression of 1929–32 had a devastating effect. According to Seidman,[4] sweatshop conditions comparable to those of a generation earlier reappeared. ILGWU membership in good standing fell to under 40,000 and "the union was at its lowest point since it had emerged as a powerful, nation-wide organization in 1910." But the hard core of unionism was there. Taking advantage of the NIRA, the ILGWU, through a series of organizing campaigns and strikes, lifted its membership from less than 50,000 in the early months of 1933 to 200,000 by the spring of 1934. Impressive degrees of expansion were also achieved by the Amalgamated Clothing Workers in the men's clothing industry, and, on a smaller scale, by the Cap and Millinery Workers Union, and by the Fur Workers. In each case, the growth occurred first in the large metropolitan centers and then in the outlying areas.

Other established unions, such as the building trades, the printing unions, the railroad organizations, and the unions of public employees, made slower and less dramatic recoveries, partly because they had held their membership more effectively during the 1920's and partly because employment in their industries rose more slowly than in mining and the needle trades. The situation in Peoria, Illinois, indicates what happened where the demand for construction went up rapidly. In this city of 100,000 population, long a center of the distillery industry, the end of Prohibition led to a revival of whiskey and beer production. A number of new plants were erected, all of them under union conditions. It was necessary to recruit building labor from out of town. As a result the membership of the building unions quickly regained and surpassed their 1929 levels. In the nearby city of Decatur, on the other hand, where building continued to lag, the union recovery did not come until about 1936.

Rise of Factory Unionism

Concurrently with the rise of the Miners and the Garment Workers and the partial recovery of some of the other older unions, there was a phenomenal movement to organize among factory workers, service workers, and other groups which had previously been outside union ranks. The exact process through which this occurred has not been studied intensively. Apparently much of the new unionism was "spontaneous." The depression had dug deep into the consciousness of workers; confidence in employers had generally disappeared; grievances were abundant. Energetic, union-minded workers in these establishments—and there were many in autos, rubber, glass, etc.—had ready audiences. The unauthorized but impressive slogan, "President Roosevelt wants you to organize," was distributed through numerous communities and had a great appeal. Newspaper, magazine, and radio accounts of reorganization campaigns by the Miners, Garment Workers, and others had a contagious effect. Unionism was in the air.

Organization of shoe workers in "Yankee City" (Newburyport, Massachusetts) in March, 1933, was probably typical of many communities.[5] Even before Roosevelt's inauguration, unorganized shoe workers had gone out on strike—in one plant for two and a half weeks in January, 1933, and in another plant in early February. Although Newburyport shoe workers were unorganized, unionism had existed for a considerable time in a neighboring shoe town. Warner and Low were not able to determine whether the union from this town took the initiative in organizing the Newburyport plants or whether the latter had called for help. In any event, on March 10, some 300 striking workers from the neighboring community came to Newburyport, marched in front of its shoe factories, and urged the workers to join in a sympathy strike. Meetings with the union's officials followed, an organization was set up, and within two days a month-long strike, involving 1,500 workers in seven factories, began.

The struggle of the nation's factory workers to achieve organizational status was crystallized between 1935 and 1937. It was waged on two fronts—in the convention halls and council rooms of the American Federation of Labor and in the plants of the nation's major industrial cities—Pittsburgh, Chicago-Gary, Detroit, Flint-Pontiac, Akron, etc. The conflict within the AFL leading to the great split and the formation of the CIO is analyzed in Chapter 2. It is important here to emphasize only that the initiative for the CIO came from the leaders of organizations whose origins extended far back into American labor history—Miners, Garment Workers, Typographers. In other words, the "new unionism" of the 1930's, like the "new unionism" of previous generations, was intimately linked to previous institutional developments and not a creation *ab initio*.

This linkage to the past was reflected on the industrial front as well as in the convention halls. After the initial burst of union enthusiasm generated by economic improvement as well as by NIRA and other New Deal measures in 1933, there was a period of uncertainty, confusion, and in many places of setbacks. Union dues-paying membership in 1935 was apparently only slightly above the 1929 level. Partly this was due to the failure of the economy to develop any sustained measure of recovery in late 1933 and 1934; partly it was due to the confusion within AFL ranks as to how to structure the new units; partly it was due to the regaining of confidence among employers and the decision on the part of many of them to try to halt the drive toward unionization by the establishment of company unions, use of labor spies, and discharge of union activists (see Chapter 8). Neither the Labor Boards established by the President to implement Section 7(a) of the NIRA nor the first National Labor Relations Board set up under joint resolution of Congress had strong teeth. And even the National Labor Relations Act of 1935 was ignored and challenged by many companies on the advice of their lawyers until the decision of the U. S. Supreme Court in April, 1937, upholding the constitutionality of the statute.

In some industries like steel and textiles, the leadership and financial support of the old-line unions were paramount in the organizational movement. The Steelworkers Union was the child of the United Mine Workers and the Textile Workers Union was at least a stepchild of the Amalgamated Clothing Workers. In other industries like the Michigan auto plants and the Akron rubber plants, leadership from within the new union groups was largely responsible for breaking through the confusion and achieving recognition, although even in autos and rubber, the advice and assistance of experienced CIO officials at crucial points were of great importance.

The turning point came in 1937 following two years of marked economic improvement, the overwhelming political triumph of the New Deal in 1936, and a wave of successful sit-down and other strikes, most notably in companies like General Motors and Goodyear. The Lewis-Taylor agreement covering the employees of U. S. Steel and the Supreme Court decisions upholding the Wagner Act were decisive factors in shaping the new trend. A number of large corporations —General Motors, United States Rubber, Jones and Laughlin, General Electric—decided to accept unionism and collective bargaining, some in conciliatory fashion, others reluctantly or with bitterness. By the fall of 1937 between 6 and 7 million members were enrolled in the union ranks, a rise of nearly 3 million since 1935 and a near doubling of the 1929 level.

Many corporations, however, did not follow suit immediately as the violent and unsuccessful "Little Steel" strikes of 1937 demonstrated. Indeed, in the cases of "Little Steel," Ford, Goodyear, Westinghouse, Swift, and others of the more resistant corporations, full union recognition and signed agreements were not to be effected until the war emergency year of 1941. Then political and economic pressures, combined with the Supreme Court decision in the H. J. Heinz Company case (requiring collective agreements to be put in the form of signed written contracts) caused most of them to yield.

The main force behind the 1936–37 drive was blunted by the unexpected and sharp recession of late 1937 and 1938. The dues-paying membership of the mass production unions was drastically reduced. Nevertheless, the new unions held firmly to the loyalty of most of their ranks despite the depletion of their treasuries. Even before the rapid economic improvements which resulted from the outbreak of hostilities in Europe in September, 1939, the CIO had regained some of the aggressiveness and initiative which the recession had checked. The CIO claim of 4 million members in 1939 certainly did not apply to dues-paying membership and probably included considerable duplication and inflation even with regard to nonfinancial membership. It is likely, however, that the organization had more "members" in a year in which some 9.5 million were still unemployed than the entire labor movement in the prosperity year of 1929.

The Start of the AFL Counter-Reformation

The rise of unionism among the large-scale, mass production factories of the nation dominated the front pages of the newspapers and generally held the limelight. And properly so. This was the "new unionism" of the day and it represented the first permanent organization of workers in these great establishments in the United States. Steel and packing-house workers had been unionized to some extent prior to World War I and packing-house and metal workers were again organized during World War I, but these organizations were short-lived and the defeat of the steel workers' strike in 1919 had pretty much ended effective union organizing among them until the New Deal period.

Behind the limelight, however, were some important developments in AFL ranks which were to have great significance for the future course of American unionism. The issue of industrial unionism initially confused the leaders of the craft and amalgamated craft unions which had traditionally dominated the Federation. The attempt to organize the new groups of factory workers into local labor unions and national councils and then to parcel them out to the respective crafts did not succeed. This failure was due, among other things, partly to the initiative seized by the proponents of industrial unionism, partly to the pressure of the new union members for action, preferably on industrial union lines, partly to the difficulties of dividing factory workers along craft lines, and partly to ineffective leadership of AFL field representatives. But the success of the CIO unions was a shock and a spur to the leaders of the old-line organizations. They realized that unless they responded to the challenge, the CIO would indeed become the "wave of the future" which its publicists were so loudly proclaiming. Unions like the Machinists, the Electricians, and, to a lesser extent, the Meat Cutters began to organize more widely on an industrial union basis in the factory sphere. The Reformation of the CIO was met by a Counter-Reformation of the AFL which was to take shape gradually in the latter part of the 1930's and very rapidly in the war and postwar years of the 1940's. This development was aided after 1937 by the decision of many employers to do business with the more conservative AFL unions in order to forestall the drives of the more radical CIO group.

The full effects of this Counter-Reformation were not immediately observed because the per capita statistics of the AFL tended to obscure them. Per capita figures seemed to indicate that in 1939 many of the leading AFL unions—in the building trades, the railroads, the street railways, among the Musicians, the Postal Employees, the Printers, and the Barbers—were at about the same level or below the levels existing in the "poor" union year of 1929 and thus were not really sharing in the great advances of the New Deal period. For example, among the building unions, which were by far the largest single group within the Federation, the Carpenters showed a net decline in paid-up membership from 322,000 in 1929 to 300,000 in 1939, the Painters from 108,100 to 100,200, the Bricklayers from 90,000 to 65,000, and the Plumbers from 45,000 to 40,000. Only the Electrical Workers and the Laborers reflected significant advances—the former moving from 142,000 to 200,300 and the latter from 91,700 to 154,400. The declines were deceptive as a measure of union strength and activity. Whereas the labor movement as a whole, and particularly such unions as the United Mine Workers, the Textile Workers, the Ladies Garment

Workers, and the railroad unions, had suffered serious losses from the post–World War I peak in 1920 to 1929, the building trades unions had benefited from the tremendous construction boom of the 1920's and had registered substantial gains. On the eve of the depression they were at their all-time peak in strength. They represented about one-third of the total AFL dues-paying membership and a far more significant proportion of the labor movement's effective strength. Thus the 1939 membership figures, which showed a slight net increase for the group as a whole, reflected a generally strong union position in the construction field—particularly since the level of construction employment (excluding the WPA relief sector) was about 20 per cent below that of 1929. The building trades needed only the expanding job market of the defense and war periods (1939–45) to extend their membership to twice the 1929 peak.

In other important sectors, such as the railroads, the printing trades, and street railways, membership stability or declines from the 1929 level likewise reflected the industries' employment pattern and obscured the improved strength of the unions. On the railroads, for example, unionism attained almost complete success during World War I, suffered a considerable setback in the twenties and early thirties after the defeat of the national shop-crafts strike in 1922 and the rise of company unionism, and then gradually returned to comprehensive coverage of the industry by 1939 (despite serious economic difficulties) with the aid of the important Supreme Court decision in the Texas and New Orleans case of 1930 and the 1934 amendment to the Railway Labor Act. As in building construction, unionism in railroads in 1939 was prepared to follow the employment trend.

Only a relatively few AFL unions, in fact, were so adversely affected by the Great Depression that they failed to be stimulated by the pro-union New Deal atmosphere and the infectious spirit of the organizing drives which prevailed throughout the land. Indeed, within the AFL there emerged a group of unions whose rise compared favorably with those of the CIO unions. Most, but not all, of these were in nonmanufacturing industries. The leader was the Teamsters Union which reported to the Federation about 95,500 members in 1929 and 350,000 a decade later. The eighth largest AFL union in 1929, it now became the first as an alert leadership took advantage of the great rise of the automobile as a source of commercial and industrial transportation. Equally impressive was the growth of the International Association of Machinists from 77,000 (mainly in railroad shops, building construction, and skilled manufacturing trades) to 190,000 (including many semiskilled and unskilled factory workers). In contrast to the Teamsters, whose jurisdiction did not seriously overlap any CIO union's (except possibly with that of the Longshoremen's and Warehousemen's Union on the West Coast), the Machinists met the CIO challenge by instituting organizing drives in the mass production industries and were particularly successful in the machinery and tool manufacturing industry and in the slowly evolving aircraft industry. When war came in the 1940's, the Machinists were in a position to match organizational strides with the dynamic UAW-CIO. A third union to achieve a phenomenal growth in the 1930's was the Hotel and Restaurant Workers Union which moved from a membership of only 38,000 in 1929 to 185,000 in 1939. A semi-industrial union covering all except the mechanical trades in its field, it took advantage of the repeal of the Eighteenth Amendment to regain an extensive membership among bartenders and waiters, which it once held, and to expand into the hotels and restaurants of the larger cities. On a smaller absolute scale but often attaining even greater percentage increases in membership were such diverse unions as the Retail Clerks, the Meat Cutters and Butcher Workmen, the Building Service Employees, the Bakery and Confectionery Workers, the two Pulp and Paper Mill Unions, and the Pottery Workers.

In a number of industries, long-time AFL unions made significant gains in some portions of the country but were forced to yield to CIO organizations in others. The maritime industry is a particularly interesting example. By 1939 the bulk of the industry's 300,000 workers were union members. On the East Coast, the longshoremen belonged mainly to the AFL Longshoremen's Union whereas on the West Coast they rejected the national AFL leadership in the 1934 San Francisco strike and later formed the Longshoremen's and Warehousemen's Union as part of the CIO in 1937. Conversely, the unlicensed seamen on the East Coast turned from the once-powerful International Seamen's Union of the AFL (it had a reported membership of more than 100,000 in 1921, although only some 6,000 in 1933) and formed the CIO's National Maritime Union, while on the West Coast the deck hands remained in the AFL and the other seamen (stewards and engineroom personnel) formed separate CIO unions. The licensed personnel was similarly divided among a number of AFL, CIO, and independent craft unions.

It is finally worth noting that while most of the "new unions" of the 1930's affiliated with the CIO, that was not true of all of them. Among the new AFL units were the Cement Workers, the Distillery Workers, the Pocketbook and Novelty Workers, the Spinners Union, and the State, County and Municipal Employees Union. Indeed, in a number of industries the AFL set up separate unions to compete with the organizations which had withdrawn to join the CIO—notably in textiles and rubber—although these unions were unable to match their rivals in strength.

As a result of these extensive developments, the AFL by 1939 had not only recovered the membership loss incurred by the withdrawal of the CIO unions but had added almost 1 million others. The AFL membership now stood almost at the same level (about 4 million) as the peak reached after World War I in 1920.

While the great bulk of the union growth during the New Deal period occurred within the ranks of the AFL and the CIO, there were also a few important developments among the so-called independents. The main body of independent unions, in the railroad industry and among federal government employees, lagged behind the general trend, achieving a moderate recovery from the low point of the depression but, for the most part, not regaining their 1929 position in terms of membership. However, in the telephone industry, a significant advance was made with the formation of the National Federation of Telephone Workers in 1939 out of the merger of over thirty separate groups in all branches of the industry. At the outset the new organization claimed over 90,000 members. Independent unionism, largely derived from former employee representation plans and company unions, also emerged after the 1937 Supreme Court decisions on the Wagner Act in such industries as oil refining, telegraph, public utility, and chemical, but remained primarily on a separate establishment or company basis.

In this brief review of organizational developments during the decade between 1929 and 1939, we have focused mainly on the major unions and the industries over which they had assumed jurisdiction. These major developments may now be summarized in the following terms: The organized labor movement as a whole was between 126 and 140 per cent [6] larger in 1939 than in 1929 despite a *decrease* in employed workers in nonfarm establishments from 31.0 to 30.3 million. The movement was between 53 and 60 per cent larger in 1939 than in 1920, the post–World War I peak, although nonfarm employment was also higher —30.3 as compared to 27.1 million. In 1929 the only major sectors of the economy which were extensively unionized were building construction, printing, anthracite mining, men's clothing, the railroads, and the street railways. In 1939 these sectors (except for the last) were again strongly unionized. But in addition unionization had swept over all or most of the bituminous coal mining, ladies garments, maritime, glass, and pottery industries; it had made phenomenal gains in steel, autos, rubber, textiles, lumber, and other large mass production industries and in trucking, hotels and restaurants, building service, and other nonmanufacturing industries; and it had made smaller inroads in practically every other industry, including agriculture, the white collar occupations, and the professions. Only about 25 per cent of the workers attached to nonfarm establishments were in the union movement, but this was about double the 1929 ratio.

The most impressive and most dramatic development of the thirties was the rise of unionism in the large, mass production industries, but upsurges in mining, trucking, maritime, and other nonmanufacturing industries were also substantial and significant. These developments were reflected in two important ways: the increased proportions of union membership to employment in the various industries and the shift in the composition (and thereby structure and locus of power) of the labor movement.

The most careful (although admittedly imprecise) estimates of union penetration of industrial categories has been made by Wolman.[7] He concluded that between 1930 and 1940, the proportion of union membership to employment in manufacturing had risen from 9 to 34 per cent; in transportation, communication, and public utilities from 23 to 48 per cent; in building from 54 to 65 per cent; in mining, quarrying, and oil from 21 to 72 per cent; in services from 3 to 7 per cent; and in public service from 8 to 10 per cent.

Obviously such changes also involved important shifts in the composition of the labor movement. In 1929 the construction unions represented a quarter and the unions in transportation, communication, and utilities, together represented another quarter of the total union membership. Another quarter was represented by manufacturing unions but mainly in small-scale industrial establishments. By 1939 manufacturing unions represented about 40 per cent of all union members, with a major proportion in the large-scale, mass production units. In contrast the construction unions and the transportation-communication group each represented about 15 per cent. Interestingly enough, the largest single union in 1939 and probably the most influential was outside of these categories—in mining.

The Geographical Distribution Pattern

As noted at the outset, union membership in 1929 was widely distributed throughout the nation, although union power was concentrated in a relatively few centers. This seeming paradox was the result of the nature of the unions which comprised the labor movement at that time. The key unions, with few exceptions, were in industries comprised of small economic units and distributed throughout the country.

The building trades, which made up about one-third of the AFL in 1929 are, of course, to be found in every community of any size, and the unions had established locals in practically all the larger and medium-sized cities and many of the smaller ones, regardless of geographical location. For example, the Carpenters Union reported in its convention proceedings that in 1928 it had 2,039 local unions, 139 district councils, 27 state councils, and 2 provincial councils (in Canada). Its membership breakdown revealed local unions in every state, ranging from 186 (with 39,345 members in good standing) in Illinois to 2 (with 297 members) in Delaware. As might be expected, the less populous and less urbanized states had the smallest memberships. Area location appeared to be a relatively minor factor. The major centers (with more than 100 locals) were in Illinois, New York, Pennsylvania, Massachusetts, California, New Jersey, and Ohio; the states with under 10 locals included Arizona, Delaware, Maryland, Nebraska, Nevada, New Mexico, North Dakota, South Dakota, Utah, and Vermont. In the South, Texas with 97 locals and Florida with 58 led the way while Mississippi and South Carolina at the bottom each had 11. Owing to the Florida building boom, there were more union carpenters in that state (3,027) than in Minnesota (2,466). This distribution of the Carpenters in the late 1920's was generally duplicated by the other smaller building trades unions.

The widespread character of the labor movement was not limited to the building trades. It was also typical of most of the other important AFL and independent unions such as the Printers, the railroad unions, the Musicians, the Street Railway Workers, the Machinists, and the Barbers. For example, the Typographical Union reported in 1926 to the Department of Labor that it had 728 locals of printers distributed among all the states, the territories (except for Alaska), and eight Canadian provinces. Within the states, the range went from 50 locals in Illinois to 2 in Nebraska and Utah. Similarly, the Barbers Union reported 910 locals which were located in every state except two (Delaware and South Carolina) and ranged from 69 in Illinois and 64 in Texas to 2 in Utah. The Railway Clerks reported 1,306 locals, with every state included, ranging from 123 in Illinois to 1 in Delaware. In 1929 the Musicians listed 743 locals. All states were represented, ranging from 75 locals in Illinois to 1 in New Mexico.

This wide distribution of union membership prior to the New Deal period is significant in revealing the national character of the labor movement despite its general weakness and its declining influence. Except for the smaller towns, there were some union members in almost every area. However, the major concentrations were in the more populous states and, within them, in the large metropolitan centers. Among the states, Illinois, New York, Pennsylvania, Massachusetts, New Jersey, Ohio, California, and Texas predominated. Among the cities, Chicago, New York, and San Francisco stood out. A few large cities, like Los Angeles, were conspicuously labeled as anti-union communities, but even in these some craft union organization existed.

During the years of deepest depression between the fall of 1929 and the spring of 1933, when a very large proportion of union members were unable to maintain dues payments, some of these locals disappeared from the scene and in some of the smaller communities unionism became nonexistent. But in the larger communities, some form of local organization continued, either retaining the earlier structure or in the shape of a new local through consolidation. Thus union nuclei remained in most of the communities and served as the basis for the recovery of most of the old AFL unions from 1933 on.

The story of the Carpenters Union is particularly illuminating because the building industry was one of the hardest hit by the depression. The Carpenters had about 2,000 locals at the start of 1929. During this year, they chartered 35 new locals but 68 others were lapsed or disbanded and 20 were consolidated. This organizational decline continued until August, 1933, when 26 new locals received charters in contrast to 10 discontinued. Thereafter expansion prevailed. The figures on local charters indicate that between January, 1929, and July, 1933, the Carpenters Union suffered a net loss of 415 local unions, but there were still about 1,600 locals in existence. No part of the country failed to suffer losses; at the same time no section remained without a sizable number of union nuclei.

In the great unionization movement beginning in the spring of 1933, the geographical distribution of union members underwent a considerable change for four reasons. In the first place, the strongest union nuclei to survive the depression were in the large cities, and these nuclei served as the basis of the initial expansion. Secondly, organization tended to spread most rapidly among the great concentrations of workers—and these were in the metropolitan areas and in special "pockets" like the mines and lumber camps. In the third place, the great upsurge of mass production unionization naturally occurred where the mass production industries were located, and the bulk of such industry was then found in the Northeastern and Middle West sections of the United States. Finally, once the initial fever of union enthusiasm had spent itself among the previously unorganized workers, the success of organization depended in large measure upon the availability of full-time, paid, professional organizers and adequate funds for organizing purposes. It was much more efficient for the unions to concentrate on the larger centers and to neglect or at least minimize assistance to the smaller communities. As a result, anti-union employers in the smaller communities were able to ward off unionism for a longer time than could those in the larger cities.

Unionization in the Metropolitan Centers

Detailed studies of union development on a city basis are unfortunately quite rare, but some data are available. Chicago provides one important example not only because it is our second greatest city but also because it has been a leading center of the labor movement for nearly a century.[8] Prior to the depression, most of Chicago's union members were to be found in six strongly organized industries —building construction, trucking, building service, street railways, men's clothing, and printing. At times, industrial unionism achieved temporary success in the great meat-packing and steel industries, but during the 1920's unionization vanished from these sectors. The depression hit the old-line unions hard in terms of dues-paying membership, but they apparently held their job territories and made a rapid recovery with the inception of the New Deal. On the other hand, industrial unionism was slow in getting a foothold. Not until 1936, when John Lewis appointed one of his ablest and most experienced aides, Van Bittner, to lead an organizing drive was any success achieved. During 1936 and 1937 the CIO made a whirlwind campaign which netted phenomenal results, favored as it was by political, economic, and judicial factors. On the Chicago South Side not only thousands of steel workers but also retail clerks, undertakers, dry cleaners, and numerous other workers in the small industries of the area joined the steel workers organizing campaign. But the CIO received a setback in the "Little Steel" strike,[9] particularly following the brutal police attack on Memorial Day, 1937, at Republic Steel, and the 1937–38 recession forced it to retrench. Although slow gains were subsequently obtained in packing, electrical products, and farm equipment, the CIO did not regain its momentum until World War II.

The AFL was not challenged by the CIO in its traditional strongholds. Outside of these industries, however, in both nonmanufacturing and manufacturing, the AFL benefited from the stimulus of the CIO challenge and the tendency of employers to prefer the more conservative organization. As a result, there was a steady expansion in AFL membership throughout the 1930's.

Across the nation in San Francisco union growth was even more dramatic. San Francisco also has long been one of the centers of union strength, particularly among the building trades and the maritime industries. However, during the 1920's the unions received setbacks in both industries. The turning point came with the longshore strike of 1934 which flared into a general city-wide strike. Following victory on the waterfront, the Longshoremen's Union moved into the warehouses of the city. The strike had a contagious effect throughout the area, and by the end of the decade San Francisco was probably the most thoroughly unionized large city in the country. Although the Longshore and Warehouse Union joined the CIO, the bulk of unionization was by AFL affiliates because of the nature of industry in the city. For the most part manufacturing was carried on in small-scale establishments outside the jurisdiction of the CIO.

The tremendous rise of unionism in the 1930's was not confined to the large cities which had long been union centers like New York, Chicago, and San Francisco. It was also visible in cities which had traditionally been "nonunion" or "open-shop" towns. The story in Detroit is in large measure the story of the Auto Workers Union, although the growth of the building trades, the Teamsters, the Street Railway Workers, and other nonmanufacturing unions must not be ignored. The story in Akron is similarly the story of the Rubber Workers Union; the story in Pittsburgh that of the Steelworkers.

In the Pittsburgh area (Allegheny County) for example, unionism had been influential until about 1928 because of the strength of the United Mine Workers, the railroad unions, and a number of the AFL craft unions. In 1928, however, an unsuccessful mine strike practically wiped out the Mine Union and the depression had a similar effect on the other organizations. In the spring of 1933 before the NRA, the UMW dues-paying membership was less than 2,000 out of an eligible group of about 60,000. The steel industry, which employed about two-thirds of all manufacturing workers, was almost entirely nonunion.

The New Deal had a dramatic impact on union organization in Allegheny County. The UMW was one of the first to revive, and by 1935 its dues-paying membership averaged about 36,000. Other unions also came to life. Klein reports [10] that by 1935 the streetcar men were completely organized, the printers and railway workers 80 per cent, the bakers about 70 per cent, the hotel and restaurant employees slightly over half. Unionism became strong in the glass industry also. On the other hand, the steel industry set up employee representation plans to forestall outside organization. Thus of the 550,000 persons employed in Allegheny County in 1935, about 100,000 were in AFL or independent railroad unions, 150,000 in employee representation plans, and 300,000 in unorganized establishments. Once the employee representation plans were destroyed by union and government action, the Pittsburgh area became very highly unionized, rivaling San Francisco in its scope.

A more complex situation existed in Los Angeles. Southern California and, in particular, Los Angeles was the "black spot" for union organizers prior to the New Deal.[11] The Merchants' and Manufacturers' Association, the chief source of union opposition, estimated that as of December, 1928, there were no more than 121 active local unions with a membership of about 35,000, mainly in the building trades. The depression hit the union group hard, and as of May 31, 1933, the AFL Central Labor Council had only seventy-five locals in good standing and a per capita tax membership of 11,139. Counting the railroad brotherhoods and unions not affiliated with the Council, the total dues-membership of unions in Los Angeles was under 20,000 in a city of 1,240,000.

During the first six weeks after the enactment of the National Industrial Recovery Act, union officials claimed that some 15,000 members joined their ranks. However, in mid–1934 the Central Labor Council reported a tax-paying membership of only 18,757 in 100 locals and by the year's end the labor movement as a whole was reported to have 171 locals and about 40,000 paid-up members. An additional 30,000 were alleged to be non-paid-up members. In the next two years, confusion in union ranks and stiffened resistance among employers appear to have checked and even slightly set back the union drive. Although the CLC increased its affiliates to 110, their paid-up membership in mid–1936 was only 17,869.

The setback was only temporary. Late in 1936 the AFL launched a big organizational campaign which was particularly effective among the teamsters, the carpenters, and the retail clerks. Early in 1937 the CIO began its first big drive in the auto, aviation, steel, and rubber industries. By mid–1937 the CLC reported the affiliation of 144 locals with 34,478 paid-up members despite the suspension of the CIO unions. In September, 1937, the CIO Industrial Union Council reported about 17,500 paid-up members.

Despite the economic recession of late 1937 and 1938, the ranks of organized labor continued to swell. By June, 1939, the CLC had 145 locals and about 45,000 paid-up members. The building trades unions claimed some 12,000 members. The Teamsters reported about 25,000 members in Los Angeles and surrounding towns. The 30,000 employees of the Hollywood movie industry were almost wholly unionized in some forty-three different craft organizations, mostly AFL. The AFL membership in Los Angeles county was estimated to be about 120,000, apparently including delinquent and partially paid members. The CIO Industrial Union Council, notwithstanding AFL and employer opposition and an internal split with the Communists, claimed sixty affiliates and 45,000 members, mainly in auto, steel, utility, warehouse, rubber, and maritime establishments. However inexact these membership figures may have been, it is clear that in 1939 Los Angeles was no longer the "black spot" of 1929 for the union movement.

If we were to go down the entire roster of the larger cities of the nation, we would find the pattern of union growth more or less generally repeated, with some cities being unionized more rapidly or more completely than others. Thus, on the West Coast, San Francisco and Seattle, old union centers, led Los Angeles and Portland, the newly organized cities. Even in the South, where unionism lagged generally, substantial advances were made in the larger cities like Birmingham, Alabama, with its steel mills and packing houses, and New Orleans with its longshore and port facilities.

There were some exceptions. A study of San Antonio, Texas (population of 254,000 in 1940), concluded that, if allowances were made for population growth, the labor movement of 1940 was less cohesive and significant than it had been in the early years of the twentieth century.[12] Whereas a few of the depression-born unions in the city like the Garment Workers and the Telephone Workers were successful in their organizational efforts, employer resistance effectively forestalled or curtailed union efforts in most other industries, including printing and publishing, residential construction, and cigar manufacture. During the 1930's the leading employer in San Antonio was the pecan shelling industry, and it was strongly unionized in 1938 after a bitter thirty-seven–day strike. But the introduction of mechanical processes after the passage of the Fair Labor Standards Act resulted in a drastic reduction of the labor force (from over 12,000 to under 1,000 by 1941) and the demoralization of the union.

The Special "Pockets"

Outside of the metropolitan areas, the major union growth in the New Deal period came in various industrial "pockets" which were often isolated from the rest of industry but represented sizable concentrations of labor. We have already noted a few of these—the bituminous coal mining towns, the lumber camps and paper mills of the Pacific Northwest, the metal mines of the Rocky Mountain area, the oil fields of the Southwest, the Alaska fisheries. Closer to the big cities were industrial valleys like the Allegheny in Pennsylvania with its coal mines and steel, aluminum, and glass plants in almost continuous line. Once the union spark was ignited in these areas and employer opposition overcome through a combination of strike action and government support, these "pockets" tended to become completely unionized. There was a good deal of class consciousness and often a long union tradition, which encouraged 100 per cent unionism.

Sectional Differences

Although substantial union gains were registered in metropolitan areas throughout the country, irrespective of area, the New Deal period witnessed some important sectional changes in the distribution of union members. In part this was due to the location of manufacturing industry. Whereas the unionized industries of the pre–New Deal period had been widely scattered—as in the case of building construction, printing, and railroads—the newly unionized mass production industries like steel, autos, rubber, glass, and meat-packing, were largely concentrated in the Northeast and Midwest sections of the U. S. But this was only part of the story. It did not explain, for example, why the lumber industry in the Pacific Northwest was unionized and that of the South was not, or why the New England textile industry was unionized and the southern textile drive failed. To account for these differences, it is necessary to note a variety of factors—community and employer attitudes toward unionism, racial prejudices, the backgrounds and traditions of the workers, the history of previous union campaigns, the political influence of the small towns and rural areas in the region, and other considerations.

The greatest growth came in three major sections of the country—the Northeast, the Midwest, and the Pacific Coast. No precise statistics are available to substantiate this statement, but an analysis by industry and union is highly suggestive. The CIO is easier to handle from this point of view than the AFL. In October, 1939, the CIO had forty-five national and international unions and organizing committees. Six of these held about two-thirds of the total membership—the United Mine Workers, the Steel Workers Organizing Committee, the United Automobile Workers, the Textile Workers, the Amalgamated Clothing Workers, and the United Electrical Workers. In all of these unions, the great majority of members were employed in establishments located in the area bounded on the west by the Mississippi River, on the north by the Canadian border, on the east by the Atlantic Ocean, and on the south by the Border states. Indeed, except for the mine and textile workers of the South, relatively few workers in these industries were to be found outside of this area. Most of the smaller CIO unions were also concentrated in this area—the Rubber Workers in Akron, Detroit, and several New England cities; the Transport Workers in New York City; the Seamen on the East Coast; the Glass and Aluminum Workers in the Allegheny and Ohio valleys; the Packinghouse Workers in Chicago and East St. Louis; the Fur Workers and the Retail and Wholesale Workers in New York City.

It is of interest to note that at this time the CIO had only twenty-eight state industrial councils. Thirteen of these were in this Northeastern-Midwest area—only Illinois (for reasons other than lack of members), Delaware, New Hampshire, and Vermont not being represented. Councils also had been established in the three Pacific Coast states, in four of the eight Rocky Mountain states, and in three of the four Border states. But among the remaining sixteen plains and southern states, only Alabama, Texas, Oklahoma, Arkansas, and Iowa-Nebraska jointly were represented. The CIO strength on the West Coast was largely in the longshore, fishing, maritime, lumber, and oil industries in addition to some manufacturing; in the Rocky Mountain area, it was mainly in metal mining and lumber; in the Southwest it was chiefly oil again; and in Alabama it was coal mining, steel, meat-packing, and some textiles.

AFL membership was more widely distributed than the CIO but its heaviest penetrations were also in the Northeast and Midwest and on the West Coast. It is quite likely that relative to the size of the labor force, the West Coast was at least as strongly unionized and perhaps even more so than the more populous Northeast. Because the West Coast had relatively less manufacturing prior to World War II than the nation as a whole, the bulk of its union members in 1939 were in the AFL, particularly in the building, printing, hotel and restaurant, trucking, metal, and retail trades and services. The paper and pulp industry of the Northwest and the movie industry in southern California were also AFL-organized.

In the vast territory between the Mississippi River and the Pacific Coast states population is sparse, and a substantial proportion of the labor force is engaged in occupations like agriculture not easily susceptible to unionization. It is therefore not surprising that relatively few union members were to be found in this area outside of the metal mines and lumber camps, and some of the larger cities such as Denver and Phoenix.

The situation in the South is different.[13] Unionism has a long history in the South, particularly among the building, printing, railroad, and metal trades. In the important coal mining, tobacco, and textile industries, unionization was more sporadic, reaching considerable proportions during World War I and then declining during the 1920's. The AFL conducted an extensive campaign in 1930, which resulted in the formation of 112 new locals, eighty-one in industries other than textiles, but the defeat of a five-month strike at the Riverside and Dan River Cotton Mills, in Danville, Virginia, broke the back of the campaign. Considerable labor unrest and a number of strikes prevailed during the worst of the depression but with little organizational success.

With the start of the New Deal, the picture changed markedly. The United Mine Workers immediately launched a drive in Alabama, Tennessee, and Kentucky which was finally climaxed in August, 1938, by the unionization of "bloody" Harlan County. A considerable although lesser success was achieved among the tobacco workers of North Carolina and Virginia. Skilled and semiskilled tradesmen in many of the cities reorganized or formed new locals. In the Florida cigar industry, the AFL found a substantial number of recruits. Organization of steel workers received a great stimulus from the U. S. Steel agreement of 1937 which included the Tennessee Coal, Iron and Railroad Company in Birmingham, Alabama. The employees of the Tennessee Valley Authority began to work under signed union agreements in 1940, although the basis for collective bargaining was laid about 1935. A considerable number of garment workers were organized. In the latter part of the decade, some successes were also achieved among the paper and pulp workers, the rubber workers, the oil workers, and the telephone workers.

The touchstone of southern unionism, however, was the cotton textile industry, and the failure of the great textile strike of 1934 (involving at peak about 170,000 workers) symbolized at least a temporary parting of the ways between the South and the rest of the nation as far as unionism was concerned. Although the CIO Textile Workers Organizing Committee, in agreement with the United Textile Workers and with a $500,000 fund supplied by the Amalgamated Clothing

Workers, launched a new campaign in 1937, progress was extremely slow and little of the industry had accepted unionism prior to the outbreak of World War II. Had textile unionism achieved the success of steel and autos in the North, it is quite likely that the result would have had an epidemic effect throughout southern industry. Its failure represented a serious setback to unionism, particularly in the smaller towns and villages where so much of southern industry is located. Lumber, furniture, chemicals, and food-processing, all leading industries, were hardly touched by union organization during the New Deal period.

If we superimpose some rough estimates on data reported to De Vyver in correspondence with most of the unions active in the South, union membership in 1938 in eleven southern states (excluding Texas, Oklahoma, and West Virginia) probably numbered about 450,000 and almost certainly was under 500,000.[14] This figure includes an estimate of 100,000 members for the Textile Workers Organizing Committee although, as De Vyver notes, the Committee had negotiated only some twenty-five contracts and union members not under contract were not expected to pay dues.[15] In addition to the Textile Workers, only seven unions claimed more than 15,000 members in the South—the UMW with 82,000, the National Maritime Union with 30,000, the Carpenters with 20,000, the Steelworkers with 17,000, and the Railway Clerks, the Railroad Trainmen, and the Machinists each with 16,000.

Thus, although the union movement of the South in 1939 was considerably ahead of its 1929 status, particularly in the coal fields and in the larger cities, it lagged markedly behind the Northeast, Midwest, and West Coast in reacting to the stimulus of the New Deal. In this respect, the geographical distribution map of unionism was noticeably changed during the depression decade.

The Lag in the Smaller Cities and Towns

Next to the widening spread between unionism in the South and the rest of the nation, perhaps the most significant negative development was the lag of organization in the smaller cities and towns behind the metropolitan centers and the industrial valleys or pockets. The reasons appear to be as follows: After the initial burst of enthusiasm had settled down, union organization depended in large measure on the availability of professional organizers and organizing funds. It was much more efficient and economical for unions to concentrate their limited resources first in the areas where substantial numbers of potential members were employed. Thus, the smaller cities and towns (except where a sizable segment of some one industry existed) tended to receive less union attention than the larger centers. The lag gave the employers who were opposed to unions a chance to recover from their initial shock and to utilize company unions and other devices to try to stem the union tide. Furthermore, the employers in the smaller cities and towns were in a stronger position to organize public sentiment against union drives because of the minority position of unionizable workers in such towns and the relatively higher density of small businessmen, farmers, and professionals.

We may illustrate this generalization by referral to some case studies of a number of Illinois and Indiana communities. In their celebrated study of "Middletown" (Muncie, Indiana), the Lynds reported that in 1929 the city had about 900 union members out of an organizable labor force of about 13,000. These unionists belonged to sixteen locals, of which the most important were the Carpenters (with 300 members), the Printers, the Molders, and the Barbers. During the worst years of the depression, the membership declined by "a couple of hundred," but with the advent of the New Deal there was a great upward spurt and at the peak in 1934 the union total stood at 2,800 in some twenty-six locals. Then confusion in union ranks combined with increased employer resistance to cause a downward trend so that by the end of 1935, only about 1,000 members in twenty-one locals were reported. The Lynds observe that when General Motors moved one of its plants back to Muncie in 1935, the mayor and the leading businessmen assured the company that the city would continue to be "open shop" and that "our people are in no mood for outsiders to come into Muncie to agitate." At the time that the Lynds closed their study, in late 1936, there was some revival of membership again in the building trades with the improvement of local business conditions and some union militancy in the unorganized manufacturing establishments following Roosevelt's re-election. However, the authors predicted, "For the immediate future it seems likely that Middletown's labor in the city's dominant automotive and glass industries will have neither the stomach nor the adequate leadership for testing its strength again soon. One suspects that militant working class organization will not come through local initiative. If and when it does come to this population, it will probably be as a lagging phase of a movement diffused from larger industrial centers." [16]

The experience in the Illinois cities of Peoria and Decatur was very similar. In 1929 unionism was confined mainly to the building trades, printing, and other craft unions and was not very strong even among all of these groups. During the depression these unions managed to hold on (a few locals like the Decatur Electricians lost their charter for lack of sufficient members), but they were totally ineffective. Nevertheless, when economic recovery came, they were quick to revive. As noted earlier, in Peoria a substantial building program in the distillery industry raised the construction unions to full power; in Decatur the revival took longer, and building unionism was not at full strength until near the end of the decade.

In manufacturing, however, the picture during the 1930's was different. With few exceptions, the factory employers were unwilling to accept independent unionism. Union organizing campaigns were opposed by the formation of company unions, the granting of strategic wage increases, and refusals to bargain collectively. A series of strikes was, for the most part, unsuccessful. In Decatur, the longest strike in the history of the women's garment industry ended in virtual failure for the union. By 1939 industrial unionism was still weak and uncertain of its future. Only after the outbreak of World War II was the situation to change.

Despite the lag of unionism in the factories of the smaller cities and towns, this was a period of union ferment and activity. Many communities to which unionism previously had been foreign witnessed organizational campaigns for the first time. There was a marked development in the scope of union organization even though agreements with employers were not immediately forthcoming. The membership of the Illinois State Federation of Labor is only partly indicative. In 1929 the Federation had 35 affiliates in Peoria; in 1939 the number was 55. In 1929, five cities in the 50,000 to 100,000 population class had 101 affiliates; in 1939, all seven were represented with 135 locals. In 1929, twelve of the fifteen cities in the 25,000 to 50,000 population class had 197 affiliates; in 1939 all fifteen had 270 locals. For the cities between 10,000 and 25,000 population, there was a drop of one city (from twenty-one to twenty) but the number of affiliated locals rose from 138 to 177. And in the towns under 10,000 population, the number of communities rose from 73 to 114 and the number of locals from 218 to 244. That the number of smaller communities is not larger is explained by the withdrawal of the United Mine Workers, which was represented in a large part of central and southern Illinois.

Implications of Union Growth in the New Deal Period for Subsequent Years

Perhaps the most important feature for the future of the tremendous growth of the union movement in the New Deal period was that it occurred in time of depression—when unemployment probably never fell below the 7.5 million mark and most of the time averaged 9 million or more out of a total labor force of between 52 and 55 million. Since unemployment was most severe in the nonfarm sector and among the wage and salaried group in this sector, a force of about 30 million, the growth of unionism was all the more remarkable. It was the first time in American history that such a growth had occurred in such an economic period. There was sound reason to believe (despite the experience of the 1920's) that when prosperity recurred, the new union movement would rise still further in strength both because of an increase in the supply of potential members and because a rise in prices and profits would stimulate union aggressiveness.

It is tempting to speculate what would have happened to the labor movement if the European war had not broken out in 1939, giving the American economy its much-needed boost. Most likely in the absence of marked economic recovery, union membership would have remained at or near the plateau established in 1938 and 1939. It is even possible that the labor movement would have been set back because of stiffening employer resistance in many areas. On the other hand, continued mass unemployment might have given the dynamic groups within the movement a chance to capitalize further on dissatisfaction with employer policies and to increase labor militancy and solidarity.

A wartime period, however, with its critical labor shortages and the imperative need for production, has always favored union growth even more than peacetime prosperity. Consequently, when the six years of New Dealism in the 1930's were followed by six of defense and war emergency in the 1940's, the growth pattern continued. The 8 to 9 million unionists of 1939 soared to between 13 and 14 million in 1945. Ten years later the union movement stood at between 16 and 17 million, having first avoided any serious decline in the immediate postwar adjustment and then benefited again from the emergency conditions of the "Cold War" and the shooting war in Korea. The ratio of unionization to the nonfarm labor force did not, of course, rise proportionately. In 1955 it was about 32 per cent, an increase of only some seven percentage points over 1939.

It is not the purpose of this volume to analyze in detail the factors underlying the continued growth of the union movement after 1939. It is important, however, in order to assess the significance of the growth during the New Deal years, to trace some of the main developments of the subsequent continued expansion.

Industrially, the expansion of the 1940's and 1950's continued and, in some cases, completed the developmental pattern laid out in the 1933–39 period. The great bulk of the new 8 to 9 million members came from the industries which were already the centers of union strength in 1939 or from new allied industries—aircraft, electronics, and atomic energy—into which the established unions expanded. For the most part, the new members were either part of the huge additional work force in these industries (the number of wage and salary employees in nonagricultural industry rose from about 30 million in 1939 to over 48 million in 1955) or were in those sections of fairly well unionized industries which had not yet been unionized in 1939. Thus the penetration ratios, as estimated by Wolman for 1947, indicated further significant rises in manufacturing to 42 per cent; in transportation, communication, and public utilities to 62 per cent; in building construction to 75 per cent; and in mining, quarrying, and oil to 84 per cent; but only to 9 per cent in services and 12 per cent in public employment. If office employees are omitted, the manufacturing ratio rises to 52 per cent. In establishments with 100 or more employees, the ratio is undoubtedly very much higher.

If we consider the industrial composition of the labor movement itself, we find that the manufacturing unions continued to grow in relative importance and that many predominantly nonmanufacturing unions, such as the Carpenters, the Electricians, and the Meat Cutters, had added substantial numbers of manufacturing employees to their membership. A crude estimate based on the top thirty-nine unions [17] in 1954 (those with over 100,000 members in the United States) and an equal number in 1939 suggests that the predominantly manufacturing unions increased their relative position from about 42 per cent in 1939 to about 44 per cent of the total union membership.[18] However, the construction unions made even larger gains, moving up from about 16 to 23 per cent. These two groups together increased their ratio from about 58 to 67 per cent of all union members.

One well-known development reflected in the rankings of the large unions was the greater growth of the AFL as compared to the CIO and the independent unions. In 1939 only twenty-one of the top thirty-nine unions were in the Federation; by 1954 the number had increased to twenty-six. The CIO, of course, lost considerable ground because of the withdrawal of the Ladies Garment Workers in 1939 and of the United Mine Workers in 1940 and the expulsion of eleven Communist-dominated unions in 1950. In contrast it gained only one major affiliate, the Communication Workers of America, during the period. Thus there were fourteen CIO unions among the big thirty-nine in 1939 but only ten in 1954. The independent group numbered four in 1939 and three in 1951.

A second major conclusion to be drawn from the rankings is that by and large the unions which had already achieved a relatively substantial size were the ones which made the greatest gains in the war and prosperity years after 1939. There were only eight unions in the 1939 list which did not appear on the 1954 list and the top fifteen of 1954 were, with two exceptions, the same as the top fifteen of 1939 although the order was changed somewhat.

Not all the union giants expanded. The Mine Workers which led the list in 1939 fell to about thirteenth rank in 1954 because of the shrinkage of mine employment. The CIO Textile Workers also lost considerable ground because of the continued migration of northern plants to the largely nonunion South, the expansion of existing nonunion southern plants, and competition from the AFL Textile union. Other major unions of 1939 which lost old members or failed to gain new members in significant numbers and fell out of the top thirty-nine entirely were: the Cannery and Agriculture Workers, the Locomotive Firemen, the Woodworkers, the Typographers, the Transport Union, the Maritime Union, the International Longshoremen's Association, and the Federation of Federal Employees. It is interesting to observe that of this group only the Typographical Union, which had very substantial coverage in its fields, was an AFL affiliate.[19]

In contrast to these few cases of reduced growth or retrogression, many of the unions leading in 1939 grew phenomenally—partly because of favorable economic conditions and partly because of aggressive union policies. The Auto, Steel, and Trucking unions passed the million mark in membership. The building trades unions, taking advantage of the greatest construction boom in American history, expanded in many cases to double, triple, or more of their 1939 size. The Machinists Union went from 190,000 members to over 800,000; the Hotel and Restaurant Workers from 185,000 to over 400,000; the Railway Clerks and the Communication (telephone) Workers each from about 90,000 to some 300,000; the Retail Clerks from 65,000 to over 250,000; and the Meat Cutters from 63,000 to over 325,000. Other unions made gains which were almost equally impressive. At least 90 per cent of the union growth between 1939 and 1954 was achieved by the unions in the top thirty-nine ranks of 1954. Close to 60 per cent of the growth was achieved by ten of the top twelve unions.

The bulk of these gains, as noted previously, came during the war years, 1939–45. However, in contrast to the experience of World War I, the gains were not only maintained in the postwar years but continued to mount notwithstanding the obstacles interposed by the Taft-Hartley law and "right-to-work" laws in the southern and other states. The increase after 1945, it should be stressed, was primarily related to the expansion in the labor force, and the percentage of union membership to nonfarm employment remained on a plateau.

The chief corollary of the fact that the large unions of 1939 were the ones achieving the main growth in the forties and fifties was that unionism made relatively smaller advances in fields which had not been substantially penetrated by 1939. Again there are a few noteworthy exceptions. In the retail field, for example, several AFL unions —the Retail Clerks, the Meat Cutters, the Teamsters, and the Building Service Employees—had made some progress, particularly among food stores, in the late 1930's; and the CIO had unionized department store workers in New York City and some other communities; but the total probably did not greatly exceed 100,000 in 1939. By 1954, however, it is estimated, retail trade union members numbered more than half a million and between 25 and 30 per cent of all food store employees were unionized.[20] On the other hand, the proportion of department store employees organized was only about 10 per cent and of all retail trade employees only 7 per cent.

In the chemical industry, there was little effective organization during the 1930's by either the AFL or CIO, and the AFL did not charter a national union until 1945. By 1953, however, the AFL Chemical Workers Union was paying per capita taxes on 84,000 members and the CIO Gas, Coke, and Chemical Workers Union, which merged in 1955 with the Oil Workers, claimed 70,000 members, while District 50 of the UMW also was active in the field. The ratio of union membership to total employment in this vast and rapidly expanding industry continued to be relatively low, however. In the laundry industry, the AFL union paid per capita taxes on about 29,000 members in 1939 and on 70,000 in 1953. In the grain milling and processing industries (corn, wheat, soy bean, etc.) unionism appeared to be insignificant in the 1930's but by 1954 most of the companies were organized by one of several unions—the AFL Grain Millers, the AFL Auto Workers, and the CIO Oil Workers Union.

Generally speaking, however, where the unions were weak in 1939 —agriculture, office jobs (both in and out of government), retail stores except for food stores, the salaried professions—their advances continued to be slow, both in terms of new members and in comparison with the other unions. The idea of unionization was apparently becoming more attractive to office workers attached to large industrial establishments, to insurance agents, and to industrial engineers, but their organizations were still of limited importance in their fields.

The geographical distribution of union members followed the same general lines as the industrial.[21] The areas where the unions were strongest in 1939 continued to be the centers of union strength and the areas of least penetration continued to lag behind. In terms of absolute numbers of union membership, the northeastern and midwestern states east of the Mississippi and the three Pacific Coast states greatly widened their margin over the southern states and the states in the Plains and Rocky Mountain areas.

Percentagewise, however, the rate of growth in the South probably matched and may have surpassed the national average; in Texas, it almost certainly did so. Comparing the reported membership of twenty selected unions in his 1948 and 1938 surveys, De Vyver estimated that the southern increase was about identical with his estimate of the national increase—about 88 per cent. De Vyver's estimate of the national increase may be challenged (for example, using Wolman's data, the percentage increase is 93.2 per cent). However, if we go beyond his twenty selected unions to his total of fifty-nine and take into account the omitted unions, it appears that in 1948, southern union membership exceeded the million mark whereas in 1938 it was almost certainly below the half-million mark.

The situation in Texas is of unusual interest. According to a well-informed observer,[22] writing at the end of 1954, Texas manufacturing industry was about half unionized whereas in 1933 there was "a state of virtual absence of unionization" and in 1938 "very little." Among nonmanufacturing industries, unionization was virtually complete in the telephone and telegraph and railroad industries, about 80 per cent in transit and interstate trucking, and 25 per cent in utilities. Surprisingly, in the traditional union industries, such as construction, printing, city trucking, and garments, unionization grew more slowly after 1938—in construction, for example, it was only about 50 per cent complete. Much of the rapid growth of Texas unionism is attributed by Meyers to the rapid expansion of industry, particularly on the part of national concerns who deal with unions elsewhere.

An illuminating picture of the distribution of unionization was obtained by the U. S. Bureau of Labor Statistics in the course of wage studies conducted in thirty-nine metropolitan areas between September, 1951, and May, 1952.[23] The survey revealed that of the four cities in which 90 per cent or more of plant workers, both manufacturing and nonmanufacturing, were covered by union agreement, two—Detroit and Pittsburgh—were in the Middle West and two—San Francisco and Seattle—were on the Pacific Coast. Of the thirteen cities with a union agreement coverage between 75 and 89 per cent, all were in the Middle West or Northeast except Los Angeles. Of the fifteen cities with a coverage between 50 and 74 per cent, eight were in the East or Middle West, one (Louisville, Kentucky) was in the Border state group, two (Denver and Phoenix) were in the Rocky Mountain area, and four (Birmingham, Memphis, Norfolk, and Richmond) were in the South. Of the seven cities with union agreement coverage of only between 20 and 49 per cent, one (Worcester) was in New England, one (Salt Lake City) in the Rocky Mountain area, and five in the South.

Although comparable data are not available for 1939, the survey clearly reflects the considerable rise in unionism throughout the country. However, the great concentrations of union membership remained, relatively speaking, where they had been before the war. Another BLS study[24] has revealed that despite some very important geographic shifts, a third of all factory jobs are still found in the nine states of the

New England and Middle Atlantic regions and "the first 15 states in size of manufacturing employment in 1939 were exactly the same 15 states in 1953." Substantially the same was true in the nonmanufacturing sector.

Another trend which occurred during the New Deal period and continued in the subsequent years was the extension of unionism to the smaller cities and towns. In many areas, as we have indicated, small-town unionism lagged behind the growth in the larger cities. During and after World War II, there appeared to be a catching-up process. Illinois cities like Decatur and Peoria are illustrative. In Decatur (population 66,000 in 1950) unionism had been re-established by 1939 in building construction, printing, and the railroad shops on a firm basis, but efforts to unionize the manufacturing establishments, despite a number of strikes, had been generally fruitless. By 1950, however, about 12,000 of the 30,000 in the labor force were union members, including about 7,000 (almost the entire hourly work force) in manufacturing. The situation in Peoria (population of 105,000) was almost identical, with the dominant manufacturing establishment becoming fully unionized only in 1942.

Not only did unionism in the smaller cities and towns grow at an accelerated rate during the 1940's, it also spread to many towns where it previously had been absent. State Federation of Labor statistics, despite the limitations noted earlier, help to illustrate this point. In Illinois, for example, the communities under 10,000 in population had 244 affiliated locals in 1939 and 499 in 1954. The number of such communities rose from 114 to 189.[25] Similarly, the number of cities between 10,000 and 25,000 population with affiliated locals rose from twenty to twenty-nine and the number of locals from 177 to 293. All larger cities had some affiliated locals by 1939. The number of such locals rose from 270 to 437 for the fifteen cities between 25,000 and 50,000 population; from 135 to 211 for the seven cities between 50,000 and 100,000 population; from 55 to 71 in Peoria; and from 223 to 378 in Chicago.

This development apparently occurred throughout the country. In California, to give another example, the AFL State Federation affiliates rose from 89 to 201 between 1939 and 1953 in Los Angeles; from 144 to 174 in San Francisco; from 55 to 88 in Oakland; from 94 to 151 in the three cities with 100,000 to 250,000 population; and from 113 to 163 in the seven cities with 50,000 to 100,000 population. In 1939, nine communities between 25,000 and 50,000 population had 66 affiliated locals; in 1953, eleven such communities had 110 locals. For the 10,000 to 25,000 population class, the number of cities rose from twenty-one to twenty-four and the number of locals from 125 to 194. For the population class under 10,000, the number of communities rose from thirty-six to fifty-five and the number of locals from 98 to 192.[26]

Summary and Conclusions

We have surveyed a considerable (if fragmentary) body of available evidence as to the industrial and geographical distribution of union members immediately prior to and during the Great Depression, the impact of events on the distribution pattern during the six years of the New Deal period, and the consequences of these developments for the wartime and prosperity years which ensued. The following conclusions appear to be supported by this evidence, although in certain respects the data are not adequate for any firm statement:

1. On the eve of the depression, the labor movement was considerably weaker than it had been immediately after World War I because of (a) the virtual liquidation of war-stimulated unionism in the large mass production industries, (b) the demoralization of the largest union, the United Mine Workers, primarily because of economic conditions in the mining industry, and (c) the near disintegration of another major union, the Ladies Garment Workers, because of factionalism and internal strife. On the other hand, the old, long-established craft unions had pretty well maintained their positions (the building trades unions, indeed, were stronger than at any previous time), and unionism was widely if thinly distributed throughout the nation in communities of every size.

2. The depression severely cut the number of dues-paying members among the craft unions and greatly weakened their fighting ability, but union nuclei continued to exist in most communities. These nuclei were generally unable to take advantage of the mounting grievances of the workers and the greatly deflated prestige of businessmen. However, they were in a position to revive rapidly with the onset of economic recovery, and past American history indicated that such a revival was highly probable.

3. The most striking initial impact of economic recovery and governmental encouragement of unionism by the Roosevelt administration was in the coal mining and garment industries where astute and alert

union leaders took advantage of the new climate to rebuild and expand their organizations with phenomenal speed. Almost concurrently there developed an enthusiasm for unionism among unorganized workers, particularly in the larger cities and in nonurban industrial "pockets," which had epidemic characteristics.

4. After its initial recovery to levels surpassing 1929 and approaching the World War I peak, the union drive was set back by uncertainties in the national economic process, structural and leadership conflicts within the AFL, the recovery of employer confidence, doubts as to the constitutionality of New Deal pro-labor legislation, and confusion within governmental and worker ranks. The setback proved to be only temporary because (a) the internal AFL conflict was decisively resolved by the formation of the CIO and the split of American trade unionism into two major segments; and (b) the overwhelming political victory of Roosevelt in 1936, with the widely publicized financial and oratorical support of John Lewis, signalized the turning back of the employer counter-drive and the regaining of union momentum. Marked economic recovery in 1936 and early 1937 added fuel to the union campaign. The Supreme Court decision to uphold the constitutionality of the Wagner Act was the final turning point. The economic recession of late 1937 and 1938 slowed down but did not reverse the trend.

5. The organization of the great mass production industries on an industrial union basis was unquestionably the paramount union achievement of the 1930's. The achievement was more than one of merely adding large numbers of new members to the union fold. These industries, although employing only a minority of the total labor force, symbolized to the nation and to the world the essential nature of the American business civilization, and their unionization indicated the coming of age of the labor movement.

6. The second major achievement within organized labor was the reformation and resurgence of the AFL. Not all of labor's dynamism rested with the CIO, even during the period when it looked to many as if the latter would swallow up all of the labor movement. In trucking, hotels and restaurants, retail stores, and building service, for example, AFL unions demonstrated a new vigor and aggressiveness quite in keeping with the new union climate. But perhaps equally significant was the decision of a number of the major AFL unions to match strides with the CIO in some of the mass production in-

dustries and to adopt the structure of industrial unionism where this seemed the effective organizational technique. The Machinists Union, the Electrical Workers, and the Carpenters were the leaders.

7. By 1939 the CIO had a membership of between 3 and 4 million, probably equalling the total strength of the labor movement in 1929. The dues-paying membership of the AFL was just over 4 million, exceeding its 1929 membership by over a million despite the loss of the original CIO affiliates. Independent union members probably numbered close to a million. Together organized labor was at an all-time high in membership despite the fact that unemployment exceeded 9 million and the number of employees in nonfarm establishments was only slightly higher than in 1920 and below 1929.

8. As a result of the growth of unionization among manufacturing employees, the major advances in union membership occurred in the eastern and midwestern states where most manufacturing was located. The AFL expansion in nonmanufacturing industries was centered mainly in the larger cities, with especially noteworthy developments in the Pacific Coast metropolitan centers of San Francisco, Seattle, and Los Angeles: Unionism made lesser advances in the South in large measure because of the failure of the great textile drive. As a result, the geographical distribution of union members shifted somewhat from that of 1929 when the concentration in the East and Midwest was less pronounced.

9. In general the larger cities unionized more rapidly than the smaller cities and towns although the trend was the same almost everywhere. Studies of a number of smaller communities indicate that the reasons for their lag (and it was in no sense uniform) were: (a) the skills and funds essential to successful organization were relatively scarce and it was more economical for the international unions to focus on the major concentrations of members and to postpone organizational drives in the more dispersed areas, (b) public opinion was more likely to be opposed to unionism, especially of the CIO variety, which was considered radical and alien, and (c) the employers tended to have closer contacts with the workers and could exert more personal appeals.

10. The doubling of union membership in the years between 1939 and 1955 was in considerable measure the consequence of wartime and prosperity conditions. The significance of New Deal developments

for the later years lay in the fact that almost all of the later gain was made by the unions which had achieved substantial growth by 1939. The biggest unions of 1939 in both the AFL and CIO were, with only a few exceptions, the biggest unions of the 1950's and, in absolute terms, they widened the difference between themselves and the smaller unions. These gains were achieved mainly along three avenues: (a) continued organization within their industrial jurisdiction, (b) the expansion of the 1939 industries as a result of the tremendous production boom, and (c) extension of their jurisdiction to wartime and new peacetime industries, such as the UAW and the IAM into aircraft and the Electrical Workers of both the AFL and CIO into electronics and television.

11. Although industrialization continued apace in the South and on the Pacific Coast, bringing with it increased union membership, the geographical pattern of industrial employment and unionism remained essentially the same in the 1950's as in 1939. Percentage increases in the South may have actually surpassed the national average, but union penetration of the South continued to lag considerably behind other areas. This was reflected in the continued failure of textile unionism in the South and the spread of the so-called right-to-work laws passed in eleven southern states.[27]

12. With a few significant exceptions—retail food stores, chemical plants, grain processing plants, laundries—unionism made relatively minor gains in the industries in which substantial footholds had not been achieved by 1939. In contrast to the 1930's unionization was mainly an exploitation of existing union territories. Farm workers, office workers, retail clerks outside of food stores, and professional salaried employees, who were largely outside the union fold in 1939, continued in this category, although some advances were made, particularly in the larger industrial establishments and in the major metropolitan centers.

13. The growth of unionism in the smaller cities and towns was accelerated after 1939, partly because the successes in the larger centers enabled the national unions to focus more of their resources elsewhere, partly because public opinion in the smaller communities came increasingly to recognize the "native" character of unionism, partly because increasing numbers of employers decided that it was fruitless and expensive to oppose unionism and that they were more

likely to get unions with which they could do business if they did not fight them, and partly because the growing decentralization of the national employers carried unionism with it.

14. The boom in unionism between 1933 and 1945 and the slower but continued growth in the subsequent decade was not entirely unprecedented in American labor history. Rather comparable conditions existed between 1897 and 1920, and the initial upsurge, although not the later decade, was matched by the 1881–86 rise of the Knights of Labor and the AFL craft unions. The difference was chiefly one of degree. The first of the great booms launched the modern American labor movement; the second insured its development as an American institution; the third raised it to power as a major force in American life.

Notes

1 Leo Wolman estimates 7.7 million in 1939 and 14.2 million in 1948, excluding Canadian members. Cited in Irving Bernstein, "The Growth of American Unions," *American Economic Review*, XLIV (June, 1954).

2 This is reflected in the generally accepted figures that union membership dropped only about half a million between 1929 and 1932. Case studies of localities and industries indicate a far greater decline of dues-paying membership accompanying the drop in employment.

3 This account is based on Charles Phillip Anson, "A History of the Labor Movement in West Virginia" (unpublished Ph.D. dissertation, University of North Carolina, 1940).

4 Joel Seidman, *The Needle Trades* (New York: Farrar and Rinehart, 1943), pp. 189 ff.

5 See W. Lloyd Warner and J. O. Low, *The Social System of the Modern Factory* (New Haven: Yale University Press, 1947).

6 Wolman estimates provide the lower figure, Peterson estimates the higher. If the U. S. Department of Labor data were used, the increases would be raised somewhat further.

7 Leo Wolman, "Concentration of Union Membership," in *Proceedings of Fifth Annual Meeting of the Industrial Relations Research Association* (Madison: The Association, 1952).

8 This account is based on a Ph.D. study (as yet uncompleted) by Barbara Newell which is being sponsored by the University of Illinois.

9 Notwithstanding the achievement of union recognition at the large Inland Steel works.

10 See Philip Klein, *A Social Study of Pittsburgh* (New York: Columbia University Press, 1938), pp. 171 ff.

11 This account is based on Louis B. Perry, "A Survey of the Labor Move-

ment in Los Angeles, 1933–1939" (unpublished Ph.D. dissertation, University of California at Los Angeles, 1950).

12 Harold A. Shapiro, "The Workers of San Antonio, Texas, 1900–1940" (unpublished Ph.D. dissertation, University of Texas, 1952), p. 329.

13 Much of the following analysis is based on facts contained in "Labor in the South," *Monthly Labor Review*, LXIX (October, 1946).

14 See Frank T. De Vyver, "Status of Labor Unions in the South," *Southern Economic Journal*, V (April, 1939). De Vyver himself makes no total estimate since he did not receive any data from several important unions, including the Tobacco Workers, the Cigar Makers, the Cannery Workers, the Hosiery Workers, the Hod Carriers, the Painters, the Locomotive Engineers, and the Teamsters.

15 In a later article, De Vyver expresses the belief that this claim of 100,000 members "probably represented wishful thinking." See "The Present Status of Labor Unions in the South—1948," *Southern Economic Journal*, XVI (July, 1949), p. 3.

16 Robert S. Lynd and Helen M. Lynd, *Middletown in Transition* (1st ed., New York: Harcourt, Brace and Co., 1937), p. 44.

17 The top thirty-nine unions accounted for about three-fourths of all union members in 1954 and about 68 per cent in 1939. The 1954 estimates are based mainly on statistics compiled by the U.S. Bureau of Labor Statistics. The 1939 estimates are derived from a variety of sources: American Federation of Labor, *Proceedings*, 1939; Congress of Industrial Organizations, *Proceedings*, 1938; and Twentieth Century Fund, *How Collective Bargaining Works* (New York: The Fund, 1942).

18 In terms of dues-paying members, the percentage increase was undoubtedly much greater. The percentage for 1954 is probably quite reliable but the 1939 figure is based on CIO membership reports which clearly overstated the dues-paying membership.

19 The Cannery Workers, after their expulsion from the CIO in 1950, merged with the Distribution, Processing and Office Workers, independent, which in turn merged with the CIO Retail, Wholesale and Department Store Union in 1955. The Longshoremen's Association was expelled from the AFL in 1953 on charges of racketeering.

20 Martin S. Estey, "Patterns of Union Membership in the Retail Trades," *Industrial and Labor Relations Review*, VIII (July, 1955).

21 This analysis was completed prior to the publication of Wolman's studies of union membership by states. On the basis of a summary report in *Business Week*, June 16, 1956, pp. 169–70, it would appear that the main findings generally correspond.

22 Frederic Meyers, "The Growth of Collective Bargaining in Texas—A Newly Industrialized Area," *Proceedings of Seventh Annual Meeting of Industrial Relations Research Association* (Madison: The Association, 1954), pp. 286–97.

23 *Monthly Labor Review*, LXXVI (January, 1953), p. 26. The study

covered manufacturing, public utilities, wholesale and retail trade, finance and selected service industries but *excluded* building construction and railroads. In the twelve largest cities the sample was limited to establishments with over 100 workers; in the others, the minimum was twenty-one workers. The inclusion of the strongly unionized sectors of building construction and railroads would undoubtedly have increased the percentages of unionization.

24 "The Changing Geography of American Industry," *Monthly Labor Review,* LXXVII (July, 1954).

25 The number of communities under 10,000 population with one or more union locals was considerably greater because many AFL locals do not affiliate with the State Federation and some have CIO or independent unions—especially the coal mining or railroad towns.

26 Twenty-three smaller towns with ninety-three locals could not be matched with the census statistics. In the case of both California and Illinois, the population frequencies are based on the 1940 census. The population shifts between 1940 and 1950 would, of course, alter the number of cities in each size class but would not affect the general picture significantly.

27 The Louisiana law was repealed in 1956. In contrast, only two midwestern states and none of the states in the East and on the Pacific Coast have such a law. In addition to the southern states, "right-to-work" laws have been enacted by Arizona, Indiana, Iowa, Nebraska, Nevada, North Dakota, South Dakota, and Utah.

2

The Split in the Labor Movement

EDWIN YOUNG

When in late 1935 John L. Lewis led several international unions of the American Federation down the path toward "dualism," it could well be regarded as the drastic but necessary method for getting the AFL out of its fifteen-year organizational and evolutionary stalemate.

The failure to organize in the twenties can in part be explained by the hostility of the government to unionism, the psychological offensive of the employers with their welfare capitalism, the rising real wages of industrial workers, etc. But our concern here is to show how this failure of the twenties affected the "will to organize" on the part of the leaders of the American Federation of Labor when a friendly government and a sympathetic public provided that opportunity in the thirties.

Gompers' Policies on Union Organization

Under the leadership of Samuel Gompers, the AFL had been highly pragmatic. At the time of its founding in 1886, it had waged a bitter fight against the Knights of Labor on the issue of dualism. The AFL leaders could see that there was no class solidarity among American workers that would prevent them from taking jobs away from their fellows in a rival organization if the opportunity arose. So Gompers had insisted that there be one and only one union for a particular group of workers. Within the Federation the AFL attempted to keep the members of the labor movement from fighting each other by trying to make careful demarcations of jurisdictions of the affiliated national unions. The concern that there be no dual organizations and that jurisdictions were property rights grew into one of the most sacred tenets of the Federation. The protection these principles afforded was the greatest inducement for a national union to become affiliated.

Most of the early affiliates of the AFL were organized along craft lines since the workers' investment in their particular skill was the bond that held the early unions together. Craft organization which had been the only practical form of organization for most members of the AFL in its early days became, after a time, the essence of Gompersism in the eyes of both the critics of the Federation and many of its own leaders. However, as early as 1901 in the important Scranton Declaration a place was made in the "constitutional structure" of the Federation for the United Mine Workers' industrial union, and the way was paved for further compromises with industrial unionism as those problems arose. That declaration said:

> As the magnificent growth of the AFL is conceded by all students of economic thought to be the result of organization on trade lines, and believing it neither necessary nor expedient to make radical departure from this fundamental principle, we declare that as a general proposition the interests of the workers will be best conserved by adhering as closely to that doctrine as the recent changes in methods of production and employment make practicable. However, owing to the isolation of some industries from thickly populated centers where the overwhelming number follow one branch thereof, and owing to the fact that in some industries comparatively few workers are engaged over whom separate organizations claim jurisdiction, we believe that jurisdiction in such industries by the paramount organization would yield the best results to the workers therein, at least until the development of organization has reached a stage wherein these may be placed, without material injury to all parties in interest, in affiliation with their national trade unions. . . . We hold that the interests of the trade union movement will be promoted by closely allying the subdivided crafts, giving consideration to amalgamation and to organization of District and National Trade Councils to which should be referred questions in dispute, and which should be adjusted within allied craft lines.[1]

Strong pressure was brought at the 1912, 1919, and 1921 conventions of the Federation for a complete change from craft to industrial unionism. Each time it was voted down with promises from the leadership that the jurisdictional problems arising from craft organization could better be solved by such amalgamations as were then taking place involving such unions as the Machinists, the Carpenters, the Meat Cutters, and others. Although amalgamation often ended a particular jurisdictional dispute, it did little or nothing for the worker without skill who belonged to no element of the amalgamation. Outside of the garment and brewery industries where a strong Socialist tradition favoring industrial unionism existed, the unskilled workers were regarded with pretty much the same disdain by the leadership of the AFL as had been the immigrants of the Knights of Labor's earlier all-inclusive organization.

Forming the Building Trades Department in 1908, the Federation tried another method of coöperation in the industry where interunion disputes were most prevalent. The Department brought into contact unions with similar interests and enabled them to discuss their joint problems. Having no authority over its member unions, this organization was not a startling success, but it and the Metal Trades and the Railway Departments which soon followed provided one of the devices that helped contain the increasing problem of jurisdictional disputes.

Another device by which the AFL tried to cope with the changing industrial scene was the federal union directly affiliated to the Federation. The federal local was intended to be a stopgap union which would take in all the workers in a particular plant on a temporary basis with the intent that after they had been indoctrinated with the ways of unionism they could be parcelled out among the internationals claiming jurisdiction over them. If no appropriate national union existed, a number of federal unions in the same industry could be brought together to form a new national union.

This recital of the attempts of the AFL to solve its structural problems in a changing industrial scene offers evidence that until World War I at least, the labor movement was alive to its organizational problems and tried to solve them by adapting to the new situations and yet preserving most of the interests of existing affiliates. In its struggle for survival the AFL had held the craft principle theoretically inviolate. In practice, some compromises with respect to the miners, amalgamations, departments, and federal unions had been made as the pressing need arose. The compromises were not long-run solutions of the problems brought by the march of industrialization, which drafted large numbers of unskilled and semiskilled workers for jobs that cut across traditional craft lines. On the other hand, these compromises had solved or contained the particular issues at hand, leaving the way open for further pragmatic modifications in structure. They embodied enough change to prove that the constitution was a live and adaptable instrument; yet the changes were not fundamental enough to shatter the House of Labor. This policy has been widely acclaimed and widely assailed as Gompersism.

Organizational Problems of the 1920's

The organizational policies and the structural evolution with which the labor movement faced the twenties were inadequate to the task. Twenty-four unions loosely banded together under the leadership of Fitzpatrick, the progressive head of the Chicago Federation of Labor, and William Z. Foster, general AFL organizer who soon thereafter became a national leader of the Communist party, had failed to crack the citadel of anti-unionism, the U. S. Steel Corporation. After that defeat the labor movement slipped into a rear-guard action.

The twenties in the United States was the decade of the employers, whose optimistic outlook dominated the whole American scene. By its noninterference, government smoothed the way of business. Not only did employers carry on their open shop drives against unionism, they tried to replace unionism with astute personnel policies, bonuses, and workers' representation schemes, all of which came to be known as "welfare capitalism." The whip of a rising cost of living was not present to push the workers to demand higher wages. Real wages of industrial workers were rising at the expense of the depressed agricultural and coal industries.

At a time when the great unorganized areas were in industries which could best be organized along industrial lines, the strongest proponents of industrial organization within the Federation—the garment unions, the Miners, and the Brewery Workers—were steadily losing ground. And across the whole labor scene determined attempts of the Communists either through dual organizations or by "boring from within" forced the more progressive and liberal elements within the unions to align themselves with the conservatives because they regarded the Communists as the greater threat to the labor movement.

So at the end of the twenties the base of the American labor movement had been considerably narrowed. Control of the executive council and the conventions of the Federation was firmly in the hands of the most conservative and craft-minded elements. No scheme of organizing had been worked out which could cope with the mass production industries and welfare capitalism.

The Opportunity Missed

It could be argued that in the climate of the twenties no form of organization could have succeeded. However, that climate changed dramatically with the great economic upheaval that shook all America at the end of the decade. The coming of the New Deal gave the AFL a chance to show if it had the dynamic leadership the new times and the new conditions demanded. Was it possible for the labor movement to go over from retreat to the offensive? Was it flexible enough to provide a place for the semiskilled and the unskilled when a friendly government set the stage for a vast organizational campaign?

Labor took New Deal laws and pronouncements, such as Section 7(a) of the NIRA, at their face value. Workers demanded unions as insurance of their rights and also as part of the great recovery effort in which all patriotic citizens were involved. Nearly all unions increased their membership, but, as indicated in Chapter 1, the growth was spectacular in mining and in the garment industries.

In June, 1933, the AFL called its international presidents to Washington for a meeting which authorized an organizing campaign. Soon offices were opened in Detroit and Akron, and Federation organizers were travelling all over the country. From August, 1933, to August, 1934, the Federation's organizing expenses tripled, and in addition there were greatly enlarged staffs of the international unions and hundreds of voluntary organizers.

But despite the increased activity, no plan was discernible. Outside of the automobile, rubber, aluminum, and radio industries, the organizers were assigned on a regional basis. This meant that the organizers drawn mostly from the older craft unions knew little of the problems of most of the workers they were trying to organize.

To take care of the new unionists in the mass production industries where no international union existed, the Federation temporarily had the federal unions directly affiliated to itself and under the direction of the executive council. However, some union leaders were suspicious of this system. A resolution condemning the federal unions was introduced at the Metal Trades Department convention in the fall of 1933 by John P. Frey and Arthur Wharton who urged that new members be immediately placed in the "proper existing organizations."

At the 1933 convention of the AFL the Federation passed on neither the resolutions supporting nor those condemning industrial unions, but it did overwhelmingly approve the action of the executive council in turning the drivers of the Brewery Workers over to the Teamsters Union. This was taken to mean that that particular convention did not strongly support industrial unionism. However, the convention authorized the executive council to call a conference to discuss ways of organizing, especially in the mass production industries.

The conference held in Washington in January, 1934, failed to alter traditional organizing methods, although it was clear by that time that such methods were not working. In addition, workers were leaving federal unions as soon as attempts were made to hand members around to the internationals, and the internationals claiming jurisdiction over the workers were powerful enough within the executive council to hold down the chartering of new industrial unions.

Perhaps the industrial union point of view and the contrary view that all existing claims, no matter how nominal, should be protected were not pushed at the Washington conference because there was hope that the problem would work itself out or at least become merely a chronic jurisdictional squabble. Many of the craft leaders believed that the mass production workers were only fair weather unionists who would come into the unions in order to get higher wages but would not stick over the long run. The proponents of industrial unions could hope that the federal unions would be used as the basis for new, industrial-type unions in rubber, autos, cement, aluminum, etc. Once the latter were established it was logical to assume that, as in the past, the Federation would be practical rather than theoretical in the matter.

As the year 1934 went by, it became increasingly clear that the AFL was losing the opportunity presented to it when the workers "at the first promise of the federal government to assure the right to union membership without discrimination" had virtually risen up and demanded union organization.[2] In reporting this demand to the 1934 convention, the executive council also reported that they could claim a gain of only a half-million new members.

Instead of an autonomous international charter, the executive council granted the federal auto unions a national council with officers appointed by the executive council. In March the auto workers threatened to strike for the reinstatement of the union leaders fired by General Motors under the "merit clause" in the automobile code which allowed the employers to "select, retain or advance employees on the basis of individual merit without regard to membership or nonmembership." Rather than face such a strike the AFL leaders accepted a White House settlement that allowed the auto companies to deal with the representatives of every group of workers in proportion to their numbers. This pluralism was accepted by William Green although it repudiated the exclusive principle on which the American Federation of Labor had been founded. The AFL was afraid to risk the militant but undisciplined strength of the auto workers in a struggle which might involve the Federation in an all-out battle with the auto companies.

Despite Green's promises no real assistance or plans for continued organization in the industry came from the executive council, and the membership of the federal unions in that industry dwindled away until only 10,000 members were left in the winter of 1935.

A very similar story of frustration and ineptness could be told about the rubber industry. Steel was somewhat different since on paper the Amalgamated Association of Iron, Steel and Tin Workers had an industrial-type charter which would allow them to organize the steel workers. The 100,000 new members that had flocked in with the passage of NIRA had quickly become discouraged by the fumbling of President Tighe. After some of the activists in the union bypassed Tighe and appealed directly to Washington for the rights granted by the steel code, the code authorities gave William Green the task of selling a special steel labor board to the workers. This board got no coöperation from the companies, and the 100,000 membership was down to 6,000 when the AFL convention met in San Francisco in the fall of 1934.

The inadequacy of the organizational activity was reflected in the number of resolutions submitted to the 1934 convention demanding organization of the mass production industries. Many of these demands came from federal locals suffering from lack of coördination, craft raids, and the threat of eventual dismemberment. John P. Frey of the Metal Trades Department brought in a counter demand that the Federation's organizers enroll workers only in those international unions already claiming jurisdiction. It took a carefully balanced resolutions committee a week to work out an acceptable compromise resolution on the question of organization. This committee reported that because of new conditions the executive council was "directed to issue charters for National or International Unions in the automotive, cement, aluminum and such other mass industries as in the judgment of the Executive Council may be necessary to meet the situation."[3] The council was ordered to inaugurate, manage, and promote a campaign of organization in the steel industry. For a provisional period the Federation was to appoint the officers of whatever new unions were established.

The task set down seemed clear enough and seemed like a victory for the proponents of industrial unionism, but management of the new unions and the organizational campaigns were firmly in the hands of the leaders of the craft organizations who controlled the executive council. The attitude of these craft leaders was displayed by speeches of such persons as Arthur Wharton of the Machinists, William Hutcheson of the Carpenters, and Joseph Franklin of the Boilermakers. Each of them questioned the resolutions committee to make sure that there was no intent to put men over whom they claimed jurisdiction into the new unions. In replying for the committee, John L. Lewis pointed out that its resolution was not an attempt to impair or to interfere in the "legitimate work or the form of structure of any existing trade union of the craft form in the American Federation of Labor. . . ."[4] Charles Howard, author of the report, argued that the time had come to fit the Federation's structure to those whom it was meant to serve rather than to try to mold millions of workers into a pattern liked by the heads of the AFL. Howard said that there was nothing in the report requiring any union to give up any members it already had. He did admit that some workers whom they had been unable to organize but who were claimed by existing internationals would go into the new unions.

Finally, the resolution, which in a sense gave the AFL its third chance in two years at mass organization, passed unanimously. The same convention increased the executive council by seven members, two of whom were strong advocates of industrial unionism, John L. Lewis and David Dubinsky. The former from his remarks made it very clear that now it was safe to leave problems in the hands of the executive council; the Mine Workers president had great faith in his own persuasive powers.

But the fine-sounding resolution and the new members of the executive council effected no change in the policies of the AFL. At the same time the climate for successful organizing was diminishing.

A number of top-ranking officials within the federal government had become uneasy about the constitutionality of the NRA codes, and many employers were sure that they were unconstitutional, thus making enforcement of their provisions well-nigh impossible. Workers were disillusioned with the failure of the government to protect the rights so grandly promised in Section 7(a). While the cost of living was rising faster than wages, millions of unemployed were prepared to take the jobs of those discharged for union activity. Many workers joined company-sponsored unions. Although between 1934 and 1935 the Federation gained a half-million members, it suffered a net decrease in the mass production industries.

During 1935 both the auto and rubber workers received emasculated charters for international unions. In the case of automobiles the skilled machine and die workers, the maintenance men, and all workers in parts plants, which embrace a large part of the industry, were excluded from the union. Nothing was done to carry out the convention's mandate to organize the steel industry.

The executive council was not unaware of jurisdictional and organizing problems at its meetings in 1935. It had on its hands the charge of the Mine, Mill, and Smelter Workers Union that its strike against the Anaconda Copper Company had been undermined by secret settlement and jurisdictional raiding by craft unions of the metal trades. After two hearings the council concluded that there was no basis for the charges. Another action which might seem inconsistent with the miners' case was the turning over of all the loggers, lumbermen, and sawmill workers in more than a hundred federal locals to the United Brotherhood of Carpenters. Considerable energy was spent by the officers of the Federation in 1935 to try to force the Building Trades Department to take back the Carpenters, Electricians, and Bricklayers, who saw gains in returning to an organization which they had deserted when decisions had gone against them in the past. They wanted to return because the federal government had raised the Building Trades Department to a semi-official role in the administration of codes for construction financed by the federal government. Small building unions made up the Department, and correspondingly small feeling for their position was shown by the AFL bosses when, cowbird fashion, the large outfits pushed back into the Department's comfortable nest.

The Crisis in the AFL

There was much bitterness against the do-nothing policies of the executive council among the 500 delegates who arrived in Atlantic City in October for the 1935 convention of the American Federation of Labor. This time the proponents of industrial organization were in no mood for compromises that would leave the ultimate decision of doing something or nothing in the hands of the executive council with its craft-minded majority. After a week's discussion, the resolutions committee divided 8 to 7 on the question of the twenty-one resolutions dealing with industrial organization that had been introduced by international unions, the state federations of California and Wisconsin, and federal unions.

In the debate that followed, all possible ideas and positions on the question of what form the future structure of the American Federation of Labor should take were brought forth. The secretary of the committee, John Frey, speaking for the majority, argued for continuing the policies laid down at the Washington conference and the 1934 convention. He said that the basis for existence of the American Federation of Labor lay in the guarantee to the international unions of jurisdiction over all workmen doing jobs covered by the charters of the respective unions and the retention by them of complete autonomy over their internal affairs. These guarantees, Frey stressed, were in the nature of a contract that could not be altered without the consent of both parties.

Charles Howard of the Typographical Union, whose concern for the unskilled workers could in no way be construed as an attempt of his highly skilled members to make gains in jurisdiction or membership, presented the minority report. Speaking for himself, David Dubinsky, Frank Powers of the Telegraphers, A. J. Myrup of the Bakery Workers, John L. Lewis, and J. C. Lewis of the Iowa Federation of Labor, he pointed out the failure of the existing structure and stated that the time had come to face up to the needs of the times. His report stated, "In the great mass production industries, and those in which the workers are composite, specialized and engaged upon classes of work which do not qualify them for craft union membership, industrial organization is the only solution."

Where the nature of the work was such that there might be conflicting jurisdictional claims, the report said, "industrial organization is the only form that will be acceptable or adequately meet the needs." Further, the minority demanded that the Federation make clear that unrestricted charters would be granted to industrial unions guaranteeing those unions the right to take in and keep any worker of an establishment without fear that some jurisdictional claim would be brought against the industrial union.[5]

There was a repetition by the minority group of the assertion that if their plan of organization were adopted no members would be taken away from any existing organization, but they did say that workers claimed by some of the craft unions would be organized into the industrial unions. Here they came directly into conflict with the doctrine enunciated by Frey that the jurisdictional claim, whether exercised or not, was a sacred and everlasting contract. This issue was a test of whether the Federation could continue to grow with changing circumstances or whether it had created for itself a strait jacket that would effectually prevent the organization into the AFL of most of the mass production workers of the country.

The motives of the men who debated at that turning point convention of the AFL were mixed and varied. John L. Lewis was a miner and the head of the strongest industrial union in the country. He believed in industrial unionism, and he also believed that industrial unionism was the only effective way to organize the giant anti-union steel industry whose ownership of the "captive" mines was a constant threat to his organization. In fact, his incisive and satirical comments on the question of organization and his year's experience on the executive council ended with a threat that if the Federation did not organize the steel industry the miners would have to do it themselves.

Matthew Woll, the scholarly lawyer of the Engravers Union, was the first speaker from the resolutions committee to support the status quo. Woll launched into a long and vague discussion which included a re-examination of the previous year's resolution, the doubts raised in his own mind by the passage of the National Labor Relations Act, and his belief that the convention should put its trust in the executive council. The speech seemed like an attempt to confuse and diffuse the issue at stake, in order to ease the task of those delegates who would be called upon to vote against the resolution.

John P. Frey recited his version of the history of the Knights of Labor, Debs, the Railway Union, and the IWW to prove the impracticality of any other organizational pattern than that being employed by the AFL in 1935. He again pointed out the sacredness of the contract which was included in the jurisdictional grant of international charters. Other speakers against the attempt to change the pattern of organization included Olander of the Seamen's Union and Wharton of the Machinists Union. The latter gave a long harangue on the values of the old ways and pointed out successes of his own organization.

Philip Murray, John L. Lewis' right-hand man, did not distinguish himself by his long, rambling reminiscences but did make a plea for the coöperation of the rest of the labor movement in organizing the steel industry. Apart from Murray's ramblings, it was clear as the hours dragged on that most of the eloquence was on the side that wanted to change. Everyone knew, however, that the votes which would make a decision were controlled by the heads of large international unions and that these votes were not being swayed by all this eloquence. After a day-and-night-long debate the roll call began. Quickly, the building trades unions, the metal unions, the railway unions, and the Teamsters rolled up the majority for conservatism. Long before the clerk reached the names of the delegates from the state federations and the city centrals, the outcome was obvious. But very few of these delegates with their single votes climbed on the winning side. Normally, they would have gone along with the majority once it was clear where the majority lay, but this time the feeling in the state and central bodies was so strong that some reform should be made that they put their names on the record against the majority. The majority position had 18,204 votes. There were 10,933 votes to adopt the industrial organization method. Almost two-thirds of these votes came from the Mine and Clothing Workers Unions.

The remaining days of that 1935 convention were filled with bitter debate in which the minority group led by Lewis did not let pass any opportunity to harangue the craft group. The leaders of the coal miners made the cause of the hard-rock miners their own when the jurisdictional quarrel between the Mine, Mill, and Smelter Workers and the Metal Trades Department came to the convention floor. It was in this debate that Dan Tobin of the Teamsters, trying to match the Lewis style of oratory, declared, "To us was given a charter of charters from the American Federation of Labor, and Gompers, McGuire, Duncan, Foster and the other men said, upon the rock of tradition, autonomy, craft trades, you shall build the church of the labor movement, and the Gates of Hell nor trade industrialism shall not prevail against it." [6]

Again, on the last day of the convention the question of the structure of the AFL was raised in a demand by the Rubber Workers that their jurisdiction be enlarged to include skilled and maintenance workers. It was at the height of this debate that John L. Lewis strode across the convention hall and struck Big Bill Hutcheson of the Carpenters. Frey said then, "This will wreck the labor movement."[7] It is quite unlikely that John L. Lewis allowed himself the luxury of hitting William Hutcheson out of pure annoyance. At this stage in the convention, Lewis must have pretty much made up his mind that those who wanted industrial organization would have to get it outside of the regular procedures of the confederation and particularly outside the control of the executive council.

Now Lewis knew that more than one-third of the convention votes and probably a much larger percentage of the rank and file membership of AFL unions wanted steel, automobiles, rubber, cement, and textiles organized, and if forming industrial unions was the method for such organizing, he could count on their support. Lewis' blow at Hutcheson was in a sense a gesture of defiance against the stand-patter and a proof to workers, particularly in the mass production industries, that John L. Lewis was their friend and was willing to strike a blow for their freedom to join unions of their choosing and not of the choosing of Hutcheson, Wharton, Woll, and Frey. If the controlling group in the AFL convention had had fewer votes and had felt less sure of their control, they would have made concessions at Atlantic City. But secure in their strength, they used their power to push through a resolution which showed no willingness to compromise and no sense that the labor movement as a whole was more important than their own smaller domains. This display of power led the progressive unionists to despair of using the machinery of the AFL for the task that needed doing. These progressives, in search of a leader who would have the courage to defy the executive council, turned to John L. Lewis, who had emerged from the debates at the Atlantic City meetings as the strongest man in the American labor movement.

Formation of the CIO

Lewis and his fellow advocates of industrial organization met immediately after the adjournment of the convention and began the formation of a Committee for Industrial Organization. On November 10, 1935, they announced to the press that the Committee membership included the following individuals: John L. Lewis, Charles P. Howard,

Sidney Hillman of the Amalgamated Clothing Workers, David Dubinsky of the Ladies Garment Workers, Thomas McMahon, president of the United Textile Workers, Harvey Fremming, president of the Oil Workers, Max Zaritsky, president of the Cap and Millinery Workers, and Thomas H. Brown, president of the International Union of Mine, Mill, and Smelter Workers. This first public announcement made it clear that the purpose of the Committee was to carry out the policies advocated by its members at the Atlantic City convention to "encourage and promote organization of workers in mass production and unorganized industries of the nation and affiliation with the American Federation of Labor." Lewis was named chairman of the Committee and Howard its secretary. Shortly afterwards, the Committee announced that it desired "to further in every way efforts of groups of workers in autos, aluminum, radio and many other mass production industries, to find a place within the organized labor movement as represented by the American Federation of Labor." [8]

Every effort was made to stress that this Committee did not intend to be a dual labor movement. Of course, such an action contained within itself, the possibility of dualism. In those first weeks, whether dualism would result from this new organization depended upon the turn of events, especially upon the attitude taken by the executive council of the AFL. The CIO organizers were trying one more tactic in the battle to organize the unorganized that had begun in the coal fields and garment factories in the spring of 1933. It was a continuation of the Washington conference and the San Francisco and Atlantic City battles for realistic organization. Since the men who controlled the apparatus of the American labor movement were unwilling to make concessions, it was necessary to invent some new device that might circumvent the conservatives and yet allow more liberal members to recognize it as a legitimate method of dynamic unionism, particularly if it were successful.

The founders of the Committee for Industrial Organization may have had some of the jubilant feeling that Franklin Roosevelt and some of his close advisers had at a later date when lend-lease was invented to circumvent a congressional barrier and save democracy. The new Committee found constitutional justification for international unions acting jointly outside the AFL in the time-honored and sacred concept of autonomy. The pale would be reached when and if the Committee should issue charters or lay claim to workers whose jobs lay within the jurisdictional territories of other unions. The provisions of the AFL's charter gave the CIO leaders further comfort. The constitution provided that unions could be expelled from the AFL only by two-thirds vote of the convention. In November, 1935, the next AFL convention was a year away and the CIO leaders already felt they had enough votes to block any expulsion.

The majority of the executive council took quite a different view of the activities of the Committee. They did not regard these activities as coming within the privileged action of autonomous international unions, and they were too unsure of their position to await developments. Within two weeks of the November 10 announcement, William Green wrote to each of the constituent organizations, pointing out the grave implications of the action and saying that the action would be regarded by some international unions as the formation of a dual organization. He spoke of the discord, the division and confusion that would result. He argued, "It has been the fixed rule both within the American Federation of Labor and national and international unions affiliated with it to decide upon organizational policies by a majority vote at legally convened convention.... When a decision has been rendered it becomes the duty of the officers and members of the American Federation of Labor to comply with it.... Those who disagree with the action of the majority are accorded the right to urge the acceptance of their point of view at succeeding conventions."[9] In reply, Howard said that the Committee's actions were necessary because the executive council had failed to carry out the San Francisco convention's mandate, and that there was no intention to raid or set up a dual organization. The January meeting of the executive council declared that the Committee should be immediately dissolved, and that the several organizations should abide by the decisions of the Atlantic City convention with respect to organizational policies. It also authorized a committee of its members to meet with the representatives of the organizations composing the CIO to present to them the executive council's point of view.

In February the Committee leaders rejected the order to disband and countered with an offer to provide one-third of a 1.5 million dollar fund to organize steel if the AFL would provide the remainder. When the executive council rejected this latter offer, the Committee entered into an agreement with the Amalgamated Association of Iron, Steel and Tin Workers whereby $500,000 would be provided by the Committee to organize steel and the control of the organizing campaign would be in the hands of a CIO-dominated Steel Workers Organizing Committee.

In the meantime, President Tracy of the International Brotherhood of Electrical Workers had filed charges of dualism against the Committee, on the grounds that it had advised the National Radio and Allied Trades to reject affiliation with his organization; the IBEW had munificently offered a Class B, nonvoting charter to the radio workers.

In the spring of 1936 the Federation of Flat Glass Workers, the United Automobile Workers, and the Rubber Workers joined the Committee, giving more impetus to the executive council's efforts to stop the Committee. These new members of the Committee brought in organizations which were both militant and immature. Most of the original affiliates of the Committee were long-time members and deeply steeped in the traditions of the AFL. Tradition was, of course, lacking in the Rubber Workers and Automobile Workers since their organizations were scarcely a year old. Their joining meant that the impetus for quick and drastic action was strengthened. Also, by way of these new organizations, leftists who had never been at all sympathetic to the American Federation of Labor and who had seized upon the new unions as an avenue for agitation were now able to get their views at least presented to the Committee.

On May 18, the executive council, from which John L. Lewis had resigned several months earlier, met secretly. Acting under Section A of Article 9 of the AFL constitution which provides, "the Executive Council shall have the power to make the rules to govern matters not in conflict with this Constitution or the Constitution of affiliated unions and shall report accordingly to the Federation," the council drastically increased its own powers to act between conventions. It gave itself power to hear charges against a union accused of violating any provision of the constitution or laws of the AFL or any order of the executive council. If a union was found guilty, the rule provided that the executive council could (a) forgive it with or without conditions, (b) suspend it, (c) penalize it in any way, (d) with the approval of two-thirds of the convention, reject its charter. Like provisions were made for the state federations, for central labor bodies, and federal locals.[10]

This was the answer of the executive council to the belief of the dissenters that they could not be expelled from the Federation without the action of two-thirds of a convention at which they were represented. This action of the council can better be defended as a wartime measure than as being within the power granted to the executive council by the constitution of the American Federation of Labor. Its drastic nature is evidence that the die-hard conservatives were in complete control of the executive council.

On June 20, President Green on behalf of the executive council sent letters to the officers of the organizations affiliated with the Committee, asking them to meet with the council so that the council could learn why they had not obeyed the request to disband, and so that the council could determine what further action it should take on the matter. No member of the Committee or the affiliates appeared to explain. In mid-July, President Frey of the Metal Trades Department brought formal charges against the Committee "alleging it was a dual organization functioning within the American Federation of Labor as such, and in administrative activities clearly competing as a rival organization within the American Federation of Labor." [11]

Again the rebels were invited to appear. Without them, on August 3, the executive council began hearings which culminated in a resolution of August 5 finding the affiliates to the CIO guilty of dualism and giving them until September 5 to withdraw from the Committee or be suspended from the American Federation of Labor.

Once the machinery had been set in motion with its elaborate provisions for trials and suspension, there was no way to get out of the situation, and on September 5, with the exception of the International Typographical Union and the Cap and Millinery Workers International Union, all internationals connected with the Committee for Industrial Organization stood suspended if the executive council could make their action stick.

Efforts to Prevent Split

The hasty action of the alarmed and furious executive council in getting the CIO unions "suspended" was soon followed by a realization that the American labor movement was really being split. Cooler heads in both groups tried to do something to patch up the situation. Early in October the Hat Workers' convention asked for the appointment of subcommittees from both groups to work out means of reconciliation. The executive council promptly appointed a committee composed of Vice-Presidents Harrison, Woll, and Knight. John L. Lewis, relishing his role as leader of the rebels, was not anxious to appoint a committee. Rather, he denounced the unconstitutionality of the suspension order. A week before the Tampa convention and after the presidential election of 1936, Dubinsky and Zaritsky forced a meeting of the CIO leaders to consider the question of peace negotiations. Lewis personally offered to meet Green, but after Green stated that he could not change the executive council policies, the meeting was cancelled. Dubinsky and Zaritsky saw such a conference as the Hatters had proposed as a possible means of getting the suspension removed and thus allowing the unions affiliated with the Committee an opportunity to take part in the Tampa convention. Lewis had invested a great sum of the Mine Workers' money and much energy in the re-election of President Roosevelt, and without doubt regarded that election as having created a climate in which labor could afford the luxury of division if he could not bring his unions back to the House of Labor on his own terms.

The convention of the American Federation of Labor that assembled in Tampa in November, 1936, lacked about 30 per cent of the membership because the "suspended" unions did not choose to come and demand their right to be seated. Such a demand on their part might have drastically altered the pattern of American labor history, for had they voted they could have prevented the two-thirds vote needed to expel them from the Federation. The power to push through its own policies in the convention was insured to the executive council when the rebels stayed away, but there were many voices in the convention that roundly criticized the action of the council in its suspension on the grounds that it was both an unconstitutional and an unsound policy that would wreck the labor movement.

Among the most articulate against the administration policies were delegates from state federations and city centrals. Again and again they argued that the primary issue was not whether a minority had refused to accept the mandate of the majority at Atlantic City, but that the real question was the welfare of the labor movement. Their position in local labor organizations that were being torn by the split made them particularly sensitive to the problem as it affected rank and file workers.

The outstanding attempt to heal the breach was made by the delegation from the Wisconsin Federation of Labor. The proposal, which came to be known as the "Wisconsin Plan," well illustrates the kind of attempt that those in the exposed positions saw necessary if the movement was to be reunited. In the late hours of the debate Delegate Friedrick, of the Wisconsin Federation of Labor, tried to amend the report of the resolutions committee by substituting a proposal that declared:

That in the interest of re-establishing harmony and unity, the suspension of the CIO organizations be lifted, and that a committee of seven members, including one representative of the state federation of labor and one of a city central body, be appointed by the President, such committee to meet with representatives of the CIO to seek an adjustment of the controversy, that such committee report to the Executive Council within 90 days and that the Executive Council be given authority to call a special convention after the committee has reported if they deem it necessary.[12]

After objections from Hutcheson of the Carpenters and Coefield of the Plumbers, Friedrick was ruled out of order and his amendment never went to a vote. Even in the watered-down form proposed to the convention, this Wisconsin Plan worried the die-hard craft unionists. As originally written and presented to the executive council in August, the plan had provided:

1. That all charges against organizations affiliated with the CIO be immediately dismissed and all plans for expulsion of such organizations from the AFL be dropped.

2. That the AFL participate wholeheartedly and completely with the CIO in the organization's drive to organize the steel industry and the rubber industry on an industrial organization basis so that this plan and the resulting organization may have a fair chance to prove its efficiency.

3. That the CIO confine its industrial organization drive to the steel and rubber industries until such time that further action is taken by the AFL.

4. That the president of the AFL within 60 days appoint a special committee of two representatives of international unions classed as industrial unions, and two classed as craft unions, three representatives of city central bodies, and two representatives of federal labor unions, to study all phases of organizational setup within the labor movement. We recommend the placing of the specified number of representatives of State Federations and city central bodies and federal labor unions on this committee because such representatives are very close to the workers in the industries of the nation. The activities of such committee to be financed by the American Federation

of Labor and such committee to take a written report and recommendations to the 1937 convention of the AFL.[13]

This proposal, presented to the executive council before the "trial" of the rebel unions, provided a face-saving escape from the position into which the council had put itself by writing a rule that gave it power to suspend national and international unions. Such a committee, weighted so heavily with representatives of state federations and federal unions, would almost certainly have found some compromise that would have continued the unified existence of the American Federation of Labor. The council rejected the Wisconsin Plan in August, and it was kept from being voted upon in its modified form at Tampa by the leaders of the craft bloc, although pre-convention rumor had reported that it would be put forward by a large bloc of the delegates and could be the basis for a settlement of the dispute.[14]

CIO Expansion and AFL Response

During the summer of 1936, John L. Lewis was more interested in the outcome of the presidential election than in any declarations by the executive council of the AFL. The Miners Union had given $500,000 to the Democratic National Committee, and Lewis, who had worked for Herbert Hoover in 1932, was working very hard to make sure that an administration favorable to unionism would be in the White House. Once President Roosevelt had been returned to office by an overwhelming majority of electoral votes, the Committee for Industrial Organization turned to organizing.

The election itself had created among workers an atmosphere comparable to the early days of NRA. There had been enough publicity about the battle within the AFL so that the CIO was regarded as the champion of mass production workers. The technique of the sit-down strike had been developed in the rubber industry in 1935 and was successfully used in automobiles in late 1936 and early 1937. By the spring of 1937 the United States Steel Corporation, which had been the bitterest enemy of the labor movement, had signed an agreement with the Steel Workers Organizing Committee without a strike. Sit-down strikes had brought agreement with the General Motors Corporation.

Early 1937 saw organizational drives in steel, shoes, aluminum, cement, radio, chemicals, transport, meat-packing, and other industries. Very often, these drives were started by the workers themselves who either went out on a strike or took over the company union and then asked for help from the hard-pressed CIO. The Supreme Court decision upholding the Wagner Act came at a very crucial time and gave new encouragement to the rebels. In the spring and summer of 1937, new member organizations of the Committee included the United Shoe Workers; the Aluminum Workers of America; the American Communications Association; the Transport Workers Union; the Architects, Engineers, Chemists, and Technicians; United Retail Employees; the International Fur Workers; the Office and Professional Workers; the American Newspaper Guild; the United Federal Workers; the National Die-Casting League; the Agricultural, Packing and Canning Workers; the National Maritime Union; the International Woodworkers of America; the Marine Engineers' Beneficial Association; and the International Longshoremen's and Warehousemen's Union. Some of these were out-right defections of a whole AFL national union. More often they were secessionist groups augmented by new locals, company unions, and federal unions. Altogether, thirty-two affiliated national unions claiming nearly 4,000,000 members and 30,000 signed agreements were reported at the CIO's October, 1937, meeting in Atlantic City.

However, all was not bright for the CIO. The Steel Workers Organizing Committee had been defeated in its strike against the independent steel companies. There was a tremendous lack of experienced leadership, particularly on the local level, and the newly organized mass production workers were most vulnerable to the recession which was on the horizon. AFL oppositional strength was growing, for the successes of the CIO had increased the bitterness of the Federation leaders and undermined their assumption that the CIO would wither away as earlier dual movements had done. In May, 1937, a special per capita tax had been enacted by the AFL, and the Federation went to work in earnest to organize. In a year it had half a million new members. By fall, 1937, when their two national conventions met, it was clear that in the foreseeable future both organizations would continue to exist and would fight each other by every known method. The standard of rebellion and civil war would prevail over any sense of belonging to a class movement.

An Attempt at Reconciliation

In both camps, thinking men were in great doubt as to where it all might end. The sit-down strikes had done much to exhaust labor's stock of public good will. The administration, friendly to organized labor, found itself constantly embarrassed by the split. As the two groups went to their conventions in the fall of 1937, the pressure was on for some sort of rapprochement. The October conference of the CIO wired the AFL's Denver convention and proposed that a committee of 100 from each group meet to consider methods and means whereby the labor movement could be unified. Finally, it was decided a committee of three from the AFL would meet with a committee of ten from the CIO at Washington on October 25. Each side brought its proposals. The CIO proposals included: (1) The AFL should declare as basic policy that workers in the mass production, marine, public utilities, service, and basic fabricating industries be organized only on an industrial basis. (2) A complete, autonomous CIO department should be established within the AFL. (3) A convention of all AFL and CIO affiliates should be called to approve this agreement.

The AFL proposed that (1) all former affiliates of the AFL resume their active affiliation; (2) conferences be held between representatives of AFL and other CIO affiliates to iron out conflicts; (3) differences in administrative and organizational policies be referred to the next AFL convention, and in the meantime an aggressive organizing campaign along both industrial and craft lines, as circumstances warranted, be carried on; (4) the CIO be dissolved immediately.

The CIO proposal was unacceptable to the AFL for it solved nothing, merely transferring the dual organization into the Federation and giving the Federation no authority to settle jurisdictional disputes to which the unions and CIO might be parties. On the other hand, if the CIO leaders had accepted the Federation's proposal, it would have looked as if they were abandoning the new organizations which they had helped form, leaving such organizations to risk whatever arrangement they might work out with their AFL counterpart.

Starting from these two unacceptable proposals the conference spent eight weeks trying to work out a solution agreeable to all parties. The AFL's executive council reported to its 1938 convention that an agreement had been negotiated which would bring the original twelve unions back into the AFL when the jurisdictional problems of each of the twenty new CIO unions had been worked out with its AFL counterpart. In addition, after all other matters had been adjusted, the AFL agreed that all affiliated organizations would have full rights and privileges and certain industries would be specifically earmarked for industrial form of organization.

The AFL council also reported that at the request of Charles P. Howard public announcement of the agreement was postponed until Philip Murray, who was absent, could be informed. Then something seemed to go wrong. The official AFL version stated that at the next meeting Murray refused to carry out the agreement and proposed that the entire controversy be referred to a subcommittee. The AFL representatives on the subcommittee argued for the agreement which had already been consented to. Lewis, for the CIO, insisted that all thirty-two CIO unions be admitted to the Federation and matters of conflict be taken up afterwards. The AFL refused to accept these terms and the attempt at unity broke down. It seems that at least an informal agreement had been reached but had been rejected by Lewis and Murray.

Cause for the Split

In retrospect, it seems very clear that in 1935 drastic action was needed to force the leadership of the American labor movement to their primary task of organizing workers. These leaders had refused to recognize that great changes in industry required some changes in the methods of the AFL. However, special circumstances had put control of the Federation into the hands of a group determined to maintain the status quo and particularly insistent upon organization along craft lines. Previously, the AFL had accommodated itself to new situations by such devices as the Scranton Declaration, amalgamations, and trade departments. Industrial unionism itself was not new to the AFL, for several large industrial unions had existed within its framework for many years. The question of industrial unionism was certainly not dead. The failure to organize steel in 1919, the continuous Socialist agitation for it on principle, and the agitation of such progressive forces as the Brookwood College kept the question of industrial unionism alive.

The creation of the Committee for Industrial Organization allowed the labor movement to escape from its self-imposed strait jacket of narrow constitutional interpretation and fit its pattern to the times as it had in the dynamic years of pre–World War I Gompersism.

The dramatic organizing successes of the CIO in 1936 and early 1937 put the AFL on its mettle and it too organized where and how it could.[15] The mass production industries could have been organized without the CIO, but they could not have been organized without leadership, enthusiasm, and insistence on industrial unions. This direction the AFL executive council refused to give, and this John L. Lewis and his followers gladly provided.

How long the labor movement needed to be split is another question. By the late summer of 1936 the craft leaders were in a conciliatory mood. Certainly by late 1937, if the CIO group had wanted unity it could have had it on honorable terms. If the AFL forced the split, the CIO seems to have maintained it.

The great contribution of the CIO—the insistence on a dynamic and forward-looking structure for the American labor movement—was made by the end of 1937. From then on the price of dualism was very high.

Adverse Consequences of Split

In 1938 the CIO was established as a permanent organization, and its name was changed from Committee to Congress of Industrial Organizations. Despite the continued attempts at reconciliation put forward by such leaders as David Dubinsky, whose own union soon withdrew from the Congress, and in spite of the attempts of the Roosevelt administration to bring unity to the labor movement, at no time before the early fifties was unity as close as it was at the end of 1937.

By the end of 1937 the political tide was running against the New Deal's domestic reform policies. The battle to reorganize the Supreme Court had given the conservative southern Democrats an excuse to get off the New Deal bandwagon and, combining with northern Republicans, they brought an end to progressive and social legislation. It is difficult to evaluate the contribution of the great labor upheaval of 1936 and 1937 to this return to conservatism at the national legislative level, but it certainly was an important factor. Many of those opposed to social reforms and labor organizations would have been so opposed under any circumstances, but the rivalries within the labor movement gave the enemies of unionism ammunition and at the same time aroused serious doubts in the minds of that part of the general public who since the depression had been more or less sympathetic to unionism. The events of 1937 had tired the public of unionism and of strikes whatever their causes. In the Little Steel strike, Roosevelt himself had said, "A plague on both your houses."

The public reaction was particularly adverse in those situations where a labor dispute seemed to be primarily a question not of whether a union should be recognized but of whether the workers should belong to the AFL or the CIO. The Wagner Act had been written before the split, and the concern of its author was to give the workers a choice between a union, presumably AFL, and no union. Once it had been established that the CIO and the AFL would both be in existence for the foreseeable future, competition between their affiliates for members became very keen, and to many union organizers it did not matter very much whether the recruits came from among the unorganized, from a plant which a rival was in the process of organizing, or from a local already an established affiliate of the rival federation.

As in most civil wars no holds were barred. Extravagant promises were made to the workers and large sums of money were spent to entice a local away from another union. When the National Labor Relations Board came into such a situation, it found itself holding an election where the workers had to choose not only between unionism and nonunionism but also between two unions. Part of the task of the NLRB was the determination of the composition of the voting and bargaining units. Often this was a choice between an AFL-preferred craft unit and a CIO-preferred industrial unit. The kind of unit chosen could often determine the outcome of the election, and this put the Board in the unenviable position of having some share in shaping the structure of the labor movement. Needless to say, whatever their decision on the bargaining unit the Board was certain to arouse the anger of one of the unions involved in such cases.[16]

In many cases a bitterly fought election was not the end to such interunion rivalry. The loser might continue to keep an organization alive hoping for a reversal in another election. Picketing of a plant by the disgruntled international union was not uncommon if by such action it believed it could bring pressure to bear on the employer or his workers to get the workers to change their bargaining agent.

Under such circumstances employers with the best of intent could not build a stable union-employer relationship and sometimes found their production interrupted through no fault of their own. Employers and newspapers were quick to bring such cases to the attention of the public.

As a result of the sit-down strikes, union rivalries, and the feeling that labor was getting out of hand, 1939 saw strong demands on Congress to revise or repeal the Wagner Act. Even the AFL sought revision of the law—hoping to get it changed to favor craft rather than industrial bargaining units. President Roosevelt refused to open the law to possible amendments that would destroy it; only his refusal preserved the original form of the Wagner Act.

The split in the labor movement was an embarrassment to the Roosevelt administration in any area where labor's counsel and assistance were needed. Both factions had to be consulted and neither could safely be given preference in such questions as appointments to governmental agencies, no matter how qualified its candidate, without arousing the ire of the other faction.

On the general political front, labor, which should have been the strong supporter of the administration, was because of its division much less influential in the important state and congressional elections. Organized labor's standing with the public and with its own rank and file was lowered by the stream of insults which issued from both camps but especially from the CIO intellectuals and John L. Lewis with reference to the leadership of the AFL. On the other side, the AFL leaders did nothing to dispel the notion that the CIO was a radical organization bent on destroying the American way of life.

When in 1916 it seemed as if this nation might be drawn into the European War, Samuel Gompers, speaking for the labor movement, had assured President Wilson that the administration could count upon the full support of the organized workers of the country. In 1940 things were very different. No one person could speak for the House of Labor. The CIO was under the domination of John L. Lewis, who believed that this country should in no way be drawn into an overseas war and who had broken with Roosevelt and was not eager to support any Roosevelt policy. Around Lewis were left-wing advisers who for very different reasons from his wanted to do nothing to aid Britain and her allies. These Soviet sympathizers, who had gained access to the labor movement and were kept in places of importance because of the split, used their positions to promote the Soviet cause and ranged themselves alongside the true isolationists until Hitler invaded Russia.

At the time of Pearl Harbor John L. Lewis was engaged in wrecking the administration's machinery for the settling of disputes affecting the defense effort.

Instead of a Gompers for a chief adviser, President Roosevelt depended heavily on Sidney Hillman in labor matters. Hillman worked very hard, but he had little standing with the AFL and was not the official spokesman for the CIO. If the labor movement had not been split in the defense period, 1940–41, labor could have given greater support to the administration, John L. Lewis' isolationism would not have loomed so large, and the left-wing minority in the CIO would have had little or no influence.

After Pearl Harbor all elements of the labor movement supported the war effort and throughout the war there was no authorized strike by either AFL or CIO. The coal miners struck several times, but they were no longer a part of the CIO. Certainly the war effort gained nothing by the split in the labor movement with the inevitable competition and comparisons between rival unions. A great deal of energy and ill-spared leadership was wasted by having two labor representatives in governmental agencies where one would have done for a united labor movement. No one charged that this was a form of featherbedding, but it was obviously wasteful of labor's scarce leadership resources. On the other hand, the war agencies and particularly the War Labor Board and its regional subdivisions did give AFL and CIO leaders valuable experience in working together and often in joining against the employers and/or the public members.

Going his own way, John L. Lewis increased demands for anti-labor legislation because of his strikes, and in 1943 Congress passed the Smith-Connolly Act over the President's veto. Again one can conjecture that as part of a unified labor movement, Lewis might not have felt so strongly the need for getting more for his miners than any other labor group was able to achieve in the midst of the war. This wartime behavior of the miners' leader was one of the most important factors in uniting support for postwar labor legislation which culminated in the Taft-Hartley law. His attempts to discredit the ability of the AFL and CIO leadership were very expensive for the whole labor movement and must in part be chalked up as another cost of the split.

Factors Leading to Reunification

In the years immediately after the war several things happened which helped pave the way for the unity that finally came in the mid-fifties. They were the enactment of the Taft-Hartley law, the eviction of the left-wing–led unions from the CIO, the experiences gained in working together on the international scene, the actual calculation by AFL and CIO leaders of the cost of competition in organizing and raiding, the signing of no-raiding agreements by some of the major international unions such as the Machinists and the Auto Workers, and finally the passing from the scene of some of the leaders who felt most bitter about the events of the thirties.

Looking back to the period just preceding the Taft-Hartley law, it is recalled that 1946 was the year of greatest labor unrest since 1919. At the end of the war both labor and management were resentful at the self-restraint they had been obliged to practice during the war period, and both wanted to make up for lost time. No matter what the reasons for the many strikes, the public which had looked to the end of the war for a great and glorious shower of consumers' goods reacted very unfavorably to the strikes and the strikers. This added to the previous anti-union sentiments, and Congress, which before the war had been prevented from amending or repealing the Wagner Act, went into action. In 1946 President Truman stopped the Case bill by a veto, but in 1947 a conservative alliance of northern Republicans and southern Democrats was able to pass the Taft-Hartley Act over his veto. The passage of this law caused labor leaders who hitherto had avoided politics to join with their more politically-minded brethren in a campaign to get the law repealed and to punish with ballots those who voted for the law. In the ensuing political experience many labor leaders and rank and file members saw the benefits of coöperation at the local level and wished for much more at the national level. Many of these workers began to question the reasons for preserving a civil war whose cause for existence had long since passed away.

Passage of the Taft-Hartley law also served notice on the labor movement that labor was a minority in the American scene and that it could not afford to be fighting itself except on those rare occasions when it had a Franklin D. Roosevelt in the White House and a pro-labor Congress on Capitol Hill.

From 1941 to 1948 Philip Murray had tried to hold the influence of the Communists and fellow travelers in check within the CIO. He was successful because during the war the immediate objective of Soviet sympathizers was no different from that of other Americans; within the labor organizations the struggle for power went on, but outwardly there was no problem. All this changed immediately after the war when Russian foreign policy began to differ from that of the United States. Some CIO unions under left-wing influence opposed the Marshall Plan and in 1948, against specific CIO policy, supported Henry Wallace for the presidency. This defiance of stated CIO policies along with the changed mood of the public and of the union rank and file gave Murray a weapon to use in forcing the left-wing–led unions out of the CIO. After the expulsions in 1949 and 1950, one large argument against unity in the minds of AFL leaders was gone. At the same time the group which had most to gain by dualism was out of the CIO and could no longer influence its policies.

Beginning in 1949 the newly formed International Confederation of Free Trade Unions provided AFL and CIO leaders a chance to work together in the international field where their interests as Americans were very similar. For the first time the AFL had agreed to work in an international labor organization where the CIO was represented. At the same time leaders from both groups were coöperating in the administration of the Marshall Plan and were coöperating in other international programs of the federal government such as the exchange of persons program and the productivity teams which brought many foreign trade unionists to the United States and took many American unionists abroad.

The Korean War brought the United Labor Policy Committee and the Wage Stabilization Board with more joint action on the part of the two federations. At the same time some of the international unions, finding the cost of raiding so great and realizing the futility of it, began to make agreements among themselves to respect each other's members and agreements. The more the representatives of the two groups worked together the more apparent were the advantages that might be achieved by organic unity.

The election of 1952 which brought into office an administration considered unfriendly by most labor leaders was another argument for a united labor movement, and by that time peace negotiations could be carried on in an atmosphere from which such personalities of 1935–38 as Murray, Green, Hutcheson, Tobin, and Wharton were absent. John L. Lewis was outside the federations, and if he had any influence, it was to push Meany and Reuther together to head off any coalitions that might conceivably be built around the old man.

So at last the new leadership of the AFL and CIO was able to bring about the unity to which all factors of the labor movement had been paying lip service for twenty years.

Notes

1 American Federation of Labor, *Proceedings,* 1901, p. 240.
2 American Federation of Labor, *Proceedings,* 1934, p. 40.
3 *Ibid.,* p. 592.
4 *Ibid.*
5 American Federation of Labor, *Proceedings,* 1935, p. 523.
6 *Ibid.,* p. 659.
7 Edward Levinson, *Labor on the March* (New York: Harper and Bros., 1938), p. 116.
8 American Federation of Labor, *Proceedings,* 1936, p. 68.
9 *Ibid.,* pp. 70–71.
10 *Ibid.,* pp. 121–22.
11 *Ibid.,* p. 78.
12 Milwaukee *Leader,* July 28, 1936.
13 *Ibid.*
14 Milwaukee *Leader,* November 13, 1936.
15 These organizational successes are described in Chapter 1.
16 See Harry A. Millis and Emily Clark Brown, *From the Wagner Act to Taft-Hartley* (Chicago: University of Chicago Press, 1950), pp. 138 ff.

3

The Impact of the Political Left

BERNARD KARSH *and*
PHILLIPS L. GARMAN

THROUGHOUT its history the American labor movement has been beset by individuals and groups whose aim was to use trade unions as vehicles to effect profound or revolutionary economic and political changes in society. These leftists have ranged from anarchists and syndicalists to Socialists of varying beliefs and finally to Communists. By "left-wing unions" we mean trade unions which have been dominated or heavily influenced by leaders holding such ideologies. The effectiveness and intensity of their efforts to transform the American labor movement varied considerably from period to period, but with the onset of the Great Depression and the birth of the New Deal, all such political left-wingers faced an almost unprecedented opportunity and achieved substantial successes.

Pre-Depression Left-Wing Unionism

Among the early leaders of the first stable, national unions were men who, though initially influenced by socialism, ultimately rejected the Marxist idea of class consciousness in favor of wage and job conscious unionism. These unionists persevered and, in 1886, succeeded in firmly establishing the American Federation of Labor.

Others who were more radical worked through the Socialist Labor party, under the leadership of Daniel DeLeon, and carried on an active fight for control of both the Federation and the waning Knights of Labor. Failing in these efforts, the Socialists began, in 1895, to split—one group, under DeLeon, ultimately deciding to go the route of dual unionism and endeavoring to set up purely Socialist unions of a more or less syndicalist nature. When these unions proved ineffective, similar efforts at a dual labor movement sprang from the Western Federation of Miners, a Socialist-led trade union made up of metal miners west of the Mississippi.

Leaders from the Socialist Labor party and the Western Federation of Miners together with some other radicals coöperated for a short time in the establishment of the Industrial Workers of the World in 1905. This left-wing offensive was directed against the unions of the American Federation of Labor—insisting that "abolition of the wage system" be substituted for the alleged goal of "a fair day's work for a fair day's pay"—as well as against the capitalists. However, the offensive emerged not from the classic proletariat in the citadels of finance and industrial capitalism of the East but from laborers affected by the working conditions and robust activism of the American West. Its program of revolutionary, industrial unionism was in reality an American version of anarcho-syndicalism.

In eight short years its leaders, including Big Bill Haywood, succeeded in organizing and carrying on violent strikes of workers who had not been reached by the regular trade unions, in lumber, metal mining, agricultural, maritime, and textile work. After the failure of the Passaic Textile strike in 1913, the influence of the IWW gradually waned, partly because of the harsh treatment accorded its leaders by public opinion and government agencies, particularly during and after World War I. Beginning about 1919, some of its leaders went into the Communist movement. Probably more fundamental, however, was the weakness resulting from the lack of interest of the IWW leaders in establishing permanent organizations to carry on systematic collective bargaining.

The more moderate Socialists abjured the ways of dual unionism and continued to work within the established trade unions in an attempt to convert union leaders and members to the acceptance of political socialism. Under the leadership of Eugene Debs and Victor Berger, these Socialists founded, in 1901, the Socialist Party of America; but the party did not undertake an organized, centrally directed program to capture the trade unions. It concentrated instead on running candidates for national and local offices. In 1912, Debs was a candidate for President and received 900,000 votes, or 6 per cent of the total vote—the highest percentage ever won by the party.[1] Although many unions had some Socialist officers (particularly among the needle trades, the Brewery Workers, Miners, Printers, and at times the Machinists) and several of these unions endorsed Socialist principles in general terms, they still concentrated largely on "pure and simple" job conscious unionism in their day-to-day programs. In addition, while they usually supported a common program, such as independent political action, they were not always in agreement on issues within the labor movement.

The Socialist party suffered heavy attack during World War I because of its anti-war program. Nonetheless, in the postwar period it seemed temporarily on its way toward increasing vigor and influence until it split, in 1919, and many of its adherents joined the emerging Communist movement.

The American Communist movement was born in part out of the previous radical heritage and parties of this country, but more importantly out of the Russian Revolution and the direction of the Bolsheviks and the Third International. Influenced by Leninism, a small, active band of American radicals attempted to wrest control of the Socialist party with the intention of preparing the country for revolution. The gradualist leaders of democratic socialism retaliated by expelling the Communists. The result, in 1919, was the Workers party, ultimately becoming the Communist Party of America, which viewed the trade unions as "schools of communism" subject to the control of the political party.[2]

The party's policy in the trade union field initially was one of dual unionism, and it had very slight success. The policy was changed in 1920, after the publication of Lenin's pamphlet, *Left Wing Communism: An Infantile Disorder*, which urged Communists to go into existing unions no matter how "reactionary," and in response the Trade Union Educational League was set up as a mechanism to "bore from within." William Z. Foster, a long-time revolutionary, became the head of TUEL. He had been in the IWW, but under the influence of French syndicalism became convinced that the policy of dual unionism was improper, and he subsequently succeeded in becoming influential before and during the war period in the Chicago Federation of Labor. With such sponsorship he became a key figure in coördinated attempts by AFL unions to organize workers in the meat-packing and steel industries. Although the attempts were well executed, they proved unsuccessful in overcoming the employers' strong resistance, and Foster openly went back to revolutionary unionism.

By 1923 TUEL's attempt to act as a revolutionary wing within the AFL proved virtually impossible. This was due, among other reasons, to the directives from the Third International to subordinate trade union policies to political objectives, the attempt to control unions by active participation in their elections, and the public exposure of the organization and its leader, Foster, as agents of the Communists. Many of the non-Communist radicals and "progressives" within the unions began to decry the party's tactics. The TUEL then opened a direct attack on the AFL and made substantial dents in such unions as the Machinists, the Ladies Garment Workers, and the Mine Workers and particularly the Fur Workers in the New York area. It was less successful in the Amalgamated Clothing Workers and the Hat and Millinery Workers.

The trade union leaders responded with drastic measures including loyalty pledges, removal of TUEL members from union office, and in some cases expulsion. In order to meet this exigency, Foster advised his followers to sign membership pledges against the TUEL in order to avoid their own expulsion. In 1925, hoping to maximize the effectiveness of boring from within, Foster urged stricter implementation of the Communist policy of organizing tightly disciplined party fractions within all levels of union structures. This program lasted until 1928, when at the Fourth Congress of the Red Labor Union International in Moscow the ineffectiveness of the attempt to capture any significant sections of the American labor movement was tacitly admitted, and the "line" was changed.

This third period of the Communist party produced a return to the policy of dual unionism, the vehicle created for the purpose in this country being the Trade Union Unity League, also under the direction of Foster. Affiliates of the TUUL were established in a number of industries, including coal mining, the garment trades, and maritime and metal products, but most of them were paper organizations with very few members and no established collective bargaining relationships. There were a few spectacular TUUL-led strikes, but otherwise the organization made scant impression on the labor front until the developments in the New Deal period and a reversion to boring from within gave opportunity for the trained cadres to operate among large groups of unorganized and newly organized workers.

The Depression and the Temper of the Times

Some of the reasons for the growth of radicalism and left-wing influence in trade unions in the New Deal period are to be found in the influence of the Great Depression on the economic, social, and ideological climate of the times. Faith in American capitalism and free enterprise as an effective way of realizing the American dream of economic freedom and independence was shockingly shattered for people in many walks of life.

The depression vented its force on farmers (who had already been suffering many lean years), industrial and retail employers, bankers, mortgage companies, and other groups, as well as on stock market speculators. Young people, just entering the labor force, found the lack of employment opportunities frustrating, and many seemed easily susceptible to the appeals of radicals. But industrial workers felt the brunt of the unemployment which increased from 4.5 million in 1930 to 13 million in 1933 (one-fourth of the labor force). Though there was some fluctuation, after six years of the New Deal the unemployment figure in 1939 stood at almost 9.5 million.

> Too deep for the average citizen to fathom, the floods of disaster had rolled in to erase ancient tide marks and tug at the moorings of inherited wisdom. This era brought a questioning into American life deeper than any other since the Civil War. Stereotypes of thought, traditional saws, the tribal wisdom of the elders, all were challenged in books, magazines and private talk. Perhaps, after all, the promise of American life would turn out merely to be propaganda, the tyranny of words or the folklore of capitalism. . . .
>
> For, after the passage of two or three years, unemployment had entered into the grain of American life. Its severity and apparent hopelessness were without parallel. Panics and bank failures, rainy days and lean years, flood and drought, had come and gone many times since the first settlers carved out a civilization in the howling wilderness. This crisis, it seemed, had no precedent. Poverty was everywhere; cornered by it, the jobless man now felt something resembling claustrophobia.[3]

In one survey of unemployed workers' opinions it was reported that nearly a quarter of them (four times as many as among job holders) felt that "a revolution might be a very good thing for this country."[4] This is not to suggest that large numbers of American workers rushed to answer the clarion calls of Communists to throw off their chains and mount the barricades, or the appeals of the Socialists to vote for Norman Thomas and government ownership of basic industries. But workers, as well as others, were confused, questioning, and willing to try new ideas, techniques, and leaders. The radicalism which existed was in the main homespun and indigenous, a diffused mixture of organized and unorganized sentiment, generally devoid of any specific programmatic doctrine. The new radicalism appeared to stem from the plain man's instinctive resentment of poverty surrounded by shops bursting with food and farms smothered under their own production surplus.

There was, therefore, some significant, if not great, upsurge in interest in the ideas and leadership offered by Socialists and Communists. This interest was greater among middle class, professional, and intellectual groups than among working class people, though in contrast with earlier periods in American history there began to appear some faint indications of a general working class consciousness, or what J. B. S. Hardman later called a "consciousness of kind." On the other hand some students have observed that, considering the desperateness of the situation, industrial workers remained surprisingly apathetic, apparently too discouraged and spiritless to be interested in the intellectuals' talk of revolution or communism.[5]

The result of President Hoover's attack on many of the veteran Bonus Marchers at the capital as "Communists and persons with criminal records"[6] and, later, of employers' "red-baiting" and violent resistance to the formation of unions in mass production industries may have been to immunize some workers from the fear of resorting to radical tactics and leaders.

Evidence of the questioning spirit and willingness to experiment with panaceas of various sorts on the part of many groups, other than industrial workers, is afforded by a look at some of the non–trade union movements of the time. Early in the decade there were efforts among some groups at self-help producer coöperatives and barter, or trading in kind.

A group of unemployed engineers, architects, and scientists calling themselves "Technocrats" furnished a serio-comic interlude for a number of years after 1932. They charged that facility in production in the power age had invalidated the price and profit system, and that engineers and their fellow specialists, serving collective efficiency rather than private acquisitiveness, must be substituted for bungling businessmen.

A movement for the Townsend Plan, an extravagant and extreme proposal for old-age pensions flourished with wide popularity beginning in 1934 and continued for several years even after passage of the Social Security Act in 1935. Upton Sinclair's writings and plan, "End Poverty in California," in 1934 helped him achieve the Democratic nomination for governor and almost to win the election. This was followed in 1938 by the "Ham and Eggs" and "$30 Every Thursday," popularly supported, flash-in-the-pan panaceas. At one point the push for "Social Credit" spilled down over the Canadian borders into midwestern states.

The support accorded to such "messiahs" as Huey Long in the South calling for "Share Our Wealth," Father Coughlin, the Michigan radio priest of "National Union for Social Justice" fame, Father Divine of Harlem ("the real God is the God who feeds us"), in the late thirties, to Dr. Buchman of the "Moral Rearmament" movement and others, gave cause for the judgment that social welfare had become the new American "religion." In literature and the arts the thirties saw the development of "proletarian" themes as well as similar emphases in books on history, economics, and sociology.

Even the normally conservative American farmer on occasion took violent and extreme action, as in some of the aspects of the Farm Holiday movement in the Midwest, sharecroppers' strikes, and the migrations and desperate flounderings of the "Okies." More effective new programs included the burgeoning development of coöperatives. The most substantial were agricultural producers' coöperatives which were established on an unprecedented scale. Even consumers' coöperatives, which had never made much headway on the American scene, became solidly formed in some areas as time went on.

Indeed the government itself broke new grounds in the extent to which it intervened in the operations of the economy. In so doing it may have encouraged radical and different modes of thinking and behavior. Witness such programs as the Reconstruction Finance Corporation's financing of business ventures (started under Hoover), the extreme step of closing banks, going off the gold standard, deficit financing, and more complete regulation of banks and stock exchanges. Consider also the paying of farmers for restricting production of crops and livestock, the establishment of government electric power facilities in competition with private enterprise (TVA), government partnership with labor and industry (NRA), the encouragement of unions and collective bargaining (Wagner Act), public relief on unprecedented scale, great public works, and social insurance programs. Mention must also be made of the recognition of Soviet Russia in 1933 and the gradual development of tolerative if not coöperative relations with this unorthodox threat to capitalism.

Even if some of these programs are regarded as New Deal tactics to steal the thunder of demagogues and scale down radical promises to workable size, the very consideration and application of such programs give evidence of a spirit of unorthodoxy and experiment.

Small wonder that in this milieu workers, as well as others, proved willing to experiment with radical ideas and left-wing leaders. The experimental temper of the times forms a variegated backdrop for the forces, events, and personalities of the remainder of this essay.

The Radicals and the Unions of the Unemployed

The dawn of the Great Depression produced an ever increasing army of unemployed. By 1933 the unemployed were conservatively estimated to number 13 million people—a naked symbol of the economic and social sickness which was sweeping America. By 1934 it was estimated that 2.5 million workers had been without jobs for two years or more; 6 million workers had secured their last employment more than a year before. It has been estimated that something between one-third and one-half of the nation's population was composed of the families of the unemployed and underemployed. The Hoover administration viewed the growing unemployment crisis as primarily the responsibility of local and state governments. As funds for direct relief became quickly exhausted, efforts by local and state agencies became increasingly feeble and fruitless. From the unpreparedness of the American communities to deal with the problems of relief emerged organizations of the unemployed. Their development was rooted in the new social environment created by the depression. When the recognized leaders of the community, including trade union leaders, failed to step into the breach, leadership fell to the professional radicals.

The actual manner in which the radicals fostered the formation of and assumed leadership in the jobless unions varied from place to place. In New York City, the various unemployed unions were little more than adjuncts to the already established radical political parties, each party having its own auxiliary of the unemployed. Elsewhere, as in Chicago, the radical organizations, such as the Socialist League for Industrial Democracy, organized unions of unemployed. And in still other places—Ohio, Pennsylvania, North Carolina, and the State of Washington—members of the Conference for Progressive Labor Action, led by A. J. Muste, organized semirural, backward unemployed workers as well as urban workers into militant jobless leagues. The effectiveness of the jobless unions varied from city to city as did the numbers of unemployed which they attracted. For the most part, they enrolled larger proportions of unemployed in the big cities, such as Detroit, Chicago, New York, and Pittsburgh. They were considerably less active in the smaller towns.

Unemployed Councils

The first demonstrations of organized unemployed to attract nationwide attention occurred in early spring, 1930, when under the leadership of the Communist-controlled Unemployed Council, hundreds of thousands of unemployed demonstrated in New York, Detroit, Los Angeles, Chicago, Seattle, Boston, Milwaukee, and several other cities. In many of these situations, particularly in the big cities, their demonstrations were met by brutal police repression. On March 6, 1930, for example, a demonstration held in New York City was reported as follows:

> The unemployment demonstration staged by the Communist Party in Union Square broke up in the worst riot New York has seen in recent years when 35,000 persons attending the demonstration were transformed in a few moments from an orderly, and at times bored, crowd into a fighting mob. The outbreak came after communist leaders, defying warnings and orders of the police, exhorted their followers to march on City Hall and demand a hearing from Mayor Walker. Hundreds of policemen and detectives, swinging night sticks, blackjacks and bare fists, rushed into the crowd, hitting out at all with whom they came into contact, chasing many across the street and into adjacent thoroughfares and rushing hundreds off their feet. . . . From all parts of the scene of battle came the screams of women and cries of men, with bloody heads and faces. A score of men were sprawled over the square with policemen pummeling them. The pounding continued as the men, and some women, sought refuge in flight.[7]

Several top leaders of the Communist party including National Chairman Foster and *Daily Worker* editor Robert Minor received jail terms as a result of this demonstration. Violence occurred in other cities such as the nation's capital where police used tear gas on demonstrators before the White House. Organizations not initially led by radicals became fertile areas for left-wing control since, among other reasons, it was generally the radicals who were best acquainted with methods of meeting police repression. These demonstrations received widespread publicity, and while their principal effect was to brand the unemployed organizations as "red," they also had the effect of enhancing the prestige of the radicals, who often demonstrated great personal courage and organizational skill in leading the demonstrations of the jobless. Further, as the jobless were met by more and more repression, the radicalism and militancy of their movement increased and the revolutionary groups were able in these years to gain over the organizations a domination which they never relinquished.

The extreme circumstances of the depression were probably more important than the existence of the radicals in producing these organizations of the unemployed. But the radicals were able to use these unions to introduce to countless workers the concept of "organization" as a strategic weapon for the solution of economic and social problems. Vast numbers of unskilled and semiskilled workers who had never before participated in organized forms of social and political protest were shown that through united group action some measure of economic benefit could be obtained.

As the situations changed, the organizations of unemployed were modified. In the very early depression years they dealt with local relief bureaus and the day-to-day task of securing direct and immediate concessions. They fought bitterly against evictions of thousands of tenants who could not pay rent. In many cases organized jobless convoked large gatherings to move furniture back into the houses of evicted families. In many places such as Akron, the Communist-led Unemployed Council organized gas squads to turn the gas back on in people's houses and electric squads to string wires around the meter after it was shut off by the local utility. Embittered and discouraged by many months and even years of being out of work, unemployed by the thousands were attracted to the Unemployed Councils which gave members an opportunity to strike back at what they considered a major source of their despair. Most of the demands made by these demonstrators were designed to meet immediate problems. A typical Chicago united front "hunger march" in 1932 made the demands described in the following report:

The delegation that waited on the mayor as the parade was passing the city hall, expected nothing and got nothing. [The demands presented to the mayor were:] cash relief on the basis of $7.50 a week for a family of two, with additional amounts for each dependent; no more evictions; free gas, water, electricity and coal; free hot lunches, clothing, text books and carfare for school children; free dental and medical care; no foreclosures; exemption from taxes; immediate release of all in jail as a result of unemployment clashes with police; immediate inauguration of a local program of public works; no discrimination in relief work against Negroes or foreign-born; all unemployment funds to be administered by elected organizations of the unemployed. The mayor said that he had nothing to do with these matters; let them be put before the relief organizations for the RFC. The committee filed out. It had put its demands, by means of listening reporters, where it wanted them to go—before that part of the public that even in today's misery had no idea how the other half is living or what it is thinking.[8]

In Chicago, the League for Industrial Democracy and the Socialist party organized in 1931 the Chicago Workers' Committee on Unemployment. At least one motive force behind this organization was the desire of the Socialists to present to the unemployed an alternative to the Communist party's Unemployed Council. Eight locals of the Committee were organized in the fall of 1931; this number grew to sixty-three locals by January, 1933. Membership was open to anyone, eighteen years of age or over, who was employed or in need of employment on a government works program or who was on or eligible for relief. Only persons who had engaged in "anti-labor activities" were barred. An initiation fee of not less than 15 cents nor more than $1 was charged, the local unit determining the amount. Dues ranged from 10 to 35 cents a month for unemployed and from 15 cents to $1 a month for employed members. Locals composed of members on direct relief were organized on a community basis, while CWA and later WPA locals were organized on a project basis. Locals met regularly, generally once a month. On July 12, 1932, the Chicago Committee became a kind of collective bargaining agency for its large membership when it established an accredited relationship with the Advisory Board of the Cook County Bureau of Public Affairs. Thereafter it grew both in prestige and in number. Its principal function was to investigate complaints of its members and present them to the district administrators of emergency relief. Each local had a grievance committee which was responsible for this activity. There was also a city-wide central grievance committee of five which took up any cases the locals were unable to adjust and which ruled upon broad matters of policy.

New York City presented a somewhat different situation. By March, 1933, there were at least four different organizations of jobless, each of them an appendage of and led by a radical political group. The four of them together conservatively claimed a membership of only six or seven thousand: (1) the Communist party's Unemployed Council, (2) the Workers' Unemployed League of New York City which was organized in 1932 under the auspices of the Socialist party in an effort to amalgamate various unemployed groups which had been originally started by individual Socialists and were later recognized as Socialist party branches, (3) the Workers' Committee on Unemployment of New York City which was organized by the League for Industrial Democracy and headed by a Socialist, David Lasser, and (4) the Association of the Unemployed, organized and dominated by the Lovestonite faction of the Communist movement, as an opposition group to the Unemployed Councils. In December, 1933, the two Socialist-dominated groups merged and a few months later the Lovestonites came in to form the Workers Unemployed Union headed by Lasser.[9]

In organizing the Unemployed Councils, the Communist party expected them to become an important center of revolutionary activity. The day-to-day economic action of the Councils was looked upon in the party as meaty bait to attract the workers and as an effective demonstration that they could hope to get nothing from "a capitalistic government which was in the last throes of decay." Such activity probably won some recruits to the party's revolutionary cadre and also must have made many more jobless workers look upon the CP and its Unemployed Councils as true friends of the down and out.

On a nationwide scale the Councils organized a national hunger march in December, 1931, when an estimated 1,200 marchers converged on Washington, D.C., from St. Louis, Chicago, Buffalo, Boston, New York, and other cities. A second such march was organized the following December. On the local scene in Chicago the Council played a major role in fighting discrimination against Negroes in relief benefits. By the end of 1932 the Chicago Council alone claimed forty-five neighborhood branches and a total membership of 22,000.

National Unemployed League

A second of the nationwide organizations of jobless, the National Unemployed League, was organized by the Conference for Progressive

Labor Action which had been established in 1929 under the leadership of the Reverend A. J. Muste. Muste, in the tradition of the proletarian preacher, had served pastorates among industrial workers for many years. He had played a prominent role in the 1919 strike of textile workers in Lawrence, Massachusetts, and thereafter became the director of Brookwood Labor College at Katonah, New York, the seedbed for some of the top labor organizers in the United States today.

Muste gathered around him in the CPLA a group of brilliant Socialist labor intellectuals such as David Saposs, Louis Budenz, Ludwig Lore, Sidney Hook, James Burnham, and J. B. S. Hardman. Their purpose initially seems to have been primarily intellectual—directed toward education rather than action. However, the CPLA found itself playing important roles in the leadership of many early depression strikes and abandoned its purely educational aims in favor of agitation and action. Like other radical groups, it looked upon itself as the "vanguard organization for American Labor." But unlike other radical groups, it was quite determined to be a thoroughly American revolutionary movement. It sought to translate the traditional international revolutionary principles into the American idiom and also to modernize the American revolutionary traditions. It advocated a "mass labor party" whose goal would be the "complete abolition of planless, profiteering capitalism, and the building of a workers' republic." [10]

CPLA's mass work was largely in the National Unemployed League. The League had its main strength in rural areas and small towns of Ohio, Pennsylvania, and West Virginia, though it was active in larger cities, chiefly in the Midwest and Seattle, Washington. It was organized as the Ohio Unemployed League when thirty-one representatives from as many counties of the state met in Columbus, February 27–28, 1935. By early summer it had organized short demonstration strikes of workers in local works projects at High Point, North Carolina; Philadelphia; New Jersey; West Virginia, and elsewhere. Fifteen hundred delegates turned up for the first national convention of the NUL at Columbus, July 1–4, 1933. With the inauguration of the Civil Works Administration's large-scale nationwide work relief program by the federal government, the NUL entered the field of organizing and representing workers on work relief projects. Among its principal demands before CWA administrators was a minimum wage of $1 an hour for CWA workers and the abolition of political and employer domination of relief benefits. In Pittsburgh, the Unemployed Citizens

League claimed 50,000 dues-paying members in fifty locals and handled as many as 1,300 to 1,500 relief complaint cases a month. In West Virginia, several thousand workers in private employment joined the League, and officials carried on the same collective bargaining activities for these workers as a regular union might seek to do. The Lucas County (Ohio) Unemployed League played a crucial role in the strike of employees of the Auto-Lite Company in Toledo in 1934. The significance of this event for the subsequent development of unionism in the automobile industry will be discussed in greater detail below.

The Workers Alliance of America

The Workers Alliance of America was organized under the stimulus of the Socialists at a convention in Washington, D.C., on March 2–4, 1935, attended by 120 delegates from various unemployed organizations. The constitution adopted at this convention provided that only organizations could become members of the WAA and that these organizations could not already be affiliated with any other organization having the same purposes. This had the effect of excluding affiliates of either the Unemployed Councils or the National Unemployed League. The convention, however, instructed the national executive board to call a conference, within three months, of the executive committees of other national unemployed organizations to discuss procedure for merger and unity. David Lasser, a Socialist, was elected president of the new organization.

The WAA apparently had a rapid growth prior to its convention in 1936, when it was augmented even further by the merger with it of the two other major organizations of the jobless. In August, 1935, the already powerful Illinois Workers Alliance voted to affiliate with the WAA. At about the same time, at a convention of more than 100 delegates, a state organization of the Alliance was established in Indiana. At that time, recent affiliates to the Alliance were located in areas as far apart as Niagara County, New York; Little Rock, Arkansas; Alameda, California; Springfield, Massachusetts, and Dallas, Texas. By the end of the summer of 1935 the secretary of the Alliance was able to report that the WAA had affiliates in thirty-one states with the likelihood of affiliations in five or six more in the course of the next few weeks.[11] By April, 1936, the Alliance claimed a membership of 600,000, while the total unemployed was estimated at 9 million.

The purposes of the Alliance were given by its president as follows:

> We organize unemployed and WPA workers in each locality to settle their grievances at the relief bureau or on the WPA jobs, to prevent discrimination, to win higher relief standards and higher wages. We co-operate in each locality and nationally with all organizations who are willing to work with us for common aims. . . . We extend our hands to the labor movement prepared to do our part in assisting them in their struggles for clean, militant unionism and for a higher standard of living for the employed. And finally, we greet all workers in the desire to unite not only economically but also politically for independent working class political action.[12]

In the fall of 1936 the Indiana WPA recognized the WAA as a collective bargaining agent for WPA employees in that state. The Ohio WPA similarly recognized the Workers Alliance as collective bargaining representative for workers employed on WPA projects.

The WAA's 1936 convention saw the uniting of the Communist party's Unemployed Councils and the National Unemployed League with the WAA. This move toward unity probably came when it did because of the change in the line of the Communist party from dual unionism to a "united front" with anybody and everybody politically left of center. In the unemployed field, the natural development was unity of the Communist party's Unemployed Councils and the Socialist party's Workers Alliance. In the new united movement, David Lasser retained the presidency, but the key position of organizational secretary went to Herbert Benjamin, a leading Communist and head of the Unemployed Council movement. The third major unemployed organization, the National Unemployed League, had in 1934 become a part of the Workers Party of the United States, which was formed by the merger of the Musteite American Workers party (an outgrowth of the Conference for Progressive Labor Action) with the Trotskyite Communist League of America. The Workers Party of the United States entered the Socialist party in 1936, and the NUL thereby became part of the united Workers Alliance of America. The Musteites were rapidly swallowed up in the internal maneuverings between the Communists and Socialists and shortly disappeared as an identifiable force.

Less than a month after the unity convention, 5,000 hunger marchers under WAA leadership descended upon the New Jersey State House when that state ran out of state relief funds. The same scene was repeated in August, 1936, in Harrisburg, Pennsylvania. The first major action involving the WAA and its members on WPA projects came in the week of October 19–24, 1936, when short "folded arms strikes" were conducted throughout the country in a campaign for "a living wage." Throughout the rest of 1936 WAA conducted demonstrations and strikes protesting inadequate relief and layoffs from WPA projects.

The third national convention of the WAA, in Milwaukee in July, 1937, brought together 600 delegates from forty-five states. From that point until its demise with the coming of the war emergency in 1940, the WAA moved increasingly away from organizing unemployed workers and "job actions" in the direction of becoming a pressure group lobbying for legislation to protect and advance the interests of the unemployed. Beginning in 1938, Socialist-led groups in WAA in many cities withdrew in protest against the domination of the Alliance by the Communist party. Splits occurred in Illinois, Ohio, New Jersey, Maryland, Wisconsin, and New York. However, as late as 1939 it was able to mount a nationwide strike of WPA workers protesting cut-backs and layoffs on relief projects. The career of the movement was terminated with the economic recovery resulting from the onset of World War II.

WAA and the Trade Union Movement

Shortly after its formation in 1935, the Alliance sought the official endorsement of the American Federation of Labor. A number of resolutions were introduced at the 1935 AFL convention calling for recognition of and support to the jobless union. The resolutions failed of passage and were instead referred to the executive council for action. There is no evidence to show that the resolutions were ever again mentioned. In convention debate it was clear that many AFL leaders viewed the jobless movement as potentially dual to the established organizations of labor, with the building trades leaders spearheading the opposition. Many of these leaders questioned the government's CWA and WPA construction projects on the ground that the lower wages paid to project workers undermined union standards. Since the WAA organized the project workers, to officially recognize it would be to lend official trade union support to these lower standards.[13] However, in June, 1936, the WAA secured an endorsement from President Green of the AFL, who cautioned in his message that the

Alliance should not function as a competitor to the Federation. Green's reservations were answered by the WAA president when he wrote:

> . . . The Workers Alliance of America teaches the unemployed their responsibilities to the labor movement to assist in organization campaigns of labor, to picket during strikes, to prevent unemployed from acting as scabs. The Workers Alliance of America is not and cannot be a substitute or rival to the trade union movement. Instead, we advise and encourage our members to resume or take out membership in their own unions as soon as possible.[14]

Even though the WAA failed to receive the official support of the AFL, some city central bodies developed close working relationships with organizations of unemployed in their communities. For example, in Grand Rapids, Michigan, the local unemployed union was directly affiliated with the Grand Rapids Federation of Labor and was being utilized as an instrument to spread the idea of trade unionism among the unemployed. Local unions were reported to have recruited many workers to their rolls through the jobless organization.[15]

The WAA worked out a detailed program for coöperation with the CIO whereby CIO locals were to set up "unemployment committees" which would engage in joint actions with WAA locals in communities throughout the country. The program adopted by the WAA national executive board on coöperation with the trade unions contained the following points:

> 1. *Strengthen the union* . . . it is absolutely necessary that . . . we assist in keeping every union member in his union.
>
> 2. *Build the Workers Alliance:* . . . it is our hope that the unions will take advantage of the opportunity to organize as members of their unions, all unemployed in their industry. But unless and until that is done, it is our task, our special responsibility, our proud privilege to undertake a great organizing drive to enroll into our organization hundreds of thousands of non-union unemployed, and bring them closer to the union movement.[16]

Evaluation of Organizations of the Unemployed

Intellectual radicals organized and dominated the unions of unemployed. The radicals looked upon the unemployed movement as primarily a vehicle through which large numbers of unemployed could be recruited to the radical program of the sponsoring party. While this purpose was probably uppermost in all of their activity in the unemployed unions, the leadership soon realized that in order to accomplish the primary purpose it was necessary to first build a mass movement which served its members well enough so that they would respect and follow the leadership of the organization. This meant that activities would center on economic and political programs and policies aimed to solve the immediate situation of the unemployed. Thus, the cornerstone of their programs always included demands for adequate relief measures, protection against eviction and foreclosures, and later legislation to promote work opportunities and the like.

The economic functions were undoubtedly the most important ones the unemployed unions performed for the ordinary member. As the left-wing leaders succeeded in satisfying the basic needs of the members, they probably were able to win their support on other issues of far less importance to the rank and file. Literally tens and maybe hundreds of thousands of American workers, who might not otherwise ever have heard of radical political parties and programs, became sympathizers of these programs. Having found that the left-wing leadership of their unemployed organization militantly fought for their benefit on a day-to-day basis and in a great number of places and instances won real measures of success, workers certainly must have been less suspicious, or even enthusiastic supporters, of left-wing leadership if they found it in local unions which they subsequently joined. This was probably particularly true in the new CIO unions organized in the mass production industries, since it was largely in these unions that the unskilled and semiskilled industrial workers of the unemployed organizations subsequently took membership.

But perhaps the greatest impact which the unions of unemployed had on the "new labor movement" was in a direction neither initially anticipated nor subsequently recognized. The unemployed groups not only helped the jobless in the everyday struggles with relief agencies, etc., but they were a very important factor in rekindling the militancy of the employed. They were a ready-organized force which could be, and in a large number of instances was, mobilized to support strikes of employed workers. The Workers Alliance, and the National Unemployed League and Unemployed Councils which preceded it, constantly pointed out to the unemployed their responsibilities to the labor movement to assist in organization campaigns of labor, to picket during strikes, and to prevent the unemployed from acting as strike breakers. They continually urged their thousands of members to join unions as soon as they left the rolls of the unemployed and returned to private industry. These organizations, in the overwhelming number of instances, locally, and certainly nationally, were organized and led by political radicals, most of whom were committed to a specific radical party, although some were unaffiliated radical intellectuals.

Thus, these left-wingers, through their unemployed unions, introduced to vast numbers of workers the concept of *organization* as a strategic weapon for the solution of economic and social problems. It seems reasonable to assume that having been members of unemployed unions, having participated in demonstrations and "job actions" in protection of existing benefits and in efforts to secure new benefits, vast numbers of workers who later secured employment in private industry were not unfamiliar with the language and tactics of unionism and were more susceptible to trade union organizing appeals than they otherwise might have been. Further, the experience which many leaders of local unemployed organizations got as members of grievance committees dealing with relief agencies was unquestionably valuable when they later found themselves as union members negotiating and administering labor agreements. In this sense, the jobless organizations, organized or dominated by political radicals, trained many of their ideological sympathizers and members to achieve positions of leadership in the new unions.

The Radicals in the Labor Unions

The efforts of workers to organize themselves into unions in the early New Deal period were born in part of the hopes offered by governmental encouragement and the despair produced by the economic chaos of the depression. This upsurge of organizing activity within the AFL is dealt with in Chapters 1 and 2. In 1934, beginning to be disillusioned with the delays and disappointments of proceedings before usually ineffective government-appointed Labor Boards, determined to win union recognition, higher wages, and better conditions, and faced with mounting employer resistance, apostles of the new unionism waged a series of dramatic struggles in their efforts to build unions.

Left-wing politicals of every shade and description, as well as trade unionists devoid of any radical political philosophy, were active in many of these struggles. Communists, Socialists, Trotskyites, members of the Proletarian party and the Revolutionary Workers League, New America supporters, Lovestonites, and even old time "wobblies" and Socialist Labor party members and syndicalists became involved, particularly in the centers of the new mass production industries.

Early New Deal Strikes

Perhaps the most dramatic of these events were three major strikes, in 1934, in which left-wingers played leading roles—strikes which had an important impact on the development of the new unions. In early 1934 the employees of the Electric Auto-Lite Company in Toledo, Ohio, struck that company for union recognition, among other things.[17] At a crucial stage, after the effects of an injunction had all but brought the strike to a collapse, the leaders of the Lucas County Unemployed League (organized and led by Musteites) defied the court by organizing a new picket line before the plant gates. Before the strike was settled, spurred on and given leadership by Muste's followers, the strike movement enlisted the support of thousands of Toledo workers, employed and unemployed. National Guard troops were called in and bitter hand-to-hand fighting developed. At one point, more than 1,300 soldiers were on duty at the plant in what was estimated to be the largest peace-time display of military force in the history of Ohio. Shortly after some 90 of the 103 locals affiliated with the Central Labor Council voted to participate in a general strike, an estimated 10,000 workers, representing nearly 100 local unions, marched through Toledo's main streets in support of the strikers. The dispute was settled the following day with the workers winning union recognition among other concessions.

While the Toledo events were developing, the longshore industry on the West Coast became the scene of a strike movement which, before it ran its course, involved a good part of the labor movement, organized and unorganized, from southern California to northern Washington, and produced a general strike in San Francisco.[18] Under the impetus of NIRA's Section 7(a) nearly 95 per cent of the registered longshoremen in the Pacific Coast ports deserted the company unions and joined newly chartered locals of the AFL's International Longshoremen's Association. At the first district convention of the newly revived ILA, the leadership was won by a group of "militants" headed by Harry Bridges, even though the old-line ILA officials retained nominal control. The core of this "militant" group under Bridges' leadership consisted of members of the TUUL's Marine Workers Industrial Union and from that point on the Communists had a vantage point in the West Coast longshoring industry which has not yet been relinquished.

Calling on all other marine unions for support of the longshoremen's demand for union recognition and control of a hiring hall, Bridges' union stretched picket lines along every waterfront from Vancouver to San Diego. The strike was soon joined by ten other marine unions and a joint strike committee was formed with Bridges as elected chairman. California National Guard troops were called in when a series of battles developed from employer efforts to move goods from San Francisco piers. An estimated 10,000 workers, forming a line a mile long, marched solemnly through the streets of San Francisco in the funeral procession for two strikers killed in these battles and in sympathy with some 100 strikers injured. As the strike wore on, more and more workers joined its ranks until the strike of 2,000 longshoremen in San Francisco erupted into a general strike involving an estimated 127,000 workers in the Bay region. When it was apparent to the leaders that the general strike movement could not be continued, they called it off and many of the participating unions agreed to arbitrate their demands. The eventual longshore settlement granted union recognition, joint control of hiring halls, and other demands.

A third great strike led by radicals in the early New Deal period occurred in Minneapolis when, under the leadership of the Trotskyite Dunne brothers, truck drivers in that city walked out.[19] Again, the basic issue was union recognition. The first of a series of strikes, this one lasting three days, was called in February, 1934. The strike ended with a contract for coal drivers, and the union's membership increased from some 200 members to over 7,000 in the next three months. In mid-May, the truckers struck to obtain union recognition and higher wages for "inside" men. President Tobin of the Teamsters International Union refused to support the drivers' efforts to organize these new workers, asserting that the organization had no jurisdiction over them. He denounced the Minneapolis teamsters' leaders as "reds" and refused to have anything more to do with them. The strike was peaceful during its first week, after which employers attempted to operate the trucks with strike breakers. For the next three months, Minneapolis was the scene of many bitter and often bloody struggles between police, National Guardsmen, and strikers. Tens of thousands of workers representing practically the entire Minneapolis labor movement were involved. The violence became so bitter that Governor Olson eventually declared martial law and ordered some 3,500 militiamen to the scene. Hundreds of workers and policemen were injured in the almost daily battles, and scores of workers were arrested. The issue was finally resolved with victory for the union in the form of recognition and other concessions.

These three strikes, all led or heavily influenced by left-wingers, occurred in the first wave of organization under the New Deal. Each involved a substantial part of the labor force of a fairly large community, taught the leaders valuable lessons in strike strategy and tactics, and endowed them with prestige in the eyes of the rank and file workers. They presented the radicals with an opportunity to forge skills, acquire knowledge, and develop leadership talents in the conduct of union organizing and strike tactics. These skills and knowledge were to play an important role in the succeeding months, particularly with the advent of the Committee for Industrial Organization. Further, since these strikes were among the first to achieve nationwide attention during the New Deal period, they must have contributed considerably to the growing union consciousness of countless rank and file workers far removed from the actual events.[20]

Communists and Socialists

The largest group of radicals in the labor movement during this period belonged to organizations affiliated with the Communists' Trade Union Unity League which in 1934 claimed a membership of 125,000 of whom 30,000 were said to be members of the Needle Trades Industrial Union. In addition to the Needle Workers, the TUUL had established an Automobile Workers Union of Detroit, the Independent Shoe Workers of New York, the Amalgamated Food Workers of New York, the National Textile Workers Union, the Marine Workers Industrial Union, and others. With the exception of the Needle Trades Industrial Union which was firmly established in the New York fur industry, the membership claimed by the TUUL was almost certainly greatly exaggerated and may not have been much more than actual party members working in these industries. Their unions, as trade unions, were hardly more than vantage points from which party organizers and propagandists could seek to recruit members to their small cadres.

With few exceptions, particularly among the fur workers in the Needle Trades Union, they achieved no employer recognition and did not carry on collective bargaining activities. Yet, as tiny as they were, they constituted a very vocal minority, constantly putting forward their program, publishing newspapers, bulletins, leaflets, pamphlets, etc., and just as constantly holding meetings and conducting training schools.

As noted, the Communist party from 1929 to 1935 was in its third period, which was characterized, in Daniel Bell's terms, by "aggressive policies of organizing unemployment demonstrations, exacerbating strikes, promoting ex-servicemen's leagues." TUUL policy was one of dual unionism, including disruption of AFL unions under any and all circumstances; the party's mechanical control over the mass organizations in which it had influence, again with the possible exception of the Needle Trades Union, prevented these organizations from becoming unions in any real sense but made them simply party units under another name. During these years the Communist parties throughout the world followed a policy of extreme verbal (and sometimes physical) aggression against democratic and socialist forces. The latter were presented as "social fascists," against whom all means, including violence, were in order. The general consequence of this ultra-left period was organizational isolation which separated the Communists from the main body of trade union members and therefore from any significant influence among them. Nevertheless, it was during this period of ultra-left propaganda and organizational isolation that an "organizational weapon" was formed that would maintain its strength when thrown into active combat.[21]

The long period of isolation and internal orientation served to consolidate the leadership of the movement, to test and train the cadres in party and trade union theory and in organizational strategy and tactics, and to intensify the commitment of individual members. It was during this period that the Communists developed to a greater extent and with more perfection the tactical use of the fraction and faction, the caucus, parliamentary maneuverings, and centralized control over rank and file party membership in the unions. The basis for later effective penetration of the mass unions stemmed from this apparently irrational period of "social fascism," "united front from below," splits and purges. After 1935 the fourth period of "united front from above" became the principal organizational strategy of the world-wide Communist movement, not only with respect to trade union work but in all of its far-flung activities. The party could now support any and all whose purposes it could use for its own ends. In the American scene, the TUUL was dissolved and the old aggression was relaxed against the "reactionary" trade union leaders of the AFL and then the CIO.

This change in basic party position on the trade union front in the United States meant that the Communists could now endeavor to work within the framework of the existing unions. However, with the emergence of the CIO, the Communists turned their attention to these new unions and new situations, largely ignoring the older established AFL unions in favor of the "wave of the future" represented by the CIO.

Their earlier training in the TUUL unions and in party and trade union theory and tactics was now directed toward the centers of mass production industries and the unions which were being forged there. Their previous isolation had fashioned a "combat weapon" which was put at the disposal of John L. Lewis and the CIO. Among the radicals in the trade unions, the Communists were the largest, the most disciplined and homogeneous group. Unlike the Socialists and the other splinter groups of the political left, their ranks were undiluted by conflicting dogmas and internal struggles for power.

The Socialist party during the early New Deal period was caught up in an internal struggle for supremacy between the "old guard" and the new young "militants" who sought to advance a more revolutionary program. In 1934 this internal conflict erupted when large numbers of the militants of the party left its ranks in disgust. A split occurred at the 1936 Cleveland convention when some 40 per cent of its membership, largely the "old guard," walked out of the SP. Shortly thereafter, Norman Thomas, the Socialist party leader, called for an "all-inclusive party."

> He invited into the Socialist Party all independent, unaffiliated, affiliated, and dependent radical homeless, the splinter groups, factions, fractions, droplets, and kibitzers. He hoped in this fashion to achieve a unity of left-wing forces against fascism. Gitlowites, Zamites, Fieldites, Trotskyites, Lovestonites and all streamed into the party, and each group of intellectual pitchmen set up its own stand. A host of previously isolated one-ring circuses was now operating under one huge billowing tent. And the result was bedlam.[22]

Only the Communists remained out, though they too agreed with the SP leadership on a program for joint work in the trade unions. But unlike the Communists, the "all-inclusive" Socialists constituted a heterogeneous amalgam of disparate radical groups, each professing a different "Socialist" ideology and each seeking to impose on their new allies their separate programs and ideological formulations.[23]

Further, many trade unionists, such as those found in the needle trades and even in the AFL's Machinists Union, were unaffiliated with any radical group though they privately or publicly professed a generally Socialist ideology. The result was that the Communists remained the largest "undiluted" and "untroubled" radical tendency. Thus, they could mobilize with much greater efficiency their small numbers than could the rest of the political left.

Radicals in the CIO

Following the dissolution of the TUUL and initial efforts to enter the AFL, its directing personnel was offered to Lewis and the new CIO. He felt he could use, if not their philosophy, at least their experience. In trying to secure a mass following for their TUUL unions, they had learned to make speeches, write leaflets and reports, run mimeograph machines, set up and man picket lines, organize violence to resist violence, and hold the chair in turbulent meetings. They were familiar with all the other mechanics indispensable when workers almost completely unfamiliar with union procedures were crowding into halls, and demanding guidance. Further, they displayed a willingness to subject themselves to all of the physical hazards of a picket line attacked by police or National Guardsmen, and a dedication to their ideology had given them a reputation for self-sacrifice and almost boundless energy. Also, they were a relatively mobile force, submitting to the party's requirement that they often pick up roots and plant them in some new and faraway community for the purpose of "colonizing" a factory or a mill.

And when the old-line AFL leadership or employers denounced Lewis and his radical support as "reds," they rubbed a good many rank and file unionists the wrong way. For it must be remembered that in the mid-thirties the Communist party was not viewed with as much distrust as it later aroused in the labor movement. It was still regarded as a legitimate radical party rather than a monolithic and totalitarian arm of the Russian dictatorship, and even the splinter Marxist groups still considered it part of the radical community. It would be several years yet before this attitude toward the Communists would change. Furthermore, the indefatigable work of the Communists, literally pouring themselves into every task no matter how small or menial, had given them the reputation of being totally dedicated to their trade union work and of being bearers of the gospel of the promised land.

From 1935 to 1941, John L. Lewis was publically idolized by them as well as by other radicals and large numbers of liberals.[24] He and his lieutenants hired known and unknown radicals of every hue as organizers for the new CIO unions. He even welcomed the aid of a group of radical unionists whom he had previously driven out of his own United Mine Workers Union because they had opposed his dictatorial regime. He called in Powers Hapgood, a militant Socialist, Adolph Germer, an old Socialist, and John Brophy. Rose Pesotta, an aggressive radical and former anarchist loaned to him by the International Ladies Garment Workers Union, and Leo Krzycki, of the Amalgamated Clothing Workers and then national chairman of the Socialist party, became among his chief organizers. At this time, there was very little comfort and less glory in organizing for the CIO. Those willing to take the risks associated with the job were, in large measure, men who were moved by a conviction that unionization of the mass production industries was a step toward a larger social end.

Lewis was well aware of the degree and proportions of the Communist power within the CIO, but he was confident that he could control it.[25] To charges of harboring Communist organizers, he would answer, "I do not turn my organizers or CIO members upside down and shake them out to see what kind of literature falls out of their pockets." Or again, speaking of Communists, "If they are good enough for industry to hire, they're good enough for us to organize." When ILGWU President Dubinsky once protested against Lewis' use of known radicals, Lewis is reported to have quipped back, "Who gets the bird, the hunter or the dog?"[26]

The effectiveness of the political radicals varied in different situations. By and large, they were most successful among the new industrial unions except in the needle trades where many Socialists were used as organizers. The radicals met with little success particularly where the AFL and already established CIO unions had strength and competent leadership. And where unions originated as organizing committees and remained for a relatively long period of time under the control of Lewis or Sidney Hillman, the Communists were less successful in establishing themselves permanently. But in those situations where there was little or no legacy of unionism or where independent leadership had made considerable headway prior to the CIO, the Communists met with greatest success. Of the eleven unions expelled in 1949 and 1950 from the CIO for Communist domination, only a few had histories which preceded their affiliation with CIO. The Mine, Mill, and Smelter Workers had a long legacy of radicalism growing out of the Western Federation of Miners and the IWW, and the Fur and Leather Workers had been controlled by Communist leadership since the middle 1920's. The Electrical, Farm Equipment, Food and Tobacco, Public Workers, Office and Professional, the American Communications Association, Fishermen and Allied Workers, and the National Union of Marine Cooks and Stewards were all new unions, created during the early days of CIO. Still other new CIO unions were found with Communist leadership at their top levels. Thus, the Transport Workers Union was for many years under Communist domination, and it was not until 1948 that its international president, Mike Quill, decided to take measures to oust them. And the National Maritime Union was likewise under Communist domination from 1938, shortly after it was organized, until its president Joe Curran broke with Communists in 1948 and succeeded in ousting them from control. The CIO's United Furniture Workers was slated for expulsion from CIO in 1949 when its international president succeeded in defeating the Communists who controlled the secretary-treasurer and the general executive board. The Communists had been established as the dominant force within the West Coast Longshoremen's Union before Lewis appointed Bridges as organizing director for CIO on the West Coast. It was into situations such as these that the Communists poured their strength and resources and were most successful.

The CIO's steel and textile unions and the new union in meatpacking were established as organizing committees by Lewis under Murray, Hillman, and Van Bittner. The two former unions were heavily staffed with personnel from the Miners Union and the Amalgamated Clothing Workers Union and remained as organizing committees under the control of the top CIO leadership for considerable time.[27] The Packinghouse Union, on the other hand, achieved autonomy relatively soon after it was set up. Where such unions originated as organizing committees, the radicals were more easily controlled and more readily removed when the top leadership desired. And the longer they remained as organizing committees, the more thorough the cleaning-out process. Hillman began quietly removing known Communists from the CIO Textile Workers Union in 1938. Yet the union emerged with a strong Socialist element among its top leadership, somewhat reflecting the political complexion of Hillman's own union. The Gas, Coke and Chemical Workers and the Retail and Wholesale as well as the Textile Workers were all in their beginning nursed by Hillman's Clothing Workers, from which they received anywhere from $80,000 to more than $800,000 in direct financial support in addition to the loan of many ACW organizers. Though some radical organizers were used by Lewis, Murray, and Van Bittner in the steel campaign, particularly in the Chicago-Gary area, Murray began purging them in 1938, and in only a few isolated local unions were they able to continue exercising any significant influence.

In the new Rubber Workers Union, the Communists made little headway. The reasons for this are not entirely clear though at least two explanations, however inadequate, can be offered. During the period of the formation of AFL federal locals in rubber in 1934, the Communists were actively boycotting and fighting them. By the time the party line had changed to permit the Communists to enter the mainstream of the labor movement, they were substantially discredited among the tire builders. Also, it may have been that the party concentrated its strength in the nearby auto centers of Detroit, Toledo, and Cleveland and lacked sufficient forces in Akron to play a significant role. Further, the Akron Communists were effectively opposed by a small group of Socialists. In any case, when the rubber workers needed help in their 1936 strike, John Lewis sent in not Communists, but Krzycki, Hapgood, Pesotta, Adolph Germer, and McAllister Coleman, all non-Communist political radicals of one variety or another.

The auto workers presented a different picture. The assembly line workers in the sprawling auto factories were for the political radicals a living embodiment of Marx's classic proletarians. With the beginning of the New Deal, political dissidents of all sorts moved into Detroit and the auto factories for the purpose of proselytizing the overworked and underpaid auto makers. The union movement in autos between

1933 and 1935 was a chaotic revolt which was substantially led by local leaders of a multitude of radical groups. After an initial burst of enthusiasm in 1933 when more than 100 strikes broke out in Detroit alone, disgust and disillusionment set in, in part as a result of the dilatory tactics of the official AFL leadership. When the rank and file again turned to unionism in 1935 they embraced the CIO with a militancy and determinism rarely equalled elsewhere in America. Part of their resourcefulness and daring in the wave of sit-down strikes may have been due to the youthfulness of the labor force, which constantly required refurbishment as a result of the terrible drain of the assembly line. It may have also been due, in part, to the lack of any legacy or heritage of defeats (unlike steel, meat-packing, and textiles) in battle with their giant employers. Though the old-line AFL leadership played some role in the very early days in the automobile industry, it never controlled the situation as did Lewis and Murray in steel. Further, greater rank and file control was possible in the Auto Workers Union since it was financed from the beginning substantially out of membership dues paid into the federal locals rather than from the resources of "outside" unions. Also, unlike the development of many of the new CIO unions, basic programmatic differences emerged very early between those who supported the AFL policy of modified craft unionism, and the grass roots spokesmen, as well as left-wingers, who pushed for an industrial structure. The conflict permitted rank and file leadership to emerge as advocates of a basic program in opposition to the program of the AFL leadership. Further, the policies advanced by Homer Martin as president of the new union were opposed by a coalition led by the "militant" Socialists and the Communists on the ground that Martin was seeking to rigidly centralize control of the union. An issue such as this, coming when it did during the still formative stages of the union's development, again gave the radicals an opportunity to exert leadership around a basic programmatic difference. It was for such reasons as these that the CIO Auto Workers Union became the largest union in America in which political radicals emerged in control. However, it was not the Communists who came out on top, but their ex-Socialist opponents who by 1949 had, for the most part, abandoned their left-wing proclivities.

Various estimates have been made of the ultimate strength of the Communists within the CIO. At minimum they controlled unions containing about 25 per cent of the CIO's total membership and at maximum they wielded powerful influence in unions having another 25 per cent. They completely controlled the third largest CIO union, the United Electrical Workers, which for many years was the main industrial base of the party. The UE was formed in 1936 from a number of independent, IBEW, and AFL federal locals which had originated as company unions. It affiliated with the CIO shortly thereafter and came under Communist control in 1936 and 1937 when Julius Emspack brought into the union a substantial group of members from an independent union and James Matles brought in another group from the International Association of Machinists. Both Matles and Emspack had previously come out of TUUL unions; Matles became the UE's director of organization and Emspack its secretary-treasurer. In addition to the UE, the Communists were strongest in the longshore and maritime fields where they capitalized on a long-time legacy of radicalism among the workers as well as unimaginative and incompetent old-line AFL leadership. In addition to their strength in the national unions themselves, the Communists wielded powerful influence in the national headquarters of the CIO where Lee Pressman had become almost indispensable to Murray and other Communists controlled some of the organization's service arms. Further, many of the CIO's state and local subordinate bodies were controlled by them. It was not until the late 1940's, after Reuther's victory over the Communists in auto, the pressure of Carey, Rieve, and others, and the onset of the "cold war," that Murray became convinced that Communist activities and influence in CIO were inimical to the basic interests of the organization. He succeeded in defeating them by setting the stage for their expulsion and aiding those unions not fully under their control to rid themselves of Communist leadership.

Communists, the NLRB, and the New Unions

The Communists also had some influence on the new unions through the National Labor Relations Board, where a small number of them apparently found employment. Their opportunities may have been greatest in the direction of manipulating and maneuvering personnel, timing of orders, scheduling of hearings, and gathering and presentation of data upon which decisions were made.

The influence of the Communists within the NLRB was at its peak during the years 1937–40. Nathan Witt, assistant general counsel, became Board secretary and chief executive officer at this time, and there is fairly clear evidence that he was either a party member or fellow traveler.[28] He knew more of the Board's operations, policies, and personnel, both in the regions and in the Washington office, than did any other employee, including the three members of the Board themselves. He was clearly in a place to influence procedures, staff members, and even, to some extent, decisions. Edwin S. Smith, a member of the Board and one of its chief policy makers, has also been closely linked with the Communists.[29] Indeed, it was the judgment of David Saposs, at that time chief economist for the Board, that until 1939 Smith dominated the actual policy-making of the Board while working closely with Witt.[30] Further, there is evidence that others among the Board personnel were committed to the Communist movement. Herbert Fuchs, initially an attorney in the review division and later a review supervisor, has testified that he was a member of the Communist party from 1937 to 1942 while employed on the Washington staff of the Board.[31] In addition, he named a number of other Board attorneys as Communists.

Lee Pressman, former general counsel of the CIO and the Steelworkers, has admitted that he and Witt had known each other as members of the Communist party in 1933–35.[32] Pressman has said that he had continuing contact with top party leaders up to the time he resigned his union position in 1948. Though Pressman allegedly broke organizationally with the party in 1936 when he left government employment, he did not make an open ideological break until 1950. Given the commitment which the Communist movement demands of its followers, it is inconceivable that the Witt-Smith-Pressman combination did not at least try to exploit the situation.

One can argue, however, that the results they tried to bring about would have obtained anyway and were desired by countless non-Communists. For, as is pointed out in Chapter 4, the National Labor Relations Board was from the beginning conceived as a device to aid union organization, and those attracted to Board employment were probably overwhelmingly pro-labor. Further, the Great Depression produced an environment in which the new unions of the CIO became for many proselytes of the labor movement "the wave of the future" to which all aid must be given. But this does not justify dismissal of some of the tactics of the Witt-Smith-Pressman combine.

In June, 1937, for instance, Witt, with the knowledge and consent of Smith, gave special and unusual assistance to Pressman in the strategy for getting a quick Board decision on the necessity of a signed collective bargaining contract between the CIO Steelworkers and the Inland Steel Company.[33] In another instance, Smith pressed William Filene and Sons, Boston department store, to urge one of its suppliers to settle with a union with which the supplier had a wage dispute.[34] When the union finally filed charges against the supplier and the Board issued a complaint and held hearings, Smith participated in the decision which found the company guilty of unfair labor practices. In another case, Witt and Smith appear to have gone to great length to help establish Harry Bridges' Longshoremen's Union by maneuvering an unusual and questionable Board decision which established a coast-wide bargaining unit. The decision aroused bitter resentment against the Board, particularly on the part of the AFL, whose West Coast longshore affiliate, a U.S. Circuit Court later said, was effectively destroyed in a large geographical area of the nation.[35]

Whatever effect the Witt, Smith, and Pressman alliance may have had in the very early years, it steadily diminished after 1939. Dr. William Leiserson replaced Donald Wakefield Smith as a Board member in 1939 and he was thereafter a militant critic of some phases of the Board administration and supervision.[36] He strenuously objected to the authority and responsibility centered in the secretary's (Witt's) office. He directed severe criticism at Witt, refusing to participate in several cases on the ground that he could not trust the evidence produced by Witt.[37] On several occasions Leiserson formally moved at Board meetings that Witt be relieved of his duties since it appeared that in some cases Witt was biased in favor of specific CIO unions. This kind of pressure brought about Witt's resignation in 1940. In 1941, Harry A. Millis succeeded Warren Madden as the chairman of the Board, and from then on the Millis-Leiserson majority was in power. With Edwin Smith dissenting, they permitted elections in three of the northern ports on the West Coast which were still claimed by the AFL's longshore affiliate. They did so on the ground that the AFL Longshoremen had never had an opportunity to vote as to whether they should be included in the broad unit. These elections were won overwhelmingly by the AFL, but the position of Bridges' ILWU on the rest of the West Coast was not subsequently seriously threatened.

That there were Communists in high places in the NLRB during the early years seems beyond a shadow of a doubt. Assessing their influence is more difficult. When in 1935 the Congress declared that, as a matter of national policy, workers should be protected in their rights to form and join unions, the Board was created as an agency which would police those rights. As sometimes happens in the unfolding of events, one of the immediate objectives of the Communists, namely the strengthening of the labor unions, ran parallel to those of the national labor policy and the overwhelming majority of non-Communist Board employees whose task it was to implement the mandate of that policy. Moreover, the new unions were products of broad social forces in which countless individuals made important contributions. And it may be argued that the NLRB was the product of these same broad social currents generated by the chaos of the Great Depression. One might even go further and argue, though the authors do not necessarily hold this view, that had the Board not been given a mandate to advance and protect union organization, and had the Board's personnel not been pro-labor, the militancy of the new unionists might have been more successfully organized by the left-wingers in the unions for more radical and wide-sweeping social change.

The influence of the Communists in the NLRB was contained by the "fish bowl" in which the Board operated during this period. It was harassed almost continually by congressional committees, employer groups, and the labor federations, and charges of bias and general poor administration were frequent. And since the Board's decisions were subject to court review, it considered it essential that it be able to show a good record should its decisions be appealed.[38] Nonetheless, the presence of Communists in the NLRB hierarchy is a part of the story of the impact of the political left upon labor during the New Deal period. History has yet to assess accurately the influence they were able to yield.

Summary and Conclusions

By the end of the New Deal period, left-wingers controlled a larger portion of the American labor movement than at any time since the formation of the American Federation of Labor in 1886. The previous high point was probably in the few years preceding World War I which saw the IWW and the Socialists at the 1912 AFL convention getting almost a third of the delegates' votes in an attempt to oust Gompers. The reasons for the left-wingers' success in the 1930's are many and complex, but this essay has focused on the following as of particular importance:

1. In 1929 the radicals' influence on American workers and unions was at a very low ebb. The temper of the times which came with the Great Depression, however, was such as to encourage American workers to experiment with "new" ideas and to put more trust in radical leaders.

2. The extended mass depression encouraged workers to participate in unions of the unemployed. These unions gave workers from industries which had previously not been effectively organized a concept of the idea of organization as a strategic device for approaching solutions to economic and social problems. The unions were organized and led by political radicals. Many workers learned an acceptance or trust of this leadership which carried over into the new trade unions as they became organized later on. Some of these workers, trained in organization, tactics, and ideology by the left-wingers, moved on into positions of leadership in the new unions.

3. Work with organizations of unemployed workers, coupled with many strikes of employed workers led by the political radicals in the first days of the New Deal, gave the left-wingers opportunity to enhance leadership skills and to develop new ones. Because these strikes attracted nationwide attention, they probably gave impetus to the growing union consciousness of workers not actually involved in the conflicts.

4. The radicals, particularly the Communists, exercised their greatest influence in the new unions of the CIO, for it was in these new and fluid situations that the talents and skills which they learned in an earlier period were most effectively deployed. They made little headway in those unions, CIO or AFL, where effective control was exercised by competent leadership in possession of the organizational machinery of the union. But the new union center, lacking an organizing staff of proportions adequate to the needs of the situation, was ready to utilize the services of speakers, writers, and organizers wherever it could find them. Where the Communists were unimpeded by a trained and experienced opposition, they managed to maximize their control.

5. The Communists were always minorities, but their success in gaining and keeping influence or control is explained in part by the strength of the Bolshevik "organizational weapon" for group manipu-

lation which they had forged. The third period of isolation from the main stream of American workers and unions resulting from ineffective dualism and ultra-left tactics was an important element in the forging crucible.

6. The Communists were the most effective of the left-wingers in controlling the new unions, but their revolutionary political philosophy was frequently deliberately concealed, and their subservience to control from Russia did not become generally obvious to other than sophisticated observers till the onset of World War II. In contrast with their earlier left-wing attempts, Communist leaders in the unions worked hard at prosecuting normal and "legitimate" trade union service functions. The leaders in this case had many followers largely because they were satisfying the economic and social needs of job conscious American workers.

7. The Communists were aided in establishing a position in some of the CIO unions by the influence they wielded for a time through key staff positions of the National Labor Relations Board. Just how extensive or significant this influence was, it is difficult to conclude, but we judge it to have been of some importance in certain situations.

8. Non-Communist left-wingers, including Socialists, Trotskyites, and Musteites, achieved holds in some of the new unions. In certain unions, such as textiles and perhaps rubber, as well as in some of the expanding AFL unions, Socialists were influential in keeping the Communists out. In autos the Socialists were a key factor in dislodging the Communists from the substantial beachhead they had achieved. In most cases, particularly by 1939 when the Socialist party had substantially disintegrated, the Socialists in the unions had lost much of their distinctive ideology and were virtually indistinguishable from other "New Deal unionists."

During World War II and particularly in the postwar period, the left-wingers lost heavily in influence. By the end of 1955 the Socialist trade unionists were almost indistinguishable from others, and the Communists no longer controlled a single CIO union. Communist control appeared limited to a couple of unions which had been expelled from the CIO, and their influence, while still extant in a few CIO unions, was exceedingly weak and almost completely underground.

Such post–New Deal developments are beyond the scope of this essay, but we may glance quickly at the New Deal period for indication of some of the factors which underlay and presaged them. These factors would appear to include the following: (1) the political and subsequent economic success of the New Deal in resuscitating American capitalism, especially as it entered the preparedness and war period; (2) the gap between basic assumptions of much of the left-wing propaganda and workers' perceptions of American realities; (3) the solid achievements of unions through collective bargaining, particularly following the judicial validation of the Wagner Act in 1937; (4) the emergence of established non-Communist leaders in many of the new unions and the consequent push toward isolation of the extreme left-wingers in the CIO; (5) the rule-or-ruin tactics of the Communists which in many cases helped antagonize other leaders and members; (6) the decision of CIO leaders, beginning in 1939, to slack off, and even in some cases to react against, their use of left-wing organizers; (7) the opposition of Communists as well as some other left-wingers, during the term of the Nazi-Soviet pact of 1939, to the preparations for national defense, highlighted by the Communist-led strikes at the North American Aviation, Vultee Aircraft, and Allis-Chalmers plants in 1940 and 1941; and (8) the sectarian splits and rabid rivalry among left-wing groups, e.g., Stalinists, Lovestonites, and Trotskyites, as well as personality and programmatic schisms among the Socialists.

In conclusion it may be of some interest to speculate as to whether the left-wing unionism of the New Deal period left any relatively permanent legacies to the American labor movement. Did the left-wingers in any meaningful measure increase the labor movement's reliance upon political action and governmental programs? Did they significantly increase the relative degree of industrial unionism (as against other structural forms)? Did they succeed in mitigating the suspicions of the "regular" union leaders and members toward intellectuals in the movement, or did the ultimate revulsion against left-wingers reinforce previous distrust of this sort?

We find it impossible to make solid conclusions on these questions, although we strongly doubt that the first two questions can be answered in the affirmative. On the other hand the left-wingers probably did have some significant effect upon the speed with which the new unions were organized and established. We doubt that the CIO would have emerged as a going concern as rapidly as it did had it not been for the ready reservoir of individuals trained in the radical movement who were eager for the multifold organizing and leadership tasks present in the mid-thirties.

It appears, however, that the left-wingers in this period, as in a few of the earlier ones, contributed a somewhat lasting tone to organizations in which they were most active. This "tone" is not easy to define or measure, but its presence may be indicated by the greater readiness of the subsequent nonradical leadership to experiment with ideas and programs not traditional to the mainstream of the older labor movement. One example might be the various service agencies now found in many of the large industrial unions which were designed to bolster and extend the collective bargaining function of the union by giving technical expertness and support.[39] Though some of these functions had developed earlier in unions which were under strong Socialist influence, the conditions of the 1930's more thoroughly ingrained them as part of the labor movement's accepted pattern. A greater union willingness to move in the direction of political action which was designed to involve rank and file workers might be a related manifestation. The class conscious unionists felt that the union's role in the larger society was a matter of great importance and that it could be maximized through an awareness of and participation in the political process by workers at the local level. Admittedly, these are speculations, but they appear worthy of further exploration.

On the question of the acceptance of intellectuals within the labor movement, many factors other than the work of the political radicals would need to be weighed and we have not attempted to do this. We are, however, inclined to give a tentative affirmative judgment on two other matters. The first is the impact of left-wing unionists on union policies with respect to racial and religious minority groups. It would appear that the radicals had some significant influence on the formulation of nondiscriminatory policies in the new CIO unions, and, indirectly, through the inter-union organizing competition, on some of the expanding AFL unions as well. Secondly, we judge that the tactics of union manipulation and control which some of the left-wingers used so skillfully were in many cases adapted by non–left-wingers, frequently in self-defense. As a result, use of these union control tools by leaders and union members' acceptance of such controls were increased and imbedded into the labor movement more deeply than would otherwise have been likely.

These are, of course, impressionistic rather than scientific judgments, but they are presented in the hope of stimulating more careful research and analysis by other students in the field.

Notes

1 He polled more than 10 per cent of the votes in each of ten western states, the highest ratio being in Nevada and Oklahoma—16.5 and 16.6 per cent.

2 "In the execution of this duty the Communists must practically subordinate the factory committees and the unions to the Communist Party, and thus create a proletarian mass organ, a basis for a powerful centralized party of the proletariat." *Theses and Statutes of the Third (Communist) International* (Moscow: Communist International, 1920), p. 35.

3 Dixon Wecter, *The Age of the Great Depression* (New York: Macmillan Co., 1948), pp. 34–35.

4 *Ibid.*, p. 36.

5 Foster Rhea Dulles, *Labor in America, A History,* (New York: Thomas Y. Crowell Co., 1949), p. 261.

6 Broadus Mitchell, *Depression Decade* ("The Economic History of the United States," Vol. IX; [New York: Rinehart and Co., 1947]), p. 110.

7 *New York Times,* March 7, 1930.

8 Paul Hutchinson, "Hunger on the March," *Christian Century,* November 9, 1932, pp. 1377–78.

9 Samuel Appelbaum, "History of the Workers Alliance of America," *Work,* September 24, 1938, pp. 8–9.

10 *Labor Age,* November, 1931, p. 26.

11 *Workers Alliance,* October 2, 1935.

12 David Lasser, "What Is the Workers Alliance of America?" *Workers Alliance,* Second Anniversary Issue, 1936.

13 For an example of this situation in a specific local area, see Milton Derber, "Building Construction" in *Labor-Management Relations in Illini City* (Champaign, Ill.: Institute of Labor and Industrial Relations, University of Illinois, 1953), I, 701–2.

14 *People's Press,* November 21, 1936.

15 American Federation of Labor, *Proceedings,* 1935, p. 678.

16 *People's Press,* December 18, 1937.

17 The Toledo events were reported contemporaneously in the following sources: A. J. Muste, "The Battle of Toledo," *Nation,* June 6, 1934; "Industrial Warfare Breaks Out Over the Country," *Newsweek,* June 2, 1934; "Street Fighting Marks Toledo Strike," *Literary Digest,* June 2, 1934; "What Is Behind Toledo," *New Republic,* June 6, 1934; also Maurice Goldbloom, *et al., Strikes Under the New Deal* (New York: League for Industrial Democracy, undated). The *New York Times* during this period reported the daily occurrences.

18 Bruce Minton and John Stuart, *Men Who Lead Labor* (New York: Modern Age Books, 1937), and Mike Quin, *The Big Strike* (Olema, California: The Olema Publishing Company, 1949), portray the career of the longshoremen and Harry Bridges, who is treated very sympathetically by the authors.

19 A detailed account of this strike is given by Charles R. Walker, *American City: A Rank-and-File History* (New York: Farrar and Rinehart, 1937). James P. Cannon, the leader of the American Trotskyite movement, discussed the strategy of the strike and the role of his political followers in *History of American Trotskyism* (New York: Pioneer Publishers, 1944).

20 A fourth major 1934 strike was the industry-wide strike of textile workers. Political radicals had played important roles in this industry beginning with Lawrence, Massachusetts, in 1913. In 1925–26, Communists led a bitter strike in Passaic, New Jersey, and played leading roles in the New Bedford, Massachusetts, and Gastonia, North Carolina, strikes of 1929. Many old-time "wobblies" and Communists emerged as local leaders in the 1934 strike which was led by officials of the AFL's United Textile Workers Union. The Socialist party, which was at the peak of its post–World War I strength, gave considerable support to the strike in the form of organizers and funds. The TUUL's Textile Union, though denouncing the AFL leadership, was active in organizing and agitating. The union's gains as provided in the settlement quickly proved to be illusory and a new organizing campaign was undertaken by Hillman of the CIO three years later. Nevertheless, this strike, like others in which radicals were active, provided them with similar opportunities, and must have contributed substantially to the growing union consciousness of workers in other parts of the country.

21 A sophisticated analytical treatment of Leninism and Stalinism as an "Organizational Weapon" is given in the book of the same name by Philip Selznik (New York: McGraw-Hill Book Co., 1952).

22 Daniel Bell, "The Background and Development of Marxian Socialism in the United States" in Donald D. Egbert and Stow Persons, eds., *Socialism and American Life* (Princeton: Princeton University Press, 1952), I, 382.

23 The "unity" of the Socialists lasted for about two years and by the end of 1938 had disappeared.

24 After Russia was invaded by Hitler, the Communists attacked Lewis in every conceivable way because of his alleged alliances with "America First" groups and other isolationists.

25 Saul D. Alinsky, *John L. Lewis: an Unauthorized Biography* (New York: G. P. Putnam's Sons, 1949).

26 Joseph and Stewart Alsop, "Will the CIO Shake the Communists Loose?" *Saturday Evening Post*, February 22 and March 1, 1947. The authors report that some years later, when Lewis himself had become a chief object of Communist attack, Lewis admitted to Dubinsky that Du-

binsky had been right all along. Dubinsky then asked, "Who was the hunter, John, and who was the dog?"

27 Indeed, the Steel Workers Organizing Committee, established in 1935, was not transformed into a national union until more than five years later.

28 U.S. House of Representatives, Special Committee to Investigate the National Labor Relations Board, *Hearings,* 76th Cong., 2d Sess. (1940); U.S. Senate, Committee on the Judiciary, *Interlocking Subversion in Government Departments,* 83d Cong., 1st Sess. (1953); U.S. House of Representatives, Committee on Un-American Activities, *Hearings Regarding Communist Espionage in the United States Government,* 80th Cong., 2d Sess. (1948); U.S. House of Representatives, Committee on Un-American Activities, *Hearings Regarding Communism in the United States Government,* 81st Cong., 2d Sess. (1950), particularly pp. 2844–2910.

29 U.S. Senate, Committee on the Judiciary, *Interlocking Subversion in Government Departments,* 83d Cong., 1st Sess. (1953), pp. 545–604; and U.S. House of Representatives, Special Committee to Investigate the National Labor Relations Board, *Hearings,* 76th Cong., 2d Sess. (1940).

30 U.S. Senate, Committee on the Judiciary, *Interlocking Subversion in Government Departments,* 83d Cong., 1st Sess. (1953), pp. 657–78.

31 *New York Times,* December 14 and 15, 1955.

32 U.S. House of Representatives, Committee on Un-American Activities, *Hearings Regarding Communism in the United States Government,* 81st Cong., 2d Sess. (1950), pp. 2844–2910.

33 See testimony of Nathan Witt in U.S. House of Representatives, Special Committee to Investigate the National Labor Relations Board, *Hearings,* 76th Cong., 2d Sess. (1940), pp. 897–919.

34 Charles N. Bufford, *The Wagner Act* (Rochester, N.Y.: The Lawyers Cooperative Publishing Co., 1941), p. 15.

35 Our discussion of the issues in this case is drawn primarily from the record in this proceeding: *American Federation of Labor* v. *National Labor Relations Board,* 103 F. (2d) 933 C.C.A., District of Columbia (1939).

David Saposs has testified that in his function as the Board's chief economist it was his responsibility to supervise a staff which would gather economic data in connection with the case. However, he did not participate in this matter, which was one of the most important to come before the Board during the late 1930's. "My surmise is that [Smith and Witt] deliberately kept me from preparing any of the material because by that time they knew what my point of view was and they knew that my general understanding was of the maneuvers, the manipulations of the Communists and the fellow-travelers." U.S. Senate, Committee on the Judiciary, *Interlocking Subversion in Government Departments,* 83d Cong., 1st Sess. (1953), p. 677.

36 Leiserson's position in these matters is taken from his testimony before the U.S. House of Representatives, Special Committee to Investigate the National Labor Relations Board, *Hearings,* 76th Cong., 2d Sess. (1940), pp. 3–141.

37 Leiserson wrote several memoranda to Board Chairman Madden, of which the following excerpt is fairly typical: "If you think immediate action is needed on this you can leave me out of the case entirely. I would rather not participate in it. I think this is another one of those cases in which the Secretary has put his fingers and balled it up." *Ibid.*

38 The record shows reversals in only two of fourteen cases taken to the U.S. Supreme Court during this period.

39 One interesting bit of evidence on this score is found in Harold Wilensky, "The Staff Expert" (unpublished Ph.D. dissertation, University of Chicago, 1955). Wilensky found that of a sample of 122 union staff experts about 30 per cent entered the labor movement as "political missionaries," originally committed to left-wing ideologies.

4

The Significance of the Wagner Act

R. W. FLEMING

WHAT conclusions can one draw, after twenty years, as to the significance and impact of the Wagner Act? A clear starting point is some understanding of both the history of federal intervention in the affairs of labor and management prior to 1935, and the context of the times in which the Act was written. The Wagner Act has by now assumed such landmark proportions that there is some disposition to regard it as the initial point of federal intervention in the affairs of labor and management. In fact, all branches of the federal government had long had extensive dealings with labor and management prior to that time.

Labor and Government Before the New Deal

From labor's point of view the judiciary presented particular difficulty. Until 1842 the courts were inclined to view labor unions as criminal conspiracies. After that view changed, the injunction came into usage. No one knows how many injunctions were issued in labor disputes, but one authority finds in his own files references to more than 500 federal court injunctions and more than 1,300 state court injunctions in the years prior to May, 1931.[1] The detailed story of the use of the injunction has been set forth in Frankfurter and Greene's book, *The Labor Injunction*,[2] and it is not one which reflects great credit on the American judiciary. Court orders designed to inhibit every conceivable kind of conduct were too often issued without proper hearing or notice. The end result was to burn the word "injunction" into labor's mind forever as a term of infamy.

Hand in hand with the injunction went the yellow-dog contract which the courts chose to honor. For all practical purposes such a contract deprived workers of the opportunity to increase their strength through organization.

Nor did the courts see fit to interpret federal legislation in the way which labor felt to be appropriate. When the Sherman Antitrust Act was passed in 1890, the Act made no specific mention of labor combinations or labor disputes. Whether the law was ever intended to apply to labor unions is debatable, but the U.S. Supreme Court decided in 1908 that it did, with the result that the Hatters Union found itself burdened with a judgment for extensive damages because it had engaged in an organizational strike and a nationwide boycott against the company's goods. The decision so alarmed the leaders of organized labor that they immediately started a campaign for the amendment of the Sherman Act. The long battle seemed to culminate with success in 1914 when the Clayton Act was passed. Section 6, on which labor's hopes were based, read:

> That the labor of a human being is not a commodity or article of Commerce. Nothing contained in the antitrust laws shall be construed to forbid the existence and operation of labor, agricultural, or horticultural organizations, instituted for the purpose of mutual help, and not having capital stock or conducted for profit, or to forbid or restrain the legitimate objects thereof; nor shall such organizations, or the members thereof, be held or construed to be illegal combination or conspiracies in restraint of trade, under the antitrust laws.

Section 6 seemed clear enough, but when it came before the courts some five years later labor's position was not upheld. Not only did the court find that "there is nothing in this section to exempt such an organization or its members from accountability where it or they depart from its normal and legitimate objects and engage in actual combination or conspiracy in restraint of trade . . . ," [3] but the Act itself permitted private parties to apply for injunctions whereas under the Sherman Act only the federal government could secure such an injunction.

Presidential intervention, which came usually in so-called emergencies, varied in its friendliness to labor but was certainly not uniformly hostile in the way the courts had been.[4] In the case of the Pullman strike in 1894, President Cleveland followed up an injunction with the use of federal troops, over the objection of the Governor of Illinois. The President later appointed a commission to study the Pullman strike, and the report read in part that "the Company does not recognize that labor organizations have any place or necessity in Pullman...."[5]

President McKinley sent troops into the Coeur d'Alene metal mines in Idaho with the end result, according to a report of the time, that they were used to destroy the Western Federation of Miners in that area.[6]

President Theodore Roosevelt felt impelled to assert the government's interest in the 1902 anthracite strike and was instrumental in bringing about a settlement.

President Wilson was called upon to intervene in more labor disputes than any of his predecessors. The mines and the railroads were the chief objects of his attention, and it was at his instance that one dispute was settled by passage of the Adamson Act in 1916 establishing the eight-hour day on the railroads.

In the West Virginia mine disputes of 1921 attempts were made by the National Guard and the State Police to suppress disturbances. When disorder increased President Harding sent in federal troops to restore the peace. President Harding also found himself involved in efforts to settle the railway shopmen's strike in 1922.

During the threatened bituminous coal strike in 1924 Secretary of Commerce Herbert Hoover sought with the approval of President Coolidge to get the parties together. In connection with the anthracite coal strike in 1925 President Coolidge sent a message to Congress in which he said that there should be authority in the President and the Departments of Commerce and Labor giving them power to deal with an emergency.

Throughout the actions of the courts and the presidents run threads of such legislation as the Sherman Act, the Clayton Act, various pieces of railroad legislation, and finally in 1932 the Norris-LaGuardia Act, which largely removed from the federal courts the power to issue injunctions in labor disputes.

The point that this bit of history brings into sharp focus is that prior to 1935 labor's experience with the agencies of the federal government was most often with the courts, which were openly hostile. Students who now explain the Taft-Hartley Act in 1947 as a reaction against the one-sidedness of the Wagner Act will do well to note that in the context of its time the Wagner Act was a reaction against another kind of one-sidedness.

The Coming of the New Deal

Chapters 5 and 6 describe in some detail the development of the New Deal recovery program which was initially crystallized in the NIRA and the industrial codes. Here we need note only that the price of labor coöperation was the incorporation of Section 7(a) of NIRA which, in its final form, reads as follows:

> Every code of fair competition, agreement, and license approved, prescribed, or issued under this title shall contain the following conditions: (1) That employees shall have the right to organize and bargain collectively through representatives of their own choosing, and shall be free from the interference, restraint, or coercion of employers of labor, or their agents, in the designation of such representatives or in self-organization or in other concerted activities for the purpose of collective bargaining or other mutual aid or protection; (2) that no employee and no one seeking employment shall be required as a condition of employment to join any company union or to refrain from joining, organizing, or assisting a labor organization of his own choosing; and (3) that employers shall comply with the maximum hours of labor, minimum rates of pay, and other conditions of employment, approved or prescribed by the President.

There was nothing new about the basic ideas contained in Section 7(a). The principal draftsman, Donald Richberg, has said that the substance of the paragraph came from his familiarity with the Railway Labor Act of 1926, the Norris-LaGuardia Act of 1932, and the 1933 amendments to the Federal Bankruptcy Act.[7] As a matter of fact the War Labor Board in World War I had professed much the same principles. Long before that the 1902 Anthracite Coal Strike Commission had endorsed collective bargaining as a device for resolving disputes in the mines. And a 1915 report of the Commission on Industrial Relations recommended that in determining unfair methods of competition, the Federal Trade Commission be given authority to take into account an employer's refusal to permit employees to become members of labor organizations or to meet with the authorized representatives of employees.[8]

Section 7(a) proved helpful in many ways but illusory in others so far as labor was concerned, for industry professed to find nothing in the law inconsistent with the formation of company unions, and defied the Board whenever it attempted to proceed against them. Senator Wagner, who chaired the first National Labor Board as a public member, became discouraged with the Board's voluntary authority with the result that in 1934 he offered a bill which in later form became the Wagner Act.[9] Opposition to the proposed legislation was strong, it had been introduced late, 1934 was an election year, and while the current steel strike convinced the President that some legislation was necessary, he wanted a noncontroversial solution. The answer proved to be Public Resolution 44 under which the President was empowered to appoint a National Labor Relations Board to investigate controversies. The Board could conduct elections by secret ballot for the selection of representatives. It also was given the power of subpoena, and penalties were provided for violators. Labor representatives were most unhappy with this result, but apparently many industry executives felt it was not a bad trade since the public resolution would automatically expire and as propitious a moment for passage of such legislation as the Wagner bill might not come again.

At the time Resolution 44 was adopted, Senator Wagner vowed to try again in 1935. Perhaps his determination and optimism were strengthened by the fact that even as Public Resolution 44 was being passed, many of the principles which he sought to apply throughout industry were being enacted for the railroads by the 1934 amendments to the Railway Labor Act. George Harrison, president of the Brotherhood of Railway Clerks, said at the time that in view of the precedent already established in the amendments to the Railway Labor Act, "I don't see how the next Congress can refuse the demand of the American Federation of Labor for more specific legislation to implement the labor sections of the National Industrial Recovery Act." [10]

The year 1935 brought fulfillment of Senator Wagner's hopes. The National Labor Relations Act was passed. We turn now to a more detailed examination of the problems which the Act raised—both then and for the future. Before doing so, however, something needs to be said with respect to the support, or lack of it, which the White House gave to collective bargaining legislation throughout the whole period.

Roosevelt and the Wagner Act

The fact that in the twenty years since 1935 a close political alliance has grown up between the Democratic party and labor, plus the enduring importance of the Wagner Act which was passed at the height of the New Deal period, has left the general impression in the public mind that the Wagner Act was a key piece of New Deal legislation and that Roosevelt was instrumental in its enactment. In fact there appears to be incontrovertible historical proof that Roosevelt himself never was greatly interested in the subject and gave the proposal his support only at the last minute and then under considerable political pressure.

Frances Perkins, who was Roosevelt's Secretary of Labor throughout his term of office, has said of the President's relationship to the Wagner Act: "It ought to be on the record that the President did not take part in developing the National Labor Relations Act and, in fact, was hardly consulted about it. It was not a part of the President's program. It did not particularly appeal to him when it was described to him. All the credit for it belongs to Wagner." [11]

Raymond Moley, at that time still a member in good standing of the Brain Trust, corroborates Secretary Perkins' appraisal. He goes further and explains Roosevelt's last-minute adoption of the Act on the grounds that the President "needed the influence and votes of Wagner on so many pieces of legislation and partly because of the invalidation of the N.I.R.A." [12]

The most thorough research into the New Deal period and its collective bargaining legislation has been done by Dr. Irving Bernstein. After an exhaustive study of the documents and interviews with all of the key personnel then concerned with legislation from Section 7(a) through the Wagner Act, he records the President's lack of support for such legislation.[13]

Finally, it is strikingly evident in the hearings before the Senate Education and Labor Committee that administration spokesmen played a very minor part in the whole proceedings. The Secretary of Labor testified and supported the bill, but the great bulk of her testimony is devoted to the question of where a labor board, established under the provisions of the Act, should be housed. When Francis Biddle proposed a fifth unfair labor practice for addition to Section 8, making it unfair for the employer to refuse to bargain with representatives of his employees, no comment on the section was ever forthcoming from the administration despite the importance of the proposal.

It should be said for Roosevelt, though this is perhaps only corroborative of the view that he was not greatly interested in collective bargaining legislation, that when he finally gave his support to the Wagner Act he was not thereafter swayed by industry pressure to change his position. Moreover in later years he often referred in political speeches to labor legislation enacted under the auspices of the New Deal.

Arguments on the Wagner Act—Pro and Con

The Wagner Act may be said to have contained three main provisions: (1) protection of the worker's right to join a union and to organize without employer interference; (2) provision for election machinery to determine union representation; and (3) a mandate that the employer bargain with the duly elected union representatives. None of these provisions was novel. Reference has already been made to similar rules and procedures under the World War I Labor Board, the various pieces of railway labor legislation, Section 7(a) of the NIRA, and the 1933 amendments to the Federal Bankruptcy Act. Nevertheless it is easy to overemphasize the fact that the provisions of the Wagner Act were all drawn from prior experience. The constitutional issue involved in regulating the nation's railroads under the commerce power as compared with regulating industry in general is obviously quite distinct. Secondly, the 1926 Railway Labor Disputes Act was an agreed bill between labor and management, and this made a vast psychological difference. Finally, in two substantive phases of the acts there were important differences. The Railway Labor Act discouraged "coercion" from any source while the Wagner Act restrained only the employer. This was the subject of hot debate, as will be shown later, when the Tydings amendment to the Wagner Act came up. In addition the Railway Labor Act prohibited the closed shop,[14] while the Wagner Act permitted it. The closed shop has ever symbolized labor monopoly to industry people; therefore it is not surprising that this difference was a red flag to them.

Aside from previous experience with similar regulations, arguments which the proponents of the Act used revolved around three main themes: (1) industrial peace would be promoted once the employer was restrained from interfering with the right of workers to join unions and to bargain collectively; (2) the democratic form of government would be given deeper roots by democratic processes in the work life of the employee; and (3) the economy would be desirably strengthened by free and independent unions which could insist upon a more equitable division of profits, thereby maintaining high purchasing power.

To these arguments the opponents responded with four main contentions: (1) the Act was unconstitutional; (2) it was one-sided in that no restrictions were placed upon labor; (3) it tended to promote class cleavage in American society; and (4) it failed to protect individual rights sacred to every American.

The above points need to be examined in some detail and, insofar as possible, subjected to the test of historical proof.

Proponents

Industrial Peace.—A primary reason for the sharp difference of opinion as to the effect which the passage of the Wagner Act might be expected to have on industrial peace was the completely different perspective from which the various interested parties approached the question. The proponents never argued that the Act would eliminate all industrial strife; indeed they considered this inconsistent with democratic principles. Their theory was that at least a quarter of all strikes arose from the refusal of employers to recognize or engage in the practice of collective bargaining. This impediment to peaceful relations could, in their view, be removed by legislation. Incidentally it was felt that by "establishing the only process through which friendly negotiations or conferences can operate in modern large-scale industry, there should be a tremendous lessening of the strife that has resulted from failure to adjust wage and hour disputes." [15]

Those who derided the notion that the Wagner Act would promote industrial peace were, in effect, emphasizing the 75 per cent portion of dispute cases which arose out of causes other than unwillingness to engage in collective bargaining. And they were insisting that the inevitable result of an act which destroyed harmonious relations then existing with "company" unions and substituted for them "outside" unions would be a decided increase in industrial unrest.

Statistical proof of the validity of either of the above positions is difficult not only because it is almost impossible to disentangle other factors affecting the strike picture as of any given moment, but because the very use of statistics involves some basic assumptions as to what one wants to prove. Moreover, the issue must not be torn from its historical context. The five years immediately after passage of the Wagner Act brought forth the greatest organizing drives ever seen in this country. At the same time employer opposition to outside unions was at its peak. Famed constitutional lawyers were openly advising that the Act was invalid. Under the circumstances a fair picture of the enduring effect of the Wagner Act can hardly be drawn from the initial period of adjustment.

On the assumption that in making comparisons one should look at those strikes involving union organization, Dr. Bernstein offered the statistics in Table 1, derived from Bureau of Labor Statistics sources.[16]

Table 1. Percentage of Strikes Involving Union Recognition

Year	Work stoppages, per cent of total	Workers involved, per cent of total
1927	36.0	13.9
1928	36.5	29.5
1929	41.3	35.5
1930	31.8	41.7
1931	27.8	33.6
1932	19.0	22.4
1933	31.9	40.7
1934	45.9	51.5
1935	47.2	26.1
1936	50.2	51.4
1937	57.8	59.8
1938	50.0	32.6
1939	53.5	54.5
1940	49.9	33.1
1941	49.5	31.5
1942	31.2	22.4
1943	15.7	11.5
1944	16.3	18.6
1945	20.5	21.8
1946	32.4	11.5
1947	29.8	43.0

From these figures Bernstein thought it was possible to suggest two conclusions: (1) that in the five years following passage of the Act there was a marked increase in the proportion of strikes over union recognition as compared with both the late twenties and the early years of the Great Depression; and (2) that between 1939 and 1947 there was a sharp decline in the relative incidence of such stoppages to a level below that prevailing prior to passage of the Wagner Act.

Charts A, B, and C throw additional light on the history of strikes over a period of years. The first, showing major issues involved in work stoppages during the period 1927–50, confirms Professor Bernstein's conclusions if one takes into account the increase in the size of the work force.

Chart A

Major Issues Involved in Work Stoppages, 1927–50

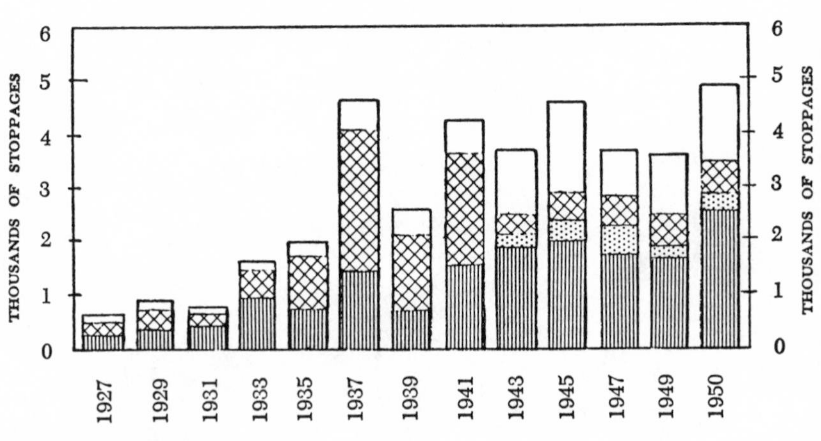

Miscellaneous Working Conditions

Union Organization

Union Organization and Wages and Hours

Wages and Hours

Source: W. S. Woytinsky and associates, *Employment and Wages in the United States* (New York: Twentieth Century Fund, 1953), p. 285. Used with permission.

The second chart shows the proportion of employed workers involved in stoppages during the period 1890–1950. The strongest single impression which this chart leaves is that strikes are unrelated to legislation. Peak periods came immediately following the two world wars, but aside from these periods the relative volume of strikes, as measured by the percentage of employed workers involved, remained about the same.

It is of special interest to compare the number of workers involved in work stoppages and union membership because there is a natural disposition to attribute an increase in strikes to the known fact that there are more union members than there formerly were. Nevertheless, if the two peak strike periods following the two world wars are compared, the figures would indicate that after an adjustment is made for the difference in the size of the work force, one in every five workers was involved in stoppages in 1919 while the comparable figure was one in seven in 1946. It is clear that the number of workers involved in

Chart B

Percentage of Employed Workers Involved in Work Stoppages, 1890–1950

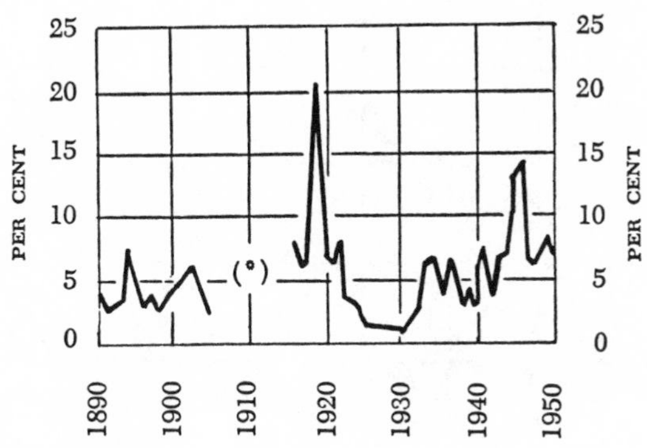

* Data not available.

Source: W. S. Woytinsky and associates, *Employment and Wages in the United States* (New York: Twentieth Century Fund, 1953), p. 292. Used with permission.

stoppages has increased much less than the growth of union membership. Total workers involved in strikes exceeded union membership after World War I, but represented only a fraction of the union membership after World War II. These comparisons are graphically demonstrated in Chart C.

In retrospect one suspects that the argument that the Wagner Act would reduce industrial strife was framed principally with an eye to the constitutional hurdle which the Act faced. The draftsmen must justify federal action on the basis of the federal government's right to control interstate commerce, and it was by no means clear that a law governing labor-management relations had anything to do with interstate commerce. If Congress in enacting the legislation recited its belief that the Act would reduce industrial strife which was, in turn, interfering with interstate commerce, this statement might contribute toward a favorable court decision. This is not to suggest that the sponsors of the Act were dishonest in their contention that industrial strife would be reduced. On the face of it they never contended that more than 25 per cent of all industrial disputes were over union recog-

Chart C

Workers Involved in Work Stoppages and Union Membership, 1897–1947

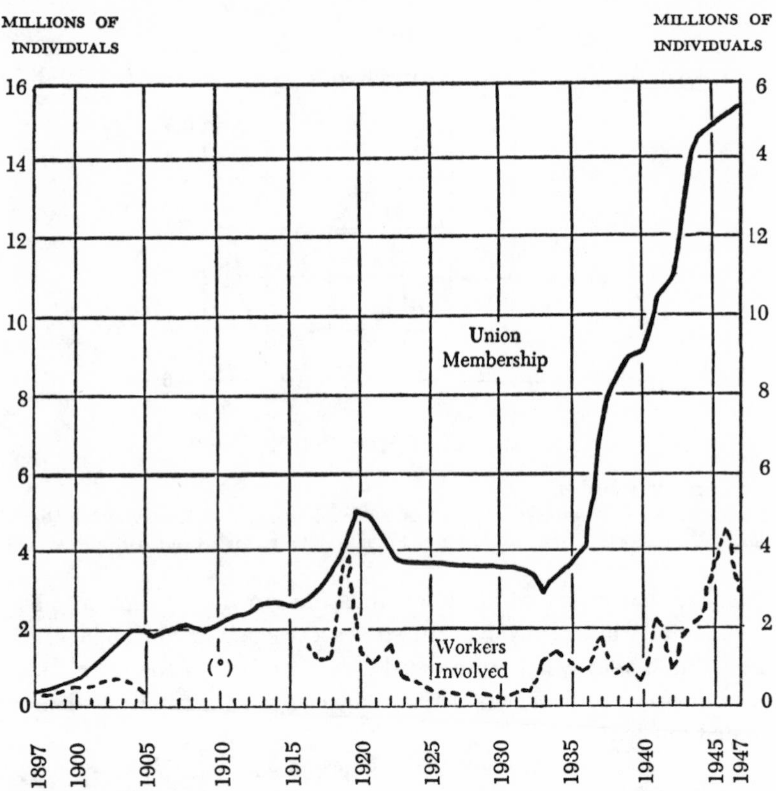

* Data not available.

Source: W. S. Woytinsky and associates, *Employment and Wages in the United States* (New York: Twentieth Century Fund, 1953), p. 291. Used with permission.

nition which was the principal area affected by the legislation. Beyond that they could have believed that friction would be reduced by the mere act of "getting to know each other better." Such an article of faith is more common than not, even on the 1957 industrial relations scene.

Industrial Democracy.—Senator Wagner ardently believed that industrial democracy was as essential as political democracy to the preservation of the American heritage. His views of this subject were perhaps best stated in 1937 for the *New York Times Magazine,* but restatements of the same idea are to be found running through his arguments during the whole period when the Act was under consideration. In 1937 he said:

> The struggle for a voice in industry through the process of collective bargaining is the heart of the struggle for the preservation of political as well as economic democracy in America. Let men become the servile pawns of their masters in the factories of the land and there will be destroyed the bone and sinew of resistance to political dictatorship.
>
> Fascism begins in industry, not in government. The seeds of communism are sown in industry, not in government. But let men know the dignity of freedom and self-expression in their daily lives, and they will never bow to tyranny in any quarter of their national life.[17]

There is, of course, no absolute proof that democracy in the shop supports political democracy. However, it is significant that the opposition did not question the desirability of industrial democracy but differed only on the level of whether the Act encouraged it. Their contention was that the company unions which were already operating in many of the shops were in fact democratically elected and that the only result of the Wagner Act would be to foist off on reluctant employees "outside" unions which would neither know nor understand the local problems. The difference in other words was not one of political theory, but of implementation.[18]

It should be recorded, by way of evaluating Senator Wagner's devotion to the proposition that democracy in the shop was an important ingredient in preserving political democracy, that our form of government may in 1935 have been in greater peril than is generally realized. The bonus march on Washington was a thing of recent memory. General Johnson's administration of the NRA on occasion raised doubts in the minds of his colleagues as to his understanding of the democratic process.[19] Hitler, Mussolini, and Franco were on the prowl in Europe. Huey Long was making a demagogic appeal in America. Millions of men were unemployed and therefore susceptible to any new philosophy which offered hope for them. In that kind of an atmosphere anything that would contribute to an understanding of the values of democracy was on the plus side.

That shop elections have been a matter of great interest to workers seems beyond doubt. The National Labor Relations Board announced in the fall of 1955 that over the past twenty years more than 75,500 representation elections were held. Approximately 13,685,000 employees were eligible to vote. Of these more than 11,658,000 voted—or 85 per cent of the total. For those who are concerned at the too frequently demonstrated apathy of voters in political elections, this is a source of great encouragement. Workers have taken a very active role in naming their representatives.

Economic Adjustment.—The most important theme in all the speeches which Senator Wagner made, as the chief sponsor for the National Labor Relations Act, was that it would effect a greater economic stability through better economic balance. In his theory, collective bargaining would promote both a higher level of real wages and a better distribution of the national income. Genuine collective bargaining could only be carried on by unions which were free from any domination by the employer. It followed that an avowed objective of the Act was to promote the growth of a free and independent labor movement. In this objective there can be little doubt that the Act has been spectacularly successful. Much of Chapter 1 is devoted to the growth of the labor movement after the passage of the Wagner Act. Suffice it to say here that from a probable figure of something less than 3 million members in 1933, the total figure climbed to between 8 and 9 million in 1939, despite a decrease in employed workers in nonfarm establishments during this period. The increase in the size of the labor movement from something near 9 million to approximately 14 million which occurred between 1939 and 1945 may very well be largely attributable to the effect of World War II. Nevertheless, it is worth noting that the wartime gains were largely accomplished by unions which had a firm foothold by 1939.

The question of whether collective bargaining does in fact raise real wages and remove inequalities of distribution is, and has been, the subject of great debate among economists. The subject matter is sufficiently complex to dissuade the noneconomist from taking part in the argument.

If there is new light to be cast on the question, it may lie in the suggestion that a debate as to whether collective bargaining is a source of real wage advantage misses the point. The evidence is fairly clear that people *think* unions do raise wages and better distribute the national income. One finds evidence of this on many fronts. Various polls indicate that the average person believes unions have forced wages up.[20] NLRB Member Phillip Rodgers, who was promoted to the Board from a position as counsel to the Senate Labor and Public Welfare Committee where he had been placed by Senator Taft, has said publicly that it is "the undisputed fact that the organized worker has progressed much more rapidly and attained a status much more enviable than has his unorganized brother."[21] Newspaper laments as to where union wage demands are leading the economy have also doubtless contributed to the impression.

If people quite generally accept the view that unions have played an important role in raising wages and in maintaining a high level economy through increasing purchasing power, this belief, whether justified or not, can play an important part in affecting the institutional role and strength of the labor movement in our society. The suggestion here is that this is what has in fact happened.

Opponents

Constitutionality.—Doubt as to its constitutionality led to what were probably the most spirited arguments over the Wagner Act at the time the legislation was being debated. Nevertheless these arguments are of only minor importance in attempting to evaluate the Wagner Act twenty years later. The reason is clear. The National Labor Relations Act was but one of many New Deal laws which raised substantially similar constitutional questions relating to the power of the federal government. Without the affirmative decision handed down by the United States Supreme Court in the Jones and Laughlin case there would be no occasion to evaluate the impact of the Wagner Act. But with an affirmative decision the net result was simply that the law became fully operative.

Prior to the decision upholding the validity of the Wagner Act there was considerable doubt as to its constitutionality. Was the commerce clause broad enough to justify the federal government's regulation of employee organization and collective bargaining? If so, was due process of law—either substantive or procedural—being violated? These were the legal questions which the Court answered.

The "One-Sided" Wagner Act.—When Professor John R. Commons wrote his opinion in the 1915 report of the Industrial Relations Commission, he said, among other things:

It doubtless has appealed to some people who consider the employer's position more powerful than that of the union, that the employer should be compelled in some way to deal with unions, or at least to confer with their representatives. But if the State recognizes any particular union by requiring the employer to recognize it, the State must necessarily guarantee the union to the extent that it must strip it of any abuses it may practice.[22]

During the 1934 and 1935 debates on the Wagner Act no more bitter or vehement arguments against it were made than those which related to its "one-sidedness." Pointing out that the compulsions of the Act ran only against management, attorney Walter Gordon Merritt argued strenuously that if management was going to be required to bargain with the elected representative of its employees the least the government could do was to require certain minimum standards of the union. By way of documentation Merritt cited various cases from his New York experience to prove that unions, "like all other human institutions," engage in wrongdoing on occasion and that it would be wrong to force companies to bargain with such unions. By way of an "extreme illustration" he pointed out the possibility that a company might have to bargain with a communistic organization, and though he somewhat apologetically observed that this was an "absurd" example, he justified using it to make the point that the Act did not discriminate in requiring bargaining.[23]

At one point in 1934 Senator Wagner appeared to agree with his arch antagonist, James E. Emery, general counsel for the NAM, that "intimidation, when it comes from any source, either a trade organization, or a company union, or an employer," should be made an unfair labor practice.[24] By 1935 Wagner had changed his mind, for reasons which will be set forth later.

There was, then, neither a lack of recognition that the Wagner Act was one-sided in nature, nor a lack of opposition to it for that reason. Nevertheless it passed without substantial change, and the causes behind that passage take more extended analysis.

A first step toward understanding the one-sidedness of the Wagner Act comes with the recognition that one-sided legislation is neither novel nor reprehensible in American history. Indeed, as Oliver Wendell

Holmes once said, "... it is no sufficient condemnation of legislation that it favors one class at the expense of another, for much or all legislation does that; and none the less when the bona fide object is the greatest good of the greatest number." [25]

A classic example of one-sided legislation in American history is the tariff. The bitter battles which a predominantly agricultural South and a predominantly industrial North fought over this issue in our early history are legendary. Moreover, the idea that fledgling industry, protected and nurtured by the tariff, should perhaps be asked to abide by certain minimum standards of wages and hours received no serious consideration.

An up-to-date example of clearly one-sided legislation on the local level is the subsidization of industrial migration in which states and municipalities are so heavily engaged. Tax concessions, municipal bonds floated to finance free industrial sites, advantageous utility rates and numerous other devices are used to attract industry to new locations. It would not be illogical to expect that if public funds and public credit are to be used to attract industrial firms to an area a *quid pro quo* might be exacted from such firms in the form of minimum standards of wages and working conditions.

There are innumerable other examples of legislation which is beneficial to one group at the expense of another or which gives advantage to a group without exacting minimal requirements from such group. There is a rational explanation of why this occurs. In each case the legislators have had an objective which they were trying to achieve. Balanced legislation may be more equitable, but it may at the same time be much less effective in achieving the desired objective. Industrial plants are not attracted to an area, for instance, by the promise of a free site accompanied by various restrictions on the operation once located. Americans are a practical people and, as Willard Hurst has pointed out, "We shall get a more realistic grasp of the part law has played in United States History if we keep in mind this readiness of Americans to use it as a means to bring about immediate practical results." [26]

The key to the one-sidedness of the Wagner Act lies in the plain conclusion of its sponsors that a more balanced approach would fail to achieve the objective. This showed up most clearly in the debates on the Tydings amendment when the Wagner Act was finally up for passage. Section 7 of the proposed legislation read as follows:

Employees shall have the right to self-organization, to form, join, or assist labor organizations, to bargain collectively through representatives of their own choosing, and to engage in concerted activities, for the purpose of collective bargaining or other mutual aid or protection.

Senator Tydings proposed that the phrase "free from coercion or intimidation from any source"[27] be added to Section 7 as set forth above. In support of this amendment he argued strenuously that if employees were going to be given the right to organize they ought to be free from interference not only by the employer, but from any source. This argument had a strong appeal to many senators who had not been exposed to the long and hard fought hearings over the bill. Nevertheless the sponsors resisted the amendment on the ground that it was exactly what industry opponents of the legislation wanted. Their reasoning was that the courts could not be trusted to interpret the word "coercion" when applied to labor organizations. Senator Wagner observed: "But how has the word 'coercion' as among employees been interpreted by the courts? The use of pickets, mere persuasion without any force, threats, or intimidation, has been deemed coercion; and employees simply trying to persuade their fellow workers to join a particular organization have been charged with coercion."[28]

The adverse role which the courts had played insofar as labor was concerned weighed heavily on the minds of the Act's sponsors. While conceding the equity of the position Senator Tydings was advancing, they feared its adoption would destroy the very thing for which they were working. Huey Long expressed this view forcefully during the debate when he said:

The Senator [Tydings] knows that we have been trying to get laborers the right to organize for quite a while, and we never have been able to draft a law yet which has not been whittled down. By interpretation the laws have always been cut down. Does not the Senator think we can take a chance for once in our lives for a little while? If the Senator from New York can draft an act that will protect labor, he will be the only man who has ever been able to do it. Nobody else has ever been able to do it with the court interpretations. I do not believe we ought to whittle away the bill and not take a chance.[29]

That the Wagner Act was one-sided in theory is beyond dispute. Its sponsors, all practical lawmakers, believed that it had to be if it was to achieve its aims despite the interpretations of a judiciary which they expected to be biased in favor of management. To use a homely comparison, the Wagner Act was like a mantel clock which for some reason will run only when tilted. Everyone can see that it is tilted but in fact that is the only way it will operate. Rightly or wrongly the proponents of the Wagner Act concluded after serious study of the attitude of the courts that the Wagner Act would work only if tilted.

Over the long pull Professor Commons' 1915 prediction has proven accurate. Through passage of the Wagner Act the state did recognize particular unions and require employers to bargain with them without at the same time guaranteeing the conduct of the unions. The reaction set in quickly. Some states, like Wisconsin with its Employment Peace Act passed in 1939, changed the rules almost immediately. By 1947 the trend was general both in the states and at the national level. Unfair labor practices on the part of unions were added and internal union affairs were no longer a matter of purely union concern. The Taft-Hartley Act established filing requirements including non-Communist oaths, financial statements, copies of the constitution and bylaws, initiation fees charged new members, names, titles, and compensation of principal officers, and a financial statement furnished both to the Secretary of Labor and the members of the union.

Delaware outdid all the other states in restrictive legislation in 1947, though it repealed the act in 1950. Under the 1947 version there were not only provisions similar to those under Taft-Hartley but a host of others. Aliens, Communists, and persons convicted of a felony were barred from holding office; no initiation fee could be over $25; no suspension or expulsion from the union was lawful except for good cause and after a fair and public hearing; elections had to be by secret ballot after at least fifteen days' notice to all members, no such election was valid if influenced by coercion or intimidation, and the results had to be tabulated by an impartial outsider; notice of taking a strike vote had to be given to all members, and an employer affected thereby "must be given the privilege of attending and stating orally the proposals made by him to the union." [30]

The closed shop was officially outlawed by the Taft-Hartley Act, and restrictions were placed on the union shop. Nineteen states had, by the summer of 1955, passed so-called right-to-work legislation making it illegal to require union membership as a condition of employment.

Other problems of union regulation loomed on the horizon for future consideration. One heard public discussions of such questions as the following: Should a patently corrupt and crime-ridden union like the ILA in New York be entitled to governmental approval as a collective bargaining agent even if it did win a duly conducted election? Should a union be permitted to picket an employer following an election in which employees voted down representation by the union? If workers could be required to join unions, was there some obligation to insure the individual against arbitrary or discriminatory treatment within the union?

Faced since 1947 with the realization that the original provisions of the Wagner Act could not continue to exist without accompanying restrictions on unions, labor leaders have had to give serious consideration to supporting the repeal of all collective bargaining legislation and reverting to sole reliance on their economic strength. Aside from John L. Lewis, most of them have apparently concluded that they are not in a position to forego the benefits they derive from such legislation. In this connection it must be remembered that despite the great growth in unions during the past twenty years, the number of unorganized workers still far outnumbers the organized. Moreover the difficulties of organizing, particularly in the South, are much as they were in some of the newly organized industries in the early days of the Wagner Act.

Out of all this one may safely predict an indefinite commitment on the part of the federal government to a major role in labor-management relations.

Class Conflict.—Somewhere in the testimony of almost every industry representative during the course of the hearings on the Wagner Act is to be found the thesis that a major defect in the bill was its premise that the relationship between employer and employee was one of conflict rather than coöperation. This view was directly related to the fact that the then existing company unions would largely be abolished. Industry was neither ready to admit that these unions were in other than isolated cases company dominated, nor that outside unions could come in on any large scale without disrupting the whole economy. The growth of a strong national union movement meant union domination such as many industrialists believed to exist in England at the time. The intensity of these views naturally varied. The Cleveland Chamber of Commerce passed a resolution which read in part:

The friendly and cooperative relationship existing between thousands of employers and their employees—existing to so large an extent that such relationships are the rule and not the exception—should not be subjected to demoralization by professional labor agitators whose primary objective is to foment antagonism, with a view to an organized power, socially, politically and economically dangerous to the American Commonwealth.[31]

At the other end of the employer spectrum were men like Henry Dennison of the Dennison Manufacturing Company who was then serving as an industry member of the National Labor Board. While conceding that many independent unions were in fact company dominated, Mr. Dennison said:

But my firm conviction is that under today's conditions, this evil will be short-lived, whereas the evils of forcing the growth of outside unions beyond the rate at which capable leaders can be discovered and can gain experience will last a generation. In few if any plans can a hog-tied company union survive more than a year or two; they will either evolve into true and independent employee representation or blow up and reform into stiff and often antagonistic unions controlled from without. But a sufficient number of new unions unskillfully led—and union leadership is one of the most highly skilled of the arts—will lead to enough fool trouble, bitter strife, and bloodshed to set the whole country blindly against unionism in any form.[32]

If industry representatives saw in the proposed legislation seeds of a new, radical unionism, the Communist-oriented Trade Union Unity League did not. Its spokesman, William F. Dunne, said:

We are against this bill just as we were against clause 7 (a), and for practically the same reasons—because it is intended to be used as another will-o-the-wisp to dance before the eyes of the working class while the employers and official labor leaders in the NRA machinery, thinking of "national recovery" in terms of "all the people," which means the capitalist class, which means mainly the big employers, trick them further into the swamp of starvation wages and permanent mass unemployment.[33]

There is little or no evidence that the Wagner Act has contributed to class conflict in the ideological sense. On the contrary the American labor movement has been among the most militantly anti-Communist forces in the nation. Evidences of this include consistent refusal to recognize "unions" from iron curtain countries as independent agencies for purpose of the ILO, affiliation with the International Confederation of Free Trade Unions rather than the Communist-oriented World Federation of Trade Unions, and the CIO expulsion of major member unions for Communist domination.

Some of the 1935 critics obviously thought of class conflict not so much in the ideological sense as in the matter of limiting management's freedom in running the enterprise. On this score the growth of a strong and independent labor movement which was clearly enormously aided by the Wagner Act has certainly had a decided impact. It can be, and has been, argued by leading American trade unionists that they exert more control over management via the bargaining table than do German trade unionists, for example, under the co-determination law. Contract provisions with respect to seniority, penalty pay, the establishment and revision of job standards, stability of employment, disciplinary review, crew restrictions, and equipment guarantees are examples of areas where unions have made substantial invasions of management prerogatives.

However much unions have succeeded in restricting the power to manage, the fact remains that in 1955 there were an estimated 125,000 collectively bargained agreements between labor and management, and even in the most strike-prone years more than 95 out of every 100 of these are settled without resort to economic force. It is noticeable also that except for parts of the South, and isolated cases such as those involving Perfect Circle and the Kohler Company, violence and bloodshed on the picket line are fading into the past. Unions have now attained an established place in American society. Whether they are too strong, or may at some future date become too strong, is another question. What is clear is that a feeling of class conflict has, if anything, been reduced rather than increased in recent years.

Failure to Protect the Individual.—Whenever machinery is provided for the election of representatives the question naturally arises as to the mechanics of the process. During World War I the National War Labor Board, with William Howard Taft and Frank P. Walsh serving as joint chairmen, speedily adopted the majority rule as the only realistic basis for designating a collective bargaining representative. In 1920 Congress passed the Railway Labor Act with a clause similar to Section 7(a) of the NIRA but saying nothing about majority rule. Nevertheless the Railway Labor Board appointed under the Act consistently applied the majority rule concept as the only workable formula. The 1934 amendments to the Railway Labor Act specifically provided for majority rule.

When the Wagner Act proposed the selection of bargaining representatives by majority rule there was a general attack on the principle by opponents of the measure. The inequities which could result from representation by a dubious majority or the case of the nonunion member were spotlighted.

In the years since 1935 the controversy has become somewhat like the constitutional fight. The concept is now so well accepted that it is hard to reconstruct the bitter atmosphere in which it was fought out. Essentially it was a power struggle and as such an ancestor of the present "right-to-work" battle. If each minority group in the plant could be separately represented, the strength of any given unit would be much reduced. From the employer point of view this was desirable. From the union view it was not.

The effect of majority versus proportional representation in political practice is sufficiently clear to predict the result in either case. Majority rule means certain inequities for minorities but more strength and stability for the unit. Proportional representation resolves most of the inequities but tends to weaken the over-all unit. France with its multiple party structure, and Israel with its proportional representation scheme are encountering these problems on the governmental front today.

The sponsors of the Wagner Act wanted to develop a strong independent labor movement which could bargain with management on a basis of independent strength. With such an objective, election by majority rule was an essential ingredient of the election process. In this light, disagreement with the majority rule principle as applied to collective bargaining more nearly reflects basic disagreement with the avowed objective of a strong independent labor movement than a concern for inequities which may be perpetrated upon minority groups.

Some Unforeseen Factors

A law in prospect and a law in being are never quite the same thing. Time and events take a toll which even the wisest may not foresee. Thus it is possible, after twenty years, to see major influences which have shaped the impact of the Wagner Act which were not discussed or even thought of at the time of its enactment.

Two major historical events in the post–Wagner Act years were the split in the labor movement and World War II. AFL leaders had not given their initial blessing to the principles of the Wagner Act without a good deal of soul-searching. Once the door was opened, the government might end up playing an ever increasing role in the internal affairs of the unions. Samuel Gompers had long warned of this danger. Nevertheless a decision was made to support the bill fully. The decision clearly presupposed a single House of Labor—the AFL. It was foreseeable that one AFL union might find itself pitted against another in an NLRB election, but if this occurred it was reasonable to suppose that the government would take the position that the question of which union should compete for votes was a matter for internal union decision. This was in fact the position which the NLRB took. In the summer of 1936 the Board was asked to conduct an election in which two AFL unions were rivals. The Board declined, calling attention to the fact that this was in essence a jurisdictional dispute which ought to be resolved by the AFL itself. In the same year the NLRB declined to intervene in a case involving two AFL affiliates where the question was one of the appropriate bargaining unit. However, a different question came up in 1937 when the NLRB was requested to intervene in a dispute involving the CIO and the AFL. This time the Board did intervene on the ground that there was no parent body to which the question could be referred.[34] Thereafter the Board found itself plagued with cases in which the AFL and CIO were contending parties. The AFL became indignant with what it regarded as rank favoritism on the part of the Board toward the CIO, particularly after all longshoremen on the West Coast were placed in a single bargaining unit to the disadvantage of the AFL. The result was that by 1939 the AFL was suggesting a number of amendments designed both to bring the "biased" Board under control and to enforce Senator Wagner's promise that "there is nothing in the pending bill which places the stamp of governmental favor upon any particular type of union."

There can be no doubt that the kinds of problems which the NLRB faced as the result of the split in the labor movement were vastly different than they would have been in the absence of such a schism. Yet neither the sponsors of the Act nor its opponents gave much attention to this possibility when the law was under consideration.

World War II brought significant changes in all aspects of our national life, including the relations of labor and management. As of the start of the war, labor union membership stood in the neighborhood of 9 million members and there was reason to suppose that it might tend to stabilize around that level. The coming of the war with its inflationary pressures, wage and price controls, manpower problems, wartime disputes machinery, and enormous expansion of companies already organized not only shot union membership up to more nearly 15 million members at the end of the war, but gave unions a foothold in certain industries where strength was weak before. Wage controls also resulted in an emphasis on fringe benefits which in turn may be said to have contributed toward exerting pressure on the NLRB to define the scope of bargaining. Some of the pent-up resentment toward unions as the result of postwar strike activities clearly contributed to a hostile Congress which in 1947 enacted the Taft-Hartley Act.

Unforeseen historical events have been hardly more important than the influence exerted by the Board's administrators since 1935. "The constitution," as Charles Evans Hughes once wisely observed, "means what the judges say it means." Much the same comment can be made about the law, and in this case the law meant what the NLRB and the appellate courts said it meant, and their opportunities for choosing alternative interpretations with quite different implications were many and varied.

The NLRB might have said, when faced with its first AFL-CIO case, that this too was a matter to be resolved by the internal union processes and not by the government. If this course had been taken might the split in the labor movement have been healed as early as 1937 instead of 1955, and if so what would have happened during the intervening years? In this connection it is worth noting that Chapter 2 suggests that merger was closer in 1937 than in any other past year.

In 1947 the Steelworkers Union charged the Inland Steel Company with an unfair labor practice because it refused to discuss pensions with the union on the ground that pensions were not a proper subject for collective bargaining. The Board chose to read that section of the Wagner Act which required the parties to bargain over "wages, hours, and other terms and conditions of employment" to require it to define the scope of bargaining. The net result was to open up a Pandora's box in which the Board found itself in later years being asked whether health and accident insurance schemes, retirement rules, rest and lunch periods, bonus payments, merit rating scores and increases, employer-owned rental housing, year-end Christmas bonuses, and stock purchase plans were similarly within the area of required bargaining. Though the Board's initial decision to define the scope of bargaining has been sustained by the courts, a good legal argument can be made that the sponsors of the Wagner Act never intended any such result.[35] During the course of the final debate on the floor of the Senate, Senator Walsh, who was the chairman of the Senate Education and Labor Committee which had conducted the hearings on the bill, said:

> Let me emphasize again: When the employees have chosen their organization, when they have selected their representatives, all the bill proposes to do is to escort them to the door of their employer and say, "Here they are, the legal representatives of your employees." What happens behind those doors is not inquired into, and the bill does not seek to inquire into it. It anticipates that the employer will deal reasonably with the employees, that he will be patient, but he is obliged to sign no agreement; he can say, "Gentlemen, we have heard you and considered your proposals. We cannot comply with your request," and that ends it.[36]

The importance which administration plays in the application of any law has been most recently emphasized by the many policy areas in which the Eisenhower NLRB has reached a different conclusion than did the Truman NLRB, though the wording of the law in each case remained the same. A point of difference of great importance has been the present Board's decision to shrink its jurisdiction so that labor-management relations in small establishments are no longer covered. It can be argued that it is this very area which is now the frontier where the provisions of the Act would be most useful and that the Board might better have declined jurisdiction over established collective bargaining relationships.[37]

One finds it difficult to think of another time in our history when the Wagner Act in its original form could have been enacted. On the other hand, post–1935 historical events and differing administrative interpretations have obviously been of major importance in writing the history of the Act.

Conclusions

In its historical context the Wagner Act represented a reaction against the predominantly unfriendly reception which labor had previously received at the hands of the government, particularly the judiciary. The hope of its sponsors that a reduction in industrial strife would follow its passage seems largely not to have materialized. Whether unions have brought about a better distribution of economic benefits is a matter of debate among economists but not among the people of the country who have concluded that unions do raise wages and benefit their members economically. The figures with respect to participation in union representation elections are an impressive testimonial to the democratic process. It seems reasonable to expect that participation in industrial elections contributes to support for democratic practices in governmental areas.

Constitutional decisions upholding the power of the federal government to intervene in labor management relations were part and parcel of a whole new trend toward increased federal power. The one-sidedness of the Act represented a calculated conclusion of its sponsors that this was the only way in which it could hope to be effective. Legislation which helps one group at the expense of another is not novel in our history. Class conflict which some critics believed would develop out of the legislation seems not to have been engendered. The principle of majority rule for the selection of bargaining agents represented the only realistic and workable approach to the basic problem of designating representatives.

In broad generalizations, the impact of the Wagner Act may be stated in four propositions:

The first is that it unquestionably contributed enormously both to the growth of a large and independent labor movement in America and, even more important, to the psychological acceptance of that movement as a desirable part of a modern American society. The attitudinal change is subtle, but nonetheless evident. Immediately after World War I, in October, 1919, President Wilson called a National Industrial Conference to help solve the problems of "labor and capital" which were giving rise to many disputes. The conference failed because the parties could not reach an agreement on the meaning of collective bargaining. To the unions it meant the employer dealing with trade unions, while to the employer the term included shop committee plans.[38] This schism persisted as late as 1935 when the Wagner Act was under consideration. It was a different story when President Truman called the post–World War II Labor-Management Conference in November, 1945. Once again the conference failed to reach an over-all agreement, but it is significant that the collapse was not due to an inability to agree as to the proper parties to the collective bargaining process. In fact the employer draft of the report read: "Collective bargaining . . . should be a process by which an employer, and the freely chosen representatives of workers negotiate. . . . "[39]

There are many other evidences of a changed climate within which the labor union as an institution exists. No presidential candidate since the passage of the Wagner Act has considered it politically feasible to urge repeal or even drastic amendment of the Act. Local agencies vie in attempting to gain labor participation in Community Chest and other activities. A number of state supported universities now offer labor education programs, justified in large part on the theory that tax money supports similar training for farmers and businessmen through colleges of agriculture and commerce.

Secondly, there is every evidence that the government is now irrevocably committed to a major though shifting rôle in labor-management relations in America. It was not long after the enactment of the Wagner Act before it became clear that at least in the states a legislative framework less favorable to labor than were the principles enunciated in that law would obtain. By 1947 the trend reached the national level with the passage of the Taft-Hartley Act. Some labor leaders, notably John L. Lewis, thought it might be wiser for labor to urge the repeal of all collective bargaining legislation and return the parties to reliance on their economic strength, rather than suffer the enactment of more restrictive legislation. Labor did not generally support this position. In point of fact there were still many more unorganized workers than organized despite the great growth in the movement during the past twenty years. Moreover, in certain parts of the country the problems of organizing were not greatly different from what they were in 1935 elsewhere. So long as the basic principles of the Wagner Act could be retained, labor obviously preferred to accept restrictive amendments rather than forego the benefits of the Act. This suggests that the path of the future is likely to involve more, rather than less, governmental intervention.[40] In this connection it is worth noting that in 1955 both the AFL and the CIO have asked for the passage of legislation designed to protect against abuses in health and welfare funds even where control over the fund is entirely in union hands.

Thirdly, it now seems clear that the Wagner Act, through its administrative interpretations, has been responsible for bringing about a peculiarly American form of codetermination. This point emerges more clearly when given a certain time perspective.

Commons and Andrews suggested four attitudes which society, acting through government, has taken toward collective bargaining.[41] These attitudes were: (1) *repression*—which meant that unions were treated as illegal conspiracies or even prohibited; (2) *toleration*—which meant that workers were to be allowed to organize and bargain collectively if they could; (3) *encouragement*—which meant that collective bargaining was good public policy and the government assumed the duty of protecting workers against interference with their right to organize and bargain collectively; and (4) *intervention*—which meant that collective bargaining was encouraged, but if no agreement could be reached the government would intervene to adjust the dispute and prevent a strike.

The Commons and Andrews framework was entirely adequate as of 1935. But from the vantage point of twenty years later it is apparent that the Wagner Act has given the policy of "encouragement" an entirely new meaning. In action the law has gone beyond simply prohibiting interference with the right to organize. It has told the parties what they must bargain about. This has, in turn, led to a dilution of management's unilateral authority over such matters as pensions, merit rating, company housing, and other items previously listed. Of even more importance for the future is the fact that no legal obstacle is in sight to restrict the Board in further defining appropriate areas of bargaining as questions arise. This being so, the government will not have contented itself with merely encouraging collective bargaining. It will have gone further and said that as a matter of public policy it is desirable to share authority over *x* items affecting the employment relationship. Such a development is of profound long-run importance.[42]

Finally, the Wagner Act by its encouragement of union growth and power has brought about a new climate within which public policy questions will be considered in the future. The kind of management intransigence recorded in the La Follette hearings is now more nearly the exception than the rule. A merged labor movement, 15 million strong, loses its appeal as an underdog agency and must rely on the development of a totally different public relations policy. In the midst of manifold pressures toward bigness on the part of both labor and management organizations, it is likely that public concern in the future will be directed more toward the individual. Advocates of "right-to-work" laws fail to capture this latent public sympathy because their motives are suspect and they have adopted the meat cleaver approach. A more moderate approach designed to protect the individual within the union was deemed sufficiently urgent and appealing to attract the endorsement of a unanimous tripartite commission appointed by Governor Bradford in Massachusetts in 1947 and might well come up again.[43]

The year 1957 finds a well established, financially sound, publicly accepted labor movement. The considerations which influenced legislators in 1935, both pro and con, have now largely disappeared. Perhaps that in itself is the greatest measure of the influence which the Act has had.

Notes

1 Edwin E. Witte, *The Government in Labor Disputes* (New York: McGraw-Hill Book Co., 1932), p. 84.

2 Felix Frankfurter and Nathan Greene, *The Labor Injunction* (New York: Macmillan Co., 1930).

3 *Duplex Printing Press Company* v. *Deering*, 254 U. S. 443 (1921), p. 469.

4 For a good summary of government intervention, see National Labor Relations Board, Division of Economic Research, *Government Protection of Labor's Right to Organize*, Bulletin No. 1 (August, 1936).

5 *United States Strike Commission Report*, Senate Executive Document No. 7, 53d Congress, 3d Session (Washington: Government Printing Office, 1895), p. xxvii.

6 See Vernon H. Jensen, *Heritage of Conflict* (Ithaca, N.Y.: Cornell University Press, 1950), p. 86.

7 Donald Richberg, *The Rainbow* (Garden City, N.Y.: Doubleday Books, 1936), chap. III.

8 For an account of these facts, see D. O. Bowman, *Public Control of Labor Relations* (New York: Macmillan Co., 1942), pp. 5–7.

9 A National Labor Board was proposed by the NRA Industrial and Labor Advisory Boards and approved by the President on August 5, 1933. However, he issued no order granting it authority.

10 "Railway Labor Act," *American Federationist*, XLI (October, 1934), p. 1053.

11 Frances Perkins, *The Roosevelt I Knew* (New York: Viking Press, 1946), p. 239.

12 Raymond Moley, *After Seven Years* (New York: Harper and Bros., 1939), p. 304.

13 Irving Bernstein, *The New Deal Collective Bargaining Policy* (Berkeley: University of California Press, 1950), pp. 25, 56, 89, 114.

14 An inaccurate inference that the railway unions were opposed to the closed shop on principle is sometimes drawn from the fact that the Railway Labor Disputes Act, which prohibited the closed shop, was an agreed bill. In fact the railway unions opposed legalizing the closed

shop at the time of the passage of the Act because they feared it would permit the companies to freeze company unions in power. Later, when this threat was removed, the railway unions sought and obtained amendments to the legislation permitting the inclusion of union security clauses.

15 U.S. Senate, Committee on Education and Labor, *National Labor Relations Board,* Report No. 573, 74th Cong., 1st Sess. (1935), p. 2.

16 Dr. Bernstein cautioned that the BLS series does not perfectly test the effectiveness of the Act because some stoppages are included where the major cause was not recognition. Moreover, the NLRA applied only to interstate commerce, while the statistics include intrastate commerce as well. However, one should note that there were many strikes where the real, as distinguished from the ostensible, issue was recognition or management's unwillingness to bargain. See Bernstein, *New Deal Collective Bargaining Policy,* pp. 143, 144.

17 "The Ideal State—As Wagner Sees It," *New York Times Magazine,* May 9, 1937, p. 23.

18 The Comments of Robert E. Lane in his book entitled *The Regulation of Businessmen* (New Haven: Yale University Press, 1954), chap. II, pp. 42–43, are interesting in this connection. Said Mr. Lane: "The proponents of regulation clearly select symbolic references which have the weight of cultural approval. For example, the National Labor Relations Act was commonly supported on the ground that it would extend the accepted right of freedom of association to the employee and substitute democratic electoral processes for violence. In this society businessmen writing for a closed circle of other businessmen did not challenge these objectives, but, accepting their validity, said that the law was confused because it would 'foment strikes,' 'cause trouble,' 'shackle labor,' and put labor under John L. Lewis who sought 'to become the virtual dictator of labor policies.' That is, at the deeper level of basic objectives, symbols, and myths, there is a remarkable consensus. Ideologically we are a high consensus society. It is dangerous to attack the stated objectives of regulation in such a society. Hence, manufacturers will say that measure will not achieve these objectives, or better will destroy them, which is the way businessmen most frequently express 'contrary to the public interest.' "

19 Perkins, *The Roosevelt I Knew,* p. 241.

20 Institute of Labor and Industrial Relations, University of Illinois, *Labor-Management Relations in Illini City* (Champaign: The Institute, 1953), I, 115–16.

21 As reported in Bureau of National Affairs, *Labor Relations Reporter,* XXXVI (October 24, 1955), p. 737.

22 U.S. Commission on Industrial Relations, *Final Report* (Washington: Government Printing Office, 1915), p. 374.

23 Walter Gordon Merritt, representing the League for Industrial Rights, in U.S. Senate, Committee on Education and Labor, *Hearings, on* S.

1958, National Labor Relations Board, 74th Cong., 1st Sess. (1935), pt. 3, pp. 309–34.

24 U.S. Senate, Committee on Education and Labor, *Hearings, on S. 2926, To Create a National Labor Board,* 73d Cong., 2d Sess. (1934), pt. 2, p. 348.

25 *American Law Review* (1873), p. 583, reprinted in *Harvard Law Review,* XLIV (March, 1931), p. 795.

26 James Willard Hurst, *The Growth of American Law and Lawmakers* (Boston: Little, Brown, and Co., 1950), p. 4.

27 *Congressional Record,* 74th Cong., 1st Sess., 79.7 (May 16, 1935), p. 7650.

28 *Ibid.,* p. 7654.

29 *Ibid.,* p. 7655.

30 See Morris B. Forkosch, *University of Chicago Law Review,* XVIII (Summer, 1951), p. 729.

31 U.S. Senate, Committee on Education and Labor, *Hearings, on S. 2926, To Create a National Labor Board,* 73d Cong., 2d Sess. (1934), pt. 1, p. 638.

32 *Ibid.,* p. 403.

33 *Ibid.,* pp. 990–91.

34 For a good discussion of this subject, see Ben Stephansky, "Structure of the American Labor Movement," in *Interpreting the Labor Movement* (Madison: Industrial Relations Research Association, 1952), pp. 54–58.

35 See Archibald Cox and John T. Dunlop, "Regulation of Collective Bargaining by the National Labor Relations Board," *Harvard Law Review,* LXIII (January, 1950), p. 389, and "The Duty to Bargain Collectively During the Term of an Existing Agreement," *Harvard Law Review,* LXIII (May, 1950), p. 1097.

36 *Congressional Record,* 74th Cong., 1st Sess., 79.7 (May 16, 1935), p. 7660.

37 See W. Willard Wirtz, "Two Years of the New NLRB," address at Annual Meeting, Labor Law Section, American Bar Association, Philadelphia, August 22, 1955. *Labor Relations Reporter,* XXXVI (August 29, 1955), p. 585.

38 Bowman, *Public Control of Labor Relations,* p. 11.

39 United States Department of Labor, Division of Labor Standards, *The President's National Labor-Management Conference—Summary and Committee Reports,* Bulletin No. 77 (1946), p. 54.

40 "Intervention" is, of course, a relative matter. In *The Age of Jackson,* Arthur Schlesinger, Jr., observes: " . . . 'intervention' is not an absolute. It is always a question of whose ox is being gored. Government *must* act; it cannot rest in Olympian impartiality. Even 'governing least' is likely to be government for the benefit of the strongest group in the community. The crucial question is not, Is there 'too much' government? but, Does the government promote 'too much' the interests of a single

group?" Arthur M. Schlesinger, Jr., *The Age of Jackson* (Boston: Little, Brown, and Co., 1945), p. 514.

41 John R. Commons and John B. Andrews, *Principles of Labor Legislation* (4th revised ed.; New York and London: Harper and Bros., 1936), pp. 374–76.

42 Cf. Neil Chamberlain, "Organized Labor and Management Control," *The Annals of the American Academy of Political and Social Science,* CCLXXIV (March, 1951), p. 159. "Whether we like to admit or not, legislation such as the National Labor Relations Act of 1935 (unmodified in this respect by the Taft-Hartley Act of 1947), providing for certified exclusive elected employee representation, is establishing a new corporate trusteeship relationship—not of present management to the workers, but of union agents to employees. . . . We might with perfect justification say that a new set of managers has been created—not duplicating the pre-existing management but sharing in certain of its decision-making functions."

43 Commonwealth of Massachusetts, *Report of the Governor's Labor-Management Committee,* House Report No. 1875 (March 18, 1947).

5

New Deal Sensitivity to Labor Interests

MURRAY EDELMAN

All political theorists recognize that governmental actions affect groups of the population in unequal fashion; but it is not easy to look at a particular historical epoch and say in what degree some groups have been favored over others and which institutions contributed to the result.

How Assess Sensitivity?

This essay undertakes to explore a small facet of that general historical problem. It will consider what institutions contributed to the degree of sensitivity to labor problems that existed in the New Deal years. It is a common charge among conservatives that the New Deal was dominated by labor; a common boast among liberals and some union officials that only in the 1930's did labor first get a fair hearing and a fair deal from our national government; a common finding of some social scientists and politicians that the New Deal did a great deal for capitalism, but that only the war rescued labor from the depression. All of these conclusions are normative judgments based upon different scales of values, and they are all couched in absolute terms. It is more important to answer the question in relative terms, relating New Deal solicitude for labor to the whole range of interests with which it was concerned.

This essay assesses sensitivity in terms of what government did. It defines public policy directly affecting labor in terms of (1) whose interests were protected or promoted; (2) whether policy varied significantly as between governmental units with different constituencies, procedures, sources of information, and economic theories; and (3) whether it varied significantly with changes in economic or social conditions.[1]

This statement of purpose suggests in some measure the conceptual framework in which data were gathered and analyzed and findings reached. It is assumed that what government does is basically a function of the group interests that are seen (or shared) by those in a position to make policy decisions. The term "group interests" is to be understood as including the values, problems, and needs of any group of people which shares them in common. So defined, the interests are unorganized; but organization, lobbying, and various collective economic sanctions are important techniques for strengthening group interests and making it more likely that they will be appreciated and taken into account by public policy makers.

Policy Directions of the Various New Deal Agencies

Representatives of all executive agencies have some voice in shaping legislative proposals and over-all administration policy, and many of them are directly responsible for administering some phase of labor policy. Because the various New Deal agencies did not always share a common outlook on important labor policies and frequently advocated conflicting ones, it cannot be said that there was any one New Deal labor policy or any one degree of New Deal sensitivity to labor or to labor problems.

At no time are the problems faced by all of America's workers the same, and they differed in important respects in the years of the Great Depression. Accordingly, public policies that benefited one group of workers might do little for another group or even hurt it. Unemployment, substandard wage levels, long hours, dangerous conditions of work, vehement employer opposition to unions and to collective bargaining were all prevalent labor problems, but not for every American worker. A skilled worker with a job had quite a different interest in relief or minimum wage laws from an unskilled, unemployed one. A craft union officer's interest in the definition of appropriate bargaining units often clashed violently with the interests of unorganized workers in mass production industries. All these interests found expression in one or another unit of the New Deal hierarchy, but with striking variations of place and time.

A review of the statements and actions of the executive agencies chiefly concerned illustrates the close relationship between the problems and clienteles over which organizational units of government had jurisdiction and their various policy directions.

Department of Labor

The Department of Labor assumed a new vigor in the New Deal years. It changed from an agency dominated by the Immigration and Naturalization Service and touching lightly or not at all the lives of America's labor force to an agency which experimented seriously and boldly with methods of gathering information about labor problems and exercised real influence in shaping the new forms of governmental protection for workers.

Secretary of Labor Frances Perkins had begun her professional life as a social worker seeking to improve labor conditions in New York State, and she had served as New York's leading public official in the labor field at a time when the state was developing an impressive program of protective legislation, but relatively little labor relations legislation. This background helps explain the Department's emphases in the thirties, though it is only a small facet of the explanation.

To increase the scope and accuracy of the information upon which its operations were based, the Department took several steps in these years. It expanded the Bureau of Labor Statistics and increased the amount of information which the Bureau gathered, laying new emphasis both on statistical techniques and on identifying additional areas in which quantitative and qualitative data would be useful. The Children's Bureau and the Women's Bureau undertook important studies of the problems of their respective clienteles.

In the depression years the reports issued by the Department reflected a continuing interest in a group of measures to cushion unemployment and to guarantee minimum standards of income and of health and safety for workers. Direct and work relief, employment exchanges, unemployment insurance, old age insurance, the elimination of child labor, and wage and hour standards are mentioned in one annual report after another, and the record is clear that the Department served as the focus of pressure for these policies within the administration. Once relief agencies and, later, the Social Security Board were established, these organizations became particularly concerned with their respective programs, but in both cases, the Department played a leading role in planning their establishment and in supporting them in the government after they began their operations. There was support in the Congress for an improved system of employment offices and for restriction of hours of work before the New Deal Department of Labor advocated these measures, and Senators Black and Wagner continued to be focal points for the interests in these policies through the New Deal period. The Department, however, helped shape the legislation to achieve these aims and took over their administration. It was evidently the Department which received and acted upon the suggestion that a constitutional method of achieving minimum wage and maximum hour regulation could be achieved in the area of public contracts. It was a Department bill, drafted largely by Assistant General Counsel Charles O. Gregory, that served as the basis for the Fair Labor Standards Act, although the Congress changed it drastically.

Apart from its representation on groups to draft labor legislation and the recommendations it made to the White House, the Department utilized two other important avenues for promoting labor interests as it saw them. For the first time it created a formal channel for dealing with state governments regarding labor matters, establishing the Division of Labor Standards for that purpose in July, 1934. The Twenty-third Annual Report of the Department described the function of the Division as, "To assist the states in moving toward greater uniformity in respect of labor legislation and to aid in developing modern standards for the health, safety and employment of industrial workers." The Division corresponded with appropriate officials of the state governments, held conferences for state labor administrators, and issued a series of bulletins on problems of protective labor standards.

Although Miss Perkins' statements and the Department's annual reports stressed the extent to which the Department relied on conferences with affected groups in shaping and in carrying out its programs, the fact appears to be that in the early years of the administration the conferences served chiefly to sell the union leaders on ideas originating in the Department rather than the reverse. In 1953, Miss Perkins provided a more candid description of these conferences of the first New Deal years than the public relations function of an annual report would permit. She declared in a public lecture at the University of Illinois that:

> The suggestions from labor leaders were practically of no consequence, in the early years, being limited to such ideas as permission for the unemployed to sleep in public buildings, the improvement of soup kitchens, and the immediate abolition of child labor.... It indicated how frustrated they were and how unable they had become to think in terms of the great public

problem because of the tenor of the depression. The best suggestions came from people from the Department of Labor who had been thinking long about some of these things.[2]

The Department did make it a practice to discuss proposed legislation with labor officials in advance of its introduction, however, and to convey their opinions to the President.

In developing specific measures the Department could rely in these years on a staff that included some highly competent lawyers, statisticians, and analysts of the labor and the economic scene, including Isadore Lubin, Charles Wyzanski, Katherine Lenroot, Grace Abbott, Arthur Altmeyer, Thomas Eliot, and Marshall Dimock.

A significant gap in the Department's interests was its relative lack of concern with measures to promote union organization and collective bargaining. Neither the Wagner Act nor the railway labor legislation of the thirties originated in the Department or was significantly influenced by it; and the Department did not display as much zeal for promoting the specific interests of unions as it did for the more general interests of workers, unorganized as well as organized. The Department's annual reports, the speeches and writings of its leading officials, including the Secretary, and its general reputation among observers in Washington and in the union movement during these years all bear out this emphasis. If John L. Lewis' occasional references to Miss Perkins as a "mere social worker" were unfair and motivated by Lewis' own frustrated political ambitions, they nevertheless played upon feelings that existed in some degree in many quarters. Doubtless the Department's emphasis is explainable at least in part on the ground that Congress never vested in it jurisdiction over any of the laws to promote collective bargaining. Those who did administer these laws —the National Labor Board under NRA and later the National Labor Relations Boards—became and remained the chief centers within the New Deal for learning about union problems and for promoting solutions to some of the major ones in a way that would protect union interests.

It is true that Miss Perkins wanted the Board in the Department, but her testimony in the congressional hearings on the Wagner Act was confined largely to this point and does not suggest that she felt enthusiasm for the principles of the Act. The President consulted her on appointments to the Board and she undoubtedly took great personal interest in NLRB policy and in the growth of unionism in the thirties.

There is little evidence, however, of active advocacy by the Department or the Secretary of policies in this area.

Because the Department's contacts were largely with labor groups and with the rising group of economists and lawyers that comprised the New Deal intelligentsia, it was only to be expected that it would not be as sensitive as some other New Deal agencies to the effects of proposed measures upon the voters and to the implications of these measures for the political popularity of the New Deal. An interesting incident that provided a clue to the influences to which the Department was sensitive and those to which it was less sensitive was that involving Harry Bridges. Miss Perkins found, late in the decade, that there was no evidence of Bridges' Communist activities sufficient to warrant his deportation. The action aroused considerable hostility from employers and from others who were persuaded that Bridges was an undesirable influence. The affair was serious enough politically that an effort was made to impeach Miss Perkins. Nevertheless, James Farley, who was highly sensitive to the political implications of policies, did declare in a Cabinet meeting that failure to deport Bridges might hurt the Democratic party and that this danger should be given consideration, regardless of the evidence upon which Miss Perkins acted. Neither the Secretary nor other officials of the Department were active in political campaigns in behalf of the party.

All this adds up to a picture of a Department of Labor highly competent in gathering the data necessary for the identification and study of labor problems, recognized as friendly to labor groups, but not particularly active in promoting the interests of labor organizations as distinct from those of unorganized workers, and not especially sensitive to the political implications of labor policies.

The Department's role and its relation to labor groups and to other governmental organizations is placed in better perspective if it is contrasted with the role of NRA. The problems which NRA was created to tackle were general discouragement regarding the chances of emerging from the trough of the depression, low price levels which drove marginal firms to the wall, low wages, and unemployment, which was basic to all the others. The formulation of public policies to deal with these problems involved pitting economic groups with adversary interests against each other, and NRA can most realistically be understood in terms of a constant endeavor to formulate policies acceptable to all the interests directly involved. A basic conflict, obviously, was that between the desire of businessmen for higher prices and higher profits on the one hand and the desire of workers and unions for higher wages and more jobs on the other hand. Included in the picture as well were consumer groups with a generalized interest in maintaining low prices, or at least in keeping them at relatively low levels, a conflict between large business organizations and small ones, and a conflict between skilled, organized workers and unskilled, unorganized workers.

In its efforts to resolve these differences, policy makers in NRA had to bear in mind that sufficient hostility by any one of several organizations concerned with its activities might very well mean the end of its existence. Widespread hostility among powerful business groups could mean lack of coöperation in preparing codes and in observing their provisions, and therefore, for all practical purposes, the end of the NRA program. Congress had the authority to terminate NRA, or to reduce or abolish its budget. The President's position was especially strong because he determined the form of the agency's administrative organization and procedures, changed the form from time to time, formally issued the codes, settled the more irreconcilable controversies, and appointed the agency's top staff. The Supreme Court was an ever-present threat and proved in the end to be the immediate cause of NRA's demise.

General Hugh S. Johnson, who served as administrator from the program's inception until the fall of 1934, became well known to newspaper readers of the time as an aggressive personality, the master of the "crack-down." His prior ties had been largely to management and to the Army, but he had also displayed a definite interest in public economic policy and a flair for strutting on a larger stage than industry or the military could provide.

Inclined to view outside groups as obstacles to be surmounted, Johnson took the position when first appointed that labor and management advisory committees would be unnecessary; only with real difficulty did Frances Perkins persuade him that their absence might bring serious problems of coöperation and compliance.

Donald R. Richberg was Johnson's deputy, and later became chairman of the National Industrial Recovery Board which headed NRA after September, 1934. He had served as a lawyer for the railroad brotherhoods and had helped defend the 1926 Railway Labor Act in the courts. During the 1932 campaign he worked on speeches for F.D.R., and after the election he helped formulate the labor and public works sections of the NIRA.

Here were two men with vastly different backgrounds and social outlooks, but NRA was to bring these outlooks close together by a process best understood through study of the pulling and tugging that went into the formulation of codes and the interpretation of Section 7(a). Significantly, Richberg moved closer to the business point of view; Johnson did not to any appreciable extent become a representative of labor's interests.

Business groups had actively sought suspension of the antitrust laws as a method of combatting falling prices, and to them it was the price features of the program that were important. Over half the codes included clauses for uniform prices, and there was often provision for limiting production and even assigning production quotas. Both these clauses and the minimum wage provisions gave an advantage to large and highly mechanized factories at the expense of those employing a larger proportion of hand labor. Many small concerns ignored code provisions in order to survive.

Industry enjoyed the huge advantage of initiative as well as economic power in code formulation. Trade associations usually prepared the first drafts of codes and were highly influential in the discussion of adjustments in them at hearings. NRA deputy administrators who presided at the hearings were drawn largely from industry, giving management a further advantage when its position conflicted with that of unions or workers. Some NRA officials and unions tried to secure equal representation for labor on code authorities, but voting membership for labor representatives was granted in only twenty-three cases and nonvoting membership in twenty-eight.

For all other codes, the Labor Advisory Board served as the workers' only spokesman. As appointed in June, 1933, the Board consisted of Leo Wolman, an economist, as chairman, Sidney Hillman of the Amalgamated Clothing Workers, Joseph Franklin of the Boilermakers, John Frey of the AFL Metal Trades Department, and Edward F. McGrady, representing the United States Department of Labor. Hillman quickly emerged as the most resourceful and influential member of the committee and as labor's chief voice not only in NRA but in Washington. Although the Amalgamated Clothing Workers did not even become a member of the AFL until October, 1933, Roosevelt saw in Hillman a man who understood the President's position at the center of conflicting pressures and who could give him accurate information as to workers' reactions to public policy. The *New York Times* reported, "the Administration turns to Hillman for advice on labor problems rather than to any old-line AFL leader." [3] Although AFL leaders' coöperation and views were solicited often and offered even more frequently, the *Times* statement continued to be true in essence until Hillman's death in 1946.

But no labor statesman, no matter how ingenious or how close to the White House, could overcome the central weakness of most American unions during this period: their inability to impose sanctions that really hurt either on segments of industry or on a political party. Because NRA policy formulation involved the pitting of private economic groups against each other, the outcome could never be too different from the parties' estimate of their chances of winning in a direct conflict in the economic arena. Business always had available the alternative of refusal to agree to a code provision, forcing either a strike or presidential intervention. The President could not intervene regularly without changing the fundamental character and rationale of NRA. He did intervene infrequently and then often supported industry. Strikes were forced upon unions in several important industries in which they were weak, with the result management anticipated. Unions won important gains in NRA codes only where they were economically strong.

In the code hearings eloquent speeches and lengthy scrutiny were accorded the labor provisions, even when complicated economic questions of other kinds were adopted with little discussion, as they usually were. In their arguments in code hearings labor representatives relied very largely on the Department of Labor for information as to wage levels and standards, industrial earnings, price levels, living costs, and other pertinent matters, but found grist for their contentions as well in materials developed by the U.S. Public Health Service and other agencies. Although the data cited did not always deal directly with the conditions under consideration, it was usually the only data to be had and therefore difficult to refute. The Labor Department unquestionably exercised some influence in labor's behalf through its virtual monopoly on technical competence regarding some relevant issues. By suggesting methods of defining substandard workers and how hours might be averaged over weeks or months, for example, and by compiling information on working conditions for women in more than 120 industries, the Department paved the way for more realistic discussion of minimum standards and somewhat strengthened labor's feeble hand.

This "informational advantage" was probably largely responsible for such success as labor did achieve in the codes' minimum wage and maximum hour provisions. The forty-hour week became the NRA standard and was adopted in 487 codes applicable to industries employing 13,000,000 workers and representing 57 per cent of the codified industries. Forty-three codes provided for a shorter work week and forty-eight for a longer one. Wage minima ranged from 30 to 40 cents an hour. As reported by Broadus Mitchell, "Three hundred thirty-eight codes covering 55 per cent of all codified workers had the basic minimum of 40 cents or more, and 14 codes covering 5 percent of all employees had a basic minimum wage less than 30 cents.... Besides the general limitations in codes, exceptions were frequently granted to individual employers."[4] Virtually all the codes called for the banning of child labor under the age of sixteen.

These gains were doubtless largely a response to the increased sympathy of Congress and the public for the problems of the unemployed and the underdog in the depression; but they were not an unmixed blessing to labor in general, and some of the industrialists powerful in NRA were doubtless more willing to grant them because their economic effects were beneficial to many industries. Thus, there were complaints that reduced hours cut earnings; that the speed-up was being imposed to compensate for cuts in hours; that systems of averaging hours over weeks or months often defeated the hope that it would spread the available work. Disputes arose because skilled and semiskilled workers were acutely aware that minimum wage provisions meant less to them than to the unskilled and that their real wages were often smaller as prices rose.

When unions tried to win standards above the general ones, and, more critically, when they tried to win recognition and collective bargaining, eloquence and supporting data proved of little use. What counted here was economic strength.

In some industries, notably in coal mining and clothing manufacture, NRA afforded a bright opportunity for unions to take advantage of the employers' weak economic position and the workers' unrest and dreams of better things to come. Active organizing campaigns in the field were reflected in the employer's willingness to incorporate into codes provisions he knew could be wrested from him by strikes. Thus, Sidney Hillman was able to insist that the men's clothing code specify a thirty-six–hour week and a 20 per cent wage increase. Hillman's hand was strengthened in these negotiations by serious divisions among the employers in the clothing trade based both upon economic position in the industry and general social outlook, including the friendship of some employers for Hillman and trade unionism.

In the textile industry the negotiating process was longer and the outcome less certain. The very first NRA code was for cotton textiles and was rushed through by Hugh Johnson. Highly disappointing to Hillman, it provided for a forty-hour week and a low minimum wage. The industry was organized at that period only by the feeble AFL United Textile Workers of America. An index to that union's strength and to the attitude of its leaders is gleaned from Miss Perkins' account of her conversation with the union president, Thomas McMahon, at this time. She consulted him prior to the code negotiations and learned he had not formulated the workers' demands, but he feebly suggested an eight-hour day. When the Secretary urged him to support a code provision for a forty- rather than forty-eight–hour week, he replied, "All right, if you say so, Miss Perkins." [5]

Hillman was incensed that a code as unsatisfactory as this should prevail in an industry closely allied to his own. He sought to have it changed, and finally succeeded by bringing to bear both higher political authority and the strength of his own union. After meeting strong resistance from textile firms and from Hugh Johnson, Hillman went directly to the White House where he warned the President that failure to revise the code would soon bring fierce strikes by textile and garment workers in many cities. On August 22, 1934, Roosevelt, by executive order, set cotton-garment workers' maximum hours at thirty-six and raised minimum wages 10 per cent. This was the first time the President had altered a negotiated code provision, and it brought threats from textile manufacturers that they would defy the order. Falling back again upon his economic base, Hillman announced that the Amalgamated Clothing Workers and the International Ladies Garment Workers would strike in support of the presidential order, which remained in effect. But few industries were organized strongly or at all in 1933 and 1934, and few unions emerged triumphant from code negotiations.

The years 1933 to 1935 saw American workers restive, impressed with the failures of the economy and of industrialists, aglow with the promise of Roosevelt's hope and optimism, willing therefore to join unions which symbolized opposition to discredited management and promise of greener pastures. The workers were nonetheless acutely aware that their position was precarious, that industry still held the upper hand. It was therefore a situation in which leadership could be crucial, whether it was the leadership exemplified by an aggressive, suddenly progressive John Lewis, or the leadership of an industry suddenly urging its work force into the protective womb of company unions.

In the automobile industry, in steel, in cotton textiles, leadership of both sorts met head-on, and in every case it was the company that won the NRA battle, even though it was to lose the war a few years after NRA had lost its own war.

The National Labor Board established to police disputes arising under labor provisions of the codes, and to mediate them if possible, showed zealous concern for protecting the right to organize and for promoting the principle of collective bargaining, as did the National Labor Relations Board which replaced it in 1934. For approximately the first year, however, it was the policy to avoid legal prosecution of violations; and even after cases were referred to the Department of Justice, there was little effective enforcement and sufficient employer evasion and resistance to convince Senator Wagner that a more far-reaching legal measure was needed.

Labor restiveness and the sharp controversies of NRA awakened the unions to their opportunity in any case and shocked them into alertness. Their indifferent success under NRA forced most of them to turn to economic tactics even before the Schechter decision drove Sidney Hillman, the most vociferous labor defender of NRA, to clean out his desk in Washington and return to union headquarters in New York to spearhead an organizing campaign in the clothing industry. The resurgency of organized labor on the economic front, combined with Roosevelt's growing realization that he could operate politically without organized business support, was to lead soon to governmental gains of a more permanent and meaningful kind for unions.

National Labor Relations Board

In the New Deal years it was the NLRB which acquired the reputation of being most responsive to union interests and least influenced by management. The Wagner Act, which established the NLRB, directed the Board to determine workers' bargaining representatives and deal with unfair labor practice charges so as to guarantee to workers the right to organize into unions and to bargain collectively. In any particular unfair labor practice case, therefore, the groups seeking to influence the Board consisted of those persons who argued that a particular act of an employer constituted an unfair labor practice and those who argued that it did not. In the early years, especially, every decision was of vital importance not only to the company and union immediately involved but also to other companies and unions similarly situated. The NLRB was highly cognizant of this wide impact of its decisions on the economy generally. By their inherent nature, however, decisions either favored union growth or permitted the status quo to continue. Under the Wagner Act they could not place the company in a stronger bargaining position than it already enjoyed for there were no union unfair labor practices. Representation decisions were also bound to increase the number and proportion of organized plants in American industry. Policy direction was therefore predictably toward the union position for institutional reasons and quite independent of the philosophies of the individuals appointed to the Board.

An additional significant institutional factor tending to move NLRB policy in the same direction was the intimate relation between the security and status of the Board's staff and the interest in guaranteeing the right to organize and bargain collectively. If this interest were weakened or died, there would be no reason for a Board to operate at all. Board and staff members therefore had a vested interest in keeping it alive. This is not to suggest that the staff leaned over backwards in favor of unions, but only that there was little likelihood that personal interests would conflict with announced public policy.

In its decisions the Board defined many types of conduct as constituting unfair labor practices, thereby inhibiting the ability of employers to engage in labor espionage, contribute to the support of company representation plans, threaten or impose economic sanctions on union members, refuse to send representatives authorized to negotiate to bargaining sessions, and so on. As important, perhaps, as the actual forms of conduct forbidden by NLRB policy was the publicity the Board's hearings gave to abhorrent employer practices, such as the use of labor spies, terrorism, intimidation, tear gas, and the manipulation of local public opinion. The publicizing of such cases identified the Board as an enemy of employers who disliked unions, earned it the friendship of much of organized labor, and therefore placed pressure upon the Board to rely on labor rather than management to support it in Congress.

That its investigations and formal hearings so consistently produced information of this kind inevitably had its effect on the Board itself. The cases were bound to develop arguments for unions as protectors of workers against employers who engaged in unfair, often quite abhorrent, practices and to produce little data on the other side. There was accordingly an institutional bent toward sensitivity to union interests on the part of the Board.

The CIO found the Board's policies more acceptable than the AFL did in these years. Craft severance in defining appropriate bargaining units and findings that some AFL locals were employer dominated were the chief issues in this dispute. The latter was inherently a temporary issue, and the Globe doctrine satisfied most AFL demands on the former; but the opposition of the AFL officials was strong while it lasted, for these policies went to the heart of the interest conflict between skilled and unskilled labor and threatened the status of the AFL bureaucracy. Unlike the AFL, the CIO did not seek to force the Board to change some of its policies through legislation; and John L. Lewis is reported to have told his biographer in 1940 that he would regard the reappointment of Warren Madden to the chairmanship of the Board as a friendly gesture to the CIO and one that might help influence Lewis to support Roosevelt's third term campaign.

Not only did the Board's decisions inevitably reflect this milieu in which it operated, but its annual reports, its personnel policies, and occasional public statements by Board members underlined the concern of the Board with extension of union organization and collective bargaining in the American economy, particularly the mass production industries.

Other New Deal Agencies

In significant contrast to the Republican administrations of the twenties and to the Eisenhower administration after 1952, agencies not directly charged with responsibility for labor problems had relatively little influence on those policies under the New Deal. They had some, however, and their activities accordingly deserve brief exploration.

As nearly as can be gathered from available memoirs, biographies, and records of governmental actions in those years, Harold Ickes, the Secretary of the Interior, and the CWA and WPA under Harry Hopkins exerted a generally liberal influence in high administration circles, though they played little direct role in the formulation or administration of labor legislation except as it concerned their own agencies. Ickes' views were notable for strong suspicion of big financial and industrial interests. To this extent he was an ally of labor when its interests were hostile to those of big business; but in no sense did Ickes represent labor organizations, nor was he close to their leaders.

The relief program was the first and most urgent effort of the New Deal to meet the problems of unemployed workers and their dependents. The relief policy problems that constituted tests of sensitivity to labor interests were: (1) the establishment, extent, and continuation of relief; (2) wage levels on work relief; and (3) reliance on unions as labor recruiting agencies for relief projects. Work relief programs were, of course, established immediately, and continued until the end of the decade. A substantial reduction just before the 1937 recession was restored in the spring of 1938. Spending for relief was a response largely to the unemployment picture and to mass purchasing power theory, but the unions did support the program. A major AFL interest in PWA was in its hiring methods, for the question whether hiring was to be primarily on the basis of need or on the basis of union membership and ability was never fully resolved. In general, however, PWA yielded very largely to union pressure on this point. Nonunion persons on relief had no preference over union laborers, whether on relief or not, if the PWA project was being built by a union contractor. Unions did not similarly control hiring on WPA.

Wage policy in PWA reflected union demands, but WPA resisted union officials' criticism of its wage rates. A statutory provision gave PWA workers the benefit of the April 30, 1933, wage even if rates had declined after that date. Officials of the building trades unions sought continually to increase wage rates on WPA, but with little success. WPA workers could join unions, but could not legally bargain on wages and hours and were legally unable to strike, though they sometimes did both.

A tripartite Labor Board of Review was established in PWA to hear all labor issues arising in connection with projects financed by the agency. Though the labor member could not be a member of a building trades union, the Board's decisions were apparently accepted regularly by the unions and the contractors.

TVA must also be listed as a generally liberal, pro-labor New Deal organ. Its contribution to labor policy was limited to the formulation of terms of employment for its own workers, but there it pioneered in public personnel administration by frankly bargaining collectively with unions representing its employees over the definition of prevailing rates for skilled labor and other relevant issues.

Proposed labor legislation was of course discussed in the Cabinet, but it was not the practice in the Roosevelt administration for the Secretary of Commerce to take a special interest in labor policy or to demand that he review proposals or be consulted about them as Republicans Herbert Hoover and Sinclair Weeks did during their respective terms as Secretary of Commerce. Secretary of Commerce Daniel Roper was conservative in his personal views, but his influence on labor policy was negligible, owing in part to the ineffectiveness of the Department of Commerce in the New Deal years. The Department was staffed with "Deserving Democrats" out of tune with the harmonies of a Washington of liberalism and the Brain Trust, but with so little impact on the total composition that it was unable even to produce a little cacophony.

Another, more influential group in the administration that can be classified with the conservatives was largely influenced by an estimate of the effect of proposed policies on the political fortunes of the Democratic party. Vice President John N. Garner, Postmaster General James Farley, and Secretary of War George Dern were all in this category. Although none of these was in any significant degree alive to labor interests or problems or sympathetic to unionism, they recognized the value to the party of a reputation for aiding the poor in the depression and consequently supported the principle of relief measures and public works. Farley and Jesse Jones were also willing occasionally to telephone employers long distance at Miss Perkins' request in order to help settle labor disputes, promote compliance with administration policies, and, far from incidentally, retain some good will for the New Deal in the business community. Dern supported the public works programs not only because he reflected the thinking of Democrats in the western part of the country, but because the Army was genuinely enthusiastic about public works, seeing in the program a vehicle for important activity by otherwise idle officers and possibly a vehicle for enhancing the War Department's depleted prestige as well.

The influence of the Department of Justice was exerted significantly in connection with the enforcement of orders of the National Labor Relations Board. In the NRA period prosecution of violators of Board orders was possible only if the Attorney General instituted action in the courts. This Mr. Cummings' Department showed notable reluctance to do, insisting upon a record more complete than any the Board was able to build, deprived as it was of the power to subpoena. In the debate on the Wagner Act, which provided for court enforcement of Board orders at the request of the Board itself, the Department of Justice favored an amendment which would have authorized the Attorney General to handle Board cases in the courts. The Department was not, of course, subject to the pro-union institutional pressures that played so potently upon the NLRB, and its record under NRA is very likely a fairly accurate indication of what it would have done had such an amendment passed.

The Brain Trust

In even the most democratic of governments the initial formulation of policy, in the sense of a plan for the solution of a specific public problem, cannot be done by the people as a whole or even by their collective, elected representatives. This is a function which must be performed in the first instance by specialized individuals whose work may then be reviewed by more representative agencies. Whether the policies suggested solve the problems effectively and whether they meet with public approval is a function of the ability of the initial formulators and of the information at their disposal: information as to both the technical aspects of the problem and public values and attitudes.

A significant distinguishing mark of the New Deal lay in the backgrounds and range of information available to its policy planners. Planning at the highest level was to some extent the function of a group of economists, lawyers, and academicians known to the public of that day as the Brain Trust. In economic roots and ties, in education, in ability and willingness to gather information, these people differed markedly from the businessmen and business-oriented politicians who dominated policy planning under Hoover and his two predecessors.[6] Though on the surface the existence and functioning of the Brain

Trust may appear remote from sensitivity to labor interests, it is an important facet of the explanation of the New Deal's responsiveness to labor.

The eminent sociologist Karl Mannheim, in a series of chapters on intellectuals, provides a conceptual framework which helps us to understand the role the Brain Trust played and the reasons it behaved as it did. The essence of Mannheim's analysis lies in his emphasis on the freedom of the intellectual from the class outlook of other economic sectors and on the intellectual's need to examine the values of all sectors critically in order to shape an effective policy which takes full account of the values of the conflicting groups concerned. Mannheim sometimes calls such a solution a "synthesis":

> A group whose class position is more or less definitely fixed already has its political viewpoint decided for it. Where this is not so, as with the intellectuals, there is a wider area of choice and a corresponding need for total orientation and synthesis. . . . Only he who really has the choice has an interest in seeing the whole of the social and political structure. Only in that period of time and in that stage of investigation which is dedicated to deliberation is the sociological and logical locus of the development of a synthetic perspective to be sought.[7]

These things are necessarily a matter of degree, of course. The intellectual is an abstraction just as the economic man is an abstraction. But to the extent that the activities of men like Moley, Berle, Tugwell, Lubin, Corcoran, Cohen, Jackson, and the others influenced New Deal policy, it was clearly in the way that Mannheim suggested. More than the policy planners of the Hoover administration,[8] these people were intellectuals. And more than the policy planners of the Hoover administration, these people examined the interests and values of all social and economic strata in an attempt to find a synthesis. The economic and the social effects of the depression and of existing institutions upon workers and their families were carefully scrutinized as a major facet of this process; and, because the attention of the men of the Hoover-Coolidge-Harding years had seldom been directed to the political aspirations of workers, the experimental, free intellectual inquiry of the Brain Trusters may have made more of a difference to labor than to most economic groupings.

Given the problem of finding a solution to economic problems which baffled the layman and the politician and which, by 1933, had reduced businessmen to pleas of impotence and cries for help, Roosevelt had nowhere to turn but to the academicians. Certainly the labor union leaders wore blinders as thick as any that business could boast. Samuel Rosenman's description of the reasons for the initial formation of the Brain Trust supports this explanation.

The Brain Trusters never constituted a homogeneous school of thought, and Roosevelt encouraged them to argue out their opposing points of view, sometimes in his presence, sometimes on committees or in agencies to which he deliberately appointed several who disagreed with each other. Their function, then, was to provide the President with ideas and arguments so that he might accept, modify, or reject them. The system worked all the more effectively because of Roosevelt's marked propensity to get information and ideas in oral conversation with people he found stimulating and to insist that they ride their own programs vigorously.

So far as labor was concerned, the first administration Brain Trusters saw it as a key economic sector whose purchasing power and living standards needed to be improved, both for humanitarian reasons and to stimulate economic recovery. Except for Tugwell they exhibited little public interest in trade unions, and Tugwell "was disturbed by their submissiveness, by their acquiescence in rule by business, and he criticized the AFL's craft structure, the backwardness of its leadership, and its failure to employ the services of experts." [9] During the 1932 election campaign no specialist in labor relations joined Roosevelt's advisers except Richberg, who dealt only with railway labor.

Although their chief contribution during the first administration was the NRA, intellectuals in various New Deal agencies began before 1936 to propound ideas in economics and constitutional law which were to have important consequences for subsequent New Deal labor policy. The basic premise that voluntary coöperation of the various economic sectors in economic policy should be promoted was urged chiefly by Tugwell and Moley and found expression in NRA, in whose formulation other Brain Trusters also participated. After 1935 this emphasis was dropped both on constitutional grounds and because Roosevelt grew increasingly skeptical that it was politically necessary to have the coöperation of organized business. The mass purchasing power theory was advanced as an important rationale for the Wagner Act. The idea of overcoming constitutional barriers to protective wage and hour legislation by setting minimum labor standards on public contracts came from Frankfurter.

In the 1936 campaign Corcoran and Cohen were assigned to maintain liaison with labor and with liberal groups. During the second administration the Brain Trusters represented an extremely important influence in the formulation of economic policy, including labor policy. Probably the most complex economic issues of these years were the impact of minimum wage legislation and the effects on the economy of spending for relief and public works, both of intimate concern to workers. In the formulation of the Fair Labor Standards Act members of the Brain Trust played central roles. The most difficult question was how to persuade the Supreme Court that Congress enjoyed the authority to regulate labor practices in plants as well as directly in commerce. The idea of defining the Act's coverage in terms of "the production of goods for commerce," which proved a successful legal formula, was conceived by Robert Jackson, Ben Cohen, Gerard Reilly, and Rufus Poole. On this point Miss Perkins also consulted Joseph Chamberlain and Felix Frankfurter, who agreed that this phraseology would improve the law's chances.

On the broader economic questions Henderson, Currie, Lubin, Oliphant, and Cohen produced a steady stream of statistical and technical data which supported policies of governmental regulation of the economy and of spending. Their theories and data on the economic impact of monopoly were influential in establishing a climate in which business was kept on the defensive.

Corcoran tried to place at least two friendly colleagues on the staff of every New Deal agency, and these men accordingly influenced policy at subordinate levels as well as in the White House. The National Resources Planning Board was an institutional expression of the New Deal's penchant for ideas and for assessing their probable long-term social and political impact.

Always the Brain Trusters competed with conservative administration counsellors like Morgenthau, Farley, and Garner, and their success or failure at a particular time was a function of Roosevelt's estimate of the relative validity of their analyses and of the political impact of their policies. Often they competed with each other. The atmosphere and in-fighting were lively, and Roosevelt thrived on the liveliness.

The White House

It was on the President that all these influences converged, and their relative strength in the presidency was in part a function of the President's own values as well as of their access to him. Franklin Roosevelt's forebears, immediate and more remote, were far removed economically and intellectually from wage labor. They were remote not only in the sense of reliance for income on other sources of wealth but also in the sense of having no adversary economic nexus with labor. It is clearly easier for one who is above the battle to see both sides.

In this happy independent status Roosevelt's sensitivity to labor interests was likely to be a function of his awareness of the social and economic problems workers faced and of his assessment of the political values of support for labor's objectives. Often, of course, the two were intermingled.

So far as contact with labor problems was concerned, Roosevelt had had some in his early career, but relatively little. As a young Democratic member of the New York legislature in 1911, Roosevelt supported progressive labor legislation, including a workmen's compensation law, a maximum hour law for women, and the establishment of the notable New York Factory Investigating Commission. Without knowing very many of the reasons for this legislation, he evidently found it exhilarating and good politics to fight on social issues. He boasted many years later that he had been an "ardent" supporter of this whole program, and he liked to recall that he had been labeled a socialist for his stand.

As Assistant Secretary of the Navy during World War I, Roosevelt was directly faced with problems arising out of the labor standards on war contracts. Although he had previously had some minor contacts with Gompers regarding social welfare legislation in New York, he probably first became well acquainted with labor leaders in the course of his Navy work, and he is said to have "liked and respected them." He supported measures to improve working conditions on war contracts.

During Roosevelt's convalescence from poliomyelitis in the 1920's, Mrs. Roosevelt sometimes brought two persuasive and likeable members of the Women's Trade Union League to visit him. Rose Schneiderman and Maude Schwartz were intelligent and could answer his questions about labor history and the economic and social functions of unions. Frances Perkins makes the interesting (and characteristic) comment, "His attitude toward trade unionism might have been different if his first contacts with labor leaders had been with some of the hard-boiled men who ran the building trade unions. But through the eyes of these girls he saw the exploitation. . . . He learned why labor leaders are sometimes rough. . . ." [10] His ability to talk realistically to union officials when he resumed public office is a tribute both to the teachers and the pupil in these extracurricular classes.

Roosevelt's attitude and behavior toward labor cannot be simply described. In his speeches and actions in New York and Washington one sees far greater attention to ameliorative measures for the unemployed, underpaid, or aged worker than to unions or collective bargaining,[11] and this facet of his behavior may well reflect a strong Perkins influence. Far more than his predecessor as President, he accepted an economic theory that included a place for labor and consumer purchasing power as important determinants of the national economic well-being, and he accepted as desirable the use of governmental powers to increase purchasing power and influence the balance of economic power among private groups.

The sources of his ideas never remained static for long. In his acute study of the New Deal years Broadus Mitchell concluded that Roosevelt "had the Tory tolerance for change. . . . Without technical economic learning he was sometimes attracted to suggestions hastily, but abandoned them as readily rather than be forced into an untenable position." [12]

As a facet of his extraordinary political acumen the President recognized that people's perspectives, ideologies, and values change with their social and economic circumstances. One consequence was his widespread use of advisory committees in the development and administration of statutes, especially labor legislation. Even if advisory committees have little positive effect on policy, they reduce the power of the groups represented to protest and probably make acceptance psychologically easier. One suspects that this manipulative function of advisory committees was the important thing to Roosevelt, though Miss Perkins saw them idyllically as a way of getting "the people into the picture."

In labor policy it would be possible by citing public speeches and reported conversations to build a case for a Roosevelt considerably more friendly to labor than the F.D.R. who in fact made recommendations to Congress and issued executive directives. The talk may have been intended to win public support for labor and was certainly intended to win labor support for Roosevelt; but before taking concrete action the President was careful to look to the right as well as to the left. He invariably failed to support labor legislation actively until he was convinced it had adequate political support, and he sometimes sabotaged pro-labor policies already declared to be the law because of strong business pressures.

In killing the Black thirty-hour bill, in his occasional pro-business interventions in NRA, in his long delays in supporting the 1934 and 1935 Wagner bills, the 1934 unemployment insurance bills, and the 1934 Railway Labor Act amendments, in his order to cut relief sharply just before the 1937 recession, and in his ambivalent statements during the sit-down strikes, he showed himself less the proponent of the things labor was demanding than a consummate politician interested in a program that would have maximum effectiveness and popularity. He showed it again in viewing the NLRB from 1935 to 1939 as unduly independent in its policies, unpredictable, and often embarrassing politically.

In shaping labor policy Roosevelt was often particularly unimpressed with the demands of top officials of the AFL. Except for a few mavericks like Lewis and Hillman, AFL leaders in the early New Deal years reserved their enthusiasm for measures that would protect the interests of the skilled crafts and give the AFL bureaucracy the procedural initiative in bringing cases before governmental tribunals. The New Deal's major, if wavering, emphasis in labor relations legislation, on the other hand, was upon measures to promote widespread organization and collective bargaining in the mass production industries. It can hardly be doubted that the President and his advisers were acutely aware that these workers had more votes than the AFL executive board.

Lewis and Hillman were leaders in the organization of Labor's Nonpartisan League in the 1936 presidential campaign, and they built an active nationwide organization to help the New Deal candidates, with regional and even precinct organizations in industrial areas. All the evidence indicates, however, that even this activity had relatively little effect so far as making Roosevelt more willing to listen to the labor officials was concerned. For one thing the very magnitude of the Roosevelt victory that fall (46 states to 2) made it abundantly clear that the ticket could have won handily without help from the League and thus, paradoxically, reduced Roosevelt's debt to it. More significantly, most of the major New Deal measures to help labor had been conceived and enacted before the campaign, and in the second term Lewis was loud in his complaints that Roosevelt, having "supped at labor's table," was unwilling to pay for the nourishment, notably during the 1937 General Motors strike. Roosevelt was still aware that winning elections depended on satisfying a much wider range of interests than was represented by any union bureaucracy.

Roosevelt came to office at a time when it was good politics to improve working conditions, increase income, and promote the organization of workers; but in all these matters he waited until it was politically opportune and possible to do them. Always fairly sure the country would follow him on relief and recovery measures, he vacillated longest on long-range reform, for business and the middle class were most hostile here. Because he deliberately cultivated contacts with the whole gamut of group interests, he knew better than his predecessors what was politically expedient and what timing was indicated. For a political office holder in a democracy there can be no higher praise.

The Change from the Old Deal

If these were the interests and major organizational groupings at play in the formulation of New Deal labor policy, it remains to be examined how the New Deal pattern differed from the prior one and how it emerged as the dominant emphasis after 1933. A brief look at the Hoover administration suffices to place the New Deal in perspective and to highlight the institutional factors that were primarily significant in explaining the change.

Perhaps the most striking difference of the Hoover administration and the other federal administrations of the twenties in respect to the formulation of labor policy was their failure to recognize or respond to the problems of many of the groups which enjoyed the greatest electoral strength in 1932 and succeeding depression elections and which were most vitally involved in the New Deal.

In his study of the background and characteristics of federal office holders, Pendleton Herring documented the widely assumed fact that in the boom years of the 1920's men with great sympathy for the business point of view, like William E. Humphrey of the Federal Trade Commission, were common in government, and that "the attitude of those in command of business and government was to let well enough alone." [13] In the agencies concerned with labor matters, which might have been expected to bring to the Cabinet and the White House some appreciation of the problems and the political mood of working people, the typical appointees were amiable politicians not particularly concerned with the acts they were administering and sharing fully the prevailing attitude that government should intervene in the economy as little as possible. Thus the National Mediation Board established by the Railway Labor Act of 1926 was described as "an asylum for needy politicians," [14] and the Secretary of Labor under Hoover, William N. Doak, voiced the orthodox Hoover doctrine when he said in his annual report for 1932, "There are indications that employment opportunities will increase in the next few months as the remedial measures provided by Congress and the Administration begin to have their natural and expected effect." [15] A hint of Doak's stature with labor and the degree to which he represented its interests is afforded by the fact that although he was himself a trainman, railway labor leaders gave their support to Roosevelt in the 1932 campaign through the National Progressive Conference organized by Donald Richberg. It is true that some of the labor leaders who had spent many congenial hours in Doak's office swapping anecdotes with him were inclined to view Miss Perkins as unapproachable, but this fact had little to do with the formulation of labor policy either under Hoover or under Roosevelt. As has already been noted, these labor officials were neither prolific nor important influences on labor policy.

Of Doak's predecessor as Secretary, James J. Davis, Hoover quotes Coolidge as saying that he was skillful at "keeping labor quiet" through friendship and associational activities.[16]

The informational and statistical services of the Department in this period were not nearly as adequate as they were to become under the New Deal. Not only was the Bureau of Labor Statistics program narrower and its techniques less sophisticated, but there was no Bureau of Labor Standards to keep in touch with state labor programs; and the Department was dominated by the Immigration and Naturalization Service, which accounted for most of the departmental budget and personnel.

President Hoover's statements and actions after the depression struck leave little doubt that from his perspective the unemployment picture was not as grave as the newspapers claimed and that direct and vigorous governmental action for relief and the creation of jobs would boomerang and deepen the crisis. There is no evidence that any influential member of the administration urged federal government stimuli to mass purchasing power or encouragement of labor organization or minimum wage laws.

In the world bounded by these theories some curious things were happening in 1930, 1931, and 1932, judging by the President's statements. The 1930 census of unemployment was misleading because the enumerators "had to list the shiftless citizen who had no intention of living by work as unemployed"; and the census accordingly, Hoover thought, really proved that there was little unusual unemployment.[17] In this world the charitable help being offered by neighbors, local governments, industry, and other organizations was so vast and so adequate that federal relief measures were "likely to stifle this giving and thus destroy far more resources than the proposed charity from the Federal Government." [18] In short, the information received by the administration was inadequate and skewed so as to underrepresent the problems of labor; and the political import of the information which was received was often missed for lack of competent economic and statistical analysis.

By what process is the change accomplished from a government inadequately responsive to dominant values to one that is more responsive? Whether or not economic interests are the most important ones to voters at other times, it is almost axiomatic that they are controlling during economic depression. In the face of widespread poverty, unemployment, and business failure there is a shift in the values of virtually all groups, which finds its political expression in the replacement of the political and economic leadership regarded as having failed to meet the groups' needs. A convincing demonstration of the relationship between economic depression and the reconstitution of the federal administration is provided by the findings of Louis Bean, a leading student of the forces that account for shifts in voting behavior. Bean's data show that, in both congressional and presidential elections, shifts in party control correlate very highly with depressed economic conditions. A drop in employment and prices means a sharp increase in the strength of the political opposition.

As for the 1930 and 1932 elections, Bean concludes: "It is not farfetched to attribute this reversal in the political balance almost entirely to the great business depression. The congressional elections of 1924, 1926, and 1928 had given no evidence of any upsurge in Democratic strength. On the other hand, the sudden rise after 1928 was strikingly paralleled by the jump in unemployment ... with every increase of a million in unemployment the Republicans lost 14 seats in Congress." [19]

Labor and a "New Deal" in government are thus virtually certain to benefit from the combination of a widespread change in values arising from depression and a built-in safety valve in our constitutional system; and they did so in 1932.

The Sensitivity of Congress to Labor Interests

In turning from a discussion of the executive branch to a discussion of the Congress, the emphasis in policy formation changes from a paramount concern with national problems which the administration is responsible for solving to an emphasis on the problems of the various districts and states the congressmen represent.

In a careful study of congressional voting and elections Julius Turner concluded that, "The great majority of congressmen . . . yield to the pressures from their constituencies, and especially to the pressures of party, in casting their votes.[20] He also found that Republicans are more likely than Democrats to lose their seats for party insurgency if the dominant interests in their constituencies oppose the party stand on key issues.[21] A Republican from a working class constituency who supported the New Deal knew that he was more likely to suffer the opposition of his party than was an insurgent Democrat who opposed the New Deal.

Some well recognized institutional characteristics of the Congress and of American political parties help convert these findings into conclusions about the sensitivity of Congress to labor. In the first place, both the House and the Senate greatly underrepresent urban areas. The emphasis on local needs therefore means that labor groups are underrepresented, for constituency pressures are more often exerted disproportionately on behalf of farmers and dominant local industries rather than on behalf of worker residential areas in the cities. This bias is greatly emphasized because the constituencies that are "safe" in the sense of predictably returning incumbents to office are also to be found almost entirely in predominantly rural areas: the South, Vermont, Maine, and some parts of the Middle West. Because an individual's influence in Congress depends so enormously on his seniority there, the congressmen from these areas gain disproportionately in influence when their parties win control. Thus a hard-fought Democratic victory in Pennsylvania, New York, Illinois, and California sufficient to enable the Democrats to organize the House and Senate does not benefit these states nearly as much as it benefits Alabama, Mississippi, Florida, and other states in which there is little hard campaigning. To this extent AFL and CIO activity in congressional campaigns in the urban areas places some of the anti-labor rural congressmen in a stronger position.

Still another institutional factor which encouraged conservatism in the New Deal years was the circumstance that it is ordinarily much easier to get agreement that a bill should be opposed than that it should pass, even if those who oppose it do so for different reasons. When the enactment of policies favorable to labor involves the adoption of new laws, this factor works against their passage.

In the New Deal Congresses of the first term, progressive sentiment was at a maximum, for the depression was at its depth and interest in reform and recovery measures maximized. In the 1934 elections this emphasis was underlined by the Democratic sweep. In the Senate the Democrats enjoyed a majority of 45 votes and in the House a majority of 219. Nor is there much doubt that it was the aggressive New Deal program of the first two years that accounted for this highly atypical midterm victory for the party in power. In the face of public values as strong and as obvious to governmental officials as those that prevailed in America during the first term, the institutional biases in favor of conservatism that have been mentioned faded into relative insignificance, for the elections indicated a leftward shift in values in most constituencies. The elections in the fall of 1930 which gave the Democrats a majority in the House of Representatives and increased their strength in the Senate had already made the Congress more accessible than the Hoover Cabinet to the depression-born interests in ameliorating the lot of the unemployed and imposing government regulations upon business discretion in labor matters as well as broader economic decisions. The record of opposition between that Congress and the White House on labor bills is the best possible evidence of their respective positions. No doubt much of the congressional opposition to the White House views on unemployment and labor policy was traceable to a fear that in the 1932 elections a record of opposition to Hoover would serve as protective coloration. Time was to endorse this view.

It was, of course, Senator Robert F. Wagner of New York who became the most prominent sponsor of labor and social security legislation in the New Deal years. Although it would be a mistake to assume that the many bills that bore his name either originated with him or were passed as a result of his influence, it does appear to be true that he personally helped shape the details of the Wagner Act to a degree that is rare for a congressman sponsoring legislation on a highly complex and widely debated subject. Under the NRA, which Wagner helped to create, Roosevelt appointed him chairman of the National Labor Board. Miss Perkins traces Wagner's advocacy of the principles of the Wagner Act largely to his discouraging discovery while on the National Labor Board that many employers would not meet or bargain with their employees in spite of Section 7(a) and in spite of clear directives from the Board. As further evidence of the institutional nature of this impetus, she reports, "Other members of the Board in part shared Senator Wagner's resentment." [22]

In the 1936 and 1937 sessions of Congress there was a loosely organized group of twenty to forty New Deal congressmen headed by Maury Maverick who met about once a week in one of the second-rate restaurants on Capitol Hill. They studied social issues, discussed pending legislation, and prepared statements and programs for release to the press and insertion in the *Congressional Record.* Coming from both urban and rural sections of the country, the members were described by Stanley High as "heavy thinkers" and as "pro-labor." [23] The existence of such a group can more reasonably be regarded as a symptom than as a cause of the liberal values of many congressmen in this period. That there should have been a clearly identified group which proclaimed itself as interested in serious study of social issues and in promoting liberal legislation with their fellow congressmen is an interesting sidelight on the atmosphere that then pervaded Capitol Hill.

In another, somewhat indirect way the interests in behalf of New Deal labor policies were forcefully presented to congressmen who might otherwise have been oblivious or indifferent to them. Once the President had decided to support a bill, his influence on Capitol Hill was well-nigh overwhelming in the first term and substantial, though considerably weakened, in the second term. After a fireside chat a congressman was likely to find his mail pouch bursting at the seams with letters and postcards urging support of the presidential position; and there were few congressmen brave or foolish enough to turn a deaf ear to the voice of the people. Roosevelt's phenomenal electoral victories supplied any added proof that may have been needed that the wave of the immediate future was likely to engulf those who identified themselves with economic royalists rather than with the champion of the forgotten man. Nor did the zeal of Farley and Roosevelt in keeping in frequent touch with the local Democratic organizations fail to make a deep impression on those congressmen whose "Potomac Fever" might otherwise have taken the form of forgetting whence their glory came.

On the basis of the actions of Congress on key labor bills and the comments of contemporary observers it appears that from 1931 to at least 1935 the interests in direct benefits to labor, in the promotion of unions, and in the encouragement of collective bargaining were stronger on Capitol Hill than in the White House. The Norris-LaGuardia Act, the 1934 Railway Labor Act amendments, and the Wagner Act all originated in Congress and were passed by considerable majorities with little influence from the President, and that belated. The executive branch did play a major role in shaping the NIRA, but Congress accepted it overwhelmingly and the Senate defeated NAM amendments to Section 7(a) by a 46 to 31 vote.

In the latter half of the decade there continued to be lingering elements of these values in Congress. The LaFollette Committee's civil liberties investigation rendered invaluable aid to the growth of unions, and especially to the organization of the mass production industries, by its revelations of blatant employer intimidation, used to prevent and destroy unionism. The passage of the Fair Labor Standards Act, though a notable New Deal benefit to workers, was marked less by controversies between labor and management than by a sectional conflict pitting both employers and workers of the organized, relatively high wage areas against the employers and politicians of the South.

In the important field of farm labor not even the climate of the early New Deal could surmount overriding congressional sensitivity to the agricultural organizations, stemming largely from the institutional factors discussed above, and benefits to farm labor did not match those provided nonfarm workers. At the beginning of the decade five or six farms of every ten in the cotton states were operated by tenants, many close to the status of peons. The Agricultural Adjustment Administration of the first term aided farm owners, but did little for tenants, for it was usually their land that was withdrawn from cultivation. They received no separate government checks in any case, but were to be paid by the landlord according to their share of the cotton. Hired labor received no benefits at all, and landlords accordingly often transferred share tenants and croppers to the status of laborers.

Again it was economic organization that ultimately produced political results. The Southern Tenant Farmers Union, founded in July, 1934, alarmed Southerners both because of its economic program and its failure to discriminate against Negroes. But it grew, and its publicity and size helped win political support. Its efforts were a major reason for the establishment by Congress in July, 1937, of the Farm Security Administration, which assisted tenant farmers by lending them money at low interest rates to enable them to buy their holdings.

The actual planning of labor legislation was undertaken by relatively few members of the Congress; and in the throes of serious emergency Congress was particularly willing to turn over to the executive the real authority to formulate economic policy, including labor policy. This latter phenomenon is illustrated not only by NRA, but by the wartime economic stabilization program as well.

The strong institutional biases in Congress that work in behalf of conservatism reasserted themselves quickly with the upturn in business trends. This development clearly affected relief policy by 1937 and was manifested as well in growing congressional criticism of the NLRB before the end of the decade and in the abolition of the Farm Security Administration.

Some Reflections on the Aftermath

Did the New Deal labor policies make American unions a more powerful political force in the years that followed the New Deal? It is quite doubtful that they did. The review of policy formulation in this essay suggests that what mattered to those who shaped policy was votes and, more specifically, an effective solution to those problems of the various groups of voters that were serious enough to result in political disaffection.

Even if it is assumed that New Deal labor policies did encourage the growth of unions, the fact that a much higher proportion of the labor force is organized has not significantly affected either of these crucial considerations. Workers have votes whether they are organized or not. We have had enough experience with labor political action to know that workers frequently do not vote as union officials recommend; that they are likely to "vote their pocketbooks" during depressions; but that, in prosperity, noneconomic interests take precedence and the "labor vote" often becomes a mirage. Governmental officials are not oblivious of this phenomenon.

This a priori reasoning is borne out by the history of labor legislation and policy formulation since the end of the New Deal. So far as labor relations legislation is concerned, the trend has consistently been toward more restrictions on unions both at the congressional level and at the administrative level, and this despite the most vigorous attempts of organized labor to repeal Taft-Hartley or amend it drastically and to influence its administration. So far as protective legislation (notably FLSA) and social security are concerned, on the other hand, labor influence has continued to be substantial. These facts strongly suggest that it is not the vigor of organized labor's stand, but the estimate of the effect of a policy on various group interests and on their votes that matters; and they further suggest doubt on the part of public policy makers that union officials can influence votes by fiat.

Even if there is reason to doubt that the New Deal made unions a more powerful political force, there is little reason to doubt that workers have remained a more powerful political force than they were before 1933. The New Deal practice of granting access to all groups that might become disaffected if ignored did not die in 1940. And even though the Eisenhower administration is considerably less friendly to labor than its Democratic predecessors, it at least knows what labor wants and makes estimates of its probable political effectiveness with a degree of sophistication that was unknown under Hoover. Government has become a somewhat readier channel for realizing those aspirations of workers denied in collective bargaining than it was before the New Deal.

Notes

1 Because of space limitations the discussion is confined to the political branches of the federal government and omits consideration of the sensitivity to labor of judicial policy makers. For a useful study that bears on the latter phenomenon, see C. Herman Pritchett, *The Roosevelt Court; A Study in Judicial Politics and Values, 1937–1947* (New York: Macmillan Co., 1948).

2 Unpublished transcript of lecture, University of Illinois, April, 1953.

3 *New York Times,* August 3, 1936.

4 Broadus Mitchell, *Depression Decade* ("The Economic History of the United States," Vol. IX; [New York: Rinehart and Co., 1947]), p. 284.

5 Frances Perkins, *The Roosevelt I Knew* (New York: Viking Press, 1946), p. 224.

6 There were, of course, some intellectuals and academicians in government posts under Hoover, but their views on important policy were not sought as they were by Roosevelt.

7 Karl Mannheim, *Ideology and Utopia* (New York: Harcourt, Brace, and Co., 1952), p. 143.

8 A committee of academicians under the chairmanship of Wesley Clair Mitchell did make an exhaustive survey for Hoover, which was published under the title, *Recent Social Trends*. It was completed in October, 1932, and was published shortly before Hoover's term ended. Although it declared that economic planning should be adopted in order to avoid future depressions, the committee indicated that the task was formidable and that it could offer few specific guides. The committee failed to function as the later Brain Trust was to do because it was not active in the discussion of specific policy questions while they were under discussion in the administration.

9 Irving Bernstein, *The New Deal Collective Bargaining Policy* (Berkeley: University of California Press, 1950), p. 26; cf. also an address by Tugwell to the American Society of Newspaper Editors, April 21, 1934, reported in *U.S. News*, April 23, 1934, p. 265.

10 Perkins, *The Roosevelt I Knew*, pp. 31–32. The comment may very well tell more about Miss Perkins' attitudes toward the labor movement than about Roosevelt's.

11 Before his inauguration as governor he authorized Miss Perkins to prepare proposed legislation for the reduction of hours of women workers, to improve workmen's compensation and child labor laws, to abolish home work, to prohibit night work for women, and to improve safety codes in mercantile establishments. Progress was made along most of these lines during his term, and in 1931 he called a conference of the governors of nearby states to discuss unemployment problems and a possible interstate compact on the subject.

12 Mitchell, *Depression Decade*, pp. 124–25.

13 E. Pendleton Herring, *Federal Commissioners* (Cambridge: Harvard University Press, 1936), p. 30.

14 Quoted in Bernstein, *The New Deal Collective Bargaining Policy*, p. 43.

15 U.S. Department of Labor, *Twentieth Annual Report of the Secretary of Labor* (Washington: Government Printing Office, 1932), p. 20.

16 Herbert Clark Hoover, *Memoirs* (New York: Macmillan Co., 1951–52), II, 101.

17 *Ibid.*, p. 49.

18 *Ibid.*, p. 56.

19 Louis H. Bean, *How to Predict Elections* (New York: Alfred A. Knopf, 1948), p. 24.

20 Julius Turner, *Party and Constituency: Pressures on Congress* (Baltimore: Johns Hopkins Press, 1951), pp. 178–79.

21 *Ibid.*, pp. 176–77.

22 Perkins, *The Roosevelt I Knew*, p. 238.

23 Stanley High, *Roosevelt—and Then?* (New York: Harper and Bros., 1937), pp. 216–40; Jerry Voorhis, *Confessions of a Congressman* (Garden City, N.Y.: Doubleday Books, 1948), pp. 30–31.

6

Organized Labor and Protective Labor Legislation

ELIZABETH BRANDEIS

Two developments coincided in the first six years of the New Deal: a spectacular growth in labor unions and an equally spectacular growth in federal protective labor legislation, with substantial gains at the state level. Was there a direct causal relation between these two developments? Did the labor movement play a major role in securing passage of the new laws? One might easily assume so.

To be sure before the New Deal the AFL had taken rather little interest in the major types of protective legislation—general maximum hour, minimum wage, and child labor laws.[1] But one might guess that the vicious downward spiral of wages resulting from mass unemployment created a labor demand for minimum wage laws; that maximum hour legislation became part of labor's program to deal with unemployment; that a desire to find jobs for unemployed men prompted an aggressive labor campaign to raise the minimum age of employment for children. In short, a priori, the historian of the New Deal might expect to find a clear reversal of traditional AFL attitudes toward protective labor legislation and to discover that the almost revolutionary advances of the thirties were due to a concerted drive by the newly expanded and strengthened labor movement. Was this the case?

Labor's role in securing the new legislation is not susceptible of precise measurement. How laws actually get passed, what are the decisive factors in any successful campaign cannot be stated with any degree of certainty. Legislative action or inaction is a form of group behavior on the part of persons with widely varying motivations. Even where the detailed record is available—the resolutions passed at conventions and conferences, the speeches made at hearings and the roll calls in legislative bodies—still the inside story remains untold. Who actually persuaded given congressmen or legislators to act as they did? No two legislative situations are alike. The ambitions and commitments of political leaders and the degree to which leaders actually control legislative bodies vary widely and are not measurable. The general climate of a time, what the newspapers and commentators are saying, all play on the legislator. He probably does not know himself why he voted as he did. Added to these difficulties for the historian, the record at the state level is far from complete. In most state legislatures, no transcript is made of speeches at hearings or on the floor. In some states, legislative roll calls are few and much action is taken by mere voice vote. Newspaper accounts, for the most part very scanty, are all that remain to tell the tale of a legislative campaign.

Despite these limitations, the story of organized labor's attitude and actions toward the major types of protective labor legislation in the New Deal period may be worth telling. The historian may properly try to determine the extent to which the AFL and later the CIO actually took the lead, or even put their backs into campaigns led by others, for the Black thirty-hour bill, NIRA, the Walsh-Healey Public Contracts law, the Fair Labor Standards Act, and for state minimum wage laws and improvements in state maximum hour and child labor laws.

As a backdrop to the New Deal story, the events of the preceding thirty years or more should be summarized, at least briefly. Over the years, state protective labor legislation had grown slowly, in the face of employer opposition, adverse court decisions, and, generally speaking, the apathy of the organized labor movement. To a large extent labor shared the general assumption that government intervention in economic affairs should be kept to a minimum, that laws if passed could not do much for workers and probably would not be enforced anyway. Unions believed that organization and collective bargaining, not laws, were the way to improve labor conditions. Child labor and safety and health laws were the only major forms of general protective legislation which unions supported wholeheartedly.

However, without much support from organized labor, a body of protective labor legislation had been built up in the industrial states—dealing with safety and health, child labor, and maximum hours—in most occupations for women, in a few special occupations for men. In addition, fifteen states had passed minimum wage laws for women and minors. Most of this legislation was the result of the efforts of middle class humanitarian reformers working in small but remarkably effective organizations, especially the National Child Labor Committee, the

National Consumers League, and the American Association for Labor Legislation.

Almost all kinds of state protective labor laws had been challenged in the courts as unconstitutional under the Fourteenth Amendment. State child labor laws to be sure had been early accepted by the courts on the ground that children were the "wards of the state" and their freedom of contract was subject to limitation for the protection of their health and welfare. After some adverse decisions, maximum hour and night work laws for women had been upheld in a series of Supreme Court decisions beginning with *Muller* v. *Oregon* in 1908. A maximum hour law for men engaged in mining was upheld by the Supreme Court, very early, in 1898, in *Holden* v. *Hardy*. But the Court subsequently, in 1905, invalidated an hour law for bakers, in *Lochner* v. *New York*. The 1917 favorable decision in *Bunting* v. *Oregon* sustained a very weak general hour law for men. But the opinion scarcely provided a firm precedent for stronger laws. It is true that hour laws for rail workers had been sustained, but on the basis that they protected the travelling public, not primarily the workers. Hour laws for men on "public work" had also been sustained, but as an exercise of proprietary power, not on broad police power grounds. Minimum wage laws for women were unequivocably held unconstitutional in the Adkins case in 1923.

So much for state protective laws. As for similar federal legislation, up to the New Deal it existed only for maritime and railroad workers and those engaged in federal public work. Congress had tried in 1916 to use its power to regulate commerce among the states to set up federal child labor standards. However, this first federal child labor law was held unconstitutional in 1918 by a 5 to 4 vote in *Hammer* v. *Dagenhart*. A second federal child labor law, based on the power of Congress to tax, met the same fate, this time by an 8 to 1 vote. This was in 1922. The demand for federal child labor protection next took the form of a proposed constitutional amendment. This went through Congress easily in 1924. But ratification by state legislatures proceeded very slowly; in fact, up to 1933 only six states had ratified the proposed child labor amendment.

Finally, it should be noted that most of the existing protective labor legislation had been secured before World War I—a lot of it in the banner years, 1911 and 1913. During the twenties almost no progress was made. The organizations which had won the gains in earlier years now found themselves singularly unsuccessful. Apparently "normalcy" for which the American people voted in 1920 did not include any further extension or raising the standards of labor laws. It was probably assumed that under "welfare capitalism" employers were voluntarily maintaining good labor conditions; that on the "permanent plateau of prosperity" there were no exploited workers needing further government protection. After the crash in October, 1929, we might think this attitude would have changed. Perhaps it did. But the depression brought a new argument against new protective labor laws—industry could not stand them. In any event, few new laws were passed in the next legislative year of 1931. Wages were falling under the pressure of unemployment, hours at least in some industries and areas were growing longer rather than shorter. In the face of mounting unemployment among men and women, children could often find jobs when their fathers could not. And state legislatures were doing little or nothing to bolster their defenses against these downward pressures.

So things stood when Roosevelt took office and the era of the New Deal began.

Summary of Protective Legislation in the New Deal

The years 1933–38 mark a period of almost revolutionary activity in federal protective labor legislation. This chapter does not deal with the more famous laws affecting labor—the National Labor Relations and the Social Security Acts. But even within the limits of protective legislation—child labor, maximum hours, and minimum wages—the federal government assumed a role hitherto undreamed of.

In the first month of the new administration the Black thirty-hour bill sailed through the Senate. In the House, however, it was held in the Labor Committee while Roosevelt introduced the far more comprehensive NIRA which was promptly put through both houses and signed by the President on June 16, a little over two months after he took office. Less than two years later this Act was held unconstitutional in the Schechter decision. As a partial substitute the Walsh-Healey Public Contracts Act was passed in 1936. Finally came the Fair Labor Standards Act of 1938.

In the states, too, 1933 was a year of action. Despite continuing doubts as to constitutionality, seven states passed minimum wage laws for women and minors. In the same year eleven states extended their hour laws for women and minors (though some of these changes were very slight). More striking, fourteen states ratified the child labor amendment. This progress continued, though at a slower pace, in the next regular legislative years, 1935 and 1937.

In order to appraise the role of organized labor in all this activity the campaign for each federal statute will be described separately, and some picture will be attempted of the forces behind the new legislation in the states.

The Black Thirty-Hour Bill

The first chapter in the federal story involves the Black thirty-hour bill which went through the Senate 53–30 on April 6, 1933, early in the special session called by Roosevelt immediately after he took office in March. The AFL claimed credit for this achievement. Certainly it did support this measure, a striking change from its long sustained opposition to general hour laws for men. In the years of greatest advance in state labor legislation, before World War I, the AFL had been explicit in this opposition.[2] The position was maintained during the twenties and even after the onset of the Great Depression. To be sure, the AFL had always urged shorter hours. As unemployment increased they offered it as their principal remedy. Unemployment was due to technological advance, they explained. The shorter work week was necessary to offset labor-saving machinery. As the numbers of unemployed grew larger month by month, labor's "share the work" demands called for shorter and shorter hours. But shorter hours were to be achieved by collective bargaining or by persuasion and the voluntary action of industry. As late as 1931 the AFL executive council in reporting to the annual convention recommended that the AFL oppose a federal constitutional amendment then pending in the House which would give power to Congress "to reduce the number of hours of service per day for which contracts for employment may be lawfully made." The executive council declared: "This is a dangerous proposal. The AFL has always opposed the fixing of hours or wages by law." The convention's Committee on the Shorter Work Day pointed out that "the proposed amendment would permit Congress to reduce but not increase the hours in a day's work; [but] it would also pave the way for fixing labor hours and wages by law." The committee agreed with the executive council as to the danger of the proposed amendment and wound up: "We recommend its disapproval." Without debate the committee's report was adopted by the convention.

This attitude toward government regulation of hours did not, of course, apply to special industries such as railroads. The president of the Railroad Telegraphers wanted to be sure that nothing in this action by the convention would stop the Telegraphers from going to Congress if necessary to secure shorter hours for themselves. President Green gave him this assurance, saying, "You possess that right and you may rely on the political and economic strength of the AFL to support you."[3]

So much for the AFL attitude toward maximum hour legislation as late as October, 1931. During the following year the leaders found it increasingly difficult to maintain that stand as the number of unemployed continued to mount. In the *Federationist* for December, 1931, Green estimated that a universal thirty-five–hour week would absorb the unemployed; by August, 1932, he estimated that it would take a thirty-hour week. But attempts to obtain shorter hours without legislation were bearing little or no fruit. In fact, in some industries and plants, hours were increasing. In July, 1932, the executive council appealed to President Hoover to call a conference of representatives of all industries and of labor to devise "ways and means by which the five-day week could be universally applied in the U.S."[4] However, the President took no such action.

Meanwhile, a few constituent unions in the AFL began calling for legislative restriction of working hours. At the convention of the ILGWU in May, 1932, Sidney Hillman, as guest speaker, declared, "National legislation for the shorter work day is the only way out," and the convention adopted a resolution "that officers continue working for legislation to universally enforce the 6-hour day and 5-day week."[5]

In 1932, the AFL convention convened on November 21. In another area of legislation the executive council report in 1932 contained a revolutionary proposal. Reversing its long maintained position, the council recommended that the AFL work for unemployment insurance or reserve laws (see Chapter 7). But as for shorter hours, the council, while urging a six-hour day and a five-day week, made no recommendation that this be achieved by law. However, several resolutions for shorter hour legislation were submitted to the convention—one by the Wyoming Federation of Labor, another by Mahon of the Street and Electric Railway Workers. These resolutions were submitted to the Committee on the Shorter Work Day. The committee presented a long report ending with a resolution. In a "whereas" it recognized that highly competitive conditions made it impossible for individual employers to put shorter hours into effect and it wound up by resolving "that we instruct our Executive Council to take all necessary steps toward having proper legislation [prepared] embracing this suggestion [six-hour day and five-day week]; insofar as possible without reduction in the daily, weekly or monthly wage, and to have the same presented to the incoming session of Congress for their consideration and adoption." [6]

President Green spoke at length on the subject of shorter hours, as did a number of other presidents of international unions. None of them endorsed the legislative approach to shorter hours in any clear-cut fashion except Mahon of the Street Railway Workers. Green said legislation was the remedy for government employees and "those governed by interstate commerce regulation," e.g., railroad workers. For private industry he called the situation "more complex" and referred to "what seemed insurmountable difficulties." We might interpret this as a reference to constitutional difficulties, but he did not elaborate. Anyway, after his speech the *Proceedings* report that the committee's resolution was passed unanimously. However, next day in a discussion of various remedies for unemployment a delegate from the Champaign, Illinois, Central Labor Union remarked, "I don't believe this Convention has reached a unanimous feeling about the question of legislation. I am quite sure a very large number of delegates are not conscious of the fact that we did adopt a resolution in favor of legislation to regulate hours of labor.... There was considerable milling around among the delegates in the hall. I believe many of them did not realize the far-reaching importance of that resolution."

About three weeks later on December 21, 1932, in the last "lame duck" session of Congress under the outgoing Republican administration, Senator Hugo Black of Alabama introduced his bill to fix maximum hours of six per day for five days per week in the production of goods for interstate commerce and asked that the bill be referred to the Committee on Judiciary because "certain legal questions will be raised." [7]

Subsequently, AFL leaders claimed that this bill was introduced as a result of their convention resolution. However, Senator, now Mr. Justice, Black is authority for the statement that it was just his own idea. He wrote out the bill at his desk in pencil. No doubt he, like the AFL leaders, believed a substantial reduction in working hours was a way to reduce unemployment. He based his bill on the power of Congress to regulate commerce among the states and the effect of unemployment on commerce.

Hearings began on January 5, 1933. To read the record of those hearings is to recapture the mood that prevailed in industry in the depression depth and helps to understand how it was possible a few months later to rally such widespread support for NIRA. The labor support for a thirty-hour law at that juncture scarcely seems surprising; it was long overdue. William Green, Philip Murray for the Mine Workers, Emil Rieve for the Hosiery Workers, McMahon for the Textile Workers, all urged the thirty-hour bill. Even John P. Frey of the Molders and Foundry Workers—probably the last of the diehards—spoke in its favor. "I have never believed," he said, "up until recent times that federal legislation was the better way. . . . [but] If those who control the credit of the country fail to find some way of working out this problem . . . the law makers have got to give us some legislation." [8]

A number of industrialists took the same position. They were largely textile manufacturers—a cotton manufacturer from New Orleans, one in hosiery from Philadelphia, another in silk from Patterson, others in plush and in worsteds. There were even some farm organization representatives, one from the National Grange and the president of the Indiana Farm Bureau Federation. The latter said they had taken no official action, "but we are all favorable to such a bill." There was much testimony that hours were being lengthened rather than shortened in many plants, because no one dared produce without an order and anyone receiving an order worked long hours to fill it as fast as possible.

Representative Connery, Chairman of the House Labor Committee, had introduced a similar thirty-hour bill in the House. The same labor leaders spoke also before the House committee on January 18, 1933. President Green led off with "I am very pleased . . . to give [this bill] my personal and official approval." When asked his opinion as to the bill's constitutionality, he pointed out that the decision invalidating the federal child labor law based on the commerce power was reached by a 5 to 4 vote. This gave hope that the Supreme Court might change its mind. However, when a committee member suggested that perhaps wages should be regulated as well as hours, Green declared, "I feel sure that courts would hold such legislation unconstitutional." This was not an unreasonable statement in view of the Adkins decision.

But it was probably not the real reason for Green's opposition to the insertion of a minimum wage provision in the Connery bill. To the suggestion that the bill might cause a reduction in weekly earnings, President Green replied that in the past shorter hours had been more apt to increase earnings than to reduce them. "Pass your bill," he said, "and let us handle the question of wages." Rieve expressed a similar view. Philip Murray testified there was a better way to protect wages than to include a minimum wage provision in the law. Congress, he declared, should offer instead "a fairer opportunity to the affected workers to protect themselves than they now have." He proposed an amendment to the thirty-hour bill to forbid yellow-dog contracts and the denial to workers of "the right to bargain collectively for their wages through chosen representatives of their own." This was perhaps the first presentation to a congressional committee of the substance of Section 7(a) of NIRA.[9]

The Black-Connery thirty-hour bill was not voted on in the lame duck session. It was reintroduced in the special session of the new Congress called by Roosevelt as soon as he took office. The Senate passed it promptly on April 6 by a vote of 53–30. In the House the Labor Committee began to hold new hearings. The new administration obviously had to take a position. In the preceding session Senator Norris had written President Hoover's Secretary of Labor asking him to state his views on the Black bill. Secretary Doak had failed to appear or even to reply to Norris' letter.[10] Now in the new administration the problem was up to Frances Perkins. She tells about it in her book, *The Roosevelt I Knew*.[11] She obviously did not like to oppose a bill backed by the AFL, but she was concerned because the hour limits were so rigid and because she feared the effect on earnings. After consulting with the President she appeared before the House Committee with certain proposals for power in a board to permit overtime up to forty hours per week, and for minimum wage fixing by representative boards on the model of state minimum wage laws. President Green opposed Miss Perkins' suggestions emphatically. He called the flexibility in maximum hours unnecessary and reiterated, in response to questions, the AFL opposition to minimum wage fixing except for women and minors. Although the question of constitutionality no longer seemed a major consideration, Green declared that boards with power to set minimum wages for men would do more harm than good. The rates set by such boards, despite the participation of alleged representatives of labor, would be so low they would weaken the attainment of higher wages through collective bargaining. He illustrated his point by the mining industry in which he declared that collectively bargained wage rates in Illinois would be undermined by wage board rates set in Kentucky. As for employers who asked protection against low wage competition, he reiterated Murray's suggestions at the earlier hearing. They would do better, he said, to urge legislation to protect collective bargaining.

> The Executive Council of the AFL [he stated] fully appreciates the commendable purpose of this suggestion [to fix minimum wage rates] . . . [but] the AFL feels that it would be a dangerous experiment. While it would help some, it would in our opinion tend to injure the efforts of the bulk of labor to raise their living standards, to bring about increases in wages. We, therefore, look with disfavor upon the proposal to establish minimum wage boards except that such minimum wage boards shall be created for the purpose of fixing minimum rates for women and minors.[12]

This obdurate adherence to the traditional AFL anti–minimum wage position in the year 1933, while the wages of men as well as women were spiraling downward, must have been discouraging to Secretary Perkins and other administration leaders. At any rate, about this time the administration decided not to tinker further with the Black-Connery bill, but to try a broader and bolder approach.

The NIRA

The exact origins of NIRA are somewhat obscure. The participants in the rapidly moving events of the first two months of the New Deal do not entirely agree as to who did what. At all events, a number of different people were working on drafts of bills designed to get the wheels of industry turning once more and the unemployed back to work. There were several ideas which seemed to be competing. Donald Richberg says he assured the President that the two main plans were not in conflict; they could be included in the same program.[13] These were: (1) the relaxation of the antitrust laws to permit industries to get together to set up codes of fair competition, including labor standards; and (2) a large public works program to create some jobs directly and more, indirectly, by creating a demand for steel and other products. President Roosevelt presented the bill to Congress on May 17. Hearings began before the House Ways and Means Committee the next day.

Was organized labor consulted in the drafting of NIRA? Miss Perkins in *The Roosevelt I Knew* (pp. 199–200) reports that when the President showed her the draft bill she told him that since hours and wages were involved, Green should be consulted. She says she then showed the bill to Green who wanted a provision inserted dealing with collective bargaining, and Section 7(a) was then inserted. She doesn't mention that he raised any question about the setting of minimum wage rates in the codes. Green's testimony before the Ways and Means Committee on May 18, and Frey's report to the Metal Trades Department a few months later, tell the story a little differently. According to Frey, "It was impossible for President Green to call a conference of international officers to study the measure until the day before the bill was introduced. At the Conference the representative of your Department [presumably himself] believing that section 7 [in the draft bill] failed sufficiently to protect labor's rights, recommended that the section be amended." He then proposed the addition which Green presented to the Ways and Means Committee a few days later.[14]

Green was the only representative of labor to appear in the three days of hearings held by the Ways and Means Committee. He presented the amendment, to be included in every code, which would strengthen the protection of collective bargaining and assure that workers would not be required to join company unions. When questioned, Green said he had had no opportunity to present his proposed amendments to the men who drafted the bill but understood that Senator Wagner accepted them. If they were included, he said, "Labor will extend to this proposed legislation its full, complete and hearty endorsement." He did not comment on the part of the bill which directed the inclusion of minimum wages and maximum hours in the industrial codes except to declare that "based upon the stabilized substantial foundation created in industry, standards with respect to hours, wages and conditions of employment can be established and this in turn will bring a revival of business." When asked whether he accepted NIRA as a substitute for the Black-Connery thirty-hour bill, Green said that he did not. "I hope the Connery bill will be passed and the AFL hopes that it will." [15] The AFL continued to urge the thirty-hour bill in the years of NRA operation—pointing out, correctly, that maximum hours under the codes had not been reduced to thirty hours nor had unemployment been ended.

On June 1, before the Senate Finance Committee, John L. Lewis spoke on behalf of the AFL and the United Mine Workers—the only labor leader to appear. He said nothing at all about the inclusion of minimum wage or maximum hour provisions in the codes. He was concerned only to prevent any change in Section 7(a) in the House bill which now included the amendments requested by Green.[16]

Apparently the AFL leaders accepted minimum wage fixing in the codes, perhaps because they expected unions to play an important part in drawing up the codes or perhaps just as an exchange for the protection for collective bargaining provided by Section 7(a). Certainly they did not originate the wage-hour provisions or even show any great enthusiasm for them.

This is not the place to attempt a description or evaluation of NRA. We are concerned only with the attitude and role of organized labor in connection with this rather amazing undertaking of the early New Deal.

Miss Perkins tells how she insisted on the creation of a labor advisory board to NRA together with counterpart employer and consumer boards. She says the labor board was very valuable and helpful (pp. 205 ff.). However, it seems clear that labor played little part in drafting the labor provisions of the majority of codes. Except in a few industries, labor's part was virtually limited to an appearance at the public hearing on each code, usually just to give approval of the draft. This was largely window dressing. (See Chapter 5 for further detail.)

The virtual abolition of child labor under sixteen through the codes was also something the AFL wholeheartedly supported, but so, to be sure, did virtually everyone else at that time. The hours set in the codes, compared with the thirty-hour week of the Black bill, were a disappointment; and the minimum wages set in the codes did very little for organized labor.

The AFL continued to urge the Black thirty-hour bill in 1934 and 1935, pointing out that the maximum set in most codes was forty hours per week, and that unemployment continued very high. They recognized that NRA had put 2 to 3 million men back to work. They argued that if a forty-hour week could do that much, a thirty-hour week would result in the absorption of the remaining 8 to 10 million unemployed. Green told the 1934 AFL convention, "This year we are making a concentrated drive [for the thirty-hour bill]; we are asking the candidates for Congress, where do you stand upon this economic measure?"[17]

What was the AFL reaction to the minimum wage rates set in the codes? Remember that they had strongly opposed a minimum wage for men as late as April, 1933, when Miss Perkins proposed adding wage boards to the thirty-hour bill. By the 1934 convention the executive council could see the results of wage setting under NRA and they were by no means happy about it. Their report declares: "Under this Act Labor expected... increasing purchasing power in the hands of millions of workers through the establishment of higher wage[s].... The codes were intended and did benefit large numbers of unskilled men and women in industry... [but the] minimum wage rates in the codes have been set so low that the purpose of the NRA has been completely nullified in a large portion of industry. Average weekly earnings have decreased in automobiles, iron and steel, paper and pulp and wool textiles." The report goes on to declare that it was "obvious from the beginning that without some protection extended to skilled workers the tendency on the part of employers would be to make the minimum wage the maximum and to reduce wages of skilled groups to compensate for increases in the wages of the unskilled." This, of course, was the old reason given by organized labor for opposing minimum wage laws. The executive council might have concluded that events had turned out just as they had feared and have urged that minimum wage fixing under the codes be abandoned. Instead, the report continues: "To protect the skilled worker it has been recommended again and again by Labor [presumably while code provisions were being drawn] that protection be given wages for groups of employees or occupations according to... the experience of the workers," and adds, "To this the Administration has been consistently opposed."

This section of its report suggests that the AFL executive council was ready for much more ambitious wage fixing through NRA—surely a far departure from the long time stand of the AFL. However, as we shall see, this position was not maintained when the Fair Labor Standards Act was proposed a few years later.

In March, 1935, the Senate Finance Committee was investigating NRA to decide whether it should be continued. Under the original Act it was to run for two years only. William Green appeared, voiced

AFL criticism along the lines of the executive council report just described, but urged continuation. Here again labor's first interest was in Section 7(a). Despite "fierce opposition," Green declared, "NRA is the first step in the establishment of real collective bargaining." As for the minimum wages established in the codes, Green spoke of the elimination of sweatshops in the garment industry where wages had been raised from 7–10 cents an hour to 25–30 cents. As for hours, he said NRA had proved that shorter hours could put men back to work. But of course hours should be further reduced. It had been suggested that the service trades be excluded from the NRA program. To this Green objected on the ground that these were the most exploited workers. "Labor," he said, "protests denying them the protection of NRA." [18]

Finally, in May, 1935 (still before the Schechter decision), the Senate was considering a very limited and emasculated extension of NRA. Green wrote a letter of protest to the President. "Your recommendation that a more effective and more constructive NRA be enacted," he declared, "... represents in our opinion the minimum legislative requirement." [19]

The Walsh-Healey Act

On May 27, 1935, the Supreme Court unanimously held NRA unconstitutional as applied to the Schechter Poultry Company. It was this decision which caused Roosevelt to ask whether we were relegated to the horse and buggy era. According to Miss Perkins, the President decided not to try to salvage any of NRA, though some administration lawyers thought it would be possible. Was there something else which could be done by the federal government to protect labor standards? Miss Perkins was prepared. She had thought it unlikely that NRA would be extended beyond its two-year duration regardless of constitutionality. Believing that some permanent legislation on wages and hours should be enacted to take its place, she had had the Labor Department solicitor draft two bills. One was a public contracts bill, based on the theory that the federal government had power to determine the labor conditions under which goods manufactured for its use should be produced. The other bill, of more doubtful constitutionality, provided for wage and hour regulation in industries affecting interstate commerce. When NRA's future was in doubt she told the President: "Never mind. . . . I've got two bills which will do everything you and I think important under NRA . . . locked up in the lower left-hand drawer of my desk." (p. 249) After the Schechter decision she took the public contracts bill out of the desk drawer. It was hastily gone over again and introduced by Senator Walsh on June 14, and by Healey in the House.

The Walsh-Healey bill provided that in all federal government contracts for $10,000 or more, minimum labor standards should be specified, including minimum wages, maximum hours, and the prohibition of child labor and convict labor. In the original form it further provided that where the federal government gave grants or loans to state or local governments the same standards should be required for work financed by such grants.

The Senate Education and Labor Committee immediately held a hearing—on June 17. Perhaps because it moved so rapidly, no one appeared representing organized labor. Various government officials in the Army, Navy, etc., explained that under existing law, when contracting for uniforms, blankets, or any other supplies, they were required to accept the lowest bid, regardless of the labor standards of the plant involved.[20] The Walsh bill was debated only briefly on the Senate floor. Senator Clark of Missouri urged that the Black thirty-hour bill be substituted, on the ground that it would cover more of industry and do more to provide jobs. Walsh read a wire from William Green endorsing the Walsh bill and urging friends of labor in the Senate to vote for it. Apparently Green knew of the plan to offer the thirty-hour bill as a substitute, because the wire ended: "I sincerely hope that no substitute, meritorious as it may seem, will be permitted to prevent the immediate passage of your bill." The Clark substitute was voted down and the Walsh bill was passed promptly without a roll call on August 12, 1935.[21]

AFL support of the Walsh-Healey Public Contracts bill was not surprising. Organized labor had traditionally urged government action, federal and state, to limit hours on "public work." Beginning with President Van Buren's executive order in 1840 establishing a ten-hour day in Navy yards, organized labor had sought to make government a model employer and had secured a succession of laws on the subject. The Bacon-Davis Act of 1931 had set an eight-hour day in the construction of public buildings and the payment of not less than "prevailing wages" as determined by the Secretary of Labor. The Walsh-Healey bill proposed to extend this kind of regulation to other kinds of government contracts—for the purchase of supplies rather than for construction. It proposed to reduce the hours to forty and to add the abolition of child and convict labor.

When the bill came from the Senate, the House Judiciary Committee immediately began hearings. Here John P. Frey appeared. He stressed the anomalous situation which had arisen since the end of NRA. The administration was urging employers to voluntarily maintain the code labor standards; but the law required government to buy from the lowest bidder, who was probably undercutting wages and lengthening hours. There were stories of sweatshop manufacturers who were winning government contracts to supply overalls for the CCC camps, etc.[22] The House Committee did not report out the bill, however, and Congress adjourned.

In the next session, the House Judiciary Committee again held extensive hearings in March, 1936. This time there was a big turn-out of labor leaders, all telling similar stories of how the existing law operated to give government work to sweatshop employers. Questions were asked as to how the Secretary of Labor could determine "prevailing wages in the locality." Green declared it was done successfully for construction under the Bacon-Davis Act and would be no more difficult for workers in factories. Both he and Frey used the traditional argument that the government should be a model employer.

The House committee was not too enthusiastic about the Walsh-Healey bill and held it up for months. When it was finally brought to the floor and debated, shortly before adjournment, one member of the committee protested against the labor pressure which was being exerted. He read a wire he had received from William Green urging him to be present at a Committee meeting (to vote out the bill). The wire ended: "Your absence from this meeting will be construed as opposition to the measure and as being unfriendly to labor." [23]

For this public contracts bill the AFL probably did do their utmost. However, the bill was an administration "must bill," which perhaps was even more important in securing its passage in the House. It was signed on June 30, 1936.

State Labor Legislation

Meanwhile what was happening in the states and what role did organized labor play? In legislative sessions in 1933 there were notable achievements—seven states passed minimum wage laws for women and minors and fourteen ratified the Child Labor Amendment. The depression had finally brought a change in the political climate. The complacent assumptions of "welfare capitalism" were shattered when under the leadership of the National Consumers League the facts were brought to light as to what was actually going on. Many small shops in the garment and similar trades were found to be migrating from the large cities to localities where unions did not exist and there was no ability to resist the breakdown of labor standards. In Massachusetts the Consumers League found some shops in the western part of the state paying as little as one cent per hour. In Connecticut the Department of Labor reported that shops in the clothing industry that had migrated from other states "employ very young girls, pay little or no wages and use the excuse of a learning period to pay nothing in some cases and then discharge the girls at the end of the learning period and take on a new group of workers." [24] In New York the Consumers League got out a pamphlet consisting of case histories of wage earners whose families were on city relief because their wages were so meager. When facts like these were brought to light, there was considerable public reaction.

At the call of the National Consumers League a Conference on the Breakdown of Industrial Standards was held in New York on December 12, 1932, and was attended by labor department officials of the principal eastern states. It was agreed to establish "industrial standard committees" to press for the enactment of minimum wage laws in the coming legislative sessions. A committee was set up to prepare a new model bill designed to meet if possible the objections raised by the Supreme Court in the Adkins decision and to enable the Court if it wished to "distinguish" the new laws from those invalidated in that case. This new type of bill was a more developed form of the "oppressive wage" law drafted by John R. Commons and passed in Wisconsin in 1925. The Wisconsin law had never been tested in the courts; enforcement had stopped before that point to avoid the possibility of an adverse decision. The new model Consumers League bill was based on the same principle of taking "value of services" into account in setting a minimum wage. This was supposed to meet the chief objection raised in the majority opinion in the Adkins case. The bill also had new procedural provisions.

On January 27, 1933, at the call of Governor Ely of Massachusetts there met in Boston an Eastern Interstate Conference on Labor

Legislation with representatives of the governors of eight states. This conference unanimously recommended immediate enactment of mandatory minimum wage laws. In New York Governor Lehman sent a special message to the legislature urging passage of the Consumers League bill. "I am confident," he declared, "that I voice the needs of industry—so as to avoid the continuous spiral of lower wages, lower prices, low purchasing power and higher unemployment."[25] Under the leadership of the New York Consumers League seventy organizations joined in support of this bill.

Employer desire for such legislation, while of course not unanimous, was nonetheless real. Three weeks after taking office as Secretary of Labor, Miss Perkins said she had already received 200 letters from employers telling how their industries were being ruined by competition from concerns paying starvation wages.

On April 12 after New York had passed its law, President Roosevelt telegraphed the governors of thirteen other industrial states urging the enactment of minimum wage laws for women and minors. It was the Roosevelt landslide which had swept Democrats into office in many states. His message naturally carried great weight. At any rate five more states promptly enacted the Consumers League bill and a sixth, Utah, passed an "old style" minimum wage law.

Did organized labor play any important part in this achievement? Articles written at the time do not give credit to labor unions or labor leaders. In New York the Consumers League did the main job, assisted by the Women's Trade Union League. Governor Lehman and Charles Poletti, his legal counsel, were actively helpful. State labor leaders gave nominal support, but the minimum wage bill was regarded as something for women and men didn't take much interest. A revealing side light on labor's role in the campaign in Connecticut is to be found in remarks made three years later by the secretary of the Connecticut State Federation of Labor. He was speaking at the third National Conference on Labor Legislation called by Secretary Perkins. In the discussion of a resolution to urge the states to pass minimum wage laws he declared: "I can well recall when we first passed the minimum wage law in Connecticut [in 1933] that our Executive Board discussed this question at considerable length and had to wire President Green who said it was all right for us to approve minimum wage for women. Therefore we put our blessing upon the minimum wage law in Connecticut."[26]

The year 1933 also saw a revivified movement to secure ratification of the Child Labor Amendment. There was rather general agreement in the depth of depression on the desirability of raising child labor standards and the opposition to potential federal action in the field was at a low ebb. Here the AFL and its state affiliates were wholehearted in their support. To what extent they should be credited with the fourteen state ratifications secured in 1933, it is impossible to say. At any rate this was amazing progress compared with the six states which had ratified in the preceding eight years, though it should be noted that the centers of opposition—Massachusetts and New York—still held out in 1933.

In state child labor legislation there were no spectacular gains. Here labor could probably have achieved considerable success if the leadership had made a real effort. With an abundance of young people of sixteen and over available for any kind of jobs, many employers really did not want to hire those under sixteen. The writer's personal experience was with a bill in the Wisconsin legislature to raise the minimum age of employment from fourteen to sixteen while the schools were in session—to apply to all children who had not completed the highest school grade available to them. (This did not affect farm work.) There was no employer opposition. Labor supported but did not initiate this bill. It passed without difficulty.

One might expect that along with their interest in the Black thirty-hour bill, labor might have been active in 1933 in efforts to reduce the maximum hours under state women's hour laws. If they tried there is very little to show for it.

What about 1935—the next legislative year in most states? By this time through its Division of Labor Standards, the U.S. Department of Labor was doing what it could to encourage the raising of state labor standards. This Division reported some progress in 1935, though nothing startling. In child labor, four states raised the minimum age of full-time employment and four more states ratified the Child Labor Amendment. No new states passed minimum wage laws. Twelve states made some improvements in their hour laws for women or minors, but many of these changes were slight. In many states forty-hour bills were introduced, but none was passed. Partly, of course, there was the assumption in 1935 that now the federal government was setting labor standards, so there was little drive for state action. By the time NIRA was held unconstitutional it was too late for that year.

What happened in the states after the Schechter decision? One might perhaps expect a rather general writing of typical code standards into state legislation. There was an opportunity to do this in 1936 in a good many states even though it was the usual off-year for legislative sessions. Because of the need to qualify under the unemployment compensation titles of the Social Security Act, many special sessions were called—twenty-eight states had special sessions between September, 1935, and September, 1936. But only one state, Rhode Island, was added to the minimum wage list. Rhode Island also reduced hours for women and minors and made sixteen the minimum age for full-time employment. More interesting was the action of South Carolina which passed an eight- and forty-hour law for the textile industry—to take effect only if North Carolina and Georgia passed similar laws. This was an obvious attempt to get concerted action to maintain or restore a reasonable hours standard for the southern textile industry, to take the place of the textile code. It may be guessed that employers favored, perhaps even initiated this measure. Certainly it is doubtful whether the union movement in South Carolina was strong enough to play an important role.

In 1936 the Supreme Court dealt another blow to minimum wage legislation. As already noted, all but one of the state laws passed in 1933 had followed the Consumers League new model which it was hoped would at least give the Court a basis for distinguishing it from the "old style" minimum wage law invalidated in the Adkins case. The Consumers League and the New York Department of Labor were working toward a court test under the most favorable circumstances possible. To this end the New York law was administered with the most meticulous care. However, regardless of all this, when a case reached the New York Court of Appeals, a majority held that the Adkins decision still applied. By a 5 to 4 vote the Supreme Court (in *Morehead* ex rel *Tipaldo*) accepted the view of the New York court and refused to reconsider the Adkins decision. Thus for the second time it held minimum wage legislation for women unconstitutional, on June 1, 1936.

The national repercussions of this decision will be discussed in the next section. To complete the story of state legislation, we should note here that the Morehead decision was overruled by a 5 to 4 vote less than a year later, in *West Coast Hotel Company* v. *Parrish.* After that decision four more states passed minimum wage laws. In one of them, Oklahoma, the law was intended to apply to men as well as women, but a technical flaw made it possible for the opposition to get court action to block this.

In 1937 there was considerable activity also in child labor and maximum hour legislation. Four more states ratified the child labor amendment. North and South Carolina made sixteen the basic minimum age for employment. Six states improved their hour laws for women. Pennsylvania took the biggest step with an eight- and forty-four–hour law applying to both men and women.

There is little evidence that organized labor in the states played an important part in the legislative gains of 1935 to 1937. The most impressive gains were made in Rhode Island and Pennsylvania where a thorough revamping of protective labor laws was a project of the state Democratic administrations, with advice and drafting service provided by the U.S. Department of Labor and its newly created Division of Labor Standards. During these years the Secretary of Labor held annual conferences of state labor department officials and state labor leaders at which the states which had made special gains in the preceding year received recognition.

The proceedings of these conferences make interesting reading. Miss Perkins usually paid tribute to organized labor as the force behind state achievements in protective legislation. But the historian should perhaps take such statements with a grain of salt—at least as applied to wage and hour laws. A straw in the wind is contained in the speech of the president of the Illinois State Federation at the 1937 conference. After reporting on other legislation secured that year (unemployment compensation, amendments to the workmen's compensation law, etc.) he added: "Then also with the help of our State Department of Labor and the Women's Trade Union League, the Illinois labor movement finally secured the enactment of a women's eight hour bill." At the same conference the president of the Pennsylvania State Federation declared that the bills passed in 1937 had been the Federation's legislative program for forty years—which seems a little doubtful in the case of the forty-four–hour law. He recognized the role of the Democratic party, declaring that only when "a party different from the party which has been in control for 40 years" won a majority in both houses of the legislature was it possible to secure labor legislation.[27]

Speaking that same year before the International Association of Government Labor Officials, the head of the Pennsylvania Department of Labor told in some detail how the state Democratic platform included a program of labor legislation and how he, with the aid of the U.S. Department of Labor, translated it into specific bills which he then shepherded through the legislature. Of course, state officials, too, may tend to exaggerate their role in legislative achievements.

However, a revealing discussion occurred that same year at the National Conference on Labor Legislation on the question: "Is there any justification for making an exception to standards established by a state hour law where an existing union contract calls for longer hours?" The Pennsylvania forty-four–hour law which had just been passed contained such a proviso, and all the labor union officials who spoke to the question approved it. Apparently they all recognized there were many union contracts for forty-eight hours or more. The secretary of the Connecticut Federation declared: "I do not think it is good policy to cut under existing contracts." The president of the Iowa Federation was even more emphatic, if a trifle unrealistic. "I do not want to see any law," he said, "that is going to tamper with labor contracts. . . . We believe in our contracts and on that we will grow and we will keep ahead of any law you may establish." McMahon, former president of the United Textile Workers, was now director of the Rhode Island Department of Labor, but he still thought as a labor union officer. "If these laws," he declared, "that so many are now working for are to supersede the agreements, the question of organizing the workers who are hiding behind legislative enactments will become serious indeed. . . . Any attempt by statute law to interfere with labor unions' rights to carry out the contract with the employer is an interference with organization in the field."

Was the real reason for these statements a fear that shorter hours by law would reduce earnings? In any case it seems clear that these union leaders still distrusted hours legislation. Along the same line it is noteworthy that at the conference in 1935 the vice president of the Illinois Federation had voiced unequivocal opposition to hour laws for men. "I am very skeptical," he said, "that legislation on hours of labor for men is advisable in any of the legislatures. . . . I believe the real hope for realizing our objective, the shorter work week, is better organization on the part of the working men of our country." [28]

As for minimum wage legislation, after 1933 organized labor accepted state laws for women as desirable. But for men they remained very dubious. At the 1936 national conference there was an animated discussion over the last clause of the report of the Committee on Minimum Wage. "When constitutional means have been devised," read the report, "the Committee recommends that states pass minimum wage laws for women and minors, and where the time seems ripe for men as well." Representatives of the Massachusetts, Connecticut, and Kentucky Federations now accepted minimum wage for men as desirable. But the president of the Pennsylvania Federation protested, declaring: "It has been the settled policy of the labor movement to refuse to acquiesce in such programs"—i.e., minimum wage for men. The director of the Industrial Relations Department of Ohio—a union man—was inclined to agree. Labor representatives from Oklahoma and California joined in. This difference of opinion among AFL leaders as late as 1936 helps to explain the difficulties of the AFL over the Fair Labor Standards bill in the following years.

All in all, the attitudes of state federation representatives at these labor legislation conferences suggest that forces other than organized labor probably took the lead in securing state hour and wage laws during the New Deal period.

The Fair Labor Standards Act

The Schechter decision in 1935 had seemed to close the door on general wage-hour regulation by the federal government. A year later the Tipaldo case went even further. It held unconstitutional a minimum wage law for women, not men, passed by a state, not Congress, so that no question of federal power was at issue. But President Roosevelt refused to accept this barrier against protective labor legislation as final. He continued to assert that such government action was needed and some way must be found to get it accepted by the courts. In the 1936 presidential campaign he spoke repeatedly of what NRA had done for the working people and promised if re-elected to find a way to restore government wage-hour regulation.

Both before and after the election there was much talk of a constitutional amendment to give Congress power in this field. However, on February 5, 1937, the President proposed instead his "court packing" plan to add up to six additional justices to the Supreme Court unless the six who were over seventy years old retired. Either way this bill would have given Roosevelt the chance to make six appointments to the Court. This proposal aroused much opposition in Congress and in the country generally. No one can say, of course, whether or not it would have been passed by Congress, if the barrier against protective and other labor legislation had remained standing. But in the spring of 1937 the judicial tide turned.

On March 29 by a narrow 5 to 4 vote the U.S. Supreme Court upheld a state minimum wage law for women and minors in *West Coast Hotel Company* v. *Parrish*. Ironically the statute upheld was not one of the "new model" laws so carefully drafted to meet the Court's objections as stated in the Adkins case and to give it a chance to "distinguish" rather than "overrule" that decision. Instead the statute involved was the state counterpart of the District of Columbia law at issue in the Adkins case and the Court stated specifically that the Adkins decision was overruled. Two weeks later by the same narrow 5 to 4 margin the Court upheld the National Labor Relations Act as a legitimate use of the power of Congress to regulate interstate commerce.

These two decisions gave hope that the Court might uphold a general federal minimum wage and maximum hours law based, like NLRA, on the power to regulate commerce. To be sure NLRA was justified in its public policy declaration by the statement that it would prevent strikes which obstruct commerce. The Court might well hold that the relation between substandard hours and wages and the obstruction of commerce was far less clear. As for the constitutionality of minimum wage laws as such, whether state or federal, the Parrish decision had upheld only a law for women and minors. Would it serve as precedent for a minimum wage law for men? In the past, beginning with *Muller* v. *Oregon* in 1908, the Court had differentiated between men and women and sustained laws for the latter on the ground that they needed special protection as compared with men. Even hour laws for men, if general in scope, rather than for specific unhealthy occupations, were not too clearly established as constitutional. The decision in *Bunting* v. *Oregon* in 1917 was somewhat equivocal and no later decision on a general men's hour law existed. So the two 5 to 4 decisions in the spring of 1937 by no means assured the constitutionality of a federal wage-hour law covering men as well as women.

However, the chance looked good enough for President Roosevelt. Miss Perkins tells us she took from her desk drawer the second of the wage-hour bills which had been drafted several years before. It was intensively reworked by the Department of Labor legal staff and by the famous Roosevelt team of Tom Corcoran and Ben Cohen.

According to Miss Perkins, the inclusion of the child labor provisions was a last-minute addition due to a plea by Grace Abbott, former chief of the Children's Bureau. Miss Abbott had administered the first federal child labor law during its short life from 1916 to 1918 (before it was declared unconstitutional in *Hammer* v. *Dagenhart*). She now asked the President if he had found a way around the Supreme Court "to give the children the benefit." (p. 257) It had, of course, been assumed for years that the only way to get federal child labor protection was through the proposed constitutional amendment which still lacked eight of the needed thirty-six state ratifications.

The FLSA was introduced by Black in the Senate and Connery in the House on May 24, 1937, accompanied by a special message from the President. It provided for a minimum wage and a maximum work week to be stated in the statute, but to be applied industry by industry by a board of five which was to administer the Act. The board would also have power to set "minimum fair wage rates" and "maximum reasonable work weeks" in industries and occupations. These could be either above or below the standards specified in the Act; but it was assumed that by this method minimum wages would be gradually raised and maximum hours gradually reduced.

The Fair Labor Standards bill provided a solution for one problem which had greatly concerned Miss Perkins in connection with the Black thirty-hour bill back in 1933. She had then opposed an absolute maximum thirty-hour week, had urged the need for some flexibility, and had suggested power in a board to permit up to forty hours by industries or areas. This Green had opposed, declaring such flexibility unnecessary. Perhaps he would have agreed to Miss Perkins' amendment if she had proposed the kind of flexibility provided four years later in the Fair Labor Standards bill. The new bill specified that hours in excess of the standard would be permitted so long as time and a half was paid for overtime. This proviso followed a pattern common in union contracts. It was used in a few NRA codes, though not in most. It was to be found in the old Oregon ten-hour law and after 1919 in the railroad eight-hour law. But most state hour laws set an absolute maximum, subject only to emergency overtime when permitted by the administrative agency.

At a joint hearing of the Senate and House Labor Committees, Robert Jackson, then Assistant Attorney General, presented the Fair Labor Standards bill and explained its constitutional basis. A number of representatives of industry appeared in support, arguing that prosperity required the raising of substandard wages to increase purchasing power, and shorter hours to absorb the unemployed. Late 1937 was a period of recession and these industry representatives were concerned. NRA had helped, they said. Since its demise, hours had grown longer and wages had gone down in some industries and areas. Some kind of government regulation was needed. Without it, employers were powerless to resist the downward pressure.

Where was organized labor while all this was going on? As far as hour legislation was concerned, the AFL had never stopped advocating the thirty-hour week. Despite the NIRA, the 1934 AFL convention passed a resolution instructing the executive council to continue working for a thirty-hour law. At the 1935 convention (held after NIRA had been declared unconstitutional) the executive council reported 11 million still unemployed and declared it would continue its effort for the thirty-hour law. However, some difference of opinion within the executive council can be gleaned from the convention proceedings. One delegate asked: "Can we . . . depend upon 100 per cent support [for hour legislation] of the personnel of the Executive Council" or at least on "a benevolent neutrality?" [29] At the 1936 convention the opposition was explicitly stated on the floor. Hutcheson of the Carpenters made the classic anti-legislation speech: "The labor movement is going far afield. . . . Insofar as Federal Employees are concerned, I say yes to the enactment of such a law. . . . When it comes to private employers, I say, establish your wages and hours by negotiation and not by law. . . . What they can give us they can take from us." President Green apparently did not dare meet Hutcheson head on. How many delegates were confused by the following statement? "I have opposed the economic doctrine," said Green, "that wages and hours of those employed in private industry should be regulated by law because, as Delegate Hutcheson has well said, if they can give it to you, they can take it away. Our policy, however, only is to secure the enactment of legislation providing for the six-hour day and the five-day week applicable to those employed in the production of goods that enter into interstate commerce. We are sure and certain that any other law dealing with the shorter work day would be declared unconstitutional." [30]

Gainor, chairman of the Committee on the Shorter Work Day, also hesitated to put up a fight against Hutcheson. He said the instruction to the executive council to get a bill introduced had been urged on their committee from many quarters. They had added it to their recommendations at the last minute because they thought a bill being debated in Congress would be educational. They would not oppose an amendment to strike out that part of their report. However, no such amendment was offered and their full resolution was adopted unanimously.

This resolution of the 1936 convention, like those in preceding conventions, dealt only with hour legislation. The AFL had never endorsed a general minimum wage law for men, unless one counts its support of NIRA. What position would they take on the new administration proposal? Miss Perkins (p. 258) does not suggest that labor was consulted in the drafting of the FLS bill. However, she apparently expected labor support. The bill was introduced May 24, 1937. On May 28 the AFL executive council met and endorsed the bill subject to additions to be offered by Green "essential to strengthen the administrative provisions and to coordinate it with other Congressional enactments"—presumably this meant the Walsh-Healey Act and NLRA. What the AFL really wanted at this stage it is difficult to understand. They must have decided that they could no longer take the position of early 1933—pass an hour law "and let us handle the question of wages." But the old fear that a legal minimum wage would weaken unionism was certainly not dead. They were more concerned that a minimum wage should not interfere with a collectively bargained wage than they were with the adequacy of the legal minimum.

At any rate, Green's testimony at the joint hearing before the Senate and House Labor Committees makes interesting but somewhat difficult reading. He supported the bill on the somewhat specious ground that it provided for wage fixing only for a very limited class of workers. "Any proposal to deal with the fixing of general minimum wage standards by government fiat for men in private industry would," he said, "be strenuously opposed by the AFL as . . . violating the cardinal principles of self-government in private industry." The bill certainly looked like a general minimum wage law, even though the minimum to be specified in the statute was to be applied industry by industry by the board, and the board also had power to vary it up or down for various industries or occupations or areas.[31]

Green presented six amendments or additions without which the AFL would not support the bill. According to the executive council's report of 1937 these amendments were to "safeguard collective bargaining and to limit the scope of government regulation to those fields wherein collective bargaining machinery is ineffective or difficult of functioning and only until collective bargaining has substantially covered the field." [32] Obviously collective bargaining can always function to set standards higher than those set as minimums by law. Apparently the real issue was whether the board should ever be permitted to set a higher minimum wage and a shorter work week than those obtained by collective bargaining. Some union agreements then in effect set wages below the 40 cents which it was assumed would be the basic minimum wage written into the Act. (This figure had been left blank in the bill as introduced.) Green's answers to questions are hard to follow. It is clear that he hated to give the proposed board any power to ignore collectively bargained wages or hours. One of the additions he urged provided that the board in setting a "minimum fair wage" or a "maximum reasonable work week" should accept collectively bargained standards "prevailing in a substantial . . . portion of the class, craft, industry or trade," unless it found that "a higher minimum wage or a lower maximum work week is necessary to prevent undue discrimination or unfair competition." Did this mean that ordinarily a collectively bargained wage below the general minimum set in the Act should prevail? This certainly looks like very lukewarm AFL support for a legal minimum wage.

The bill set an upper limit to the board's power to set "minimum fair wage standards." It could not set a minimum fair wage which in the judgment of the board would yield "an annual wage income in excess of $1,200 or an hourly wage in excess of 80 cents except for overtime, night or extra shift work." Strangely enough this limitation seemed to please Green. "The proposed act," he said, "deals only with the fixing and regulation of wages of men as well as women in that very limited class of workers with total income under $1,200." Disregarding the quibble involved in this statement, one may wonder how limited this class of workers actually was in 1937.

Perhaps because he knew well the attitude of many AFL leaders, Green was apparently trying to minimize the scope of the proposed law and to make it look like a minor exception to the general rule against government minimum wage fixing. This is borne out by the AFL *Newsletter* which headed its account of Green's testimony: "President Green . . . approves as a temporary measure minimum wage regulation by the government for those earning $1,200 or less per year, but opposes the general principle of government wage fixing for men in private employment."[33]

As for the CIO, which by 1937 was an important part of the organized labor movement, its support of the proposed FLS bill was not 100 per cent either. John L. Lewis, testifying at the joint hearings, recommended that the whole section giving the board power to vary minimum wages and maximum hours was too complicated and would lead to general wage fixing. He urged that the bill just specify a 40-cent minimum wage and a maximum week of say thirty-five hours, with very limited power in the board to go up to forty hours or down to thirty. He said the bill as drafted gave too much power to the board, would interfere with collective bargaining and might lead to a struggle in the courts "to determine whether after all American workmen are freemen or indentured servants."[34]

Sidney Hillman of the Amalgamated Clothing Workers was the only labor leader who approved the bill substantially as introduced, including its provisions for varying the minimum wage and maximum hours up or down. He commended its "carefully drafted administrative machinery" and declared it would aid, not retard, the process of collective bargaining. When asked why he endorsed the bill wholeheartedly in contrast to the qualified and limited endorsements by Green and Lewis, Hillman replied: "I think if there is any difference it is because of our experience. . . . I am speaking from my experience of the many industries . . . such as the garment industry, the shoe industry, textiles and others."[35] Possibly that is not the whole story. He was certainly far less afraid of government action all along than were the AFL leaders. Perhaps he had been consulted during the drafting of the bill. He was closer to the administration than Green or Lewis.

The Senate Labor Committee reported out the bill in amended form. It contained no wage or hour standard. The board was to set such standards, but no wage above 40 cents or week below 40 hours could be set. The amendments which Green had requested were not included. When the bill was debated on the floor of the Senate the varying opinions within the AFL were exposed to public view. Black read a letter from Green which said the bill before the Senate did not "meet the expectations of labor" but that "it would seem advisable to pass the best bill possible in the Senate with the hope that it can be revised and amended in the House." However, his opponents in the AFL did not accept this view. A New England senator read a story from a Boston paper quoting the president of the Massachusetts Federation of Labor. The president said that they in Massachusetts did not favor the bill in its present form and that "many labor men in high office in Washington" agreed with them. This was borne out by letters read on the floor asking for recommittal of the bill. These letters came from important AFL leaders—Frey for the Metal Trades Department, Williams for the Building Trades, and Ornburn for the Union Label Trades. Ornburn declared he was "unalterably opposed to [the bill] in the present form." Frey and Williams urged recommittal because there had been "no adequate opportunity for consideration of the measure by Labor or the Senate."

Senator Black in reply reminded his Democratic colleagues that their platform of 1936 had pledged action on maximum hours and minimum wages and pointed out that Hutcheson of the Carpenters (who presumably dominated the Building Trades Department) was "about the only leading representative of the AFL who could be secured to fight under the Republican banner." [36] So he rallied the Democrats and the Senate passed the FLSA on July 31, 1937, by a vote of 56 to 28.

In the House, the Labor Committee tried to meet the AFL demands. Representative Wood, a member of the Committee, told about it in the subsequent House debate. "I personally worked with the president of the AFL and two attorneys of the Administration in an attempt to work out amendments which would make the bill acceptable to the AFL. Six out of seven, the principal ones, were accepted by the Committee." The amended bill was reported out on August 6, and on August 9 Green wrote a letter to all members of the House saying: "The wage hour bill as reported by the House Labor Committee is reasonably acceptable and satisfactory to Labor. . . . I request you to support this proposed legislation . . . without any substantial change." [37]

However, the Rules Committee refused to let the bill go to the floor of the House and Congress adjourned without acting on it.

The *Proceedings* of the 1937 AFL convention show clearly the divided opinion among union leaders and indicate there was opposition to any federal wage-hour law. The executive council report tries to explain why Green had not demanded recommittal of the bill in the Senate. The administration, according to the report, urged that the bill be allowed to go through the Senate and promised support for labor's amendments in the House. The adoption of these amendments by the House Labor Committee, the report declares, "reduces government control over industry to a minimum" and merely gives "the Board power to deal with chiselers and those employers who through company unions or . . . fake collective bargaining agencies maintain sweat shop conditions." This interpretation of the amended bill might look somewhat questionable to one who read the bill as recommended by the House Committee. At any rate the AFL convention was not satisfied. It is interesting to note that the California Federation of Labor, which had actively opposed a state minimum wage law for women and minors in 1913, now in 1937 submitted a resolution "that we stand unalterably opposed to giving over to lawmakers the power to fix wages." More significant was a resolution introduced jointly by the groups which had registered their opposition in the Senate. The Building Trades and Metal Trades Departments submitted a resolution which declared that the Fair Labor Standards bill "was not prepared . . . by the American Federation of Labor nor was Labor consulted as to its several provisions." It therefore "justly comes under suspicion." The Resolutions Committee in its report declared that "the experiences of our movement with the authority exercised by N.R.A. and . . . under the National Labor Relations Act

. . . .

make us reluctant to approve the creation of any additional boards or commissions having to do with industrial relations." [38]

President Green was certainly reprimanded for going as far as he had in supporting Fair Labor Standards legislation. The convention adopted a resolution which read that "the officers and Executive Council be directed before taking any further action . . . to call into consultation the officers of the Building and Construction Trades Department, the Metal Trades, the Railway Employees and the Label Trades Departments." John P. Frey of the Metal Trades had moved adoption of this resolution and it was seconded by Matthew Woll of the Photoengravers.

Despite the AFL attitude, President Roosevelt continued his efforts to secure a federal wage-hour law. He called a special session of Congress for November 15, 1937, and declared in his message: "I believe the country as a whole recognizes the need for immediate Congressional action if we are to maintain wage increases and the purchasing power of the nation against recessive factors in the general situation." He recommended immediate passage by the House of the Black-Connery Fair Labor Standards bill. This time a discharge petition brought it to the floor of the House and it was debated on five days in December.

Mrs. Norton, now chairman of the Labor Committee since the death of William Connery, tried her best to secure AFL support. At the last minute she changed the bill to provide a single administrator in the Labor Department in place of the five-man board. Green had said they would rather have the law enforced by a single administrator in either the Department of Labor or the Department of Justice. But opposition in the AFL had hardened. Green in a letter to Mrs. Norton on November 27 tried to justify his about-face since August. He spoke of changes in economic conditions and the unfairness of the NLRB, though neither seemed relevant to the issue of opposition to the FLS bill. On December 10 he wrote to all members of the House opposing the current draft of the bill. "It is inconceivable," he wrote, "that Congress would vote to confer upon a single government administrator such broad, definite and comprehensive power. If the board is dangerous . . . certainly the administrator is even more dangerous." [39] Now the only form of legislation the AFL would accept was a short bill fixing a flat 40–cent minimum wage and an absolute eight-hour day and forty-hour maximum week, with no overtime permitted except in emergencies. Since they now opposed any federal administrative agency, their substitute bill provided for filing statements as to emergencies with the proper state agencies and left it to the Attorney General of the United States to prosecute in case of violations. The leaders of the AFL surely knew enough about labor legislation to realize that this substitute of theirs was completely unworkable. Without enforcement machinery it would be a dead letter, besides being so rigid as to hours as to be completely impracticable. And incidentally there was nothing in this substitute to safeguard collectively bargained wages and hours, the subject Green had been so concerned about six months before.

Meanwhile, the CIO was demanding enactment of the bill as recommended by the House Labor Committee.

While the rival labor groups rallied their supporters, spokesmen for agricultural groups were busy demanding and securing further and wider exclusions for occupations related in any way to agriculture. And while the "differentials" possible under the administration bill were said by the AFL to be a chief reason for their opposition, Southerners in the House were declaring that the differentials were not guaranteed and that the bill did not adequately protect southern industry, which would be destroyed by forcing wage increases. Amid a plethora of speeches pro and con there is irony to the historian in the words of Congressman Hartley (of later Taft-Hartley fame). "The leadership of the AFL," he declared, "wisely recognizes that the passage of this bill may easily sound the death knell of the organized labor movement in the United States; for what will be the incentive to join a union if the government is going to set wages and hours?"

Finally, the so-called Green substitute was defeated by a vote of 131 to 162—killed by administration orders, the AFL charged. Southern Democrats voted against it, of course, because it allowed no "differentials." But the Committee (or administration) measure fared only a little better. It was ordered recommitted by a vote of 216 to 198—the first major administration measure defeated on the floor of the House.

Still President Roosevelt did not give up the fight. When Congress reconvened in January, 1938, he again urged passage of a federal wage-hour law. As this was still the Seventy-fifth Congress, the bill as it had passed in the Senate was still pending. The House Labor Committee again tried to produce a bill which would satisfy the administration, the CIO, and the AFL. A subcommittee prepared what was known as the Ramspeck bill, a new version of the Department of Labor's bill. However, the full committee turned it down, probably because of the continuing AFL opposition. Miss Perkins comments on the spectacle of the AFL and NAM joining in opposition to the Ramspeck bill The Labor Committee finally reported out a bill somewhat resembling the so-called Green substitute of the preceding session. It provided for an initial flat 25-cent minimum wage to be raised 5 cents each year till it reached 40 cents. It provided for a standard work week of 44 hours to be reduced to 42 and 40. Presumably to satisfy the AFL the law was to be enforced only by prosecution by the Department of Justice.

The Rules Committee again refused to let the bill be brought to the floor and for a time not enough names could be secured for a discharge petition. Apparently it was two southern Democratic primaries in May which turned the tide. Lister Hill of Alabama and Claude Pepper of Florida—two outspoken supporters of the wage-hour bill—were nominated by spectacular majorities. When this became known, more than enough congressmen hurried to sign the discharge petition and the bill was brought to the floor of the House.

The attempt to substitute the Ramspeck bill was defeated. Maury Maverick of Texas made a strong speech for the Committee bill which he said was supported by the AFL, the CIO, the four railway brotherhoods, and hundreds of other organizations. "It is opposed," he declared, "by all reactionaries." It was, of course, opposed by many of the Southerners in the House. Maverick gave them an effective warning. "The people of the South," he said, "are for the minimum wage bill and there is plenty of proof of this. Lister Hill, our good colleague, just beat the socks off his opponent and that was the only issue. Down in Florida . . . Senator Pepper was elected on the same issue." Next day the House passed the Labor Committee bill by a vote of 314 to 97.[40]

The final form of the FLSA of 1938 was written by the Conference Committee. The power granted to a board in the original administration draft to vary rates from a statutory standard survived in somewhat attenuated form. The administrator (to be head of a division in the Labor Department) was given power, on recommendation of an "industry committee," to set rates above 25 cents the first year and 30 cents the second, but not above 40 cents. At the end of seven years the statutory standard was to become 40 cents, with power, however, through industry committee procedure, to set a rate below that figure down to 30 cents. According to Miss Perkins, the chief controversy in the Conference Committee was over regional differentials. The Southerners urged language which would make it mandatory for the administrator to set lower rates in regions where the prevailing wage pattern was below the national standard. However, the Southerners ultimately yielded, the Conference Committee report was unanimous, and the bill directed that "no minimum wage rate shall be fixed solely on a regional basis."

The AFL claimed credit for this prohibition of regional differentials. On the whole, the executive council in their report to the 1938 convention congratulated themselves on the ceiling for hours and foundation for wages written into the statute and the absence of a board with power to set wages. However, they said the administrator had too much power and pledged themselves to seek amendments to the law "as soon as the insufficiency of some of its provisions has been shown." [41]

One who tries to piece together the story of how the FLSA was achieved should give Miss Perkins the last word. "Everybody," she writes (p. 266), "claimed credit for it. The AFL said it was their bill and their contribution. The CIO claimed full credit for its passage. I cannot remember whether the President and I claimed credit, but we always thought we had done it. Certainly he gave a sigh of relief as he signed it. 'That's that,' he said."

How shall we explain the AFL attitude toward FLSA? It probably delayed passage of the law for nearly a year and weakened it materially. In 1937 with strong AFL support a 40–cent minimum wage and a forty-hour week might have been written into the statute. In 1938 the statutory wage was set at 25 cents, with no assurance of reaching 40 cents until the end of seven years. Hours started at 44 and went down to 40 only after two years. This was a big price to pay for a reduction in the power vested in a board and the elimination of possible regional differentials.

The heart of the AFL was the building trades unions. Did they have nothing to gain from a federal wage-hour law applying to private employment and does that explain the long AFL opposition? The building trades (and the AFL generally) were strong for the Bacon-Davis law for public work. They also supported the Walsh-Healey bill for other kinds of public contracts probably because (like Bacon-Davis) it provided for "prevailing wages" as the basis for minimum wage fixing. Labor leaders probably assumed that union contract scales would be accepted as "prevailing wages" even in industries in which there were virtually no union contracts.

But as for a wage-hour law for private industry, the building trades were by no means alone in their opposition. Hutcheson of the Carpenters was perhaps the most extreme opponent; but the Metal Trades Department and the Union Label Department joined in trying to prevent passage of the FLS bill in the Senate in July, 1937. John Frey moved and Matthew Woll seconded the resolution reprimanding Green in the 1937 convention a few months later. Of course at that time the AFL leaders were bitter against the NLRB, which they alleged was favoring the CIO. But it is hard to see this as a rational ground for opposing a board to administer a wage-hour law. How could such a law have been used to strengthen the CIO as against the AFL, even assuming the board wanted to do that?

AFL opposition, or at best indifference, to minimum wage legislation has a more basic explanation. Wages are the best area for collective bargaining. Things difficult or impossible to deal with by that method—restriction of prison labor as an obvious illustration—were seen as desirable areas for government action. But wages and to a slightly lesser extent hours are the heart of collective bargaining. If government enters this field it competes with collective bargaining. So AFL opposition to minimum wage laws, at least for men, was old and well entrenched. Even the events of the depression years did not really dislodge it. On the one hand, AFL leaders honestly did not expect legal minimum rates to be high enough to do most of their members any good; on the other hand, they feared that if minimum rates did equal or exceed union rates, unionism would thereby be weakened. Some of them still felt the same way about a maximum hour law—despite the official support of the thirty-hour bill.

The CIO from its inception was somewhat more favorable to wage-hour legislation than the AFL. Lewis was by no means enthusiastic about the FLS bill when it was first introduced; he, too, was afraid of general minimum wage fixing by government. But other CIO leaders took a different position. They were less influenced by traditional AFL thinking. They saw unions in the role of an effective pressure group in the political arena, and they probably thought it would be possible to build union membership on legislative as well as collective bargaining achievements. Anyway they supported the administration bill most of the time in 1937–38. But the CIO was not the prime mover. The Roosevelt administration certainly played that role.

Conclusion

Over-all it appears that organized labor was not primarily responsible for the revolutionary gains in protective labor legislation achieved in the years of the New Deal. Two principal factors account for these new laws—the depression and the Roosevelt administration.

The depression brought a dramatic worsening of labor conditions, a vicious downward spiral which not only caused suffering for workers, but also augmented the depression by a constant reduction in consumer purchasing power. But earlier depressions had brought no legislation to maintain or raise labor standards. This depression brought such laws because of new elements in the situation: the greater industrialization of the country, an enhanced recognition of the importance of consumer purchasing power, and more experience with state labor laws. All these contributed to create a new climate of opinion propitious for new protective legislation.

Experienced, able, farsighted, and daring leaders took advantage of that favorable climate. President Roosevelt and Secretary Perkins had both had long experience with labor laws in New York. Miss Perkins (and to a lesser extent the President) had been strongly influenced by the Consumers League, one of those small middle-class organizations which had worked so effectively to improve the lot of workers through legislation. At the outset of the new administration, labor's demand was for a maximum hour law only. It was Miss Perkins, after consultation with the President, who injected the minimum wage idea (as well as more flexible maximum hours) into the picture and who saw that it became part of NIRA. The AFL withdrew its positive opposition to minimum wages, probably in exchange for the famous Section 7(a). Later, on the advice of Miss Perkins, the President made first the Walsh-Healey bill and later the FLS bill "must" legislation.

The Walsh-Healey public contracts bill did have wholehearted labor support. On the FLS bill, however, labor's objections to one form after another of the administration proposal (added to the opposition of other groups) nearly caused final defeat of the measure. Ultimately the President's supporters in the House secured passage of the bill. Conservative Democrats and the AFL "went along."

So it was that between 1933 and 1938 those big steps were taken to use the federal government to put an end to child labor and to establish a "ceiling on hours" and a "floor under wages."

Postscript Since the New Deal

What has happened to protective labor legislation since 1938 and what has organized labor done about it?

As for the FLSA, both AFL and CIO representatives participated in the industry committees through which rates above 25 cents were set in 1939 to 1941. As one who served as a public representative on three of these committees, the writer can testify that union officers on these committees handled themselves well. Their participation in setting legal minimum rates made these committees a real experiment in tripartite minimum wage fixing, very different from the wage boards under most state minimum wage laws for women of earlier years. In the earlier years if unorganized women workers served on wage boards, they were quite unable to cope with employer representatives; if men union leaders were used, they really did not represent the women to be affected and were apt to know and care little about their problems. Both AFL and CIO should have been pleased with the way the industry committee procedure operated under the FLSA to raise the minimum wage industry by industry.

During the war of course this procedure became unnecessary as wages, even in low wage industries and areas, reached and passed the 40–cent figure beyond which minimum rates could not be set. After the war, labor, both AFL and CIO, pushed for amendment of the FLSA. However, they wanted a higher statutory rate without bothering with industry committee procedure. They were also demanding extension of coverage. In 1947 the AFL was demanding a 65–cent rate, by 1948 and 1949, $1 per hour. In the latter year FLSA amendments were finally passed. Seventy-five cents became the statutory minimum, the industry committee procedure was abolished except for Puerto Rico; but the coverage of the Act was narrowed rather than widened.

As prices and wages rose in the following years, the 75–cent minimum wage became increasingly outmoded. Both AFL and CIO supported amendments to raise the minimum further. Organized labor no longer opposes minimum wage legislation, or fears that the minimum will become the maximum. No doubt in some quarters at least the old belief survives that real gains in wages are achieved through collective bargaining, not through legislation. But the value of a legal minimum wage is increasingly recognized, especially among national labor leaders. Testifying for the CIO in April, 1955, Walter Reuther took a broad view. He urged a $1.25 minimum wage chiefly because "it would constitute the best kind of public interest legislation." "No minimum wage which Congress would conceivably adopt," he declared, "would affect the great majority" of CIO members. But he pointed out that only about one-third of America's wage earners are in unions—due largely to the "tremendous obstacles in the way of new organization" contained in the Taft-Hartley Act. Hence the importance of an increase in the minimum wage.[42]

Some unions, in industries where unorganized areas remain and where new unorganized competition can easily develop, took a very active part in the 1955 campaign. The Textile Workers, the United Hatters, the Amalgamated Clothing Workers, and the International Ladies Garment Workers joined together for this purpose. Among other activities they brought union people to Washington from all over the country to call on their congressmen and senators and urge a $1.25 minimum wage. This probably helped materially to secure final passage of a $1 rate; though it must be remembered that even the Eisenhower administration was urging an increase to 90 cents.

As for hours, in 1955 the AFL recommended that the standard work week be reduced to thirty-five hours, to replace the present forty-hour week—with time and a half for hours above forty—which took effect in 1941. Perhaps automation will produce a strong new drive for shorter hours, but that has not developed yet.

What of state minimum wage legislation to supplement the federal act? Hotels, restaurants, laundries, retail stores, agriculture, and much agricultural processing are outside of the federal act. Coverage was narrowed in 1949 and no widening was achieved in 1955. It has been estimated that 20 million out of a total of 54 million wage and salary earners are now excluded from the wage-hour provisions of FLSA. Under these circumstances state supplements would seem an appropriate legislative demand for organized labor, expecially in states which do not even have a minimum wage for women and minors. But there has been surprisingly little labor activity in this area. In 1949 the AFL executive council declared: "Labor must buckle down to a real fight for decent wage and hour laws in the 48 states." [43] But there is little evidence that many state federations have taken this admonition very seriously.

If Wisconsin is typical, both AFL and CIO state organizations have been apathetic toward raising state minimum wage standards. Apparently the minimums that might be enacted by state legislatures are so far below wages achieved by collective bargaining that union leaders and union members see little reason to make efforts along these lines. Of course they might well find it difficult to secure gains in minimum wage no matter how hard they worked. For state legislatures in which rural and small town areas are overrepresented are afraid that even very moderate minimum wage rates would force up wages in small businesses and in small towns—so the opposition is strong. From 1942 to 1955 no new state minimum wage laws were passed. Surprisingly in 1955 three mountain states, Idaho, New Mexico, and Wyoming, passed laws applying to men as well as women and minors. This brings the total to thirty-three laws (in twenty-nine states and four other jurisdictions). But only ten of these cover men. There is still much to be done.

Labor and the New Deal

In the first flush of enthusiasm in the New Deal period, some observers saw no further role for the "humanitarian" groups which in the past had played so important a part in securing protective labor laws. It was said in the thirties that now the government, with adequate funds for research, would collect the facts as to exploited groups or dangerous conditions and do a much better job than had been possible for private organizations like the Consumers League or the National Child Labor Committee. Then the strong expanding labor movement would see that bad conditions were remedied, either through collective bargaining or through legislation.

But a more sober appraisal of what has happened since the New Deal throws doubt on any such conclusion. The Labor Department's appropriations have shrunk; its investigations are restricted. Employer organizations oppose improvements in protective laws even more vigorously than in the twenties. The Chamber of Commerce for example, ignoring the much higher price level, opposed in 1955 any increase in the federal minimum wage; it also urged an important reduction in the law's coverage. If Wisconsin is typical, state Chambers are vigorous along the same line as regards state minimum wage laws.

As for child labor legislation, the recent trend in an era of full employment has been to nibble at child labor restrictions. Public support of child labor laws has weakened. A concern about juvenile delinquency has brought a rather strong swing back in some quarters to the old view that work is good for children, that "Satan still finds mischief for idle hands to do." Part-time work for children attending school is now called "work experience," and many high schools give credit for it as a part of education. How far should this be allowed to go?

So today there is a big job to be done in most states even to maintain present protective standards, which of course includes raising minimum wage rates to keep pace with rising prices. Besides, many states lack minimum wage laws altogether, and most of the women's hour laws are completely outmoded. But for organized labor in most states this job does not get a high priority. State labor groups lobby energetically to increase benefits under workmen's compensation and unemployment compensation. They are zealous about bills which affect collective bargaining. But mostly they are not very much concerned about bills dealing with child labor, maximum hours, or minimum wages.

Today adult labor does not fear child labor competition because the jobs for which children are sought (in bowling alleys and drive-in restaurants, as newsboys and the like) are marginal jobs which men and women do not want. Perhaps, then, it is natural that union leaders are somewhat apathetic about bills which would weaken or strengthen child labor laws. As for wage and hour laws, it must be conceded that they directly benefit chiefly the unorganized; and in many states even today organized labor tends to treat the unorganized as stepchildren. Bills which won't benefit union members are not apt to get top rating.

So perhaps there is still an important role for the "humanitarians." Despite the expanded labor movement and its increased awareness of the value of government action, there is still a need for active pressure groups motivated by social conscience, with no personal or group axes to grind. Without such groups it is doubtful whether the body of protective labor laws could withstand decay and inevitable attacks, much less grow and change to meet the new needs of changing times.

Notes

1 This statement does not apply to minor protective laws—those relating to prison labor, garnishment of wages, etc.—nor to hour laws for special groups such as railroad workers, nor to what might be called indirect protective laws, such as contract labor and other immigration laws. Safety laws were also the concern of organized labor in at least some states.

2 For an account of this earlier AFL attitude toward men's hour legislation, see Elizabeth Brandeis, "Labor Legislation," in *History of Labor in the United States, 1896–1932,* vol. III of John R. Commons and associates, *History of Labor in the United States* (New York: Macmillan Co., 1935), especially pp. 554–59.

3 American Federation of Labor, *Proceedings,* 1931. For quotations see pp. 113, 277, and 281.

4 American Federation of Labor, *Proceedings,* 1932, p. 291.

5 International Ladies Garment Workers Union, *Proceedings,* May, 1932, pp. 201, 51, 90. See also International Union of Mine, Mill, and Smelter Workers, *Proceedings,* August, 1931.

6 For the quotations in this and the following paragraph see American Federation of Labor, *Proceedings,* 1932, pp. 284 ff., and especially pp. 296, 291, 317.

7 *Congressional Record,* 72d Cong., 2d Sess., 76:1 (December 21, 1932), p. 820.

8 U.S. Senate, Committee on the Judiciary, *Hearings, on S. 5267,* 72d Cong., 2d Sess. (1932–33), pp. 298, 425.

9 U.S. House of Representatives, Committee on Education and Labor, *Hearings, on H.R. 14105,* 72d Cong., 2d Sess. (1933), pp. 1–22, 176.

10 So reported in Senate debate on Black thirty-hour bill, *Congressional Record,* 72d Cong., 2d Sess., 76:4 (February 17, 1933), pp. 4304–11.

11 Frances Perkins, *The Roosevelt I Knew* (New York: Viking Press, 1946), pp. 192–97. Future references to this source will be given only in the form of page numbers in parentheses in the text.

12 U.S. House of Representatives, Committee on Education and Labor, *Hearings, on S. 158 and H.R. 4557,* 73d Cong., 1st Sess. (1933), p. 66. See also pp. 3, 61–69.

13 Donald Richberg, *My Hero* (New York: G. P. Putnam's Sons, 1954), p. 164.

14 American Federation of Labor, Metal Trades Department, *Proceedings,* September 27, 1933, p. 15.

15 U.S. House of Representatives, Committee on Ways and Means, *Hearings, on H.R. 5664,* 73d Cong., 1st Sess. (1933), p. 118, 128.

16 U.S. Senate, Finance Committee, *Hearings, on S. 1712 and H.R. 5755,* 73d Cong., 1st Sess. (1933), p. 404–7.

17 For this quotation and those in the following paragraph see American Federation of Labor, *Proceedings,* 1934, pp. 89–91, 381 ff.

18 U.S. Senate, Finance Committee, *Hearings, on S. 79,* 74th Cong., 1st Sess. (1935), pp. 610 ff., especially p. 628.

19 *Congressional Record,* 74th Cong., 1st Sess., 79:6 (May 3, 1935), p. 6841.

20 U.S. Senate, Committee on Education and Labor, *Hearings, on S. 3055, Government Purchases and Contracts,* 74th Cong., 1st Sess. (1935).

21 *Congressional Record,* 74th Cong., 1st Sess., 79:12 (August 12, 1935), pp. 12883 ff.

22 U.S. House of Representatives, Committee on the Judiciary, *Hearings, on S. 3055,* 74th Cong., 1st Sess. (1935), Ser. 12, Part 1, p. 78; Part 2, pp. 211–21, 360–90.

23 *Congressional Record,* 74th Cong., 2d Sess., 80:9 (June 18, 1936), pp. 10002 ff.

24 Quoted from article by Ethel Johnson, "The Drive for Minimum Wage," *Current History,* Vol. 38 (September, 1933), p. 688, which gives the best account of the 1933 campaign for minimum wage.

25 *Ibid.*

26 U.S. Department of Labor, Division of Labor Standards, *Third National Conference on Labor Legislation, November, 1936,* Bull. No. 12, p. 88.

27 For the references in this and the following two paragraphs see U.S. Department of Labor, Division of Labor Standards, *Fourth National Conference on Labor Legislation, October, 1937,* Bull. No. 18, pp. 12–13, 20, 101 ff.

28 U.S. Department of Labor, Division of Labor Standards, *Second National Conference on Labor Legislation, October, 1935,* Bull. No. 3, p. 11; and *Third National Conference on Labor Legislation, November, 1936,* Bull. No. 12, pp. 79 ff.

29 American Federation of Labor, *Proceedings,* 1935, p. 397.

30 American Federation of Labor, *Proceedings,* 1936, pp. 719–22.

31 For references to hearings in this and following two paragraphs see U.S. Congress, Joint Committee, *Hearings, on S. 2475, Fair Labor Standards Act,* 75th Cong., 1st Sess. (1937), pp. 211, 219, 222, 271–308.

32 American Federation of Labor, *Proceedings,* 1937, p. 165.

33 American Federation of Labor, *Newsletter,* June 12, 1937.

34 U.S. Congress, Joint Committee, *Hearings, on S. 2475, Fair Labor Standards Act,* 75th Cong., 1st Sess. (1937), p. 286.

35 *Ibid.,* p. 948.

36 *Congressional Record,* 75th Cong., 1st Sess., 81:7 (July 30, 1937), pp. 7892, 7939, 7945.

37 *Congressional Record,* 75th Cong., 2d Sess., 82:2 (December 13–17, 1937), pp. 1484–85.

38 For quotations in this and the following paragraph see American Federation of Labor, *Proceedings,* 1937, pp. 166, 500–502.

39 *Congressional Record,* 75th Cong., 2d Sess., 82:2 (December 13–17, 1937). See especially pp. 1393, 1398, 1405, 1591–92, 1604, 1664, 1835 for the references in this and the following three paragraphs.

40 *Congressional Record,* 75th Cong., 3d Sess., 83:7 (May 23, 1938), especially pp. 7292, 7388, 7449.

41 American Federation of Labor, *Proceedings,* 1938, p. 155.

42 U.S. Senate, Committee on Labor and Public Welfare, *Hearings, on Amending the Fair Labor Standards Act,* 84th Cong., 1st Sess. (1955), pp. 110, 306, 713–52, 1473–78, 1867–71.

43 American Federation of Labor, *Proceedings,* 1941, p. 247.

7

Organized Labor and Social Security

EDWIN E. WITTE

WHETHER the New Deal is thought of as the legislative program for recovery and reform of the Roosevelt administration or as the period in American history of the first two terms of the presidency of Franklin Delano Roosevelt, social security must be accorded an important place in the New Deal story. And any account of the history of social security in the United States must give attention to labor's role in its development.

To relate accurately how and where labor figured in this important story, the entire history of social security in the United States must be sketched, followed by a detailed account of labor's role in each stage of development. It was not until after the end of the New Deal period that labor became the strongest force for the improvement of social security in the United States, but at no stage was it uninterested or its influence negligible.

Early History of Social Security

Social security was not a New Deal invention. Nearly all forms of social security now existent in the United States were in operation in western European countries for decades before they developed here. In a significant sense, our social security legislation was copied from Europe, particularly from England and Germany. But invariably the copying was with modifications, and the differences have become greater with the lapse of the years.

As in Europe, the earliest form of what is now known as social security was poor relief. In nearly every colony (and later in the territories and states) a poor law, adapted directly or indirectly from the (English) Elizabethan Poor Law of 1601, was one of the first legislative enactments. In these poor laws all people in immediate want were treated alike. They were to be provided necessary food, shelter, and clothing to sustain life, but on a basis which treated them as inferior citizens, little better than criminals.

Differentiation in the treatment of people without other means of support, in accordance with the causes of their poverty and their peculiar problems, began shortly after the Revolution. One by one, groups among the people in immediate need were distinguished, and specialized forms of public assistance were developed. Before the Great Depression which began in 1929, there had been developed in the United States, in addition to the old poor relief, aid to the needy families of veterans (soldiers' aid), aid to the needy blind (blind pensions), aid to dependent children (mothers' pensions), and old-age assistance (old-age pensions). All these programs were established by state law, but generally were locally administered and mainly locally financed. Many states, however, had no such laws, and in some states laws on the statute books were not actually operative or they were optional with the counties. In none of these programs was there any participation by the national government.

Social insurance, the other principal type of social security institutions, was of much later development than public assistance. On the national scale it began in Europe with compulsory health insurance in Germany in 1881. By the onset of the Great Depression, social insurance institutions existed in literally every European country, although no country as yet had a complete or unified social insurance system.

Some interest in social insurance was manifested in the United States in intellectual circles and by some radicals almost immediately after Germany instituted its pioneer national systems in the 1880's, and much more after the National Insurance Act of Great Britain in 1911. The American Association for Labor Legislation gave considerable attention to social insurance from its organization in 1906; in 1913 it conducted the first National Conference on Social Insurance and organized a standing committee to promote this cause.

The first form of social insurance to actually come into operation in the United States was workmen's compensation. Legislation bearing some resemblance to workmen's compensation was enacted in Maryland in 1902 and in Montana in 1909, only to be held unconstitutional. Congress enacted a workmen's compensation law for some federal employees in 1908, but this had narrow application. New York in 1910 passed a broadly-inclusive, compulsory workmen's compensation law, but this act was held unconstitutional. Finally in 1911, nine states passed elective laws and one state a compulsory law, all of which were sustained by the local courts. In the following years workmen's compensation spread rapidly. By World War I nearly all northern states had compensation laws and by 1929 all but five states, all of them except Missouri in the South. The national government enacted liberal workmen's compensation laws for three groups of employees within its jurisdiction between 1916 and 1927. In 1917 the Supreme Court of the United States upheld the constitutionality of both elective and compulsory workmen's compensation laws.

Following the widespread adoption of workmen's compensation, the American Association for Labor Legislation and other leading advocates of social insurance directed their efforts toward winning compulsory health insurance. In 1915 to 1918 more than a half-dozen states had reports favorable to health insurance by legislative study commissions. At that time it seemed probable that this form of social insurance would soon be as widely adopted in the United States as workmen's compensation. But this first health insurance movement collapsed when its opponents during World War I raised the cry "Made in Germany."

The first bill for unemployment insurance was introduced in 1916 in Massachusetts. This form of social insurance received a good deal of attention after a new type of unemployment insurance law was devised by John R. Commons in 1921 and came close to passage in Wisconsin. Variations of this proposal were introduced in Wisconsin in every legislative session of the 1920's and also in about a dozen other states, but no unemployment insurance law was enacted until Wisconsin passed its pioneer act of 1932.

Old-age and survivors' insurance was little discussed in the United States prior to the Social Security Act. However, Governor Franklin D. Roosevelt, in signing the New York old-age pension (assistance) act of 1930, put himself on record publicly as believing that a social insurance approach was needed in old-age security. Public interest in the problem of economic security in old age was great in the twenties, but was restricted to "old-age pensions," as old-age assistance was then known. Most active in promoting this interest were the Fraternal Order of Eagles and the American Association for Old Age Security, organized in 1927, which became the American Association for Social Security in 1933.

Beginning also had been made before the Great Depression in the third major type of social security legislation, social service and miscellaneous social security legislation. Important among such services are veterans' services, public employment offices, public health and medical care services, particularly for the medically indigent, vocational rehabilitation, and a variety of child health and welfare services. Most of these date from the second and third decades of the present century. Federal aid for social security purposes began in the early twenties with aid for infant and maternal health services, vocational rehabilitation, and public employment offices.

Note must be taken also of the beginnings before the New Deal of private economic security institutions: industrial pensions, health and welfare plans, voluntary health insurance, company unemployment insurance and dismissal wage plans, group insurance for employees, and still others. The first such private security programs date from the late nineteenth century, but it was in the 1920's that they became quite common and important.

Labor's Role in Social Security Before the Great Depression

The role of organized labor in the early social security developments was secondary but of some importance. Unions lacked the strength to exert a decisive influence; moreover, they gave major attention to economic rather than political activities. Not one of the social security programs originated with organized labor nor can be said to have been put over through its influence.

There was a good deal of suspicion in labor circles of workmen's compensation when it was first proposed. Many labor people, particularly labor lawyers, preferred a modified employers' liability system. Some labor organizations, for instance the Chicago Federation of Labor,[1] continued their opposition until the enactment of the first workmen's compensation laws. In most states, however, the labor unions were among the strongest supporters of the legislation. Once the laws were on the statute books, the state federations everywhere became the principal advocates of improvements.

The American Federation of Labor was an early supporter of "old-age pensions," although it was not the first or most active advocate. In conventions early in the present century, the Federation regularly voted down resolutions of the Socialist minority endorsing old-age pensions to be financed from general taxes. A little later it endorsed the "home guard" bill of Congressman William B. Wilson, later the first Secretary of Labor. This was a fanciful proposal to enroll all aged citizens in a "home guard" and pay them monthly for nonperformed services. When the more realistic old-age assistance plans made their appearance after World War I under the designation of "old-age pensions," the state federations of labor everywhere supported them, but the American Federation of Labor did not endorse such legislation until 1929.

On forms of social insurance other than workmen's compensation, the attitude of organized labor at first appeared sympathetic. Samuel Gompers and other leaders of labor were members of the executive council of the American Association for Labor Legislation. In 1915, however, Gompers took strong objection to the successful campaign conducted by that organization for the reorganization of the New York State Department of Labor, headed by an AFL member.[2] He then withdrew from the Association and denounced it as a group of "outsiders" meddling in labor matters. At the AFL convention of 1916, he denounced both compulsory health insurance and unemployment insurance. In the 1918 convention, the executive council of the AFL called for an investigation of the relations which the advocates of social insurance "may have with those interests who are opposed to the best interests of the labor movement."

That continued to be pretty much the position of the American Federation of Labor up to the Great Depression. During the depression of the early twenties, Gompers denounced unemployment insurance as a "dole" and called, instead, for the use of the credit of the national government to launch a large public works program.[3] He opposed compulsory health insurance almost as strongly, but was not supported in this position by all members of the executive council, with William Green, then secretary of the Federation, one of the dissenters.[4] A committee to study health insurance further was recommended in 1921, but as interest had waned, no further action was taken on this subject by the Federation until well into the thirties. Unemployment insurance, in contrast, was condemned in several of the executive council reports of the twenties, in lieu of which an efficient system of employment exchanges was advocated, along with the stabilization of employment by private employers.

While such was the official position of the American Federation of Labor on unemployment insurance, many affiliated state federations and international unions gave support to the bills before the state legislatures for this form of social insurance. The strongest popular support for unemployment insurance in Wisconsin, the first state to pass such a law, came from organized labor, and much the same situation developed in nearly every state where such bills made their appearance.

Social Security in the Early Years of the Depression

The Great Depression which began in 1929 profoundly affected the development of social security in the United States. One of its most striking effects was an enormous increase in relief expenditures—a hundredfold increase in many areas by the middle thirties as compared with the 1920's. It became simply impossible for a majority of local governments to continue alone to shoulder this burden, which often exceeded their total tax levies. First the state governments, beginning with New York in 1931, and then the national government had to come to the rescue. The first national relief act, passed in July, 1932, during the Hoover administration, provided for loans to the states, by the Reconstruction Finance Corporation, for relief purposes—repayment of which was later cancelled. This was followed in the next year, at the beginning of the Roosevelt administration, by legislation setting up a Federal Emergency Relief Administration and providing for outright grants to the states for this purpose. The FERA was terminated in 1935, but was succeeded by the WPA (Works Progress Administration). At that time the national government withdrew from all participation in direct relief, a policy continued to this day. Through the WPA, the national government bore the largest part of the costs of relief for the unemployed from 1935 through 1941. It also operated a number of other emergency public assistance programs for selected groups of the many millions of people in distress—the CWA, CCC, NYA, FSA, food stamp plan, and still others. Altogether, the national government spent more than 16 billion dollars for relief purposes from 1932 to 1941—its largest expenditures in this period other than loans to distressed business corporations, farmers, and homeowners, which, unlike the relief expenditures, were mainly repaid.

Thanks to the large governmental expenditures, starvation, impairment of health, and permanent damage to morale were avoided, but the experience of being unemployed and on relief was one few people found satisfying. While no exact statistics are available, it appears that at least one-third of all American families were on relief at one time or another during the depression. The immense total of the relief expenditures and the growing national debt caused great alarm among taxpayers. About everybody looked for some better way of meeting the unemployment and consequent relief problems than poor relief and the quickly concocted emergency programs. The British unemployment insurance system, widely ridiculed in this country in the twenties, became popular almost overnight. It then was apparent that the worst forms of the dole were in the United States, and the British unemployment insurance system seemed a vastly preferable method of meeting the economic consequences of widespread unemployment. As the depression continued, many realized that unemployment insurance alone could not meet the situation, but even so it was recognized to be a valuable first line of defense against this great hazard. At the same time, the need for institutions to provide economic security in old age became much more widely recognized. An abnormally large percentage of the old people were on the relief rolls, and older people, once they had lost their jobs, found it quite impossible to get others. At this time, too, appeared the extensive studies of the Committee on the Costs of Medical Care, financed by foundations but suggested by President Hoover and headed by Secretary of the Interior Wilbur. These studies established that millions of Americans did not receive the volume and quality of the medical care which the medical schools and all good practitioners deem necessary to be adequate.

In the legislative sessions of 1931, unemployment insurance bills were introduced in seventeen states; in 1933 in twenty-five states and in Congress for the District of Columbia. Six states in 1931 created legislative commissions to study unemployment insurance, and several more were established by governors. An Interstate Commission on Unemployment representing six major northeastern states was established in this year on the initiative of Governor Roosevelt. This Interstate Commission and the study commissions in six states, either in 1932 or 1933, reported in favor of the immediate enactment of unemployment insurance laws. The Democratic national platform of 1932 included a pledge for "unemployment insurance through state action" as well as for "old-age pensions." But only Wisconsin in 1932 enacted an unemployment insurance law, and in 1933 it postponed the beginning of the collection of contributions until July 1, 1934. The principal argument against such legislation was that any state going it alone would handicap its employers in interstate competition.

Several proposals to overcome this difficulty through federal action made their appearance at this time, but none was adopted prior to the enactment of the Social Security Act. As early as 1928 a Senate subcommittee headed by Senator Couzens conducted hearings on the advisability of tax concessions to encourage employers to stabilize their employment. A more comprehensive study of unemployment insurance was undertaken in 1931 at the initiative of Senator Wagner by a special Senate investigating committee. This committee in June, 1932, endorsed the enactment of "unemployment reserves" legislation by the states, but divided upon how the national government should promote such legislation through tax concessions. Significantly, practically everybody at this time deemed a federal system of unemployment insurance to be unconstitutional. Following the 1932 committee report, Senator Wagner introduced several bills for financial and other aid to the states to encourage them to enact unemployment insurance legislation, none of which was even accorded a hearing.

Early in 1934 a new proposal, the Wagner-Lewis bill, was presented in Congress, which the author believes originated with Supreme Court Justice Louis D. Brandeis.[5] This measure proposed the levy of a federal tax on the payrolls of employers of labor throughout the country, against which an offset (credit) would be allowed for amounts paid by the subject employers into state unemployment insurance funds. Hearings on this bill were conducted by a subcommittee of the House Ways and Means Committee in the early spring of 1934. Most of the witnesses, including, among others, William Green, president of the American Federation of Labor, Secretary of Labor Perkins, such "experts" on the subject as Abraham Epstein, Paul Douglas, and John B. Andrews, and a goodly number of "progressive" employers, endorsed the bill. So did President Roosevelt in a public letter to Chairman Doughton. Opposition was manifested only on the grounds that industry would not be able to stand the extra burden until recovery had progressed further, and that the necessity of having to liquidate reserves when unemployment became widespread would increase the seriousness of the depression. No report was made by the subcommittee, but the Wagner-Lewis bill may well be regarded as the first stage in the development of the Social Security Act of 1935.

In contrast with the failure to get unemployment insurance legislation on the statute books except in one state, very considerable progress was made in the early depression years in old-age security legislation. The number of states with old-age assistance laws increased from seven in 1928 to twenty-seven in 1933. The first bill for federal aid to the states for old-age assistance, sponsored by the American Association for Social Security, made its appearance in 1932. This Dill-Connery bill passed the House of Representatives in both 1933 and 1934 and also won favorable reports from a Senate committee but did not come to a vote in that house.

Noteworthy among the developments of these years, also, was the change in the position of the American Federation of Labor on unemployment insurance. Unemployment insurance was a major subject of debate in both the 1930 and 1931 Federation conventions. In both conventions positions unfavorable to unemployment insurance taken by the resolutions committee and the executive council were endorsed, but some important leaders expressed views to the contrary. In 1932 there was again extended discussion of the subject, but on this occasion the executive council took a position in favor of unemployment insurance to be "paid by management as a part of the costs of production," which was approved unanimously by the convention. President Green followed up this convention action by bringing together a group of university people to make recommendations on an unemployment insurance bill to be suggested for enactment by the states.[6]

At this conference, differences developed along the lines of the controversy which divided the supporters of unemployment insurance during the following years. In the 1920's all advocates of unemployment insurance stressed the differences between the then unpopular British system and the American proposals, emphasizing that the latter were designed to reduce unemployment and not merely to provide compensation. After enactment, early in 1932, of the Wisconsin law and the promulgation later in the same year of the "Ohio Plan" by the study commission of that state, a bitter controversy developed over "pooled funds" versus "individual employer reserves" and over variations in contribution rates in accordance with the employer's employment record. This controversy was more emotional than factual,[7] but served to delay the enactment of unemployment insurance legislation and was an obstacle in the preparation and passage of the Social Security Act.

At this time, the AFL avoided commitments on the type of unemployment insurance law that should be enacted, except that it insisted that employers alone should be required to contribute. On numerous occasions, both before and after its change of position on unemployment insurance, it called for the stabilization of employment. In 1934 it supported the Wagner-Lewis bill and President Green took the position that unemployment insurance serves two purposes: (1) the stimulation of more regular employment, and (2) the payment of unemployment compensation to those temporarily out of work.[8]

Development and Passage of the Social Security Act

In the spring of 1934 both the Wagner-Lewis and the Dill-Connery bills were before Congress. The President had publicly endorsed the first of these bills and administration leaders were supporting the second. But there was a good deal of feeling that both measures needed to be modified in important respects and also that a more comprehensive approach to social security was called for.

This entire matter was discussed at a Cabinet meeting late in May.[9] At this meeting it was decided that no further attempt should be made in that Congress to secure the enactment of social security legislation but that the administration would present a comprehensive social security program at the opening of the next Congress, to be elected in November. A promise to this effect was made by President Roosevelt in the first of his social security messages, on June 8, 1934. In this message, the President said that the administration would in January, 1935, present to Congress a comprehensive program for the protection of individuals and families on the occurrence of the personal hazards of life. He promised further that this program would include both unemployment insurance and old-age security and that health insurance and all other institutions for protection against the personal hazards of life would be thoroughly studied, with a view to determining whether they should be included in the administration's program. To this end the President further announced that he was setting up a Committee on Economic Security to study the entire problem and to make recommendations to him on the program to be presented to Congress.

The complete story of the development of the administration's program [10] lies beyond the scope of this chapter. Labor's role was still a secondary one. Suffice it to record that the President, early in July, by executive order, established the Committee on Economic Security, consisting of five top Cabinet members, with Miss Perkins, Secretary of Labor, as chairman. The Committee had a staff of less than fifty research, statistical, and actuarial employees, who included, however, a majority of all people in the country who were considered to be specialists on any aspect of social security. In addition, there were nine advisory committees, composed of people (not on the staff) interested in some or all of the problems with which the Committee had to deal. The most important of these advisory committees was the Technical Board, composed of government officials and employees, headed by Arthur J. Altmeyer, then an Assistant Secretary of Labor. This Board, acting as a group and through subcommittees, kept in close touch with the staff and the Committee on every phase of its work and probably had more to do with the final recommendations than any other group or individual not a member of the Committee. More publicized but distinctly less important was the Advisory Council on Social Security, appointed by the President and composed of people representing leading nongovernmental organizations interested in social security. The other seven advisory committees were more specialized, concerned with specific problems or aspects of the social security program. There was also a two-day National Conference on Economic Security, attended by several hundred men and women from all parts of the country, at which specialists not otherwise connected with the Committee presented differing views on major social security problems. Literally almost everyone in the country who ever had discussed any aspect of social security had some part in the work of the Committee on Economic Security, although all decisions reached were those of the Committee.

Early in the functioning of the Committee on Economic Security, the President asked it to present its recommendations by December 1, so that he would have time to make his own decisions before Congress was scheduled to convene. It was not quite able to keep this schedule, but on December 24 it informally presented its principal recommendations orally to the President and followed this within a few weeks by its final report and the draft of an administration bill. Both were approved by the President, with an understanding that the Committee would present an amendment during the congressional consideration of the bill making old-age insurance fully self-financed. Both the report and the administration bill were sent to Congress with the President's endorsement in a special message on January 17, 1935.

Labor had relatively little to do with the development of the administration's social security program. The American Federation of Labor had four representatives on the Advisory Council on Social Security, one of whom was William Green. These representatives took only a minor part in the deliberations of the Advisory Council. Thomas Kennedy of the United Mine Workers was a speaker at the National Conference on Economic Security, in which he advocated a federal system of unemployment insurance. The executive director and members of the staff of the Committee on Economic Security consulted Federation officers informally on several occasions. But that was just about all of the direct participation by labor in the development of the administration's social security program. Organized labor then had no staff people specializing in social security and its leaders had too many other duties to give much attention to the details of the program. It was assumed by just about everybody, however, that whatever the administration might propose, labor would go along with it, so long as it assured increased protection against the personal hazards of life.

In his message of January 17, the President urged that Congress act promptly on the administration's proposals, as they called for state action after Congress had acted and the state legislatures would be in session only for a few months. Pursuant to this request, both houses promptly began hearings on the administration bill and these were concluded within a few weeks, after which the House Ways and Means Committee immediately began consideration of the measure in executive session. But then the bill bogged down. It was not until late in March that the Ways and Means Committee favorably reported a substitute for the administration bill. This substitute passed, after extended debate and consideration of many amendments, on April 19, by a vote of 371 to 33. Thereafter there was further delay before the Senate Finance Committee acted upon the measure, and for a considerable time it seemed doubtful whether that Committee would act favorably upon the proposed federal old-age insurance system—which by the time of congressional consideration had become the most debated part of the social security program, in contrast with the earlier major interest in unemployment insurance. However, late in May, the Senate Finance Committee by a narrow majority favorably reported the House bill, with relatively minor amendments.[11] Then on June 19, the Senate passed the bill, with only six votes in opposition, although only after it had adopted the Clark amendment. This amendment, which would have exempted employers with industrial pension plans, was strongly opposed by the administration, as it would pretty much have wrecked the federal old-age insurance program. During the next six weeks in which the bill was in conference, each house insisted on the position it had taken on the Clark amendment. Finally, in August, the Senate conferees yielded and the conference report was approved by both houses, without a roll call vote. The President signed the Social Security Act on August 14, 1935, and under its terms it was immediately to become effective. But it was then so late in the session that when Senator Huey Long staged the longest of his filibusters it was impossible for the Senate to act on the bill providing money for social security purposes. The President promptly appointed the members of the Social Security Board, but it had no appropriation until February, 1936.

As the legislative history establishes, the large majorities ultimately mustered for the Social Security Act are deceptive. Actually it had a close call in Congress, particularly with respect to old-age insurance. This was due to many factors, among them concern about placing new financial burdens on industry, division of opinion on details of the program among "experts," growing restlessness in Congress over "administration dictation," and, above all, the Townsend Plan. Advocated as a measure to end the depression, this was a proposal for pensions of $200 per month for everybody over 60, to be spent within the month. It originated with southern California promoters and did not become a proposal for action by the national government until after President Roosevelt's social security message of June 8, 1934. But then the idea spread like wildfire in all parts of the country, and while the social security measure was before Congress in 1935 its members were deluged with letters, telegrams, and petitions for the Townsend Plan. Although there were few members who thought this proposal at all possible, the great support it appeared to have among older citizens made many hesitant to vote for the moderate administration bill. Whether the bill would have passed without the President's insistence and intelligent administration leadership in Congress is doubtful.

Labor's role at this stage was still secondary, although more important than when the administration's program was being developed. William Green testified before the congressional committees in both houses. He confined his testimony entirely to unemployment insurance, urging action on this subject but criticizing the administration's proposals on two major grounds. He urged that Congress increase the employer contribution rates to 5 per cent and that the Act should prescribe quite in detail what the state laws must provide. The counsel of the AFL was the only other labor witness and he reiterated what Green had said.

At that time labor was greatly dissatisfied with the administration's WPA bill, which, in a sense, was a companion measure to the Social Security bill. Its concern was that there were not sufficient safeguards against having the WPA projects replace normal public works projects, and it feared that the program would operate to lower wage rates. Bitter debate developed over the WPA proposal and it was not until this bill was out of the way that the Senate would act on the social security measure.

At the crucial stage, before the vote in the Senate, William Green made it clear that the American Federation of Labor wanted the House bill passed, and its lobbyist did some work among the members to bring about this result. Throughout the long battle over the Clark amendment, the AFL consistently opposed exempting companies with industrial pension plans from the old-age insurance system.

The American Federation of Labor also gave valuable support to the social security program through its vigorous opposition to radical proposals, which Paul Douglas has described as "thunder from the left." [12] One of these was the "Lundeen bill," which under various titles and with different authors was before Congress from 1934 to 1936. Usually referred to as an "unemployment insurance bill," it proposed that full compensation should be paid from the United States Treasury on the occurrence of any of the personal hazards of life to workers, farmers, and self-employed persons, with the funds to be raised through a tax on large incomes and estates. A nationwide campaign was put on by left-wing groups for endorsements of this measure by labor unions, farmers' organizations, councils of the unemployed, etc. Some local unions affiliated with the AFL adopted resolutions endorsing the Lundeen bill, but when the Federation realized what was going on, it denounced the proposal as a Communist-sponsored measure designed to block, rather than promote, social security. Early in March, 1935, at a slimly attended meeting, the House Labor Committee endorsed this bill by a majority of one. But that is as far as it got, as it never had a chance of getting on the House calendar. Communists continued for another year to make as great a noise for this bill as they could, but, thanks to labor's clear denunciation, the "thunder" for this measure never became more than a tinpan disharmony, which fooled scarcely anyone.

The Townsend Plan had much more genuine support, including many endorsements from bona fide unions and leaders of labor. Most serious was the fact that many members of Congress made pledges to the Townsend organization, which most of them hoped they would never be called upon to fulfill, but which also made them hesitant to vote for any other social security measure. The Social Security bill came up in the House of Representatives in 1935 under an open rule, which made it inevitable that the Townsend Plan had to be voted on as an amendment to the committee bill. That was done by a division, not a roll call vote, in which 50 votes were cast for the Townsend Plan among the 435 members. In every subsequent Congress some version of the Townsend Plan was introduced, and discharge petitions were circulated to withdraw this measure from committee and bring it up for a vote on the floor. On several occasions these discharge petitions lacked only a few signatures, which, however, were never forthcoming. Considerable actual, although clearly minority, support for this measure existed in Congress in the years immediately following the enactment of the Social Security Act, and there are Townsend Clubs to this day.

The American Federation of Labor never took an official position on the Townsend Plan, but at all times its most influential members regarded it as chimerical. Its executive committee, on at least one occasion, referred to this plan as "a rainbow pot of gold," contrasted with the substantial benefits under the Social Security Act. Organized labor is entitled to much credit for at all times making its influence felt against impossible proposals labeled as programs for social security.

Developments in the Early Years Under the Social Security Act

For nearly two years after the Social Security Act became law, serious doubts continued to exist about its ever coming into full operation. For the first six months there was no appropriation from Congress for putting into effect any part of the Act. During this period the Social Security Board had only personnel loaned by other agencies and no funds whatsoever for payment of any of the federal aids to the states for social security purposes. After appropriations were made, grave doubts regarding the constitutionality both of the old-age insurance program and of the provisions for unemployment insurance continued to prevail. These doubts were not resolved until the Supreme Court in May, 1937, upheld both of these major programs. Political opposition to the legislation became much stronger than it had been before its passage, coming both from radical groups and from commercial insurance and other business interests. This opposition reached its peak in the presidential election of 1936, in which the Republican candidate took a position of outright opposition to almost the entire program. Even after the Republican defeat, business organizations determinedly fought for a reduction in the contribution rates in the federal old-age insurance program, while the Townsend Plan manifested its greatest strength in the congressional elections of 1938.

As nearly all of the 1935 state legislative sessions had adjourned by the time the Social Security Act was passed and promised federal aid actually was not available, not much progress was made in the enactment of necessary supplemental state legislation until after Congress made appropriations for this purpose in February, 1936. Thereafter, state after state acted in special sessions, and by 1937 nearly every state had qualified for federal aid under every program for which aid was provided in the Social Security Act.

While the Social Security Act was still before Congress, the Committee on Economic Security prepared several alternative drafts of model state unemployment insurance bills. Six states enacted laws before passage of the federal act and another did so within a month thereafter, as did Congress for the District of Columbia. In the more than a year prior to the election of 1936 only six more states were added to those having unemployment insurance laws. The attack made by the Republican candidate on the Social Security Act and its vigorous defense by the President and his supporters made that election something of a referendum on the legislation. Because the taxes on employers for 1936 became payable in March, 1937, and because only contributions paid to state unemployment insurance funds before the end of 1936 could be offset against them,[13] a veritable rush developed to get approved state laws into effect. In the last six weeks of 1936, more than twenty states passed unemployment insurance laws in special sessions. In a few states, notably Illinois, the manufacturers' association, relying upon legal advice that the federal law would be held unconstitutional, was able to delay action until the Supreme

Court held otherwise. By the end of the summer of 1937, literally every state had an approved unemployment insurance law, under which contributions were collected from the year 1936 on and benefits became payable, in the last states, in January, 1939.

More than any other social security program, old-age insurance was under attack in the first years of the Social Security Act. There had been little popular support for this program, which owed its enactment principally to the fear that noncontributory old-age assistance would become financially run-away, unless it was supplemented by a contributory insurance program. The entire concept of minimum necessary support only, of course, was not satisfactory to the Townsend Plan supporters. Many of the staunch advocates of social security felt that the old-age insurance program was seriously defective in not providing for contributions from general tax funds, retirement benefits before 1942, and survivors', dependents', and invalidity benefits. But most serious of all was the attack, made by insurance men and business organizations, on the financing of old-age insurance, centering in the slogan "pay-as-you-go." This popular slogan was used to justify a reduction in contribution (tax) rates because the total tax collections in the early years of the system greatly exceeded the total benefits paid, although far below the true costs of the promised benefits.

The many criticisms of the old-age insurance program, particularly the outcry about large and misused reserves, led the Senate Finance Committee to suggest an advisory committee to restudy the subject. This advisory committee of 1937–38, whose chairman was J. Douglas Brown of Princeton, was constituted of people not connected with the administration of old-age insurance, representing industry, labor, and about every other shade of opinion, except for the extreme radicals.[14] After many meetings and wide disagreements, this committee arrived at a report signed by every member, but with indicated dissents from some recommendations by some members—principally industry and insurance company representatives. All members joined in a clean-cut statement that the program established by the Social Security Act involved neither misuse of funds nor double taxation. All members also favored beginning payment of retirement benefits on January 1, 1940 (two years earlier than originally contemplated), increasing the benefits payable during the early years of the system, adding wives', widows', and children's benefits, limiting death benefits, and reducing promised benefits in future years unless the national income should increase sufficiently to warrant larger benefits. All members also concurred that provision of benefits to persons permanently and totally disabled before attaining retirement age "is socially desirable," but the final report indicated disagreement over whether such disability benefits should be introduced immediately. There was complete agreement on the extension of coverage to substantially all employees, including farm workers and domestics and the employees of nonprofit organizations. All members also were in agreement that full reserve financing was not feasible,[15] but that the inevitable large increase in total benefit costs in future years should be anticipated and a plan of financing adopted which would insure that adequate funds would always be at hand to pay all promised benefits. All concurred in the recommendation that tripartite financing of old-age and survivors' insurance should be introduced, with regular contributions from general tax funds, rendering unnecessary an increase in the ultimately contemplated combined tax rate of 6 per cent. The sharpest division developed over the question whether the increase in contribution rates to a combined 3 per cent provided in the original law to take effect in 1939 should be eliminated. By a majority of more than two to one, the advisory council rejected any reduction in tax rates, but suggested that the entire problem of the necessary contribution rates be restudied before the further increase in contribution rates to a combined 4 per cent was to go into effect in 1942. The dissent of some members from the recommendation that there should be no reduction in contribution rates was noted, but these members signed the report along with all others. Unlike other members, however, they did not feel that they were bound to support the recommendations of the report (which represented a compromise on many issues) and continued to agitate for the positions they had taken originally. As the Congress elected in 1938 was much more conservative than any other of the New Deal period, the dissenting members of the advisory council had more influence on the Social Security Act amendments of 1939 than did the majority.

The 1939 amendments amount to a pretty complete revision of the original old-age insurance program. Old-age insurance became old-age and survivors' insurance. Benefits for dependent survivors, as well as for the wives over sixty-five and for the children of primary beneficiaries, were added to the original retirement benefits. The time of the beginning of benefit payments was advanced to January 1, 1940.[16] The benefits of workers in the system only a short time before reaching retirement age were increased quite substantially. But the total benefit costs over time were not increased. This apparent miracle was accomplished by cutting out most lump-sum payments, reducing the future benefits of long time contributors, and more than all else, by changing the eligibility conditions so that millions of people who were subject to the old-age and survivors' insurance taxes were cut off from all prospect of benefits. Instead of broadening the coverage of the system, Congress narrowed coverage by extending the agricultural exemption. It never gave real consideration to the recommendation that the government should pay a part of the costs from general tax funds; instead, the 1939 Act eliminated the contribution to old-age insurance from the Treasury involved in the provision of the original law under which the government paid 3 per cent interest (considerably above the average rate on the public debt) on the special securities in which the reserve of the old-age insurance fund was invested. Despite the failure to provide for government contributions, Congress initiated the first of the many tax freezes, which kept the combined contribution rates of employers and employees at 2 per cent until 1950.

The 1939 amendments were acclaimed as a very great improvement over the original program for old-age insurance. Today, it is generally recognized that not all changes made were improvements. Few people now regard the narrowing of coverage to have been desirable. More serious was the reduction in contribution rates, occurring as it did just a few weeks before the start of World War II. The lowering of the contribution rates had the effect of increasing by many billions the actuarial deficit in the old-age and survivors' insurance fund and the levies which will have to be made in the future years. And this occurred at a time when in the prevailing war and postwar prosperity the original higher rates would have produced no hardship and would have had the wholesome effect of keeping down inflation. Worst of all was the stiffening of eligibility conditions, the effects of which became progressively worse as the years elapsed.

Offsetting the features of the 1939 amendments which the author deems unsound were many changes which have stood the test of time. Among these were the two-year-earlier start of retirement benefits, the increase of benefits in the early years of the Act, and above all, provision for survivors' benefits and for benefits to some dependents. On balance, the gains more than offset the losses, particularly as they have proved enduring while the unsound policies have since been reversed.

Clearer than the improvement through legislative changes in the early years under the Social Security Act was the excellent administration of the federal old-age and survivors' insurance program. When the law was passed there were many doubts whether it would prove possible to keep straight the records of the many tens of millions of Americans with credits in the system. There was also fear that the workers would resent having to contribute to the costs of a program from which most of them would get no direct benefits for many years. Worker opposition never developed, and confusion of records has never become a problem. Administration costs from the outset were much lower than anyone had hoped for or than those in any form of private insurance.

The other major social insurance program, unemployment insurance, also was well established and in at least reasonably successful operation in every state by the end of the New Deal period. The payment of unemployment insurance benefits began in most states during the sharp business dip of 1937–38, which interrupted recovery from the Great Depression. The laws of many states were such that over a million workers then unemployed became immediately eligible for benefits. Many states were poorly prepared to assume the administrative burden involved and the federal administration gave them little aid. The consequence was that in some states, notably New York, considerable confusion and delay developed in the payment of unemployment insurance. But most states met the challenge and even in New York payments were being made promptly by the fall of 1938.

In the early years of unemployment compensation, bitter controversies continued to be waged over the provisions of the state laws. The old controversy among the advocates of unemployment insurance in the period before most of the state laws were enacted over "pooled fund" versus "reserve" plans was replaced by the more realistic issue of merit or experience rating. Other issues involved federalization of unemployment insurance and federally prescribed standards in the state laws. On experience rating, a sharp cleavage developed between industry and labor and between the federal and the state people concerned with the administration of unemployment insurance. By the end of the New Deal period, the battle over this issue had not yet been finally decided although experience rating was definitely in the ascendancy. By 1941, thirty-eight states had provisions for experience rating in their unemployment insurance laws. In Congress, the McCormack bill, making experience rating impossible, came close to passage in 1939. After its defeat, the opponents of experience rating placed their main reliance upon the substitution of a federal system of unemployment insurance for the federal-state system provided for in the Social Security Act. This issue did not come to a head until the World War II period, following the taking over of the public employment office by the national government after Pearl Harbor.

As has been noted, with the enactment of the Works Progress Act of 1935, which in administration thinking was a companion measure to the Social Security Act, the national government withdrew from all participation in direct relief. But in the WPA and other work relief programs, the national government continued to carry the largest part of the relief costs until our entrance into World War II.

In this period, also, the national government carried, as it has done ever since, a large part of the expenditures under the three specialized public assistance programs for which the Social Security Act provided federal aid: old-age assistance, aid to dependent children, and aid to the blind. Within a year after federal aid actually became available, practically every state had qualified for such aid. Under varying state laws, these forms of public assistance were in full operation everywhere in the United States for several years prior to the end of the New Deal period. All types of public assistance costs combined continued to be very great, reaching peaks in 1936 and again in 1938. Both in amounts and still more as a percentage of national income, public assistance expenditures were far greater in the second half of the 1930's than at any time since. Because the national government assumed the major part of those costs, however, the United States got through the depression period without serious impairment of the health, efficiency, and morale of its population, as was demonstrated in the succeeding war period.

In the years immediately following enactment of the Social Security Act, there seemed to be fair prospects for the extension of social insurance into a new major field, health security. Health insurance was studied thoroughly by a group of staff experts of the Committee on Economic Security, flanked by its medical advisory committee, among whose members were the presidents of the major medical organizations. When the Committee on Economic Security had to make its report to the President and the Congress, this group was not ready with its recommendations. So the Committee merely recommended further study of the subject—a recommendation which led the American Medical Association to charge the administration with some devious plan to secretly foist socialized medicine on the nation. Later, when the congressional consideration of the Social Security Act was nearly completed, the staff presented a report for the establishment of compulsory health insurance through state action, on the same basis as unemployment insurance. This recommendation was endorsed by the Committee on Economic Security, but was never presented to Congress because the President felt that, coming at that stage, the proposal would only endanger the entire social security program.

Almost immediately after passage of the Social Security Act, the President created the Interdepartmental Committee to Coördinate Health and Welfare Activities, with Miss Josephine Roche, Under-Secretary of the Treasury, as chairman. The Interdepartmental Committee in 1938 sponsored a National Health Conference and thereafter presented a report to the President stressing the need for a national health program and making recommendation for legislation. These recommendations contemplated federal leadership in a unified attack on a coöperative basis by the national and state governments on the nation's health problems. It called for large federal aids to the states, which they might utilize in many different ways, including extensive public health and medical care programs, disability compensation, and health insurance.

These recommendations were incorporated in a bill introduced in the 1939 Congress by Senator Wagner. This bill met bitter opposition from the American Medical Association and never had the slightest chance in Congress, not even being accorded a hearing. The New Deal period ended without any health insurance legislation being enacted either nationally or in the states. But voluntary health insurance, particularly hospital insurance, really got started at this time.

Social Security Developments in the War and Postwar Periods

The above will suffice to complete the general account of social security in what may be called the formative period for the present-day social security institutions of the United States. To appraise the impact of social security on labor and vice versa, however, a sketch of the general development of social security in the United States since then seems necessary.

During World War II, social security received only slight consideration from the Congress and the American public. A long report of the National Resources Planning Board on *Security, Work, and Relief Policies* was publicized as an American Beveridge Plan. But this report did not catch on, not even a bill being introduced to put its recommendations into operation. In the next session (1943) and for several years thereafter, a comprehensive measure for the revision of the nation's social security program was introduced, known as the Wagner-Dingell bill, which provided for something like a unified social insurance system, extension of old-age and survivors' insurance, federalization of unemployment insurance, and a national health program including compulsory health insurance. Although reportedly favored by the Social Security Board and the administration, it was not endorsed publicly by the President and was never accorded a hearing.

As early as the enactment of the Selective Service Act in 1940, the President recommended that the men called to service be protected in their rights in the OASI system. But Congress did nothing until 1946, when it made the survivors of deceased servicemen eligible for survivors' insurance benefits, and it was not until the Social Security Act amendments of 1950 that provision was made for counting all time spent with the colors as covered employment. Congress in 1944, however, enacted the generous G.I. Rights bill which included unemployment insurance allowances for discharged servicemen and greatly extended public health services for veterans and their dependents. During the Korean War similar legislation was enacted for the veterans of that war. In the Social Security Act of 1956 this was replaced by coverage of all men serving with the colors on substantially the same basis as civilian employees.

Under the Social Security Act amendments of 1939 old-age and survivors' insurance benefits first became payable on January 1, 1940. No major changes in old-age and survivors' insurance were made thereafter until 1950. In the 1940's, amendments freezing old-age insurance tax rates were passed every three years and coverage was further slightly narrowed. The conditions for eligibility introduced in 1939 operated more restrictively with each advancing year and the unchanged benefit formulas resulted in smaller real benefits because of the wartime and still greater postwar inflation. Congress, however, increased the federal aid for old-age assistance, creating a situation in which needy old people who had made no contributions to the costs of their benefits received more, on the average, than the beneficiaries in the contributory old-age insurance system. These inequities resulted in the organization of the Social Security Advisory Council of 1947–48 by the Senate Committee on Finance of the Eightieth Congress. This Advisory Council, composed largely of businessmen, made recommendations for many improvements. The Eightieth Congress did nothing with these recommendations, but they became the basis for the Social Security Act amendments of 1950 enacted by the Eighty-first Congress.

The 1950 amendments broadened coverage to include most employees and also most of the self-employed other than farmers and some of the professional groups. This legislation restored easy conditions for eligibility and increased benefits somewhat more than enough to offset the decline in the purchasing power of the dollar. At the same time contribution rates were increased to again make old-age and survivors' insurance fully self-financed. The Social Security Act amendments of 1952 further increased benefits, both in old-age and survivors' insurance and in old-age assistance, by another $5 per month. The Social Security Act amendments of 1954 made greater changes, increasing the coverage of the old-age and survivors' insurance system by 7 million persons, particularly the farmers,[17] and providing for modest increases both in benefits and in contribution rates. In 1956 Congress changed the old-age and survivors' insurance system quite fundamentally by including benefits for the permanently and totally disabled from age fifty on and by lowering the age for eligibility to benefits of women from sixty-five to sixty-two, but retaining the feature of lower benefits for women than for men. While the several amending acts of the 1950's have greatly improved the old-age insurance system, its general framework to this day remains that of the original Act of 1935 and the Social Security Act amendments of 1939.

As regards unemployment insurance, the predominating factor since our direct involvement in World War II has been the economic condition of near full employment. Despite a few setbacks, unemployment has been much smaller than was thought possible in the 1930's. Unemployment reserve funds (except recently in Alaska) have proven more than sufficient, despite the adoption of experience rating in all states, which has resulted in low average employer contribution rates. Although this feature of the unemployment insurance laws and the related questions of the federalization of unemployment insurance and of federal standards with which the state laws would have to be put into compliance continued to be hotly debated in the 1940's, there never was any doubt after the New Deal period about the continuance of unemployment insurance. Considerable publicity in the postwar years about frauds committed by claimants in some metropolitan areas resulted only in some tightening of administrative rules.

In the 1950's, discussion of unemployment insurance has centered around the meagerness of compensation benefits and the numerous and increasing disqualifications. While benefits have been frequently increased in most states, so that they have more than kept pace with the decreasing value of the dollar, they today represent a smaller percentage of average wages than when first enacted—a consequence of the great increase in wages. This situation led President Eisenhower to appeal with some success to the states, both in 1954 and 1955, to increase unemployment insurance benefits. Considerable progress also has been made in the extension of coverage of unemployment insurance, through making the federal employment tax applicable to employees of the national government under the state systems. Unemployment insurance remains the most controversial of the existing social insurance programs, but with little likelihood of fundamental changes in the near future.

For the third major social insurance program, workmen's compensation, the recent story is similar. Workmen's compensation has always been exclusively a state responsibility, except for employees under federal jurisdiction. Until fairly recently workmen's compensation enjoyed almost universal approval. In the 1950's, however, it has come under heavy fire from labor and investigators of its operations on the score of illiberality of benefits and legalistic administration. No strong sentiment, however, has developed for federalization of workmen's compensation and only extremists have suggested that the workers would be better off under the old employer's liability system of compensation for industrial injuries. But the railroad employees have preferred to remain under the modified liability system for injuries occurring in interstate commerce which Congress established as long ago as 1908.

In the several public assistance programs, the most important development of the war and postwar years has been a decline in the percentage of Americans receiving assistance. This has been a result of good employment conditions and, more directly, of the rapid increase in the 1950's of the number of old-age and survivors' insurance beneficiaries. Despite marked increases in benefits, the total costs of the assistance programs have increased only slightly. Proposals to provide federal aid for general assistance, strongly urged by the social workers after the enactment of the Social Security Act, failed to get congressional approval. On the other hand, the federal aid in the specialized public assistance programs has several times been increased and broadened. A new program was launched in the Social Security Act amendments of 1950, aid to the permanently and totally disabled, and has since been put into operation in three-fourths of the states. A new federal aid program was provided for in the Social Security Act amendments of 1956 under which the national government will bear part of the costs of necessary medical and hospital care for the recipients of public assistance and the "medically indigent"—people who, although generally self-supporting, need help with doctor and hospital bills, when serious illness strikes their families.

During the immediate postwar years, the most discussed social security subject was compulsory health insurance. President Truman, unlike President Roosevelt, boldly endorsed this form of social insurance. But despite administration support, compulsory health insurance never got beyond the hearing stage. The American Medical Association branded compulsory health insurance "socialized medicine" and launched a most effective advertising and lobbying campaign against the proposal. In 1951, the administration shifted its ground, bringing forward what was known as the Ewing plan for hospital insurance for people covered in the OASI system. But this, too, was "socialized medicine" to the American Medical Association and got little consideration in Congress. In its uncompromising opposition to all forms of compulsory health insurance, the AMA has been greatly aided by the rapid growth of voluntary forms of health insurance since the close of World War II. Tending in the same direction was the development in the 1940's of cash sickness compensation, now more commonly called "disability insurance." Rhode Island in 1942, California, New Jersey, and New York, and the national government (for railroad men) enacted laws by 1949 providing for partial compensation for wage loss resulting from nonindustrial illness. Since then no state has enacted a disability insurance law and in the last years there has been a slowing up in the growth of the most widely prevalent form of voluntary health insurance, hospital insurance. But American public opinion is still strongly opposed to any sort of governmental compulsion in insurance protection against the economic costs of illness. Even the very mild proposal of President Eisenhower for a national system of reinsurance of voluntary health insurance plans, presented to Congress both in 1954 and in 1955, never got out of committee, despite the popularity of the President. On the other hand, each Congress since the close of World War II has provided some new form of federal aid for public health and medical care services.

Labor's Role in Social Security in the Past Twenty Years

Organized labor's role in the developments of the early years under the Social Security Act was considerably greater than in the period of the passage of the legislation, although it can scarcely be described as a role of leadership. In those years of rapid growth in membership and collective agreements and of the AFL-CIO split, unions, their officials, representatives, and employees had so many things to do that social security could be given only limited attention. Neither federation nor any international unions, as yet, had any social security staff. Both federations organized committees on social security, constituted of important union leaders, which watched developments on both the administrative and legislative levels and adopted and publicized views on social security subjects.

Six union officials (three from each federation) represented organized labor on the twenty-seven–member Social Security Advisory Council of 1937–38. These representatives played an even lesser role in the work of this Advisory Council than labor had had in the development of the original Social Security Act, most of them not even attending meetings. They all signed the majority report, and in the hearings on the Social Security Act amendments of 1939 the labor people who testified generally supported the administration bill. Despite their mutual distrust and rivalry, the AFL and CIO agreed pretty well on everything pertaining to social security. Some statements of the CIO social security committee and testimony by its spokesman in the congressional hearings sounded somewhat more radical than those of their AFL counterparts, but the substantive differences were minor. On practically every issue, both groups supported the position taken by the Social Security Board. This included unqualified opposition to the extremist Communist and Townsend proposals and to experience rating in unemployment insurance, and support for broadening and liberalizing old-age and survivors' insurance, liberalization and federalization of unemployment insurance, and the establishment of compulsory health insurance.

In the 1940's organized labor became much more active in relation to social security than it had been earlier. This has been true particularly since 1944 when the American Federation of Labor established a Social Security Department, with Nelson H. Cruikshank as its director. The CIO soon followed suit, but its influence in social security matters on the congressional level was not quite as great. The 1956 merger of the two federations resulted in a consolidated Social Security Department, with Nelson Cruikshank as its head.

Not only has labor been represented on all advisory groups, as it was earlier, and been heard from at all congressional hearings on any aspect of social security, but the social security departments of both federations have been in constant touch with the Social Security Administration and have carried on a vast amount of publicity work to better acquaint union members with social security legislation and problems. It is impossible to speak with certainty about labor's part in the preparation of amending legislation, but there is at least some evidence that labor, particularly the Social Security Department of the AFL, had an active role in formulating bills presented to Congress as administration measures. A large percentage of all members of Congress, although generally only a minority, have rather consistently followed the leadership of labor on all social security questions. In recent years it has become doubtful whether even the private insurance companies whose influence earlier was often determining, have been listened to on social security matters by the congressional committees as much as has organized labor.

In part, the respect shown in Congress for the views of organized labor seems due to the generally conservative position it has taken on social security matters. It has always pressed for extensions and improvements but has never lost sight of the costs and has always insisted on sound financing. It is to labor's credit that it has never objected to the workers having to pay one-half the cost of OASI or to increases in contribution (tax) rates necessitated by increases in benefits. It has staunchly supported a contributory system based on insurance principles. It opposed the tax freezes of the 1940's and all "pay-as-you-go" (really "owe-as-you-go") proposals. It has favored raising the amounts above which no payroll taxes are collectible, with a view to ending the injustice of exempting nearly a fourth of all wages and salaries from any contributions to the costs of the OASI benefits, with the exemptions coming at the upper end of the pay scale. Its efforts in this direction have been only partially successful, but it scored a great victory in its opposition to the proposal of the Chamber of Commerce of the United States in 1953 for a low flat rate payment from OASI funds to everybody over sixty-five, in lieu of all federal aid for old-age assistance. This proposal, coming at a time when the new administration apparently had not yet made up its mind what to do about old-age security, was most vigorously opposed by labor as a subtle method of destroying OASI and died aborning. Along with sound financing, labor has favored universal coverage, liberal eligibility conditions, moderately increased benefits, and inclusion of benefits for the permanently and totally disabled in the OASI system.

On unemployment insurance, organized labor since passage of the Social Security Act has unqualifiedly opposed experience rating in the state laws and has been very critical of their low benefits and their severe disqualifications. It vigorously supported the federalization of unemployment insurance, when this was a live issue before Congress. Even since the federal administrators have abandoned this proposal, labor has continued to endorse it. Its major effort, however, has been directed toward the inclusion of standards in the Social Security Act to compel the states to abandon experience rating, to liberalize benefits, and lessen disqualifications. But all these efforts have pretty much fallen on deaf ears in Congress.

This has also been the result of the staunch support accorded by labor to compulsory health insurance and the several national health programs presented to Congress with the tacit or expressed approval of the Roosevelt and Truman administrations. No other politically important organizations have so consistently favored compulsory health insurance as have all labor groups, but their influence in Congress has never been as great on this issue as that of the American Medical Association on the other side.

State social security legislation has been largely left by both major labor federations to their state affiliates. Both the AFL and the CIO have adopted many resolutions at their annual conventions, and their executive boards have freely expressed themselves on what the states should do in such matters as unemployment insurance, workmen's compensation, public assistance, and other social security legislation within state control. But all lobbying and related activities on such matters have been left to the state federations of labor and the state industrial councils, and there are quite a few instances where these affiliates have pursued policies different from those favored by the federations. At the present time there are indications that top labor leadership at last realizes that social security in the United States is largely a matter within state control. There are distinct possibilities that the merged AFL-CIO will give more attention to state action on social security than the heretofore rival federations have paid to the subject. Failure to give more attention to the state capitols is at least one reason why labor has not exerted the influence on social security in this country which its numbers would lead one to expect.

On the other hand, labor has had a large role in the truly phenomenal growth of industrial pensions, health and welfare plans, and other private economic security institutions during the post–World War II years. While by no means the attitude of all affiliated unions, the official position of the American Federation of Labor was one of opposition to industrial pensions and employer welfare programs. These were regarded as being designed to keep out the unions. A changed attitude was produced by governmental wage control during World War II and still more by NLRB and Supreme Court decisions which made fringe benefits a matter about which companies had to bargain collectively with their unions. Beginning with the largest CIO unions, organized labor now aggressively sought industrial pensions, to be paid for by the employers, and health and welfare plans, in which it was willing to have the workers share the costs. OASI benefits were made deductible from promised industrial pensions, a provision favored by organized labor not only to make the industrial pensions, for which organized labor claimed credit, seem larger but also to give employers a direct interest in the improvement of the federal system. This device, generally credited to Walter Reuther, is believed to have been a major factor in the enactment of the Social Security Act amendments of 1950, which ended the long period in which there were no improvements in the OASI system. The same motive figured in the development in 1955 of supplemental unemployment insurance in the collective bargaining agreements of the automobile manufacturers and other large companies. Whether this will result in the improvement of the state unemployment compensation benefits remains to be seen. The spread of collectively bargained health and welfare plans appears to have had a retarding effect upon proposals for compulsory health insurance. As one important labor leader put it privately: "The benefits workers get under the health and welfare plans are so much greater than those we have dared to include in health insurance bills that it has become an anomaly for us to continue to favor compulsory health insurance."

Conclusions

Summarizing the story of labor and social security in the New Deal period and since, the first important fact is that the American Federation of Labor in the early years of the New Deal changed its official attitude on social insurance, shifting its position from opposition to endorsement. It was but natural that it did not at once assume a position of leadership in the social security movement, as both its leaders and members had only vague knowledge of the subject. Further, after enactment of the National Industrial Recovery Act in 1933, its energies were engrossed in the promising effort to spread union organization.

When the great split in the labor movement developed in 1936–39, the frantic rival organizing and union raiding demanded all of the time of the union leaders, making improvement of social security but a secondary matter. With no specialists in this field, it had only vague ideas what was needed, and, while some increased attention was given the subject, it was not until near the end of the war period, when the labor federations established social security staffs, that labor became reasonably well informed on social security and deeply interested in its improvement.

Labor supported the Social Security Act on passage in 1935, but it did not originate this legislation nor act as its strongest supporter. The major credit for this legislation belongs to President Roosevelt, Miss Perkins, and many others in the administration, and to the Congress of that day, particularly the able, conservative leaders of the congressional committees which had charge of this measure.

In the subsequent improvement of the original legislation, the Social Security Board and its successor agencies have had the greatest influence. Organized labor, however, has had a growing role in these developments, principally as a supporter of the proposals of the administrations, but also as a prod and critic. Despite a change in the national administration, today it probably has a greater influence on social security legislation than ever before. The greater influence of organized labor can be ascribed only in part to greater economic and political strength resulting from growth in union membership. At least equally important has been the increasing popularity of social security among workers, as more of them have become beneficiaries and a better understanding of the entire subject has been achieved, particularly by the labor leaders.

Organized labor has not had its own way, even approximately completely, in relation to social security or sought merely its own ends. Its influence upon social security legislation has been limited, but conservative, wholesome, and to the benefit of the entire nation. In recent years it has more and more resorted to collective bargaining to gain additional protection for its members against the personal risks of life, which it has found impossible to win through legislation. In doing this, it appears, also, to have strengthened the prospects for further improvement in social security legislation.

Notes

1 Eugene Staley, *History of the Illinois State Federation of Labor* (Chicago: University of Chicago Press, 1930), pp. 253–54.

2 This account is based upon an examination of the correspondence files of the American Association for Labor Legislation, which are now in the Library of the New York State School of Industrial and Labor Relations, Cornell University.

3 AFL Weekly *News-Letter*, January 7, 1922.

4 William Green, *Labor and Democracy* (Princeton: Princeton University Press, 1939), p. 37.

5 This bill came to Senator Wagner from Secretary of Labor Perkins. The essentials of the proposals were suggested to Secretary Perkins by Elizabeth Brandeis and Paul Raushenbush, the daughter and son-in-law of Justice Brandeis.

6 The author was one of the participants in this conference. Among others were Francis B. Sayre of Harvard, Joseph P. Chamberlain of Columbia, Mary Gilson of the University of Chicago, and Paul Raushenbush of Wisconsin.

7 The Wisconsin bill provided for a pooled fund for investment (and after 1937 also benefit) purposes, but also for variations in contribution rates in accordance with the employer's unemployment record. At a late stage of the legislative enactment of this bill, the supporters of the measure had to accept an amendment allowing employers to set up their own unemployment insurance reserves on approval of the Industrial

Commission, provided they paid benefits at least as good as the state law. Some employers did so, but before benefits became payable this privilege was withdrawn.

The "Ohio Plan" as presented by the Ohio Study Commission (which failed of adoption) differed from the Wisconsin law in that variations in the contribution rates in accordance with the employers' unemployment experience were to be postponed for three years. In the controversy which followed, the fact that the Ohio Plan like the Wisconsin bill also provided for experience rating (on a somewhat different basis) was overlooked.

8 William Green, "Why Labor Opposes Forced Worker Contributions in Job Insurance," *American Labor Legislation Review,* XXIV (September, 1934), pp. 101–5

9 Frequent references to this Cabinet meeting were made in the meetings of the Committee on Economic Security when the time came for decisions on its recommendations to the President. The fact that all members had agreed on the program decided upon at the Cabinet meeting and thereby had gotten "the President out on a limb" was skillfully used by Chairman Perkins to get agreement on the Committee's report.

10 The author was the executive director of the Committee on Economic Security. In 1936 he prepared a confidential, detailed (unpublished) report for the Social Science Research Council and the Social Security Board on "The Development of the Social Security Act," a copy of which is in the library of the U.S. Department of Health, Education and Welfare. In August, 1955, he dealt with the same subject in his address at the observance of "Twenty Years of Social Security" by the U.S. Department of Health, Education and Welfare, which was published in the *Social Security Bulletin,* October, 1955.

11 The most important changes made concerned unemployment insurance. The most discussed of these changes was the LaFollette amendment, which, in substance, restored the provisions of the original administration bill permitting experience rating. These had been stricken in the House Ways and Means Committee under conditions not going to the merits of the proposal. They were restored in the Senate without dissent and readily agreed to by the House conferees.

12 Title of Chapter III, in Paul Douglas, *Social Security in the United States* (New York: McGraw-Hill Book Co., 1936, 1939).

13 Congress later provided for crediting employers with the tax offset in states which had no law in effect in 1936 but which enacted such a law in 1937.

14 The author was a member of this advisory committee and of its steering committee.

15 The original law did not provide for full reserve financing or anything approaching such a program. Opponents of the legislation, however, constantly so charged.

16 Previously only lump sum benefits had been paid, amounting to a refund

of taxes paid by contributors who died before retiring or who were ineligible for benefits at the time of retirement. These refunds, provided for in the original law, were done away with in the Social Security Act amendments of 1939 and 1950.

17 The potential increase in coverage is 10 million but the actual increase to date is considerably smaller.

8

Industrial Management's Policies Toward Unionism

RICHARD C. WILCOCK

A DRAMATIC and far-reaching change in American labor relations occurred in 1937 and in the years immediately following when a large number of leading companies in the mass production industries recognized and began to bargain with organized labor. This essay is an attempt to explain and evaluate both the evolutionary development of managerial policies toward unionism in the years prior to 1937 and the almost revolutionary changes which of necessity accompanied recognition.[1]

Although the significance of this switch from policies which were built around the open shop and individual bargaining to policies which accompanied collective bargaining with organized labor has often been noted, surprisingly little has been written which helps to explain how and why industrial management accepted unionism. What has been written generally falls into two categories. On the one hand, many accounts of industrial relations in the New Deal period analyze either labor's spectacular gains or the government's unprecedented influence on industrial relations. In the process, management either goes unexplained or tends to be cast in the role of an adversary in the exciting drama of the worker's struggle for his rightful place in industrial society and of the government's fight to give workers equal bargaining power with management and the right to have unions of their own choosing. Those reports which have focused on the industrial relations policies of management, on the other hand, have generally failed to provide a full assessment of the origins and impact of these policies and of the factors which shaped them. The tendency has been to portray management as a hard-pressed group fighting against unprincipled union power and unnecessary governmental interference.

Although neither approach should be disparaged, the fact remains that there has been relatively little analysis which could accurately be labeled as nonpartisan. In an attempt at objectivity, this essay is based on the premise that the men who were management leaders in the thirties were, for the most part, neither heroic nor villainous but were instead men trying to manage industry in accordance with their concept of the job and its responsibilities. Going further, it is assumed that management policies in labor relations, even though defensive in the sense of being opposed to the advance of unionism, nevertheless greatly influenced and shaped in direct ways not only the character of labor relations in American industry but also the size and even the nature of the American labor movement.

With these assumptions, two major propositions are advanced. The first is that the labor relations policies of management in the thirties can be interpreted meaningfully in terms of who and what management was. In examining this proposition, we shall take a brief look at the goals and philosophy of modern corporate management and the development of labor relations policies in the early decades of the twentieth century.

Management, however, could not and did not operate unaffected by contemporary economic, social, and political forces. The second proposition, therefore, is that management policies in the New Deal period, while heavily affected by the depression, the New Deal, and the activities of organized labor, were purposeful and rational when examined in the light of management's knowledge, experience, and concept of its role. This proposition calls for an analysis of management policy on the primary questions of whether, when, and how to recognize and deal with the freely-chosen representatives of employees. This analysis will draw upon the political and economic events of the New Deal years, the findings on the nature of management, and the historical development of labor relations.

Industrial Management and Its Basic Position on Unionism

In recent years "management" has been used to mean the collective grouping of those who make the policy decisions in business enterprises. The term thus embraces all individuals whose opinions and knowledge are directly involved in the formulation of policy and who could be considered as part of the management group. Included are "top management," other corporation executives in particular areas of policy, and, depending upon the circumstances, at least some of the outside directors, key stockholders, and representatives of financial interests. Unless otherwise stated, however, the term "management" is used in this essay to mean, more specifically, the top policy-making executives in manufacturing companies.

Management decisions are of course not entirely within the control of the managers or of the management group. The individual manager cannot be the freebooter that the nineteenth-century capitalist was supposed to be. He must operate within an established political and economic system with increasingly restrictive formal and informal pressures from outside interest groups. These groups include industry itself (as represented by competitors, trade associations, general management associations, and major customers and suppliers), money-market institutions such as banks and insurance companies, various governmental agencies, and organized labor.

While management policies are necessarily the product of a resolution of conflicting interests within the management group and between management and outside pressures, policies are nonetheless formulated and the over-all result has been undeniably impressive. Management, it is generally conceded, has become in the past few decades an indispensable institution in our society and perhaps the dominant one. If it is agreed that our society and its institutions, whether cultural, political, or economic, are largely dependent upon the functioning of the private enterprise system, the importance of management leadership becomes obvious. Even though this argument may overstate the case, the private enterprise economy, in an era of monopolistic competition and technological change, does depend upon leadership to keep it dynamic and expanding. Much of this leadership has been supplied by management.

In fact, management must assume leadership to survive as an institution. Because American business has had much change forced upon it and is subject to many uncertainties, leadership is necessary to assess the uncertainties, to adjust to change, and to create change. The creation of change, through the continuous discovery of new markets and the introduction of new products and more efficient methods of production, has long been thought to be an essential and perhaps the key factor in the successful operation of the dynamic American economy.

The essence of the managerial "revolution" can be described, therefore, as the assumption—by a class of professional managers—of the responsibility for directing individual enterprises in such a way that the collective result of their individual management decisions determines the direction of the economic system. Important also is the fact that management believes its decisions are crucial not only to the success of individual enterprises but also to the success of the enterprise system. One result of this belief is that individual managements have been, from the beginning, extremely reluctant to share their authority and responsibility with any other major institution, such as government or labor.

Whether management has been correct in its conviction that trade unions want to share, or by their very nature inevitably would share, the responsibility for management is beside the point. The mere belief that unionism means or would mean the loss of some of management's authority and prestige is a sufficient explanation for much of management's opposition to unionism over the years. Certainly, the history of industrial relations shows that, at least until recent years, management not only has preferred to do without unions but also has believed that unionism interferes with management's right and duty to manage.

Management's approach to labor relations, therefore, has always been based on the conviction that management must have the authority to manage. The approach is the same whether particular managements bargain with affiliated trade unions, independent unions, or individual workers. Today, while the principle of collective bargaining is widely accepted, it is accepted only to the extent that it be limited to the joint determination of the wage level, details of the wage structure, the schedule of hours, and specific conditions of work. On such questions as what to make, who to hire, and whether to expand or contract, most managements believe strongly that their authority should prevail.

This discussion has necessarily been limited to the broadest possible analysis of the goals and philosophy of management as they relate to labor relations. Much more could be said about the individual problems of managers faced with the introduction of a union or the problem of developing a satisfactory labor-management relationship. Managerial attitudes toward unions have rarely entailed a completely logical and informed assessment of the probable results of a bargaining relationship. Misconceptions, misinformation, misunderstandings, and fear of the unknown play an important part. In addition, the individual manager may see the union and the union leader not only as a threat to orderly, unimpeded formation of business policy, but as a threat also to his achievement of such personal goals as the respect of fellow managers, economic security, and independence in ordering his own affairs. The basic position of management on the question of unionism, however, has been, within the limits of information and understanding, a product of management's concept of its role and responsibility.

Labor Relations Before the New Deal

A review of labor relations prior to the New Deal period could encompass almost any type of labor-management situation and almost any type of labor relations policy that existed in the thirties and later. Collective bargaining relationships, mature and immature, company unions, welfare capitalism, personnel administration, and scientific management all enjoyed long histories before the New Deal began. Even a degree of understanding and application of "human relations" is far older than the studies begun in the late twenties by Elton Mayo and his group.

The purpose here, however, is to describe only the major elements in the development of managerial policies toward unionism which, continuing into the thirties, helped to shape management policies under the New Deal. But first a word should be said about the type of labor relations approach which was perhaps the most prevalent in the twenties and earlier, particularly in small firms. In most small firms and in many larger ones, the managers were not only untouched and unworried about unionism in any form, but also were quite innocent of such notions as scientific, personnel, and welfare management. Management was largely "personal," and the art of management often lay primarily in the "business" end of buying and selling and not in directing production and the work force. Labor and personnel relations, such as they were, were handled by the foremen, who knew what the boss wanted, although the big boss himself might, on occasion, "interfere" in either the handling of production problems or in settling the personal problems of workers.

"Personal" versus Personnel Management

Although "personal" management existed in some large companies —the Ford Motor Company being a notable example—this general type of management was for the most part limited to the smaller firms. The smaller firms, however, were gradually losing their importance in the economic scheme of things. From the Civil War on, corporations had been growing both through individual firm expansion and through merger. This expansion in the size of firms was accelerated during World War I and during the twenties. In the larger companies and in the companies which grew out of the small shop class, "personal" management was rarely sufficient to the needs of the business, both because of internal problems of control and because of outside pressures. Management developments in these firms were important because of their size, the proportion of the labor force involved, and the unmistakable trend toward the dominance of the large firm in the American economy.

As "personal" management waned in the early decades of the century, "scientific management" grew rapidly. Scientific management was more than the "rationalization" of jobs and production processes; it embraced the philosophy of the worker as an "economic man." With the use of time and motion study, wages were related with presumed exactness to the amount and value of production. "Law and science," as Frederick W. Taylor explained it, would not only solve all shop problems but would create higher wages, shorter hours, and steady employment. In the Taylor philosophy, the worker needed no more and would want no more when he understood the system. Under Taylorism unions were, in a word, unnecessary.[2]

Scientific management provided management with a relatively simple approach to labor relations. Workers had no cause to complain about change because the engineers were creating new jobs and higher wages. In fact, the extraordinary measures used by some managements to keep unions out of their plants can be explained at least in part by this faith in the benefits of scientific management. These benefits, however, were often not enough to keep workers from joining unions or to prevent labor unrest and dissatisfaction.

With general agreement, therefore, on the undesirability of unions, management's response to unionism and labor unrest was normally of two kinds—welfare and personnel programs, and programs of direct opposition to unions. The latter involved all of the methods later familiar in the thirties, such as aggressive open-shop policies, which often meant closing the shop to any union members, discrimination against union members through discharge and blacklisting, the use of temporary injunctions, the employment of strikebreakers and labor spies, the mobilization of public opinion, and in some cases, the actual or attempted control of local government and newspapers.

The alternate approach of personnel and welfare management often had the same objective of keeping the unions out. Welfare management included such devices as recreational facilities, employee publications, Americanization programs, medical departments, and company housing. In some cases, it also involved various types of health, pension, profit-sharing, stock ownership, savings, and credit plans. Early personnel departments were often set up primarily to administer such programs. In addition, these departments would administer cases arising under the relatively few laws affecting workers such as workmen's compensation and protective legislation for working women and children.

Management often found, however, that scientific management and welfare management combined were not enough to solve its labor problem. One result was that some companies, in the twenties and earlier, experimented with various forms of employee representation plans and shop committees. These plans, which permitted employee representatives to discuss their problems with management, were few in number [3] yet had a great influence on the growth and characteristics of company unions in the thirties. Finally, some companies did recognize and bargain with trade unions, particularly in the clothing and printing industries, but in the great mass production industries, management, with the aid of favorable or at least complacent public opinion and the limited interest of the AFL in industrial unionism, was able to maintain successfully a policy of being anti-union or even in large segments of industry a policy of nonawareness of unions.

The Business Cycle, the Labor Market, and Labor Relations

As companies grew in size and as management became more professional and impersonal, the policies and philosophy of management with respect to controlling the work force were increasingly reflected in the programs of scientific, personnel, and welfare management. At least two other influences, however, were important in shaping the thinking and policies of management as it entered the thirties and faced the depression, the New Deal, and a revived labor movement. These were the changing characteristics of the American labor force and fluctuations in the business cycle.

Both of these influences assumed particular importance during World War I when the war-induced prosperity and a dramatic decline in immigration created drastic changes in the labor market. Labor became scarcer than it had been for many decades, and among the results were the dilution of skill requirements for factory jobs, an acceleration of mechanization and job simplification, and substantial migrations of rural, and in large part southern, Negroes and whites into the industrial centers.

The labor shortage, together with some governmental sanction of union organization from 1917 through 1919, contributed both to the expansion of the labor movement, and, concurrently, to greater managerial awareness of personnel and labor problems. This awareness was strengthened for many managements both by the high incidence of labor turnover in their own plants and by a spate of studies which demonstrated the high costs of labor turnover. One of the results was the first major period of growth of professional personnel management. Many companies, particularly the larger ones in the basic industries, established centralized personnel departments for the first time and hired "professional" personnel managers who were charged with the orderly recruiting, selection, training, and discharge of workers. The objectives were to reduce labor turnover, to increase labor productivity, and to alleviate frictions between management and the work force.

The history of personnel management in the twenties, however, illustrates that personnel administration was often considered a necessity only when labor was scarce and the company could not afford to lose workers. In "ordinary" times a personnel department was regarded as something of a luxury and during a recession the personnel department was apt to be the first to go. Thus, while the personnel men were trying to establish a body of principles and practices and were forming professional organizations, such as the Industrial Relations Association of America (1919–22), the ground was being cut from under them as management observed that the recession beginning in mid-1920 increased the supply of qualified labor and reduced quit rates. Most managements apparently believed during the twenties that the state of the labor market had more to do with labor dissatisfaction and labor turnover than did their particular personnel policies.

As the twenties progressed, a number of personnel departments were re-established, or started where they had never existed, for a different set of reasons. Welfare programs needed to be supervised. In many companies, the very complexity of operations made it impossible for foremen to do an adequate job of selection and training of workers. Moreover, scientific management, in some of its forms, called for certain functions, like personnel administration, to be handled on a staff rather than a line basis. Finally, the character of the work force was changing.

As the great waves of immigration became a thing of the past, as the former rural dwellers became accustomed to urban life, and as real wages and the standard of living increased, American workers were developing more of a middle-class orientation. On the one hand this made the workers more susceptible than they might otherwise have been to management's attempts to secure their good will and perhaps less susceptible to union organization. But, on the other hand, it made the workers more independent, more demanding, and less satisfied with the mechanized nature of factory employment, the arbitrary decisions of foremen, and the general assumption in the factory system that the worker was a hired hand who could not be expected to contribute in ideas and imagination to the productive process. The result was often both a general feeling of unrest and the existence of many specific grievances, expressed or unexpressed. Some managements recognized the changing characteristics of their work forces by establishing shop committees; others turned to personnel management to handle grievances and to try to keep the work forces contented and coöperative.

In at least some companies, however, employee relations were based on the assumption that the worker is a complex being whose problems cannot be entirely solved with the arbitrary rules of scientific management or the paternal gifts of welfare management. Such were employee relations at their best, but personnel programs of any kind were still relatively rare in the late twenties.[4] For the most part, management did not give the personnel men the necessary status, prestige, and responsibility, or the necessary policies, to build the kind of mature worker-management relationship which is an important goal of many managements today. With the benefit of hindsight, it seems quite apparent that management in the twenties failed to perceive the potentials of personnel management in improving the productivity of an enterprise both in the short and in the long run.

When the stock market collapsed in 1929, management was prepared, at least in one sense, for the labor relations events of the depression decade. Various managements had had experience in practically all phases of dealing with employees and with unions which became important in the thirties. By 1929, scientific, welfare, and personnel management had each had an extensive history. Indeed, examples could be found to support the claim that in none of these fields were there significant innovations after the twenties, although there may have been changes in terminology. In addition, many managements had had extensive experience in resisting unionism, and, again, all the weapons later used in fighting unions had been employed in the twenties and earlier. At the other extreme, some managements had made a beginning in the application of "human relations" techniques and others had developed constructive and mature relations with organized labor.

In most respects, however, management was poorly prepared for the impact of the depression and of the New Deal on labor relations. A majority of all managements had had no experience with personnel departments, with collective representation of their employees of any kind—whether company union or organized labor—or even with scientific management. Personnel management in the twenties scarcely resembled its more advanced forms in today's industry. Little was known about such matters as vertical communication, training beyond the manual skills, or counseling and testing. More generally, the kind of teamwork in decision-making attempted in management today was virtually absent.

Even more important perhaps, management had been operating since 1919 with relatively little governmental interference and since 1922 in a period of general prosperity. The public, furthermore, even though it was not clamorous in its praise of business leadership and many groups may have been disgruntled, had at least accepted the business world as it was and tolerated the prevalent labor relations policies and practices. Management, therefore, was not fully prepared mentally for the change which took place in the attitude of both the public and the government, and perhaps could not have been prepared in view of its concept of its function in the economy.

As the depression years multiplied, the changed attitude of public and government became manifest in many ways, including a growing public sympathy for the aims and objectives of organized labor, a general feeling that business was to blame for the depression, and widespread popular support for the early New Deal measures. Management was unwilling to accept the blame for the depression, believing that business cycles were inevitable and in the natural order of things. Moreover, management was determined to protect and maintain the free enterprise system, in spite of its loss of prestige and the considerable confusion and even fear which the early years of the depression created in its ranks.

The Early Years of the New Deal, March, 1933, to April, 1937

While the origins of NIRA have been discussed in Chapters 5 and 6 and our concern here is primarily with management's reaction to Section 7(a), it is worth noting that management was not opposed to recovery legislation as such. In fact, the structure and objectives of the NRA were influenced by plans prepared by the U.S. Chamber of Commerce in 1931 and 1932 and by the suggestions of such business leaders as Gerard Swope, president of General Electric, and Bernard Baruch. Many industrialists believed that industry-wide planning and coöperation were necessary to permit price and wage adjustments that would stimulate production and employment. Such planning would require a relaxation of the antitrust laws.

The NRA, as it worked out, was more than management had bargained for, however; Section 7(a) and the creation of the various labor boards meant much more interference in management-labor relations than management had anticipated. The immediate reactions, nevertheless, appear to have been mixed. In a survey in the fall of 1933, the National Industrial Conference Board found only a few managements willing to state "with finality that they did not approve of dealing with a union," while most of the executives who replied indicated they regretted the change in conditions but were determined to observe the spirit as well as the letter of the law.[5]

Observing the spirit of the law did not, however, in the minds of most managements, mean the recognition of an "outside" labor organization, or, if there were trade unionists in a plant, agreeing to a collectively bargained contract. There was, in fact, nothing in the law to compel employers to make concessions or to sign agreements. Moreover, since the signing of an agreement with representatives of a trade union would mean recognition of the union, management, particularly in the manufacturing industries, was very reluctant to bargain at all with organized labor.

Section 7(a), while it gave employees the right to choose their own representatives without interference on the part of their employers, also meant, according to General Johnson, the right to make either collective bargains or individual agreements. The result was that, when employees did not have the economic power to insist otherwise, management was able to retain individual bargaining. Where the pressures were sufficiently strong, however, it became necessary for management, willingly or unwillingly, to discuss with organized groups of employees issues of wages, hours, and working conditions. These pressures came from the government, through the code-making machinery and the labor boards, public opinion, the employees themselves, and the rapid increase in trade union membership. By the end of 1933, sizable new groups of trade union members existed in a number of manufacturing industries, including automobiles, steel, electrical machinery, rubber, meat-packing, and leather, as well as in industries where unionism had been strong, such as men's and women's clothing, and printing.

The Rise of Company Unions

Under these circumstances, there was an understandable impetus on the part of hundreds of managements to form or encourage "company unions" of various types. In late 1933, the National Industrial Conference Board reported that more than 60 per cent of surveyed company unions were founded after NRA, and in April, 1935, according to the Bureau of Labor Statistics in another study, almost two-thirds of the reported company unions had been introduced in the NRA period.[6] Significantly, company union coverage grew even more rapidly than trade union membership between 1932 and 1935—from 1.25 million workers covered or about 40 per cent of the membership in trade unions in 1932 to 2.5 million or about 60 per cent of the number in trade unions in 1935.[7]

Although the new company unions were accepted by hundreds of thousands of industrial workers as a means of collective representation, there is little doubt that their existence was the result of top management policy. In some cases, management merely had to authorize their adoption but more frequently management took specific steps to assist in their creation.

The company unions of the NRA period, however, could not be duplicates of the old employee representation plans because of Section 7(a) and labor board rulings. Largely as a result of interpretations of Section 7(a), the company unions began to resemble trade unions in structure and operation. They had elected officers, membership, constitutions, and other attributes of formal organization. In addition, they usually had formal grievance procedures and a certain amount of collective dealing with management on wages, hours, and working conditions, although few achieved written contracts. Finally, although the companies rarely gave them direct financial support, the company unions often would have their meetings on company time and property with the personnel director or other management representatives present.

Company unions were not, however, an unmixed blessing for the industrial managements who sponsored them. While most company union elections were private affairs with no other organization on the ballot, companies could not always avoid government-run representation elections which the trade unions won more often than not. In addition, many of the company unions were able to take advantage of trade union pressure on management to gain concessions which the companies were not willing to grant to organized labor.[8] This was particularly true in the 1933–35 period when there was an active struggle in many plants between trade union and company union adherents. Finally, some of the company unions declared their independence of company influence or affiliated with established international unions.

For the most part, however, managements with company unions preferred this arrangement to either individual bargaining or recognition of trade unions. The employee organizations provided a two-way channel of communications and often were highly valuable to management in the efficient settlement of grievances. Collective dealing was largely discussion since management retained almost complete discretion in hiring, firing, seniority, wage rates, and similar matters and did not as a rule permit written agreements. The Bureau of Labor Statistics, for example, in its 1935 survey, found that in 592 establishments with company unions less than 15 per cent had written agreements and, of these, almost half made no mention of wages, hours, and working conditions.

The Bureau survey also indicated that three of every four manufacturing firms still practiced individual bargaining. Most of these firms were small, however, as is illustrated by the fact that they employed less than half of the workers in manufacturing. About one-fifth of the manufacturing firms, employing about one-fifth of manufacturing workers, were dealing with trade unions and these firms included small as well as large establishments.[9]

The company unions, however, were found almost exclusively in large firms. Only one in twenty of the manufacturing firms had company unions or a company union along with one or more trade unions at the same time, but the firms in this group had one-third of all the workers in manufacturing. To a large extent the management problem of what kind of unionism to have, if any, was a problem for the larger firms. For the most part company unionism was not an alternative in the small firm. With exceptions, such as the garment industry, most small companies were not threatened by unionism in the mid-thirties. If their employees joined a union, the usual choice for small-company management was between recognition and nonrecognition.

Management and the Wagner Act

In the congressional hearings leading to the passage of the National Labor Relations Act, only a few employers spoke in favor of the bill. Most of the management representatives and the important management associations vigorously opposed the bill, as did a number of company union officers. Specific objections were made against the majority-rule provision, the barring of company support of company unions, and the lack of provisions on union control. The basic objection, however, was the belief that the proposed law would do more to foster trade union growth than had the NRA.

Management efforts to defeat the Wagner bill failed for a number of reasons. The climate was not propitious for management to receive a sympathetic hearing. Congress reflected a growing public sentiment in favor of giving workers "equal bargaining power" with management. In addition, the management objections to the bill were weakened in the eyes of many congressmen as a result of the instances of management defiance of the labor boards and the apparent widespread use of such anti-union tactics as espionage, blacklisting, and the storage of weapons.

The immediate impact of the NLRA on the extension of union organization in the mass production industries was slight, largely because management was convinced that the law would be declared unconstitutional and therefore continued to refuse recognition. Widespread opposition to the Act is described in the first annual report of the National Labor Relations Board. The Board refers to a publication of the National Lawyers Committee of the American Liberty League and says:

> This document, widely publicized and distributed throughout the country . . . can be regarded only as a deliberate and concerted effort by a group of well-known lawyers to undermine public confidence in the statute, to discourage compliance with it, to assist attorneys generally in attacks on the statute, and perhaps to influence the courts. . . .
>
> The process [of filing injunction suits] was like a rolling snowball. The allegations in a pleading filed by an employer in Georgia, for example, would show up in precisely the same wording in a pleading filed in Seattle.[10]

The Wagner Act did not ban, any more than had the NIRA, either company or "independent" unions, but it made it an unfair labor practice for management "to dominate or interfere with the formation or administration of any labor organization [including company unions] or contribute financial or other support to it." As a result, company union growth was drastically curtailed although relatively few employee representation plans were abandoned prior to 1937.[11]

The nature and characteristics of company unions, furthermore, continued to change under the impact of governmental activity in labor relations, continuing organizational activity of trade unions, and public opinion. As the company union plans were "readapted," they became increasingly independent of management influence. More frequently than before, membership was optional, meetings were held without representation of management, provisions for "outside" arbitration were added, and in some cases, signed agreements between management and company unions were made. By and large, however, company unions in 1936 and 1937, while more independent than they had been, remained relatively weak in bargaining power. The reasons were that the company unions, with little treasury and no ties with large organizations, not only did not have the economic power to force their demands, but also did not have the technical services available to them which would have been useful in formulating their demands.

In the period prior to the Supreme Court validation of the Wagner Act, therefore, the company union continued to be a device through which a number of managements were able to maintain a type of labor-management relationship which was consistent with managerial control over output and wages.

The "Belligerent" Approach to Labor Relations, 1933 to 1937

The policies of management with respect to the acceptance and recognition of trade unions changed relatively little in the early New Deal years. In spite of the New Deal, management in 1937 was for the most part no more inclined to engage in collective bargaining with trade unions than it had been in 1933. This early New Deal period did differ from the years immediately preceding 1933 in that the managements of half or more of American factory workers were forced, or became persuaded, to do something about the organizational aspirations of their employees. Many managements, however, while hard pressed by trade unions and the government, found themselves either unable or unwilling to accept the notion that they could be told to bargain "in good faith" with representatives of their workers. As a result, the total amount of activity in resisting union organization was greatly increased in the mid-thirties.

Leaders in the fight to restrict trade union advances were a number of those trade associations, whether local, state, regional, or national, that were called "belligerent associations." The most important of these, on a national level, was undoubtedly the National Association of Manufacturers, whose labor relations efforts were primarily in lobbying and publicizing. The extent to which the NAM has truly represented manufacturing management has often been questioned, but its influence has nonetheless been great. The NAM led the fight against the Wagner Act from the time of the original hearings to the passage of the Taft-Hartley Act. In the period before April, 1937, it not only claimed that the Wagner Act was unconstitutional, but encouraged noncompliance and injunction suits on the part of its members.

More important, perhaps, in this period than such associations as the NAM, since the legislation they fought was for the most part passed, were those management associations which provided various types of direct assistance to their members. A leader among these was the National Metal Trades Association, which had a large membership among major manufacturing firms. This association, as did a number of others, furnished strikebreakers to members. Indeed, it was specifically stated in its constitution that strikebreakers would be supplied to the extent of seven-tenths of the number of workers for which the member had been paying dues. Penalties were established for members who settled labor differences without the consent of the association's administrative council. In addition to national groups such as the NMTA, there were many regional and local associations of the so-called belligerent type which furnished industrial spies, conducted strikes, and planned campaigns to frustrate attempts at labor organization.

The greatest amount of detail about the activities of these associations and of individual managements who used belligerent methods to keep unions out of their plants is contained in the voluminous hearings and the several reports of the LaFollette Committee. The importance of the hearings lies in the revelations of the lengths to which a number of managements and their associations were prepared to go in attempting to prevent trade union expansion. In reading the reports today, one is struck by the vehemence and conviction of some managers in their belief that it would be impossible to combine collective bargaining and successful management.

Although not all companies resorted to professional spies, strikebreakers, mass discrimination, and similar tactics, there is little doubt that most of the managements in the mass production industries were opposed in principle to the recognition of trade unions and could be classified as "anti-union." A list of anti-union industries, as of 1935, would include steel, automobiles, electrical machinery, meat-packing, agricultural machinery, and chemicals.

One technique used during this period deserves special mention because it was applied by a number of companies and because variations of the technique have continued in use since that time. This is the famed Mohawk Valley Formula, which was first used to break a strike against Remington Rand in Ilion, New York, in the summer of 1936. The essential steps of the formula were to form a "citizens' committee" in the community, label the union leaders as outside agitators, stir up violence or the fear of violence, have a "state of emergency" declared, organize a back-to-work movement, and finally have the back-to-work employees march into the plant protected by armed police.[12]

Techniques such as industrial espionage and "professional" strikebreaking did not end in 1937, but in the 1933–37 period they were at their height and exacted a tremendous price from companies, workers, and the public. The more indirect, intangible costs continued for years afterward in many plants in a heritage of unsatisfactory and bitter labor relations.

The "Constructive" Approach to Labor Relations, 1933 to 1937

Few managements have ever limited their labor relations policy to the simple negative of opposing unions. While strikes and strike-breaking were making news and receiving the attention of congressional committees, the courts, and government agencies, many managements were more or less quietly developing or continuing positive programs in their labor relations. These programs not only helped shape the character of labor relations at the time but in many of their aspects have also continued to the present day.

The personnel management movement, for example, while it suffered a setback in the first years of the depression (as it had in the 1920–22 recession) grew stronger in the mid-thirties as more and more companies found it necessary or desirable to "deal" in some way with their employees. In 1935, the BLS found that half of the reporting establishments with company unions also had personnel managers, and in companies with 500 or more workers a large majority had personnel departments. In some companies, the industrial relations function was separated from the personnel and employment functions. Industrial relations directors and vice presidents in charge of industrial relations became more numerous.

A growing number of managements also came to believe that employee organization was valuable to the enterprise quite apart from any question of preventing "outside" organization of the employees. An organization would give the workers both a sense of status and a channel of communication which could not only reduce grievances and discontent but also lessen labor turnover and contribute to the quality and quantity of output.

Most of these managements sincerely believed that these purposes could not be achieved with a trade union, and management publications of the thirties reflect this belief. The industrial relations manager of Socony-Vacuum, for example, had this to say in 1937:

> The thing to bear in mind is that there is an important distinction between bargaining under pressure and dealing through discussion. The two groups may have differences of opinion, but after all they are both interested in

the success of the company, and are not primarily engaged in trading concessions.

. . . .

> Where employee representation is set up on a basis of genuine cooperation, there is no major weakness. It is not a militant fighting machine, and if progress depends on winning battles rather than adjusting differences such a plan might be called weak. Employee representation as it has been conceived has strength of spirit, and of character, but not of force or strategy.[13]

On the other hand, some employers believed that company unions should have some bargaining strength and should incorporate "the best features" of trade unionism, but the emphasis was on "dealing" and the "conference method" as opposed to "bargaining," and on "coöperation" as opposed to "conflict." The belief was widespread that company unionism was synonymous with coöperative relations while trade unionism was not, but, as in the quotation above, it was also recognized that the bargaining power of company unions typically was relatively weak and that, by its very method of organization, the company union was tied for better or worse to the success of the individual firm.

It is worthwhile emphasizing, however, that, except in cases where company unions were no more than an anti-union expedient, company-union employers were for the most part "relatively good employers" and often through their efforts had a positive effect on the improvement of labor relations. Also, the experience of managers and employees with company unions influenced to a considerable extent the character of labor relations when trade unions began more frequently to replace the company unions. Finally, the company-union movement without doubt limited severely the forward advance of the labor movement by establishing a substitute for organized labor in large segments of industry.

Management's Response to the Validation of the Wagner Act

The year 1937 has been considered by many to have been a major turning point in labor relations. The Supreme Court decisions in April, 1937, made it clear that the Wagner Act was, at least for the time being, the law of the land. In addition, the re-election of Roosevelt and of a Democratic Congress in 1936 led management to believe that for another four years governmental agencies would in their decisions tend to promote union development. More important, there was a growing belief that a strong labor movement would be a part of the American scene for the indefinite future. While the changes in labor relations policies after 1937 certainly cannot be traced entirely to these factors, they were of major significance.

The impact of the Wagner Act can be measured in part through the decisions and orders of the National Labor Relations Board. After validation, the proportion of company and independent unions on the ballot in NLRB elections gradually dropped. For the period from October, 1935, through June, 1941, the company unions and independents were in 1,101 elections and they won slightly less than half, but the elections they won represented only 9.2 per cent of the total number of NLRB elections in this period.[14]

In addition to elections, there were a large number of cases, particularly in 1937 and 1938, of alleged violation of Section 8(2), in which employer domination of or interference with labor organization was charged. In many cases, company unions were disestablished either through agreement or by order. The dissolution of company unions and their frequent replacement with independents, free from company domination, or with trade unions was not limited, however, to situations involving unfair labor practice charges. A large but unknown number of managements changed their labor policies to conform to the law without any direct action on the part of the government. The net result was that after April, 1937, the company union was eliminated or became relatively unimportant in a number of major industries, such as steel, agricultural implements, electrical machinery, meat-packing, and rubber. The process, however, took a number of years and was not substantially complete until well into the war years. The conscious policy of many managements was to adjust to the new era as slowly and as deliberately as possible.

The process of conversion from company union to trade union, therefore, included in a number of companies a stage during which the employees were represented by an "independent" union. A number of these independents were "legitimate" in that they were entirely free from company control, and some of them are still in existence—for example, some of the independent unions in Standard Oil of New Jersey. In such cases, management policy was to encourage continued independence. Others of the independents, such as those at Westinghouse and International Harvester, were declared to be company-dominated and were ordered disestablished. For several years, therefore, the managements who were most reluctant to deal with organized labor and who could persuade enough of their workers to go along were able to continue, in effect, with company unions. Organizations were even formed, such as the Independent Organizations' Service, to assist workers in the establishment of independent unions.

In a 1939 study of sixty independent unions alleged to be company-dominated, the National Labor Relations Board found that a large majority of them had been newly formed as independents or had been readapted after April 12, 1937, most of them between April and August, 1937. Also, in the majority of cases, one or more of the following methods were used in organization: use of company time and property for recruiting (with supervisory permission), recruiting by supervisors, and supervisory attendance at organization meetings. Even more significant was the fact that, with one possible exception, all of these unions were formed when an "outside union" was attempting to organize the plant. In a number of the cases, the independent was formed during a strike or while a back-to-work movement was in process. Finally, only a few of these independents obtained formal agreements from the managements.[15]

When a management first recognizes a labor union, the event is usually dramatic and represents a significant change in the company's labor relations policy. The subsequent development of a working relationship between management and the local union is perhaps more significant, but the first crucial step is the formal recognition of the union. To illustrate the process of recognition, a brief account is given here of the events leading to the acceptance of collective bargaining in key companies of several of the mass production industries.

Meat-Packing Industry

In meat-packing, the NRA did not disturb the employee representation plans which were in effect in most of the large plants. The position of the meat packers is illustrated by remarks made by the industrial relations director of Swift at the October, 1933, convention of the American Meat Packers.

> Some of the units in this industry have had plans for employee representation in effect for 12 years or more. They have proved an effective means of

employee-employer relationship. . . . The NRA does not require the giving up of previous industrial relations policies except as modifications may have been necessary in hours and wage rates. Whether or not we go into new forms of collective bargaining depends at least in some degree upon the satisfaction of employees in existing arrangements. Our destiny is still partially in our hands.[16]

The Wagner Act, however, brought about some changes and the representation plans, as in other industries, began to resemble trade unions in structure and operation. They remained company-dominated, however, and a number were involved in NLRB cases on charges of unfair labor practices both before and after the Supreme Court decisions of April, 1937.

The first major concession of the Big Four (Swift, Armour, Cudahy, and Wilson) came in the fall of 1939 when Armour recognized the Packinghouse Workers Organizing Committee, CIO. The Armour management did not publicly state its reasons for recognition, but an analysis by the union undoubtedly touches upon some of the important ones. One was "public pressure" through a union-inspired mail and telegram campaign, along with the threat that CIO members would boycott Armour products. Another was government pressure. Finally, there was the economic situation. World War II had begun in Europe and it was believed there would be large orders for meat products from European governments. A long strike would have put Armour at a serious disadvantage.[17] While these may not have been the only reasons, the ice was broken, and in the early months of 1940 collective agreements were reached in the Armour meat-packing plants.

Wilson was the last of the Big Four to recognize the PWOC. On March 27, 1943, the company entered into a master agreement with the organizing committee in compliance with National War Labor Board directives. James D. Cooney, president of Wilson, said in 1955, in an interview, that had it not been for the intervention of the WLB he doubted whether the CIO would have been able to obtain representation in a majority of the Wilson plants.[18]

Automobile Industry

In the automobile industry, for many years a center of the "open shop" movement, the major companies had not had experience with employee representation plans when the NRA came into being. The major firms with the exception of Ford, however, established company unions during the NRA period.

In the spring of 1934, the AFL organized a number of federal locals and threatened a general strike for recognition, but with the intervention of the federal government and even of President Roosevelt most of the managements agreed to meet with all representatives of their employees on a proportional basis. The Automobile Labor Board was set up to administer the agreement and supervise elections. The net result, however, was a continuation of management's open shop policy.

Because of its size and prestige, it is not surprising that General Motors was the first major target of the newly formed United Auto Workers, CIO, in late 1936. After a forty-four–day strike, including the first major use of the sit-down technique, General Motors on February 11, 1937, recognized the union and on March 12, 1937, signed a contract which gave the UAW sole bargaining rights for six months in those plants which had been on strike.

Several related reasons can be advanced for this major change in the labor relations policy of GM. The sit-down strike itself, with its attendant publicity, demonstrated that large numbers of GM employees very much wanted unionism. Management, particularly Knudsen, was worried about the effect of further violence if the strike continued. The strike was also harming the competitive position of the company in what promised to be the best production year since 1929. Related to this was the decline in both earnings and dividends, and key management officials were large holders of stock. In addition, management felt that government at all levels was supporting the goals of the strikers. President Roosevelt, Frances Perkins, Jesse Jones, and James A. Farley all intervened in various ways; Michigan's Governor, Frank Murphy, refused to use state troops to enforce court orders; and various city officials in the Detroit industrial area were sympathetic to the strikers. At the same time, the LaFollette hearings were giving GM unfavorable publicity. Some management officials, such as Thomas Lamont, a Morgan partner, and Myron C. Taylor of U.S. Steel, who was then meeting secretly with John L. Lewis, were reported to have urged the General Motors management to recognize the UAW. Finally, the GM management, which was relatively inexperienced in bargaining, may simply have been "worn out," as Frances Perkins believed, as a result of the protracted negotiations with John L. Lewis and his colleagues and the tremendous tension generated by the fast-moving events in early 1937. William Knudsen is quoted in his biography as saying: ". . . all this talk about collective bargaining could have been made a good deal easier for all of us, if we had a few ground rules as to how we should proceed. There were several stages in the conflict. The whole thing looked something like a ball game, without an umpire, and everybody in the grandstand telling you what to do. That was about the way it was."[19]

The Chrysler Corporation, once GM had made the initial concessions, did not have the economic strength to resist the UAW. After a relatively short sit-down strike in March, 1937, an agreement with the union was reached on April 6. Although neither Chrysler nor General Motors was forced to grant exclusive bargaining rights to the UAW for several years, the 1937 agreements represented the major change in policy on unionism.

The Ford story is somewhat different. For years Henry Ford had been saying that he would have nothing to do with any union and in 1937 he said: "There shouldn't be any bargaining or dealing necessary between employers and employees. . . . We're all workers together, the men and I."[20] The beginning of the end for this policy came on February 10, 1941, when the Supreme Court upheld a lower court enforcement of NLRB orders concerning the bargaining rights of Ford employees. In April, Ford consented to NLRB elections when the NLRB agreed to call off a new series of hearings on unfair labor practice charges. On May 21, 1941, the UAW handily won elections in the River Rouge and Lincoln plants and on June 20, 1941, a contract was signed. With his flair for the dramatic, and perhaps to confound his competitors, Henry Ford accepted the union demands in full, including a wage increase, a shop steward system, seniority provisions, the union shop, and a checkoff. The union shop and the checkoff were the first in a major automobile company. Because of the Supreme Court position and the evidence available to the NLRB, the only alternative to Ford's capitulation might have been his going out of business.

Steel Industry

In contrast to the automobile industry, unionism in iron and steel has had a long, if turbulent, history. The Homestead strike in 1892 and the failure of the 1919 steel strike are major events in American labor history. Over the years, however, steel managements quite frankly did not want to deal with trade unions and were largely successful until the New Deal years in maintaining their version of the American Plan. Before the NRA, individual bargaining was the crux of their labor relations policy and of the major firms only Bethlehem and Youngstown even had employee representation plans.

As a producer of basic industrial products, the steel industry was one of the hardest hit in the depression and was anxious to have a steel code under the NRA. As a result of Section 7(a), almost all of the major firms established company unions, with an estimated 90 per cent of steel workers covered by the end of 1934.

In June, 1936, the Steel Workers Organizing Committee was set up by the CIO and over the next few months absorbed a number of the company union organizations. On March 17, 1937, Carnegie-Illinois, a major subsidiary of U.S. Steel, signed an agreement recognizing the SWOC as the bargaining agent for its members, and within three months agreements were reached with fourteen U.S. Steel subsidiaries and with a number of other companies, including Jones and Laughlin.[21]

Several immediate factors undoubtedly influenced the decision of U.S. Steel to change its policy on recognizing an "outside" labor union. The defection of a number of the company unions meant that a strike for recognition could very well have had some success. Indications were that prolonged court battles would only delay the necessity of permitting NLRB elections, which the company unions would almost certainly not win, and delay the time when bargaining with the Steel Workers Organizing Committee would be ordered. In this situation, there were sound business reasons for recognizing the union. In 1936 and early 1937, business was getting better and the corporation had a chance to recoup some of its losses of the early depression years. Not foreseeing the sharp recession which began in the summer of 1937, the assumption was that business was on the way up. Recognizing the union and avoiding a long, costly strike meant that U.S. Steel could gamble on an advantage over its competitors if they were struck over the issue of recognition.

A number of the large producers refused to follow the lead of U.S. Steel and decided to fight the union. Some of the management people were highly annoyed at the abandonment of the "open shop" policy by U.S. Steel and this annoyance may have been a factor in their decision. The result was the so-called Little Steel strikes against Republic, Youngstown Sheet and Tube, Inland, Bethlehem, and Weirton, and several years of active opposition to the union, numerous NLRB hearings, and court cases. Finally, in 1941 and 1942, largely as a result of court orders, most of the companies which had been holding out recognized the Steel Workers Organizing Committee and began to bargain. Weirton, however, continued with an independent union and was involved in unfair labor practice charges throughout the forties.

The managements of a number of steel companies came closer to fighting unionism to the bitter end than was true in most manufacturing industries. This may have been in part because the steel industry has a tradition of highly individualistic leaders, whose individualism included the belief that a worker could only lose if he joined a group whose leadership was outside the company.

In his autobiography, Tom M. Girdler of Republic Steel attributes full recognition of SWOC to the Supreme Court ruling that union agreements must be written contracts.

> In our private discussions my associates and I find ourselves unreconciled. We can't help but feel that if the checkoff, which is now a fact in the steel industry, had been resisted by business generally as effectively as we and our employees resisted it in that so-called strike in Little Steel, everybody in the country would have been the gainer. . . .
>
> There is little comfort for me in the realization that my warnings of 1937 have been justified by subsequent events. When our plants were being besieged I was saying that C.I.O. leaders simply wanted to force workers to join their unions and pay dues. I said they wanted, not to help labor, but to gain for themselves tremendous political and economic power. . . . I do not believe a majority of workers in this country want such a system. But in the present circumstance, what are they going to do about it? [22]

That Tom Girdler, and others with similar convictions, did not fight unionism to the last ditch demonstrates that he and other industrial leaders had other principles and interests stronger than their belief that unionism was bad for their companies. One can only conclude that by 1940, in those companies and industries where the pressures were sufficiently strong, managerial labor relations policy had to be built around the existence of unionism and collective bargaining.

A New Era Emerges

Similar accounts of the change in management policy inherent in the process of recognition could be given for other mass production industries. Although the pattern varied both in timing and in the degree of union penetration, it was the same pattern. Recognition and acceptance of unionism were, however, far from universal. In the first place, recognition did not always mean acceptance of the principles of collective bargaining or a belief that collective bargaining had become a permanent feature of the industrial scene. Secondly, a majority of plants in the late thirties were not organized, and, therefore, it was relatively easy for their managers to take the position that they did not believe in bargaining. Only about a third of manufacturing employees were trade union members by 1940, although the proportion was much higher in such key industries as basic steel, automobiles, rubber products, and electrical machinery.

Since the central concern of this volume is the labor movement, however, it is pertinent to emphasize the labor relations policies of those managements who began to bargain with trade unions. The story of these policies is reasonably representative of the state of managerial labor relations because the unionized companies, like the non-union companies, varied in their approach to the management of the worker from the most minimal type of management-worker relationship to very elaborate structures of personnel services, welfare programs, and communication techniques. This means an emphasis on the larger firms since the unions tended to be concentrated in the larger companies.

Among the firms that recognized trade unions, two distinct trends emerged after 1937. One trend is represented by those managements who attempted to build a constructive and harmonious relationship with organized labor, and the other trend by those who remained unreconciled and who dealt with unions, when necessary, at arm's length. It was not a clear-cut dichotomy, however, since some managements were in both camps to the extent that they bargained in good faith and sought a good relationship but at the same time actively participated in association campaigns to delimit the scope of bargaining and to regulate union activities through legislation. In the period after 1937, also, "human relations" began to come into vogue, although its uses varied from attempts to improve management-union relations to attempts to circumvent local unions.

The Changing Character of Labor Relations, 1937 to 1941

For any one company, recognition of a trade union was the most obvious change in labor relations policy, although recognition by itself did not always mean much of a change in the character of labor relations. Initially, recognition was often merely formal and was limited to recognizing the union as representative only of its own members. Until the Supreme Court decision in the Heinz case in 1941, a number of companies refused to be committed to a signed, written contract and fostered the impression that agreements reached in bargaining were in effect unilateral company decisions arrived at after consultation with employee representatives. The habit of having the final say was strong, as was the belief that it was essential for management to retain the ultimate authority over all policies affecting employees.

These habits and beliefs led to a continuation of anti-union practices in some segments of industry long after the Wagner Act was upheld by the Supreme Court. These practices included continued domination of "independent" unions and discrimination against members of "outside" unions, going through the motions of collective bargaining with no intention of making concessions or reaching an agreement, and attempting to create a public opinion hostile to organized labor. Concern over the unknown and seemingly unpredictable results of genuine collective bargaining also meant that the more extreme forms of fighting unions did not immediately diminish. Industrial espionage, back-to-work movements, vigilante groups, citizens' committees, and the Mohawk Valley Formula were all used after 1937. NLRB records, however, show a gradual decline in the number of cases involving the more flagrant forms of unfair labor practices. Also, as the extent of union recognition grew, there was a higher proportion of representation cases and a declining proportion of complaint cases.

The belligerent type of labor relations, therefore, was gradually fading away after 1937. In its place, in unionized companies, was a growing amount of the kind of "good faith" bargaining that usually fails to make the headlines. Many a management discovered for the first time that it was possible to "live with" a union and even that there could be unsuspected virtues in the process of collective bargaining. Many such managements not only became reconciled to the new order in the industrial scene but also achieved a smooth transition to the new relationship with labor. Paul G. Hoffman of Studebaker, Jay C. Hormel of the meat-packing firm, James D. Zellerbach of the Pacific Coast paper industry, and Gerard Swope of General Electric are but a few of the many individuals in top management who have been credited with such an accomplishment.

The orderly and successful transition to a collective bargaining relationship, however, did not always mean complete acceptance of the new political and economic power of the labor movement. Management in general, and many managements with reasonably good labor relations in particular, fought for changes in federal and state labor law that would restrict and circumscribe union activity. Willingness to bargain was not inconsistent with believing that unions in general were being given too much power, that jurisdictional disputes should not be allowed to create costly strikes, and that many trade union practices placed unnecessary restrictions on efficient production.

The basic fact of an enlarged and vigorous trade union movement was, nevertheless, increasingly accepted, even though not widely welcomed, in management circles. Only a few years before, in October, 1935, a *Fortune* survey had shown that a substantial majority of the "prosperous," "proprietors," and "salaried persons" (groups that presumably would include all of management) believed that labor in general was treated fairly in the United States. Since for the most part workers were unorganized in 1935 and many union members were not represented in industry, the implication is that groups other than the "poor" and "factory labor" thought that labor relations of that day were adequate. In February, 1939, however, the *Fortune* survey asked individuals whether they thought it wise or foolish for the management of businesses to try to keep unions from organizing in their plants. A majority of both the "prosperous" and "poor" thought it was foolish. Moreover, "executives" thought it foolish in greater proportion (68 per cent) than did "factory labor" (61 per cent). By 1939, therefore, a large segment of American industry had apparently come to believe that unionism was here to stay. This was particularly true in the larger firms. Although there were serious reservations about the aims of the CIO, to a substantial proportion of management the AFL now appeared almost respectable—though this may have been in part the viewpoint of those dealing with the CIO.

The entrance of a union in a plant and its recognition had effects both upon personnel administration and on the relationships between management and worker in the shop. The union had only a moderate effect upon the techniques of personnel administration, however. Such techniques as selection tests, job evaluation, and efficiency ratings were sometimes subject to modification as the result of the management-union relationship, but their introduction or continuance was typically determined by other factors. Similarly, the relative decline of indirect financial incentives, such as stock purchase plans and various forms of welfare benefits, can be attributed more directly to the impact of the depression than to the rise of trade unionism. It was not until the war and postwar years that the unions significantly influenced the size and scope of benefit plans. As was true both before and after the thirties, the fluctuations in the personnel management movement were more directly influenced by the business cycle and the state of the labor market than by the relative strength of the labor movement.

To the extent, however, that personnel departments undertook such industrial relations work as grievance handling and union negotiations, the unions did affect personnel administration. It would be more correct to say, nevertheless, that unions greatly changed industrial relations and that personnel departments were sometimes used to carry out some or all of the industrial relations functions of management. Policy determination remained, however, in the hands of top management and the character of labor relations in any company tended to reflect the beliefs, convictions, and labor philosophy of the chief executive officers, even though some practices might be the result of labor law rather than the result of management conviction.

At least a few top management people in the late thirties accepted the idea of unionism to the point of believing that strong unions were better than weak ones on the ground that a weak union is forced into excesses and a strong union is able to accept responsibility and work with management in improving productivity for the betterment of both company and worker. Techniques of union-management coöperation designed to increase productivity and reduce costs, while not new, received renewed interest, particularly during the defense period starting in 1939 and later during the war. Considerable attention was given to such examples of union-management coöperation as existed in some parts of the clothing industries, the steel industry, and a few others.

But union-management coöperation was not then, nor has it been since, as popular as "human relations"—the "discovery" that the factory is a social system in which the norms of social groups, formal and informal, are major determinants of the accomplishments of the entire organization. The rapid growth and interest in human relations research and practice, as exemplified by the Hawthorne experiments of Elton Mayo and his group, have been too often described to need any summary here, but it is pertinent to note that it was in the late thirties that the work of the human relations school began to have an effect on management thinking in some companies. It was little more than a beginning, however. The meaning and implications of the human relations findings are still imperfectly understood, and before 1940 human relations, then in its formative years, was probably more generally misunderstood and more frequently misapplied than it is today.

To some managements, human relations was a set of principles, quickly learned and easily applied, which would have magical results on the behavior of the work force. The results sought were not only a "better" attitude toward work and increased productivity but also the creation or strengthening of loyalty to the company, sometimes with the hope that thereby there would be less loyalty to the union. This view was probably more popular in some of the nonunion firms whose managements wished to remain nonunion than it was in unionized companies. Attempts to remain nonunion, however, did not necessarily mean "poor" human relations or dissatisfied workers. On the contrary, a number of managements were able to achieve remarkable results in improved morale and worker satisfaction by adapting the human relations findings to the particular circumstances found in their plants.

In unionized plants, those managements who were least reconciled to unionism tended to be so because they believed in the individualistic approach, and as a result they were not apt to be receptive to human relations or they would see human relations only as another anti-union tool. For the growing number of managements, however, who came to believe that union-management relations could be coöperative and constructive, human relations was more likely to have an appeal. In many such cases, management believed that human relations was a technique to be applied quite separately from the union relationship. To them the union's interests were strictly economic and workers joined unions primarily to gain economic power commensurate with that of the employer. Human relations, while its ultimate goals for management were economic, involved recognition and manipulation of informal groups in such a way that workers would better enjoy their work place, their fellow workers, and their work. For many managements, in other words, the union was still an outside agency, and it did not occur to them that the union might be an important part of the social scheme within the factory.[23]

In some companies, however, the union was recognized as an important, and perhaps even the key, group in affecting worker attitudes toward the firm and toward productivity. Management in such firms, instead of working around and outside the union, found it worthwhile to seek and obtain the union's coöperation in attempting to increase production and lower costs. That kind of relationship in the late thirties was relatively rare, but it was nonetheless important because it helped to establish a model of successful union-management relationships.

Opposition to Unions Through Legislation and Public Opinion, 1937 to 1941

After the first flush of major union gains in mass production industries, highlighted by recognition in such leading firms as U.S. Steel, General Motors, and General Electric, opposition to unions, while continuing in many plants in increasingly subtle forms, moved to a greater extent and with increased vigor into other areas—namely, legislation and public opinion. The sit-down strikes, the tremendous publicity given to the more violent aspects of labor disputes, the belief that union power had reached a point where it was harmful to the average consumer, and the split in the labor movement, culminating in the expulsion of the CIO unions from the AFL in May, 1938, all contributed to a shift in the public's attitude toward organized labor. The associations representing management, using all the devices of modern communications, did all they could to encourage this shift.

Oversimplifying the picture greatly, one might say that labor was, figuratively, being pushed into the doghouse so long occupied by management. It was not, of course, a complete reversal, since management's prestige itself was still at a low ebb; but there was a tendency, revealed in public opinion surveys, for large segments of the public either to be neutral in questions involving labor and management or to blame both sides in industrial disputes.

The factors which were causing a shift in public opinion, together with the Wagner Act validation and the 1937–38 recession, also stimulated a renewed effort on the part of the major management associations to change federal and state labor legislation. Further, the reassertion of the normally conservative tendencies of legislative bodies led the associations to believe that the time had arrived to obtain clauses more favorable to management and more restrictive to unions.

Support of these moves, however, was far from uniform among individual managements. A minority of managers remained opposed, on principle, to the entire Wagner Act and favored its outright repeal. At the other extreme were those management people who believed or knew from experience that they could work within the bounds of the law. These managements were of the opinion that collective bargaining could work to the mutual benefit of company and worker and were not convinced that union power would get out of hand. A far larger group than either of these, however, was composed of those managements who either had accepted or were willing to accept collective bargaining but who insisted that the Wagner Act needed to be amended in order to make its impact more equal on labor and management and to make illegal such union demands as the checkoff and the closed shop.

The associations which represented management in the legislative and public relations areas reflected this majority view, although they differed in the degree to which they wanted the labor laws amended. The American Management Association, for example, for the most part left national labor policy to other groups and instead concentrated on promoting the spread of scientific management and personnel administration. By focusing on methods of handling in-plant problems arising under national labor policy, the AMA probably had the net effect of furthering the acceptance of collective bargaining. The NAM and the Chamber of Commerce, on the other hand, once the Supreme Court upheld the Wagner Act, increased their efforts to amend that Act.

Whether the drive to amend had widespread public support, as the associations claimed, is questionable, but there is little doubt that management in general believed that amendments were both desirable and necessary. In September, 1939, in its "forum of executive opinion," *Fortune* reported that the Wagner Act was the least popular of major New Deal measures affecting business, with less than 10 per cent of the businessman respondents approving the Act as it stood. The survey also indicated, however, that at least two-fifths of the executives thought the law should be kept in modified form.

The objectives of this legislative drive reflected at least some change in management thinking and in managerial policy toward unionism. For one thing, the principle of collective bargaining was now more generally established in the managerial mind. The NAM, for example, which has tended to reflect the most conservative management thinking, in late 1938 for the first time fully committed itself to the collective bargaining principle and stated that an employer should deal with the chosen representatives of the employees unless there was a strike for illegal purposes or by illegal means.[24] While unionism was being accepted, the NAM and a large proportion of management believed that the scales had been pushed too far in the direction of labor, both in the Wagner Act itself and in its administration by the NLRB.

These beliefs were strengthened by the Smith hearings which began in July, 1939, and which convinced many in management that the NLRB had fostered the cause of organized labor and more particularly the cause of the CIO beyond anything called for in the Wagner Act. The following year, when the Smith bill was passed by the House, it contained amendments that covered most of the major objections of management. These included removal of the implication in the Wagner Act preamble that employer denial of organizing rights and refusal to bargain necessarily led to strikes and industrial strife, protection of "freedom of speech" for employers, provision for employer requests of representation elections, and separation of the judicial from the prosecuting functions of the NLRB. The Smith bill, however, failed to survive in the Senate, although many of its provisions were finally adopted in 1947 in the Taft-Hartley Act.

Employer associations had more immediate success in some of the state legislatures. In 1939, four states (Wisconsin, Pennsylvania, Michigan, and Minnesota) adopted laws which placed restrictions on unions as well as on employers. Wisconsin and Pennsylvania had had "baby Wagner Acts," but in 1939, Wisconsin replaced its Labor Relations

Act with an Employment Peace Act and Pennsylvania adopted drastic amendments to its Labor Relations Act. By 1947, all but three states which had had laws similar to the Wagner Act, limited largely to labor's right to organize, had amended these laws to restrict unfair labor practices of both unions and employers. Typical provisions banned massed picketing, secondary boycotts, sit-down strikes, and coercion or intimidation of workers in their right to join or not to join unions. All of these legislative changes were the result of the lobbying of state and local employer associations, with the backing of both individual managements and the NAM and Chamber of Commerce.

Conclusions

The analysis of managerial policies toward unionism in the thirties leads to two general conclusions. The first of these supports the proposition that a meaningful interpretation of labor relations policies requires an understanding of the goals and philosophies of managers. The available evidence indicates that during the New Deal period management's self-concept of its role in the economy and in society did not permit it to change its basic philosophy and belief about unionism, namely that unions would interfere with and compromise management's full and rightful authority to manage. The second major conclusion is that management, when the pressure of events made the acceptance of unionism and of the principle of collective bargaining increasingly mandatory, attempted to adapt itself and its labor relations policies and practices in such a way that the maximum amount of managerial authority and control would be retained. Looking backward, the labor relations policies of industrial management seem to have been for the most part purposeful and rational when examined in the context of the times and of management's knowledge and experience.

The turning point in management resistance to recognition of unions did not come until the Supreme Court validation of the Wagner Act in 1937. The Wagner Act validation meant that almost any management, when faced with a union effort to obtain recognition that was fully supported by money and membership, had as the only alternatives either capitulation, perhaps delayed for some years through vigorous legal fights and anti-union tactics, or serious business losses and even the collapse of the enterprise. This basic dilemma for unreconciled managements is illustrated again and again by the history of union organization between 1937 and 1941 as company after company in such industries as automobiles, basic steel, meat-packing, and rubber recognized trade unions and began to bargain. The largest firms were the favorite targets and were the most vulnerable to concerted campaigns.

After 1937, collective bargaining became increasingly accepted, especially where there was no clear-cut alternative. Two distinct trends emerged, however, with one group of managements attempting to build constructive and harmonious relationships with organized labor and another group remaining unreconciled but bargaining with labor, when necessary, at arm's length. In addition, managements in both camps, either individually or through trade associations, attempted to limit the scope of bargaining and to regulate union activities through federal and state legislative amendments.

At the end of the depression decade, few managements were any more convinced than they had been at the beginning of the decade that unions were a good thing for business. Management had come to believe, however, that workers, collectively represented, should be at least a subordinate partner in the determination of questions of immediate concern to the workers, such as wages, hours, and working conditions. Management had not, at least for the most part, accepted the notion that both management and worker are better off under a collectively bargained agreement. Significantly, though, managerial efforts to curb union power were shifting, in the late thirties, from direct opposition in the factories to opposition in legislatures and in the forum of public opinion.

Finally, the analysis of historical change in managerial labor relations leads to the conclusion that the development of labor relations policies has been for the most part evolutionary. Although it is outside the scope of this essay to review the events after the thirties, a careful analysis of the period since 1940 would undoubtedly show a further evolutionary change. While "revolutionary" changes may have occurred in a number of individual firms, the over-all change has been gradual. Most industrial managers today look upon collective bargaining as a normal, established, and necessary aspect of industrial life. And in the vanguard are those managements who not only have accepted collective bargaining but who believe also that it pays in worker morale and productivity and in their own prestige and satisfaction to work diligently for a labor-management relationship which is both constructive and mature.

Notes

1 In addition to its focus on policies towards unionism in mass production manufacturing, this essay is further limited in scope to an analysis of top management policy formation. Labor relations practices are not discussed in detail. For example, policies on union recognition are discussed but not details on management positions in collective bargaining; management policies on legislation and government regulations are examined but not many details of specific National Labor Relations Board rulings as they affected industry; trade associations are discussed to the extent that they reflect managerial policies toward unionism but not with respect to their bargaining activities. Some of these matters are covered in Chapter 9.

2 Many of Taylor's followers, including Robert G. Valentine and Morris L. Cooke, differed from him in their recognition of the importance of securing union consent and coöperation. See Milton J. Nadworny, *Scientific Management and the Unions: 1900–1932* (Cambridge: Harvard University Press, 1955).

3 In 1926, for example, there were fewer than 450 known plans and less than 1.5 million workers covered. See National Industrial Conference Board, *Collective Bargaining Through Employee Representation* (New York: The Board, 1933), p. 16.

4 A study made in 1928 indicated that only 12 per cent of all wage earners were in plants with personnel departments. Of 4,500 plants surveyed, with over 4 million wage earners, 34 per cent of the firms with 250 workers or more had personnel departments but less than 3 per cent of the plants with less than 250 workers. See National Industrial Conference Board, *Industrial Relations in Small Plants* (New York: The Board, 1929), p. 20.

5 National Industrial Conference Board, *Individual and Collective Bargaining under the N.I.R.A.* (New York: The Board, 1933), pp. 32–37.

6 *Ibid.*, pp. 23–24, and U.S. Bureau of Labor Statistics, *Characteristics of Company Unions, 1935*, Bulletin No. 634 (Washington: Government Printing Office, 1938), p. 50. The term "company union" is used here, as it was by the Bureau of Labor Statistics, to mean any type of employee representation plan or independent, unaffiliated association of workers whose membership is limited to one plant or one company.

7 Based on data from National Industrial Conference Board, *Collective Bargaining Through Employee Representation* (New York: The Board, 1933), p. 16; Leo Wolman, *Ebb and Flow in Trade Unionism* (New York: National Bureau of Economic Research, 1936), p. 16; and Twentieth Century Fund, *Labor and the Government* (New York: McGraw-

Hill Book Co., 1935). Comparisons of trade union and company union membership should be treated with caution because many company unions at this time did not have "members" as such. The data above refer to the production workers employed in plants with company unions and thus the use of the terms "coverage" for company unions and "membership" for trade unions.

8 In representation elections held by federal Labor Boards between August, 1933, and September, 1935, trade unions received two-thirds of the valid votes cast and company unions less than 30 per cent. See Harry A. Millis and Royal E. Montgomery, *Organized Labor* (New York: McGraw-Hill Book Co., 1945), Table 20, p. 847.

9 *Monthly Labor Review,* XLI (December, 1935), pp. 1450–51, and Bureau of Labor Statistics Bulletin No. 634 (1935), pp. 36–45.

10 National Labor Relations Board, *First Annual Report* (1936), pp. 46 and 48.

11 E. Marks and M. Bartlett, "Employee Elections Conducted by National Labor Relations Board," *Monthly Labor Review,* XLVII (July, 1938), p. 37; National Industrial Conference Board, *What Employers Are Doing For Employees* (New York: The Board, 1936), p. 10.

12 It is of interest to note that in the fall of 1955 Remington Rand concluded a union agreement containing the union shop, climaxing ten years of relatively peaceful labor-management relations.

13 C. R. Dooley, "Collective Dealing Versus Bargaining," in *Collective Bargaining for Today and Tomorrow,* Henry C. Metcalf, ed. (New York: Harper and Bros., 1937), pp. 35–43.

14 Millis and Montgomery, *Organized Labor,* pp. 852–53. The "independents" referred to include only nonaffiliated unions representing more than one plant or employer.

15 National Labor Relations Board, *Characteristics of 60 Company-Dominated Unions,* Research Memo No. 70 (December, 1939).

16 Address by Frank I. Badgley, Industrial Relations Director, Swift and Company, at the Twenty-eighth Annual Convention of the Institute of Meat Packers, October 23, 1933.

17 *CIO News,* Packinghouse Workers edition, October 2, 1939.

18 An interview with James R. Holcomb. An outstanding exception to the resistance of the Big Four occurred in September, 1933, when George A. Hormel Company recognized an independent union in its Austin, Minnesota, plant.

19 Norman Beasley, *Knudsen: A Biography* (New York: McGraw-Hill Book Co., 1947), p. 182.

20 *Time,* April 19, 1937, p. 16.

21 The Jones and Laughlin Steel Corporation has a claim to fame because the Supreme Court decision on April 12, 1937, upholding NLRB orders to cease unlawful discrimination, also involved the constitutionality of the Wagner Act. The outcome for Jones and Laughlin was compliance

with the order, NLRB elections in May, 1937, and recognition of the Steel Workers Organizing Committee.

22 Tom M. Girdler in collaboration with Boyden Sparkes, *Boot Straps, the Autobiography of Tom M. Girdler* (New York: Charles Scribner's Sons, 1943), pp. 374–75.

23 Human relations may also have been, for some managements, a way of implementing their own belief that their employees should consider themselves a "big, happy family." The paternalistic instinct has traditionally been strong in American management.

24 Forty-third Annual Congress of American Industry, *Industry's Platform for 1938* (New York: National Association of Manufacturers, December, 1938).

9

Collective Bargaining Developments

DORIS E. PULLMAN *and* L. REED TRIPP

TRADE UNION activity, with emphasis upon the "new unionism" which emerged in the mass production industries, is a much-told aspect of the New Deal period. How new the "new unionism" was, and how much its subsequent development owed to the earlier labor movement tradition in this country, is explored in other chapters of this volume. This chapter deals with the form and content of the collective bargaining which developed with positive measures of governmental support, such as the National Industrial Recovery Act and the Wagner Act.

Just as the discussion of the expansion of unionism in the 1930's has shown that the new unionism was grafted upon an older labor movement, a consideration of collective bargaining developments must recognize the prior existence of collective bargaining structures with the older unions in a number of industries including the railroads, construction, printing, coal mining, men's and women's clothing. New Deal legislation gave protection to labor's right to organize and enabled trade unions and companies to negotiate thousands of additional agreements, in the above-mentioned industries and also in new fields such as automobiles, rubber, chemicals, electrical equipment, and steel. Certainly one of the most important aspects of trade union activity in the 1930's was the extension of collective bargaining to firms of very large size.

During the decade, collective bargaining changed in many ways: The National Labor Relations Board determined the proper unit for bargaining purposes and thus set limits for the coverage of contracts. Management, with some reluctance, accepted majority rule in determining labor representation and gave exclusive bargaining rights to the union which won a plant election. The Board developed definitions of "good faith" bargaining and determined that contracts should be put into written form. Through the bargaining process, unions and management agreed upon working conditions, seniority rules, discharge practices, and procedures for interpreting the contract and settling grievances. Agreements were made involving union status and management prerogatives. Within units brought under collective bargaining contracts for the first time, new roles developed for paid union representatives, shop stewards, foremen, industrial relations managers, and arbitrators.

Emergence of Collective Bargaining Processes from Competing Concepts

In the early 1930's, opinions differed as to the meaning of collective bargaining. By the middle of the decade it was by no means clear that traditional private bargaining arrangements with independent unions, or collective bargaining as we know it today, would emerge from the concepts competing for legal and factual acceptance as to the basic nature of collective bargaining. Under the NIRA, workers were encouraged to organize into unions of their own choosing. However, the predominant method of handling employee relations in large mass production plants was the individual bargaining basis. It was not until after the Supreme Court upheld the constitutionality of the Wagner Act that collective bargaining in these plants took firm hold.

Employee Representation Plans

As in the previous decade, employee representation plans continued to grow, and they were considered by many to fulfill the collective bargaining concept of the NIRA and the first National Labor Board. The NRA boards allowed company unions to appear on the ballot and to attain recognition, as long as they were not forced upon the workers by the companies. After observing several months of NIRA experience, *Business Week* reported a faster growth of employee representation plans than of trade unions.[1]

When the Wagner Act, in line with the Texas and New Orleans Railroad decision of 1930, prohibited company-dominated unions, strenuous efforts were made to demonstrate the facade of "independent" unions, confined to a single plant or company and not affiliated with the outside labor movement. These attempts were marked with varying degrees of success. The swing-over of workers' councils to the

Steel Workers Organizing Committee is well known. In 1935, the United Automobile Workers invaded employee representation plans at Chrysler Motors and took over the majority of offices. At the Schenectady Works of the General Electric Company, the United Electrical, Radio and Machine Workers Union won an NLRB election over the company union, which was then disbanded.

Some companies found independent unions difficult to bargain with because there was no possibility of calling upon more responsible international union leadership to temper occasional extremism at the local level. In other situations, local employees' associations continued to maintain their members' allegiance despite repeated election challenges through World War II and the postwar decade. Other local unions, as in the case of federal labor unions within the AFL, resisted direct ties with national unions and carried on collective bargaining largely at the local level. Thus, while company domination was clearly rejected, much heterogeneity remained as to whether the local or the national union was to have the major role in bargaining.

The National Labor Relations Board, in a long series of cases, ordered the disestablishment of company-dominated unions. For example, the International Harvester Company was ordered to withdraw recognition from the Harvester Industrial Council plan, which provided for monthly meetings of employee and management representatives, and to disestablish the council. A ruling of the NLRB ordering the disbanding of a ten-year-old company union at the Newport News Shipbuilding Company was upheld by the United States Supreme Court in 1940.

Legislated Terms of Employment

A further concept which competed with collective bargaining in the New Deal period was governmentally legislated terms of employment. Most of the codes under the NIRA provided a forty-hour week, but some such as bituminous coal mining, blouse and skirt manufacturing, fur dressing and dyeing, electrical manufacturing, shipbuilding, rubber tire, dress and men's clothing industries provided thirty-five to thirty-seven and a half hours. The codes set minimum wage rates for unskilled and semiskilled workers; rates for higher classifications were left to collective bargaining between companies and unions.

After the codes were invalidated by the United States Supreme

Court in the Schechter case, Congress restored the legislative method of setting minimum work standards in the Walsh-Healey Act of 1936. This law, called the Public Contracts Act, provided that manufacturers and contractors bidding for government contracts in excess of $10,000 value had to agree to an eight-hour day and forty-hour week, and overtime after these hours. Wage rates were to be at or above the prevailing minimum as set forth by the Secretary of Labor. In practice, a single minimum wage rate was usually set for an entire industry.

Congress then set new underpinning requirements for working conditions and the content of collective bargaining agreements in the Fair Labor Standards Act of 1938. This law provided for minimum rates, gradually rising to 40 cents an hour, for all goods produced or carried in interstate commerce. Work over forty hours per week was to be paid at the overtime rate of time and one-half. This provision applied to all wage rates, not just those at the minimum level. The law also contained certain prohibitions against child labor.

Apart from these minimum standards set by legislation, however, conditions of work remained subject to negotiation by union and management after the NIRA codes were invalidated, although some of their features were continued through collective bargaining. For example, in 1936 the Millinery Stabilization Commission was set up in an agreement between the Employers' Association in New York City and the Millinery Workers' Union to formulate and put into practice some policies intended to rehabilitate the industry. This Commission of three citizens drawn from outside the trade was appointed by the parties to the contract to develop a code of fair practices, including wage and hour standards. The Commission's activities were financed through the sale of a consumers' protection label, and this label became a symbol for compliance with the Commission's standards.[2]

Generally, both labor and management preferred direct negotiations to any further legislative effort to dictate conditions of work. In sketching the various phases of collective bargaining during the 1930's, however, it is important to note the continued role of the federal government in the otherwise bilateral process, as illustrated, for example, in the recognition and negotiating processes associated with the establishment of the new collective bargaining relationships.

Negotiating Processes in the 1930's

For significant developments in the process of negotiation, we may look to the firms of very large size in mass production industry brought within collective bargaining for the first time during the 1930's. These developments, however, occurred in the latter half of the decade after the earlier opposition and company union maneuvers had given way before the mounting organizing drives and judicial affirmation of the new law. The 1937 agreement of the Steel Workers Organizing Committee with Carnegie-Illinois, the largest U.S. Steel subsidiary, broke the open-shop tradition of the steel industry. This agreement was largely the outcome of the personal negotiations of two men, Myron C. Taylor, chairman of the board of the corporation, and John L. Lewis, president of the United Mine Workers. They were brought together through a mutual friend, Thomas Moses of the H. C. Frick Coal Company, after the personal urging of President Franklin D. Roosevelt.

The General Motors and Chrysler contracts, which were signed in the spring of 1937 after bitter sit-down strikes, were made in recognition of growing CIO strength and the power of the National Labor Relations Board to compel recognition if the employees decided to organize. Many subsequent agreements in the mass production industries were reached because the NLRB certified a union as bargaining agent, after an election, and ordered an end to discriminatory practices against union members. Thus, early CIO contracts represented a shot-gun marriage between an aggressive union and a subdued but unwilling company.

Negotiations in the newly organized plants reflected the struggle for recognition. The Lewis-Taylor agreement in steel set a pattern for highly personalized negotiations, and this continued through the Murray-Fairless settlements of the post–World War II years. In other instances where organizers negotiated the settlements, the transition from the bitterness of organizing drives to mature agreement presented difficulties.

The highly personalized negotiations of the CIO bore some resemblance to the work of business agents in the old established AFL craft unions. In contrast, in some of the new industrial unions, rank and file negotiating committees took a prominent and sometimes stormy part. The election procedure was often accompanied by rivalries for union office, political rifts within the membership, and suspicion of international representatives. Union democracy was going through the turmoil of new leaders and inexperienced members. Only gradually did the pattern of joint participation of local and international officers emerge. Men had to learn to weigh, adjust, and accommodate to local and national union needs in the bargaining process.

Practices which developed in a pragmatic manner were bound to show great diversity. Even today, negotiating committees and practices differ widely. The 1930's were different from the present time because they were the turbulent formative period, during which aggressive organizing and opposition campaigns predominated.

The National Labor Relations Board came to have strong influence on negotiations. Section 8(5) of the Act made it an unfair labor practice for an employer to refuse to bargain collectively with the representatives of his employees, subject to the provisions of Section 9(a). The NLRB began to spell out different aspects of the obligation to bargain with a validly certified union. The employer had to meet and to seek an understanding in good faith. There were to be personal conferences, at reasonable times and places. The Board's *Second Annual Report* discussed the expected steps in the bargaining process: meetings, submission of employees' demands, bargaining, making a collective agreement which would "stabilize employment relations for a period of time," adjusting differences, and reaching a common ground.[3]

The Board stated that an employer's unilateral determination of terms of employment, when a recognized representative of the employees was attempting to bargain, was a refusal to bargain collectively within the meaning of Section 8(5).[4] In a long line of cases, beginning with St. Joseph's Stockyards Company in 1936, the Board explained the employer's duties, including the obligation to accept the procedure of collective bargaining as historically practiced, and to place the agreement in writing. The written contract was further supported in the Inland Steel case in 1938. The Board said that it was an unfair labor practice for the company to announce in advance that an agreement would not be signed, and that once an agreement was reached, it had to be put in writing. In the H. J. Heinz Company case, the Supreme Court supported the NLRB in its contention that a unilaterally posted statement was not enough; the employer had to enter into a signed contract.

Related also to recognition were cases where the Board found that an employer was not complying with Section 8(5) unless he accorded exclusive recognition to the statutory representative. He could not fulfill this obligation by offering to bargain with the organization for its members only.[5] Beyond the recognition clause, other substantive matters soon came before the Board. In the matter of the Singer Manufacturing Company and the United Electrical, Radio and Machine Workers of America (1940), the Board held that an employer's refusal to negotiate concerning paid holidays, vacations, and bonuses constituted an infraction of Section 8(5). Later developments, in the postwar years, brought government further into the determination of contract terms and negotiating processes.

Negotiating processes in the 1930's may be viewed as a result of a combination of forces. They revealed the aggressive organizing campaigns and bitter opposition struggles. In the midst of turmoil the government agency seeking to carry out the objectives of the Wagner Act found itself engaged in administrative control of the bargaining process, verging even on the scope of content of the agreement. In the sense that such compulsion was widely necessary to recognition and the establishment of bargaining, it is assumed that government activity facilitated the bargaining process. In another sense, however, the government's compelling actions, with frequently accompanying bitterness, may have actually aggravated the barriers to acceptance of what is in the final analysis a voluntary bargaining relationship. In any case, the role of the Board necessarily stimulated recourse to legal procedures which have characterized American collective bargaining ever since.

Collective Bargaining Structure

A significant characteristic of the current collective bargaining scene in the United States is great diversity of structure. A study by the Bureau of Labor Statistics in 1950[6] showed that two-thirds of all collective bargaining agreements related to the employees of a single plant. These tended to be the smaller contracts in coverage, as only one-third of the workers were covered by such contracts. While only one-eighth of the contracts were multi-plant agreements, these applied to about 40 per cent of the workers covered. Multi-plant contracts prevailed in the steel, transportation equipment, and rubber industries. Multi-employer or association-type contracts were fewer in number and were common in the printing and publishing, coal mining, apparel, and building trades, and among hotels and restaurants. Multi-employer bargaining practices existed of course where separate contracts were executed by the participating companies, just as multi-plant bargaining took place at times when separate plant contracts were maintained. The extent to which events of the 1930's contributed to this complexity warrants brief review.

The older AFL organizations were heavily craft-oriented, although some were industrial organizations. In any case, the AFL had stressed the sovereignty of individual unions over given job territories. Government-sponsored elections were used under the NRA and the Wagner Act to provide support and teeth for the employees' right to organize. The principle of majority rule became an important bulwark against proportional representation, which unions viewed as divisive. The AFL became suspicious of the election procedure, however, as a threat to its precepts of union legitimacy, and proposed amendments to the Wagner Act on this point. With the split in the labor movement, however, the election procedure inevitably became solidified in formal, legal processes. Structure of bargaining then became a resultant of action by government as well as by unions and employers.

Recognition for Members Only, or Sole Bargaining Rights

Basic to developments in collective bargaining structure was the issue of exclusive bargaining rights for a particular union. Although practice in the older bargaining relationships had generally conformed to this principle either for particular crafts or for larger groups of employees, the legal clarification of sole bargaining rights in large firms under the new legislation was not accomplished until the very end of the 1930's.

As noted in Chapter 8, the Automobile Labor Board, under the NRA, worked out a system of proportional representation under which committees from the various unions would bargain jointly with the same management.[7] Then the NLRB in the Houde Engineering Corporation case in 1934 decided that majority choice by the employees gave a union exclusive bargaining rights. The employer was not to bargain with a minority of workers, if the majority had chosen another union as its representative. However, the minority could present grievances or confer with employers.

After invalidation of the NIRA and the subsequent passage of the Wagner Act, many employers again took the position that they would not give exclusive bargaining rights to any union. When the General Motors contract was signed in 1937, the union was demanding much stronger security. The agreement to recognize the union as bargaining agent for its members was a compromise. The company indicated good faith by promising no discrimination against employees because of union activity. Governor Frank Murphy of Michigan, in helping to settle the sit-down strike which preceded the contract, brought a company concession that it would not bargain with another union for six months.

During the business slump in late 1937 and 1938, unions appeared to be marking time. Then, in April, 1938, the CIO entered a second phase of its organizing drive. Important developments of this phase were the strikes of the United Automobile Workers Union against ten plants of General Motors and against all of Chrysler in the summer of 1939. Both had as a main objective the improvement of the union recognition clause.

At General Motors, in contrast to the plant-wide strike of 1937, only the tool and die makers, maintenance men, and engineers were on strike. Announced union objectives were for the company to cut down on work "farmed out" to machine shops (the so-called alley shops of Detroit), to regularize production schedules, to smooth out wage differentials between plants, and to clarify the issue of sole bargaining rights. The union newspaper claimed that the strike settlement provided sole and exclusive bargaining rights, but this actual wording did not appear in a General Motors contract until the following year.

In the fall of 1939, the Chrysler situation became a test case to make the grievance machinery more workable and to improve the union recognition clause. As a consequence, 50,000 workers were away from their jobs for fifty-five days in a dispute which was called a strike by one side and a lockout by the other. The settlement which followed recognized the union as exclusive bargaining agent.

Multi-Plant Units

Intertwined with the issue of sole bargaining rights was the demand for plant-wide bargaining units. By far the most important issue for the NLRB in the 1930's was whether multi-plant units were appropriate for collective bargaining. A step in this direction was taken in 1935 by the Sinclair Oil Company and the International Association of Oil Field, Gas and Refinery Workers representing their field workers. As large-scale mass production firms became organized, the CIO began to insist that other companies sign one contract for all plants.

In establishing multi-plant units, the NLRB considered the history, extent, and type of organization of the employees; the history of their collective bargaining, including any contracts; extent and types of organizations and collective bargaining of other employees in the same industry; the relationship between proposed units and the employer's organization and management. The Board considered also the geographic location, skill, wages and working conditions, and the present extent of organization.

In the cases of two major glass companies in 1939, the Board established multi-plant units. In the Pittsburgh Plate Glass case, the majority of employees at one plant opposed their inclusion in a company-wide contract, but the Board found such a contract appropriate because the majority in the company wanted it. The Board said: "Such units tend to place the employees on a basis of equal bargaining strength with the employer and to prevent any disharmony in the bargaining process and the temporary advantage of one section of the employees as against the others, without rational justification based on differences in the nature of their work." [8] Likewise, in the Libbey-Owens-Ford case, the Board submerged the desires of the employees of one plant by forming a unit to include all the plants. However, in 1941, after the chairmanship of the NLRB changed, the Board granted a separate unit for one plant of Libbey-Owens-Ford and the local union won the election and was certified for this plant only.

Several developments in 1939 brought a shift to company-wide bargaining units in the automobile industry. On the one hand there was the drive for exclusive union recognition, mentioned in the preceding section. Then too there was the matter of a split between two factions within the United Automobile Workers. Both Chrysler and General Motors asked the NLRB for new elections to determine which union represented the workers. The NLRB set up single plant units for the election, over the objection of the UAW-CIO, which wanted company-wide or multi-plant units. However, in 1939, Chrysler workers voted overwhelmingly for the UAW-CIO in all plants. The next year, the CIO won NLRB elections at forty-nine plants of General

Motors, and lost to the then nonaffiliated faction in five plants. After these elections, the NLRB certified that a corporation-wide unit was appropriate for bargaining in the case of each company. The 1939 strike settlement with Chrysler included a statement that the union was to be recognized as exclusive bargaining agent for all the employees in the twelve-plant unit.

Association-Wide Bargaining Units

When the National Labor Relations Board began its work of determining appropriate bargaining units, a number of trades were organized on an association-wide basis. The building trades, which had had collective bargaining for over fifty years, generally made agreements between a contractors' association and a union local. In one locality, often forty or fifty agreements were to be found, one for each trade. There were some country-wide agreements with large construction companies and a very few national agreements with employers' associations, among specialized groups such as elevator constructors, sprinkler fitters, and tile layers.

There was a trend in the early 1930's toward broadening the area of building trades contracts. An area-wide agreement made in 1935, for example, covered seventeen counties in Pennsylvania, sixteen in West Virginia, and five in Ohio. Area wage agreements were made supplementary to the construction code, under the NIRA, for mason contracting, plumbing, painting, paper hanging, and electrical contracting.

Another development in the direction of a broadened basis for collective bargaining was the agreement signed by the Metal Trades Department of the AFL with the Sinclair Refining Company in 1935. This agreement was signed by thirteen national and international unions which negotiated as a group for production, construction, and refining employees. Included among these were blacksmiths, boilermakers, technical engineers, operating engineers, firemen, hod carriers, bridge workers, machinists, molders, pattern makers, plumbers, and sheet metal workers. Another contract, covering fourteen crafts at the Wood River, Illinois, plant of Shell Petroleum Corporation was also signed in 1935. This was followed by the agreement mentioned above between the International Association of Oil Field, Gas, and Refinery Workers of America and three Sinclair companies for all oil field workers of the company on a national basis.

Then in 1937 the Amalgamated Clothing Workers signed their first national agreement covering 135,000 workers or 85 per cent of the coat and suit industry. The anthracite industry had a single agreement covering all operations, while bituminous mining had agreements with regional miners' associations. The most prominent among these was the Bituminous Coal Pact for the Appalachian area which covered 300,000 miners in eight states. As other contracts expired on the same date as the Appalachian pact, the union developed the practice of signing first with the Appalachian Conference of Operators, and then negotiating almost identical agreements with the other regions.

The railroad unions traditionally bargained with the individual railroad systems. After 1931, questions of wage increases or decreases were taken up by the Association of American Railroads and the Railway Labor Executives Association, an organization formed in 1926 of representatives of twenty unions of railroad workers. The American Flint Glass Workers Union and the Glass Bottle Blowers Association had a long tradition of industry-wide bargaining, through conferences held annually, and these resulted in industry-wide agreements.

In approving association-wide units for collective bargaining, the NLRB considered whether an association was authorized to act and was acting for the employers and whether a broad unit was feasible. The Board placed considerable emphasis on past collective bargaining history. It found association units to be appropriate in clothing, fisheries, fish-packing, stone-working, and motion picture industries. One of its significant decisions was the establishment of a coast-wide unit for the Pacific Longshoremen, CIO, in 1938. This decision was challenged by the AFL, and in 1941 the Board permitted elections in three ports which were unwilling to be included in the coast-wide contract of the CIO. In these ports the AFL won the election and received bargaining rights.

Agreements with Maritime and Longshoremen's Unions on the West Coast showed acceptance by the employers of a plan for "One Big Union for Employers," which was advanced by Roger Lapham, president of the American-Hawaiian Steamship Company, after 1936–37 maritime strikes. A blanket contract, with uniform expiration dates, could be suspended by all employers if the union engaged in a contract violation against one company. Thus association-wide bargaining on the West Coast gave small-scale employers a greater measure of resistance against "quickie" or "hot cargo" strikes.

Craft Units

The question of whether or not particular crafts should be included within a broader bargaining unit, such as a plant-wide contract, proved a thorny one, as it was the essential issue between the AFL craft and the CIO industrial patterns of organization. In the Globe Machine and Stamping Company case in August, 1937, the Board stated that in cases where all other considerations were evenly balanced, the desires of the disputed group of employees should be determining. Thus the Board ordered an election within the disputed craft to determine whether the majority wished to be represented by the craft or the industrial union, and then permitted the craft to organize separately when it appeared that this was the majority desire within the craft. A number of cases were handled in a similar manner following the Globe decision, although the question was always one of controversy within the Board itself. Edwin S. Smith dissented in cases which followed the Globe decision. His position was that to set the craft off, contrary to the wishes of the larger majority of the company's employees, weakened the collective bargaining rights of the majority.

Later in 1939, William Leiserson, who had been appointed to the Board recently, and Smith agreed in limiting the Globe Doctrine. In the American Can case, the Board refused to determine a small unit by which one group could break from an appropriate unit already established and maintained as part of a collective bargaining contract, against the will of the majority of the employees. For the next five years, the American Can decision was generally applied by the Board, limiting much more narrowly than before the circumstances under which a Globe election would be held. The issue of whether a craft could break away was the subject of legislative enactment by Congress in the Taft-Hartley law. This provision did not lead to wholesale craft severance as some predicted.

In summary, in the late 1930's, the development of bargaining units depended in large measure on the organizational efforts of the unions themselves. A great diversity developed, although both the AFL and CIO tended to organize, where possible, on a plant-wide or multi-plant basis, according to the industrial union pattern. The NLRB tended to find appropriate whatever units existed, where there was no sharp conflict between unions, and for its criteria looked to the history, extent, and type of collective bargaining and the desires of the employees. The Board moved slowly in certifying multi-plant units, but did so when it was evident that the majority of workers desired broad units; they were certified in a small number of cases which involved many thousands of workers. Association-wide units were recognized where the employers had an organization set up for the purposes of collective bargaining. Craft groups were permitted in some instances to splinter away from the industrial groups, although no large-scale disintegration of bargaining relationships occurred.

Thus under the government-supported expansion of collective bargaining in the 1930's, the principle of AFL union legitimacy over a given job territory gave way to the election procedure. Majority rule was applied in a great diversity of units of different sizes and shapes. Relatively few moves toward multi-employer or association bargaining took place, and these were mainly in industries with prior traditions of unionism as in clothing, glass, and water transportation groups. Many of the conspicuous examples of "industry-wide" or regional bargaining antedated the New Deal and reflected older drives for bargaining terms to cover the extent of the product market.

Government policy was a more important factor in facilitating multi-plant or company-wide bargaining arrangements, though these developments came only at the very end of the decade of the 1930's. It was only after second or third rounds of negotiations that company-wide or nearly company-wide coverage appeared in some segments of heavy industry, in autos only after the 1939 challenges of multi-plant-unit determination by the NLRB, involving intra-union rivalry.

The most prevalent pattern, however, of government-sponsored establishment of collective bargaining in the 1930's was on the basis of the individual plant or fractional part of a plant or establishment. This pattern was perhaps to be expected by the nature of the union organizing drives, which spread pragmatically in response to various degrees of success or employer opposition. Consolidation, however, had to be accomplished in the 1940's.

The new unions of course did not secure recognition throughout the steel, meat-packing, machinery, and chemical industries until the decade of the 1940's was under way. Ford and Bethlehem Steel did not sign agreements until 1940 and 1941, respectively, and recalcitrants in other industries lagged even further. It was only in the post–1930 decades then that contracts of indefinite duration or various termination provisions gave way to the practice of common expiration dates, sometimes accompanied by industry-wide strikes, such as occurred in the post–World War II years. The decade of the 1930's constituted the infancy and early adolescence of much American collective bargaining as it was developing its form and structure—a stormy and rebellious phase accompanied by employer opposition, inter- and intra-union struggles, and government agency decisions affecting all parties.

Terms of Employment

Although the expansion of collective bargaining in the 1930's sprang from an earlier American labor movement, with considerable governmental stimulation, it is significant to note certain contrasts between the older labor agreements and the newly emerging contracts. The older collective bargaining agreements themselves varied as to length and nature. Most commonly, the older unions, such as the men's and women's clothing, teamsters, miners, and building trades, had short, simple contracts with emphasis upon standardization of labor rates among competitors, often within local or regional markets, but otherwise with flexible rather than rigid terms. The long-established collective bargaining arrangements in the branches of the glass industry had evolved more elaborate "legislated" agreements from their group or associational bargaining, but much of this complexity resulted from the union's efforts to standardize the wage scale among competitors after a complicated piecework history. The agreement was often called "the scale." Terms were set in the national bargaining, but most administration took place locally and the local plant was even exempted from the national rules on rare occasion when circumstances were extreme. Meanwhile local unions were kept under strict national union orders against wildcat strikes.

The hosiery workers' bargaining on a national scale resembled more closely the other branches of the needle trades in the respect that they relegated their complicated piece-rate wage scale to a separate, large, and detailed volume, keeping their basic agreement on other terms to the simple skeletal-type contract. The printing trades had rather more detailed and rigid contracts, incorporating many of their job rules and rate standardization policies. These contracts reflected a curious mixture of local autonomy for wages and rules along with strong international policy measures and strike control.

In all of these illustrations of older bargaining agreements, however, whether long or short, whether incorporating the all-important wage scale or relegating their wage standardization attempts to a separate document, they were usually drawn up by union and management negotiators with a highly practical flavor and with little reliance upon legal advisers. Even the Typographers' rigid rules and concern with the Priority Law (their name for seniority) reflected job-saving power bargaining rather than legal statements of position. The other older agreements left much more room for building up local practices on layoff, discharge, benefits, and even working rules—often covered only very generally, if at all, in the contracts themselves. The outstanding exception to this pattern of generalized working agreements was the voluminous, detailed-type contract of the railroad unions, working within a governmental regulation framework since 1926. They had built up elaborate seniority regulations and rules, incorporating in their agreement volumes many grievance adjustments as they were made. Administration of this kind of agreement and subsequent negotiations required legalistic and detailed techniques.

The new agreements signed with the CIO were originally short but very limited—reflecting barely the nod of recognition. Consequently they were relatively rigid. In some new bargaining situations, both parties felt that unless rights were expressly stated, the other side would take advantage of an omission. Unions demanded safeguards against discriminatory acts and efforts to undermine the union. Management feared the inclusion of statements which would whittle down its right to run the business. Whereas the emphasis of the older contracts had been on rate standardization among competing employers, sometimes actually welcomed as a stabilization measure by the companies, the newly organized firms, often giants themselves, adopted individual defensive or arm's-length positions. In an effort to foresee all possible consequences, lawyers were more and more frequently entrusted with the traditional role of the parties to the contract—the writing of a clear agreement.

In the second round of negotiations in the newly organized basic industries, which took place in 1939 after the dormant recession year of 1938, substantial improvements were made as compared with the original 1937 agreements. Several signs of maturity appeared. The later agreements were more practical and workable than the earlier ones, as they covered situations arising out of day-to-day plant operations; and they were consequently more flexible and less vague and rigid. More matters were left to joint discussion in the grievance procedure. Another important change in 1939 was that many contracts were arranged to run indefinitely, instead of for one year only. Either party could terminate a contract after specified written notice, but the contract implied that there was an expectation of continued collective bargaining.[9]

A greater measure of union acceptance was shown by the 1939 contracts, as the shop steward systems were enlarged and made more workable and other refinements were made in the grievance procedures. In addition, unions benefited from the provision of bulletin boards within the plant, time off for union representatives for negotiating, top seniority for shop stewards, and access to the plant for union officials. Certain union practices showed signs of growth. Where the 1937 agreements were negotiated by top union leadership, many 1939 contracts were an outgrowth of meetings between union committees and management. More contracts were offered to the membership for ratification in 1939 than in 1937.

In spite of the impelling factors leading to the development of grievance procedures and other measures to meet the day-to-day operating needs of the new bargaining relationships, there was still a noticeable stress in the new agreements of the late 1930's on formal, legalistic language. This often included the spelling out in detail of the rights and responsibilities of both parties. In later negotiations and administration both sides emphasized the letter of the contract. Many relationships were clouded by ambiguities of interpretation and often by feelings of mutual distrust.

Job Protection—Old and New

In describing a transition in the content of job protection provisions during the 1930's, it is relevant to recall the patterns which were already established. The strongly organized trades prior to the new wave of union growth included many skilled workers in small shops where there was a long history of collective bargaining and an accord existed between labor and management. This could not readily be duplicated in the newly organized, much larger plants.

Throughout the earlier years of bargaining, the AFL crafts had endeavored to protect their wage standards and working conditions "from any competitive menace," to use the terminology of John R. Commons. Thus we find that practically all the agreements of the

Carpenters, Electrical Workers, and Painters in the 1930's prohibited or controlled contracting by employees and provided fines if these provisions were violated. Certain exceptions were made for superannuated or incapacitated members. These unions regulated conditions under which their members might become contractors. They had to apply to the union for a withdrawal card, give security for weekly wages, and were prohibited from re-entering the union for a period of time. The ban on contracting by employees served to protect the organized workers from an undercutting of their working conditions, and guaranteed to the employers that men from within the union ranks would not compete with them.

The building trades also forbade employers to use tools, and the Ladies Garment Workers and Bakers Unions endeavored to prevent employers from filling the jobs of members. The ILGWU required that no member of the firm or foreman could do any work except instruction and supervision. If union members were laid off and members of the firm were found working, fines were levied on the firm to reimburse the members for lost earnings. The bakery workers permitted an employer to work in his own shop, but required that he promise to give at least two nights a week work to union members. Only one member of the firm could work at the trade. Fines were levied on union members if they worked where more than one member of the firm used tools.

Through the 1930's, the International Ladies Garment Workers Union gradually secured greater control of the contractors within the industry. At the start of the decade, the dress industry operated on a closed shop basis; for the first time the 1932 agreement provided that jobbers were to be responsible to the union for the maintenance of wage rates by contractors. In addition, this contract established a union-management price settlement committee for the contract shops. This provision was a forerunner of the NRA code requirement that each jobber was to designate his contractors and to distribute work only to those on his list. The 1936 contract, which set up a uniform system of settling piece rates within the whole New York market, gave the jobber the responsibility of standardizing the labor costs of dresses manufactured for him in the contract shops. The jobber had to pledge to pay the contractors enough to make it possible for them to pay the union wage scale.

The Machinists controlled their job market through the use of working rules. Their contracts usually provided one apprentice for every four journeymen, and only one apprentice per job. Apprentices had to register with the union before being admitted to work and to serve six months before admission to the union. They worked on a five-year graduated wage scale, and this five-year period had to be completed before they could become journeymen. The Typographical Union and the building trades also regulated the ratio between apprentices and journeymen. They often provided an apprenticeship committee to work out methods of training, standards, and terms of apprenticeship. The Teamsters had no formal apprenticeship program, but encouraged their members to guard against "those who would tear down our wage scale." [10]

The closed shop issue in this context requires consideration not merely as "union security" in a narrow sense but as part of the varied job control efforts of unions and the power plays of the labor and management sides of collective bargaining. The closed shop clause, which provided that only union members were to be hired, was quite common in the building trades, printing trades, mining, and clothing industries. Other highly organized groups, such as breweries, motion picture production, fur manufacturing, metal trades, glass, millinery and hats, also quite commonly had the closed shop.[11] In semiskilled industries like clothing and millinery, employers would hire on the open market if all qualified union members were employed. The new workers then applied for union membership. The measure of job control provided by the closed shop, however, was considered essential to protect craft groups from an undercutting of wages by unorganized workers, and the closed shop offered employers the assurance that costs would remain fairly standard within the industry.

A typical closed shop clause in 1935 was that of the Cleveland Chapter of the National Electrical Contractors Association and the International Brotherhood of Electrical Workers, Local Union No. 38, to the effect that the employers who were members of the association agreed to hire for electrical work only members of the union in good standing. The union agreed to issue work permits to additional men if the employees could not be supplied from the union ranks. Thus the union controlled the supply of labor and entrance into the trade.[12]

In the above-mentioned craft groups, employers and workers had a common interest in standardizing costs throughout industries composed of many small firms. Hence, employers accepted a strongly organized union which could control its membership and organize the unorganized. The employers appeared less concerned with management prerogatives. They did not feel that the closed shop or other regulations pertaining to the labor supply restricted their freedom of action.

In the larger industrial plants which came within the area of collective bargaining during the 1930's, both management and unions faced a very different situation. Management feared chiefly the encroachment of unions into areas of decision-making. Management wanted the sole right to promote, discharge, lay off, or transfer employees, and to decide methods of work. The unions sought chiefly a voice in determining the destinies of their men—a reasonable method for handling discharges, layoffs, and other grievances. They wanted protection for their members from the arbitrary caprice of immediate supervisors and recognition of rather vaguely defined job rights.

Strong union security demands generally fell by the wayside in the new industrial union bargaining. Negotiations were preoccupied with legal struggles over recognition for members only and exclusive bargaining rights. Few instances where union security was strengthened beyond this occurred. World War II brought struggles over maintenance-of-membership clauses, and the postwar period saw the extension of the restricted union shop.

An exception to the general pattern of union security clauses, in the newly organized industries, was shown by the Ford contract of 1941. The company agreed in its very first contract to the closed shop, with union membership within thirty days as a condition of employment. All present and new employees were required to join the union. Persons losing membership in the unions were not to be retained in the employ of the company. In addition, the checkoff was provided. Thus, after many years of resistance to the union, Ford Motor Company accepted a stronger union security clause than was the practice in the newly organized mass production industries. And yet subsequent history of the bargaining relationship demonstrated neither the wisdom of the closed shop clause here nor the necessity of its application to other mass production situations.

Job protection rules in the new agreements of the 1930's emphasized the individual job right against arbitrary discipline and discharge, seniority rules, and occasionally work sharing or layoff benefits. Management's disciplinary treatment of employees was usually qualified, in CIO contracts, by the statement that discharge was to be accompanied by a list of reasons, and discharge was not to be for reason of union activity. The Carnegie-Illinois agreements provided first for suspension for a five-day period, during which there was an opportunity for a hearing by the grievance committee. Grievances were to be carried through to the final step of arbitration, with the understanding that the company would reinstate discharged employees with back pay if the arbitrator ordered this action. Steel, aluminum, and automobile contracts provided that disciplinary actions were within the employers' right, whenever infractions of company rules were considered serious enough to warrant discharge, but that management had to be prepared to defend the discharge through the processes of the grievance machinery. Gradually time limits were placed on each stage so that discharge cases would be handled promptly.

As to the seniority principle applied in the evolving collective bargaining relationships in the mass production industries, it became apparent that the unions were chiefly interested in seniority with respect to layoff, transfer, and rehiring, and to a lesser extent, in the matter of promotions. The stated union objectives were to initiate fairness, to end discrimination of a capricious nature, and to protect the jobs of their membership. Because of the desire for specific content, contract provisions covering these matters became longer and more involved than those formerly negotiated by the old, established unions, with the conspicuous exception of railroad agreements.

A clause was developed in the Carnegie-Illinois agreement which later became known as a "standard CIO seniority clause." In layoffs, the following were to be considered: length of service, ability to perform the work, physical fitness, family status, and number of dependents. Where ability, fitness, and family status were equal, men were laid off on the basis of seniority. In recalls, men were to be called back in reverse order of layoff. Management retained the right of initiative, and the union exercised the right of appeal through the grievance procedure. The automobile industry adopted this type of clause, but did not include the consideration of marital status and dependency.

As collective bargaining matured, management came to prefer departmental seniority, as being easier to administer, while unions often wanted plant-wide seniority. Management gained "escape clauses" which excluded certain probationary employees and others judged to be of "exceptional service." Unions received other safeguards, such as placement at the top of the seniority list for shop stewards, regardless of their actual length of service.

With respect to promotions, the union's interest in emphasizing length of service interfered with the companies' desire to retain and advance men of skill and ability. In some of the older contracts, such as the Teamsters', management was willing to include the clause "seniority shall prevail." In the mass production industries, personnel departments were more highly developed with systems of merit rating and selection, and management was unwilling to have arbitrary seniority rules. Generally, unions were less forceful and successful in applying seniority principles to promotions than they were in the case of layoffs.

Some abortive efforts were made toward job or income protection on a broader scale in the face of heavy unemployment during the 1930's. The Full Fashioned Hosiery Manufacturers Association and the American Federation of Full Fashioned Hosiery Employees had established an unemployment benefit plan, with joint contributions from employèrs and employees, in 1930. Between 1930 and 1935, unemployment benefit plans were introduced into collective bargaining agreements in the clothing, wallpaper, millinery, cleaning and dyeing, and street railway industries.[13]

Progress made in the 1930's, in the mass production industries, in regularizing employment, however, was generally limited to the setting forth of company policy concerning layoffs. In the first Chrysler contract, in 1937, the company and union agreed on a plan which was later applied to other automobile plants. In the case of layoffs, probationary employees were to be laid off first, and then hours were to be reduced to thirty-two per week; next, employees were to be laid off according to seniority, with transfers made to other departments where possible. Managements were given the right to retain "valuable employees" to the extent of 10 per cent of the seniority list.

The Libbey-Owens-Ford contracts showed an evolution in practice; the early contracts contained a statement that in layoffs, first consideration was to be given to length of service, if this was not offset by the consideration of competency or dependency. The company promised to make hiring and layoffs on a "sensible basis" consistent with "fairness and freedom from favoritism." By 1940, the contract was changed to include the provision that seniority should determine, subject to the grievance procedure. However, in a slack period, all work was to be divided equally among the regular employees in any department, provided that they had worked for the company longer than six months. Hours would be dropped as low as twenty-four per week before the company determined to have a layoff. A combination of distribution of work with layoff rules was used in other contracts as well.

Wages and Wage Practices

It was pointed out above that the wage scale (even called a price list in earlier bargaining arrangements) had been a traditional focus of older AFL collective bargaining. This scale had encompassed the dual union objectives of establishing standard rates among competing firms and endeavoring to achieve "more and more" in job benefits for the members. Yet the central focus of wage bargaining was not clearly discernible in the new unionism of the 1930's. It was overshadowed by the tactical developments of seeking recognition, establishing bargaining relationships, and explorations in the new environment of unionism in mass production industry. It is not surprising that substantial wage gains were difficult if not impossible in the face of deep economic depression with millions of unemployed. However, a comparison of the new unionism's wage program with the older "Standard Rate" may prove significant and may reveal the origins, in the 1930's, of such post–World War II developments as wage patterns and package bargaining.

The facts themselves are surprising. The largest percentage short-run increase in average hourly earnings during the 1930's was between 1933 and 1935. The NRA codes, together with some subsequent attempts to preserve their gains through collective bargaining in some industries, were undoubtedly a major factor.[14] Even in this period, however, wage increases granted by large manufacturing companies were probably influenced in part by the threatened stirrings of collective bargaining.[15] Similarly in November, 1936, U.S. Steel granted a 10–cent-per-hour increase just prior to the successful organizing campaign of the Steel Workers Organizing Committee. This increase was copied by other firms in the industry. A second 10–cent-per-hour increase in steel accompanied the first union contract in 1937. Wage adjustments in other industries came with the improving business conditions in 1937 either prior to unionism or as an outcome of collective bargaining negotiations. Meanwhile bargaining in older relationships as mining and building trades made such gains as the economy would permit along traditional lines.

From 1937 to 1939, after the major contracts were signed in the mass production industries, the newly organized firms made only small changes in wage rates. For the first time in American history, wages were not generally reduced during a severe recession such as occurred in late 1937 and most of 1938. The part of the steel industry under union contract made no major change until April, 1941, when, under the impact of war orders, wages went up 10 cents per hour. In General Motors bargaining, the 1939 contract included no general upward wage changes, although increases were given to tool and die makers and maintenance employees. The 1940 contract included only a small wage gain associated with the re-evaluation and reclassification of jobs. The first substantial change was a 10–cent-per-hour increase in 1941, for all employees, plus 6 cents additional for tool and die makers and maintenance men.

In generalizing about wage changes through the 1930's, it would appear that business cycle improvement and legislation exerted direct influences. As Professor Slichter points out,[16] the 1937 round of collective bargaining brought improvements for the organized workers, and gains for nonunion workers where management acted to offset the possibility of union activity. As far as the CIO effort was concerned, emphasis was placed largely on securing union recognition, union and job security, and the settlement of grievances. From 1937 to 1940 business conditions were not conducive to strong demands for wage improvement. The upturn in defense activity in 1940 was to be noted mostly in the improvement in weekly pay, as overtime provisions began to operate. Contracts in 1941 were the first to include substantial wage gains in many industries.

The practice of emulating industry leaders in determining wage policies began in pre-union days in the basic steel industry. Similarly, the 1930's saw nonunion companies matching or exceeding collectively bargained wage settlements, as a reaction to the organizing struggles of the period. The practice of pattern bargaining, however, among units of an organized industry or even between industries emerged only in later periods.

Only gradually during World War II and the postwar period did some approach to the older standard rate concept emerge as the steel industry jointly established a standard wage scale over a national market, slowly wiping out the southern differential. Sporadic attempts to narrow differentials in other firms or between firms in other industries were occasionally made, but the problems encountered here were much different and more complex than the largely local or regional wage bargaining of older relationships. The new wage-bargaining was to develop along pattern-following lines. Attempts to "sell" settlements (reached in power centers) to smaller firms in the same or similar industries would at times conflict with the older Standard Rate orientation of wage bargaining. The subtle strains in the directions in which the collective bargaining of wages would develop probably have their origins in the period of the 1930's. They were lost to view at the time, however, in the struggle of the power plays under government-sponsored unionism.

Wage practices were also more complex in the new bargaining relationships. Some of the older objectives of weekly pay practices, minimum call-in or report pay, and overtime provisions, were sought. New ones began to appear dealing with equal pay for women, holiday and vacation provisions, foreshadowing the great growth of fringes during the war and postwar periods. It is noteworthy that many of the fringes appeared first in the newer industrial union bargaining relationships. They probably reflected in part the new unionism's bargaining with large companies which had themselves given more attention to employee benefit programs than was typical of the smaller industry which had been unionized before.

Time rates were used in construction, printing, and service trades. Apparel, clothing, millinery, hats, and shoes continued on a straight piecework basis; coal mining was paid on a tonnage or hourly basis. Many of the newly organized mass production firms operated on a bonus or point-incentive basis or measured day rate. Where incentive methods of wage determination were used, unions directed attention to securing participation in the setting of the rates, or the standards on which the rates were based. They asked for advance notice of rates, before they went into effect, and the right of appeal through the grievance procedure after rates were established. They strove for less complicated incentive systems, an end to secret time studies, the right to have union observers or to make independent time studies.

One frequent cause of controversy within the large plants concerned time study, bonus, and incentive plans. The first contract of Libbey-Owens-Ford in 1934 stated merely that the company would coöperate with members of the industrial relations committee of the union on improvements in the bonus system, and would discuss upward or downward revisions before putting them into effect. This wording had the disadvantage that it was rather indecisive, and yet management had possible limits. By 1940, the clause on this subject read that controversies over the bonus system would be subject to the union's right to appeal through the grievance machinery.

One issue in the 1939 strike at Chrysler was an alleged speed-up of the production line; the company, on the other hand, charged the union with purposely slowing down production. The Chrysler contract in 1939 provided that in establishing rates of production, management would make studies based on "fairness and equity, consistent with the quality of workmanship, efficiency of operations, and reasonable working capacities of normal operators." If workers felt that the timing was unfair, a restudy could be requested, with a union representative present. If matters were not settled by agreement, disputes on timing were to be carried through the grievance procedure.

The General Motors contract in 1940 contained a similar provision, with the additional statement that disputes on timing were not to be carried to the last step of the grievance procedure, which in this contract was submission to a permanent impartial umpire. Grievances concerning timing were to be referred back to the parties to the contract by the umpire, management was to restudy the jobs, and discussions were to continue with the grievance committee and plant management. Committeemen were given the right to examine jobs.

Did the New Unionism Mean Encroachment?

In contrasting old and new collective bargaining relationships on job protection devices and wage scales, it is apparent from the preceding sections that job control had long been a focal interest of collective bargaining. The AFL unions, in accordance with the traditions established by Samuel Gompers, engaged in "bread and butter" trade unionism to improve wages and conditions of work. It is sometimes said that they did not interfere with the right of the owners to manage and to decide what to produce or how to produce except as direct effects on jobs were involved. But unquestionably the tight job control described above, including the closed shop as well as job rules, and requirements such as those in the building and printing trades stating that foremen must be union members had an impact on the managerial process. This impact must, of course, be gauged in the light of the circumstances and characteristics of the industries in which the earlier unions operated. They were generally highly competitive industries often made up of small firms where a standard scale enforced by a strong union was considered as having stabilizing effects in an otherwise turbulent labor situation. When accompanied by union-management confidence, accommodation, and even coöperation, as for example in the needle trades and in some branches of the glass industry, positive benefits could be discerned by the several parties on the labor terms of trade in the industry. The rigidities of the old relationships—the standard scale, the closed shop, and tight job control—with their accompanying impact upon management rested largely on the economic circumstances of the industries described above. These industries were highly susceptible to the need for some stabilization program, even though its level and specifications would be left to bargaining power. The entire relationships then, leaving much to practices as they developed, could be handled with a practical, problem-solving orientation. Such matters as seniority or work-sharing on layoff, job transfers, discipline, and discharge were worked out flexibly in practice as in giving content and meaning to such vague contract phrases as provision for discharge for "just cause."

In many AFL contracts, no statement of management prerogatives was included. Managerial rights were modified only to the extent that the agreement specified procedures concerning seniority or job allocation, discharge, and the appeal of grievances. Management retained the right, unwritten in the contract, to initiate changes within the plant. The union's right became one of appeal if it was claimed that management reduced the job security of the members.

A thorny problem in many AFL contractual relationships concerned the displacement of men by labor-saving devices. Many instances were reported in which building trades employees and their unions interfered with new methods, in an effort to protect the jobs of their members. Few labor agreements contained specific limitations on new methods. Interferences, when they occurred, were usually beyond the scope of the agreement. However, in industries where collective bargaining had matured to a state of industrial government, the contracts frequently specified that complaints concerning labor-saving devices were to be taken up through the grievance machinery. Management retained the right to determine proper production methods, subject to appeal if union members suffered loss of earnings.

In the contract between the Full Fashioned Hosiery Manufacturers of America and the American Federation of Hosiery Workers, and in the body of "common law" developed by the various impartial chairmen, certain fundamental rights of management were maintained such as the right of administrative initiative, and the right to make all decisions without interference from the union. Management had the right to carry on such experiments with equipment and methods as it deemed practicable, the right to buy, and use, and dispose of property, to let property stand idle, or to discontinue operations. The union, on the other hand, had the right to protest and appeal, in order to secure fair treatment and to maintain the earning power of its members. If the impartial chairman decided in favor of the union member, retroactive pay adjustments were ordered. The union was further protected by the closed shop and the right to have control over internal union affairs, without management interference.

In the contract between the cloakmakers' division of the International Ladies Garment Workers Union and the manufacturers and jobbers in the New York metropolitan area, the union shared functions which in other industries were the exclusive prerogative of management. In 1932, an impartial chairman was given the power to limit contractors to the number necessary to perform the employer's or jobber's business; contractors were forbidden to work for more than two jobbers. All jobbers agreed to pay contractors enough to cover the minimum costs of production. The impartial chairman received the power to police and limit the operations of contractors.

A further limit on management was the setting of piece rates by a labor bureau, to be supported by the union and the companies as part of the impartial chairman's office. The labor bureau determined piece rates, after consideration of time requirements for workers of average skill. A system of union-management coöperation for the standard grading of coats and suits was worked out, with appropriate piecework prices for operations of a similar nature. The 1933 contract specified that while any employer could make the decision to operate on piecework, no employer could abandon this decision without the consent of the union.

Two years later, after the abandonment of the NIRA code for the industry, the employers and union set up a new joint agency, similar to the NRA board, for the enforcement of labor standards. This board was empowered to grant or withhold a Consumers' Protective Label depending on compliance with labor standards. Thus through the board and the labor bureau, both of which operated under the authority of the impartial chairman, the manufacturers and the union engaged in union-management coöperation in areas usually believed to be exclusively management prerogative.

The experiments in union-management coöperation, developed in industries where collective bargaining was at a mature stage and where management was for the most part small-scale and highly competitive, could not possibly be reproduced in the mass production industries which were organized by the CIO in the last three years of the decade. At General Motors and Chrysler, for example, there were huge investments of capital; management considered itself as having a trusteeship function for thousands of common stockholders in scattered parts of the country. Management did not have the incentive of the smaller shops in the hosiery and garment trades to raise the labor standards of the entire industry through an agreed-on system of self-policing. The early contracts with CIO unions were made because the Wagner Act forced collective bargaining, if the employees desired it. Under the circumstances, management feared any statements which would weaken its rights to run the business.

In the late 1930's, in the newly organized mass production industries, two views developed concerning statements on management prerogatives. One group desired to include within agreements a definition of the absolute rights of management, in the belief that this would clarify the relation between union and management and thus reduce conflict. The other group refused to include any statement, because of the possibility of incompleteness and the thought that enumeration would limit management.[17] Both attitudes reflected fear of union encroachment.

Typical of the protective clauses was one included within the 1941 contract between Bethlehem Steel, Shipbuilding Division, and the International Union of Marine and Shipbuilding Workers, CIO, that "the company is not to be limited in any way in the exercise of regulations and customary functions of management, and the making of rules on operations." Similarly, a contract between Lockheed Aircraft and the International Association of Machinists, AFL, gave the company unquestioned and exclusive right to manage the plant and direct the working force.

While the new CIO contracts reflected the managerial desire not to be limited in authority, the second round, in 1939–40, showed some interesting changes as compared with the 1937 contracts. The General Motors contract of 1940 included for the first time a statement of general objectives quite reminiscent of that found in the traditional AFL contracts, suggesting that there was no longer just a grudging acceptance of union status. The company and union agreed that the objective of the contract was to provide orderly collective bargaining relations between the corporation and the union, and to assure prompt and fair disposition of grievances, without interruption of the company's business.

The second contract also included new material in a statement of management prerogatives: the right to hire, promote, discharge or discipline for cause, and to maintain discipline and efficiency of the employees, but without discrimination against the union. In addition, products to be manufactured, location of plants, schedules of production, and methods of manufacturing were solely and exclusively the responsibility of management. The company received certain promises from the union: strikes of any kind were barred pending recourse to the means of settling differences provided in the agreement; no strikes were to take place without authorization of the international union; the union would not intimidate or coerce employees in their right to work or to refrain from joining. The union agreed, furthermore, that the corporation had full right to take disciplinary action against employees for violation of the union guarantees.

The Chrysler contract of 1939 differed from the 1937 one in spelling out in more detail the responsibilities of the union: the members would not cause any sit-down, stay-in, slow-down, or curtailment of work, nor take part in any strike or stoppage until the bargaining procedure was exhausted, and in no case until negotiations had continued for at least five days. Management reserved the right to present to the secretary of the local union as grievances any abuse of the bargaining procedure by the union or chief stewards. If management was dissatisfied with grievance handling by the local union, it might take its complaints to the international union.

The first Carnegie-Illinois agreement, and subsequent ones, included the clause that management of the works and the direction of the working force, including the right to hire, suspend or discharge for proper cause, and relieve employees from duty for lack of work or other reasons, were the corporation's right. However, it was stated that this right would not be used to discriminate against anyone for reason of union activity.

In the mass production industries organized by the CIO, management generally resisted clauses which provided for consent of the union before promotions, layoffs, discharges, and changes in piece rates, bonus, or incentives could be made. The companies were reluctant to agree to union-management committees or to share their basic decision-making powers. They were unwilling to entrust to arbitrators the power to change the content of an agreement or to determine the labor practices of the companies.

By 1940 contracts in the newly organized industries showed the increased legalism and attention to detail that they carry to the present time. The important results of the bargaining for the CIO were exclusive bargaining rights, plant-wide contracts, and management's recognition of the union as the agency for settling employees' grievances. On the surface, the unions began to function much as AFL unions had in the older organized trades. They negotiated agreements with improved conditions and then adjusted grievances brought by the membership.

The newer unions did not reach, and perhaps did not find necessary or even appropriate in the different economic circumstances involved, the extent of job control characterizing the older relationships. By 1940 there were indications that management's resistance to the "encroachment" offered by union organization gave way to permanent union recognition, and for the most part, strict observance of contractual obligations. It is apparent, however, that these relative positions entailed legalistic sensitivity with sometimes outright suspicion of a practical, problem-solving approach to collective bargaining. Probably far less invasion of management prerogatives was permitted than in the old structure if job control is considered within such a sphere. However new rigidities crept in—defensive sparring, narrow and literal constructions of the new individual plant job rules, attempts at legal enforcement of human relations conduct—particularly as strictures against the older union methods of closed shop, unionized foremen, and other traditional job control techniques were embodied in statute in the post–World War II period. The later 1930's saw the beginning of the uneasy dilemma (which has not yet been resolved generally in American collective bargaining) of how to develop constructive two-way bargaining agreement to solve industrial relations problems by the parties without recourse to legalistic procedures or the maneuvering and tactics associated with the new role of government launched by the Wagner Act and extended further in subsequent legislation.

Agreement Administration

In the 1930's, as management and labor in the newly organized industries worked out methods of settling grievances on the interpretation and application of the contract, great emphasis was placed upon the settlement of grievances through the direct negotiation of parties to each contract, as might be expected when relationships were new. By 1940, only a little more than half of the union agreements on file with the Bureau of Labor Statistics had provision for referring disputes not settled by the parties to an impartial arbitrator or board. The General Motors, U.S. Steel, Firestone Tire and Rubber Company, and Sinclair Oil Company contracts had submission to an impartial outsider as the last step of the grievance procedure, but most other major contracts in the automobile, steel, electrical equipment, metals, fabrication, rubber, and flat glass industries were without this provision.

Within the newly organized mass production plants, the main achievements of the decade were the right to carry grievances through to the main office of the corporation and to have members represented by union officials outside the employ of the company. These were privileges which the organized trades had enjoyed for some time. Once these principles were established, certain differences in bargaining practices, as compared with those in the longer-unionized areas, were to be observed. These differences arose primarily because of the extreme size of the firms and their component parts and the still prevalent atmosphere of hostility. A contributing factor was surely the lack of experience of shop stewards and committeemen, and foremen, in the joint handling of problems.

Three trends in agreement administration seemed to characterize the newly developed bargaining relationships in the mass production industries and to contrast with the longer-unionized areas. The first concerned the detailing in the contract of a stage-by-stage grievance procedure, often with as many as five steps in the typical CIO contract, each designed to fit into existing levels of plant administration. The second trend was evidenced by an evolutionary development from a cautious, even grudging acceptance of arbitration as a possible, though little used, last step to the more advanced stage of permanent arbitration machinery. Third, many of the new contracts gave a narrower definition of the arbitrator's scope of duties than had been characteristic of older collective bargaining contracts.

Grievance Procedures

The first Carnegie-Illinois Steel Corporation agreement with the Steel Workers Organizing Committee outlined a five-stage grievance procedure, with arbitration as a possible, though remote, last step. According to this 1937 contract, a grievance was first to be discussed between the employee and foreman, and then to be taken up by a plant-wide grievance committee and the foreman or plant superintendent. As a third step, the grievance committee presented the matter to the general superintendent of the plant. Problems not settled at this stage were referred to a representative of the national union and an executive of the corporation. As a fifth step, a grievance could be submitted to an impartial umpire, appointed by mutual agreement and paid jointly by the union and the company. Essential to the process was the election of a grievance committee of three to ten union members within each plant. The committee members were given time off, without pay, and permission to visit departments to handle grievances.

The strengthening of the Carnegie-Illinois agreement that was apparent in 1941 was typical of improvement brought to many other CIO contracts. Grievances were to be reduced to writing at the second stage, and then to be submitted to the foreman by a member of the grievance committee. As experience was gained, many grievances were weeded out at the first stage, and the union had to develop policies to prevent the processing of nuisance and otherwise unsupported claims. Various time limits were set: three days for the first step, ten for the second, and ten for the third. More important than this was the regular scheduling of plant-wide grievance meetings for once a month, with a written grievance agenda. Disputes not settled at the committee meeting were to be answered by management not later than one week before the next regular meeting. If the decision was not acceptable, the union could ask for the fourth stage, which was the same as in the 1937 contract. In 1941 both parties wrote into the contract their mutual desire for prompt, equitable settlement.

Within the automobile manufacturing industry, the first UAW-CIO contract at General Motors provided the skeleton five-step arrangement, with referral to an impartial arbitrator mutually chosen, as the last step. In 1938–39, the UAW-CIO had as its goal throughout the industry the greater recognition of the shop steward system. This became the major issue in the 1939 strikes at Briggs Manufacturing Company and Chrysler Motor Company. After these strikes, the major automobile manufacturers agreed to a system which included chief stewards, shop stewards, assistants, and plant committees, with pay for the stewards by the corporations. Many more union members were involved in the grievance structure than in the 1937 contracts. Weekly conferences between plant shop committees and labor relations representatives were provided, time limits were set, and more bulletin boards were made available for union use. In the UAW, as in the Steelworkers and other CIO unions, programs were instituted to train stewards and committeemen for their new duties.

The 1940 General Motors contract broke with precedent for the automobile industry by providing a permanent arbitrator, to serve for one year and to be jointly paid, to render decisions on cases submitted to him within thirty days. By the time of the next contract, in 1942, the five-step procedure was further refined: the grievance was to be written out at the second stage. If it was not settled through discussion by the committeeman and plant supervision, the stewards' council was to decide whether to appeal to stage three, which included discussion between the shop committee and plant management. After this, the regional director of the union decided whether to appeal further, and if he did, the regional director and chairman of the shop committee then discussed the grievance with two management representatives. If this failed, and the question was one on which the permanent arbitrator had jurisdiction to rule, the grievance was submitted for his final and binding decision.

The Libbey-Owens-Ford contract with the Federation of Flat Glass Workers moved more slowly through the various phases of development in this respect than the contracts in the automobile manufacturing industry. Not until 1946 was arbitration provided as the last step in the Libbey-Owens-Ford contract. Then the parties included a clause that grievances which could not be settled were to be submitted for final and binding decisions to an arbitrator selected by the Conciliation Service of the U.S. Department of Labor. Each side was to have a representative who would sit with the arbitrator during the hearing but would have no vote in rendering a decision.

The patterns which existed in the late 1930's were far from uniform. On the one hand, the clothing, hosiery, millinery, fur, coal mining, and West Coast longshore industries had arbitration machinery for the entire industry, on a continuing basis. Arrangements varied as to whether a single arbitrator, an impartial chairman, or a bipartisan arbitration board was used and as to whether the parties made frequent or occasional use of the procedures. Many of the building trades had city-wide arbitration boards, set up on a permanent basis, usually with five union and five employer representatives. In some places these were on a single craft and in others on a multicraft basis. Under some contracts, a permanent arbitrator was designated to sit in on the deliberations of an arbitration board when a deadlock arose. In others such a person was chosen only on an *ad hoc* basis.

The Machinists relied on *ad hoc* arbitration in many of their contracts. Typical of these was the one between the union and a California aircraft corporation. The steps in this contract included discussion of the grievance by an aggrieved member and the foreman, then by the union business agent and the industrial relations office, and lastly by a plant-wide subcommittee of three union and three management members. Following this, as a fourth step, the grievance was sent through to a company-wide labor relations committee consisting of seven management and seven union members. If this group deadlocked, the U.S. Conciliation Service was asked to name an impartial person to arrive at a final and binding decision.[18]

A single permanent arbitrator or impartial chairman was characteristic in the 1930's of the long-unionized clothing, hosiery, and West Coast longshore industries. These situations were similar in that they included association-wide bargaining, and both employers and unions had an interest in maintaining certain labor standards throughout the trade. The General Motors contract of 1940 was the first among the large corporations bargaining with the CIO to include the principle of the single arbitrator. This permanent single arbitrator was later specified in several of the large CIO contracts during the decade of the 1940's.[19]

The Chrysler contract, which in 1937 had only a vague grievance procedure, in 1939 included nine steps, the last of which was a conference between two executives of the corporation and two executives of the union. If this step failed, there was no recourse to arbitration. This contract was unique in that it permitted the union to process grievances on the abuse of the collective bargaining procedure, and management could present grievances on such matters as dissatisfaction with individual workers, discipline problems, abuse of collective bargaining, disruption of work in soliciting new members, irresponsible charges against management, and union rules which interfered with production. Plant shop committeemen, the chief steward, and union officers were to be subject to the same discipline as other employees for the violation of shop rules.

By and large, within the newly organized mass production industries at the turn of the decade, arbitration either was not mentioned at all in the contracts, or it was provided for on an *ad hoc* basis. The conclusion to be drawn is that it was visualized as a somewhat remote possibility. The unions placed their emphasis on establishing workable channels for handling grievances, and management carefully guarded their areas of prerogative and hesitated to agree to submit problems to arbitrators.

Scope of Arbitration

Within the older segments of organized activity, it was customary to give the permanent impartial chairman very broad authority. For example, in the men's clothing industry, the impartial chairman, while not especially active in the late 1930's, nevertheless had the power to hear any and all controversies and to settle disputes on machinery, piece rates, and the use of contractors. While his main duties were to interpret and apply the agreement, sometimes he was given matters to decide which were outside the scope of the contract. Certain understandings were included: that the union would not oppose new machinery or restrict output, that management would protect workers displaced by new machinery by transferring them to other jobs, and that the union and management would coöperate on matters of production and efficiency.

Rather similar rights were accorded to the hosiery industry's impartial chairman, except that he adhered to the strict rule of never adding to the agreement nor dealing with general wage levels and other disputes which arose at contract renewal. The union agreed on its part not to interfere with management's right to initiate changes, and it emphasized its own right of appeal if its members were adversely affected by the changes. It was understood that the union would not oppose work changes and new machinery, but that management would not reduce the conditions of work of the union members. Piece rate adjustments on the occasion of cost reducing innovation deliberately provided for a sharing of productivity gains between higher employee earnings and savings to the employer.

Within the mass production industries, this spirit of accord did not exist, and management was jealous of its prerogatives concerning the running of the business. Hence interpretations of the words within the contract and alleged violations became the bulk of the arbitrator's work. Management's fear of encroachment was shown by restrictions on the arbitrator's functions. Thus, wage rates, wage systems, methods of production, installation of machinery, and in fact any matter "wholly within the management function" were often excluded from the grievance procedure. The 1940 General Motors contract gave the arbitrator the following specific areas for activity and in effect excluded the ones mentioned above: He could hear cases on discrimination for union activity, use of the grievance procedure, seniority, discharge, layoff, call-in pay, working hours, leaves of absence, bulletin boards, physical exams, strikes and stoppages, and alleged violations of local agreements. He was not to add to or subtract from agreements, or to rule on timing or on any sections not enumerated. On discrimination and discharge cases, he was to rule only on the guilt or innocence of the person involved, and not on the company rules.[20]

By 1940, observers noted a legalistic view of contract administration as well as of the agreements themselves. The parties to contracts in the mass production industries seemed to be searching for hard and steadfast rules, and in the presentation of cases before the arbitrators, there was frequent controversy over how much weight should be given to such factors as the intent of the parties, practice in the plants, and equity of the situations. In searching for a legal basis for decisions, they seemed to be making a literal analysis or interpretation of the written words of the contract, without regard for human relations values.

Within older-unionized sectors, such as hosiery and clothing, seldom was there noncompliance or nonacceptance of arbitrators' decisions.

In contrast, the newly organized plants in the 1930's and 1940's witnessed many challenges of authority of arbitrators. At the end of the thirties, this trend was just beginning to be evident. A great burden was placed on the parties to the contracts to negotiate in good faith, and in their inexperience and with their sense of insecurity in the collective bargaining relationship, certain grievances continued to be unresolved and to fester.

It should be mentioned, of course, that basic to all grievance procedures was the union's renunciation of the right to strike, at least for those issues subject to arbitration and excepting cases of noncompliance with the arbitrator's decisions. As an outgrowth of bitter experiences in the late 1930's, such contracts as those of Ford and Chrysler companies specified no strike, lockout, stay-in, sit-down, slowdown, or curtailment of production, nor interference with the company's plants and premises, until the grievance procedures had been fully used. Observance of the no-strike clauses left something to be desired in the newly organized plants, which were subject to a variety of wildcat strikes and slow-downs in the first few years of union organization.

We may note that by 1940, at the end of a decade of great change in the extent of collective bargaining, old principles of grievance settlement had been transferred in large measure to the mass production industries, though with somewhat narrower and more legalistic scope. After a period of time, the new procedures worked out in some relationships with much the same degree of smoothness as in the older unionized areas. In others, continued strife, reluctance to use arbitration, and frequently over-use of arbitration characterized the newer bargaining relationships.

Summary and Conclusions

The decade of the 1930's had critical influence on the shape of collective bargaining in the United States. Competing concepts of collective bargaining, such as company unionism and government determination of employment terms, were rejected in favor of collective bargaining between independent unions and employers in a wide heterogeneity of forms. The federal government nonetheless adopted an active and far-reaching role which had lasting and penetrating effects.

Building upon an older labor movement, then reduced to a modest but well entrenched institution, the New Deal made many changes. Governmental election procedures supplanted voluntary or bargained recognition. While the election procedures brought governmentally imposed recognition where previous bitter organizing strife had often failed, they also left a legacy of legal maneuvering and heterogeneous bargaining groups. Majority rule within legally established units supplanted the traditional job territory of older unionism. Rival unionism added to the structural difficulties of the New Deal period. As unions advanced pragmatically, some established strong bargaining relationships, while elsewhere unionism remained localized, weak, and divided.

The National Labor Relations Board's decisions affected negotiating processes, and to some extent the nature of contract terms. The requirement of a written contract became mandatory and the parties to the new relationships sought to work out the job conditions requested by the unions, while managements generally sought to protect managerial rights in the contract language. From the earliest shotgun agreements, the parties experimented with clauses which would provide sufficient flexibility and would apply to practical situations. Yet their agreements were more formally structured than older bargaining relationships. Wage adjustments were of less importance to the new unions than was the establishment of bargaining, but reflected also the characteristic strategies of the period as well as direct governmental and business cycle influence.

Perhaps the greatest heritage of legalism arose from the administrative sections of the new contracts. Grievance procedures had to be developed to make the contracts "working documents" in day-to-day bargaining relationships. Rather elaborate procedures were devised, not only specifying steps but setting forth exactly the privileges and responsibilities of grievance committeemen. Sometimes contracts provided for full-time paid grievancemen and carefully spelled out requirements for written grievances and specified grievance meetings, according to a highly formalized process.

Perhaps most noteworthy of all were the carefully circumscribed provisions for arbitration as the use of voluntary dispute settlement machinery spread. The arbitrator's jurisdiction was often considerably more limited than in older bargaining relationships, and the stage was set for legalistic, formalistic attempts to resolve contract problems.

The decade of the 1930's thus sowed the seeds for more recent collective bargaining in the United States, extending through World War II and the postwar decade. Perhaps the New Deal's positive role of government was necessary to the expansion of collective bargaining that took place. Its legacy, however, included much legalism that is in many ways strange to the industrial relations climate. If collective bargaining rests upon agreement between the parties and mutually acceptable accommodation, a review of developments in the 1930's must question the extent to which voluntary agreements can be forced by government and what characteristics accompany such compulsion. One can recognize the possibility of influencing attitudes by law and public opinion and may concede the essentially pragmatic fashion in which collective bargaining was extended under the aegis of the NLRB. One may also see, however, that aspects of the conforming accommodation involve inherent contradictions to the voluntarism traditionally associated with free collective bargaining. As proponents of democracy throughout the world seek the appropriate role of government in industrial relations, the American experience of the 1930's warrants careful and penetrating consideration.

Notes

1 *Business Week,* January 20, 1934, pp. 22, 23.

2 "Stabilizing the Millinery Industry," *Monthly Labor Review,* LII (February, 1941), pp. 355–59.

3 National Labor Relations Board, *Second Annual Report,* 1937, pp. 82–89. The *Third Annual Report,* 1938, pp. 96–100, sums up the earlier cases on bargaining in good faith.

4 *Whittier Mills Company and Textile Workers Organizing Committee,* 15 NLRB 487, 111 F. (2d) 474 (1940).

5 Cases cited in the NLRB's *Third Annual Report,* 1938, pp. 100–102.

6 J. C. Nix and L. C. Chase, "Employer Unit in Collective Bargaining," *Monthly Labor Review,* LXXI (December, 1950), pp. 695–97.

7 Membership of employees in various unions in the same plant without regard to job group is common in European countries today.

8 National Labor Relations Board, *Fourth Annual Report,* 1939, p. 91.

9 A study by Harold F. Browne, Managing Research Director of the National Industrial Conference Board in 1939, emphasized the "more serious acceptance of the CIO and an end to the preliminary stage of 'instinctive combativeness' in the relationship between unions and management." Bureau of National Affairs, *Labor Relations Reporter,* September 11, 1939, pp. 3–4.

10 *International Teamster,* April, 1937, p. 5.

11 "The Closed Shop and Check-Off in Union Agreements," *Monthly Labor Review*, XLIX (October, 1939), pp. 830–35.

12 "Cleveland Chapter of National Electrical Contractors' Association and Local Union No. 38, IBEW, 1935," *American Federationist*, XLII (October, 1935), pp. 1079–83.

13 General Motors announced, in 1938, a plan for cash loans to hourly-wage workers in slack times to the extent necessary to bring weekly income up to 60 per cent of what they would receive for a forty-hour week, including unemployment compensation. These loans were to be repaid through a payroll deduction plan. Alfred G. Sloan emphasized, "The Corporation is not guaranteeing work for which there is no need." The United Automobile Workers greeted the plan without enthusiasm and stated it was for freezing the work week at 30 hours. *New York Times*, November 19, 1938.

14 Average hourly earnings for all manufacturing industries stood at 64.8 cents per hour in 1937, as compared with 56.7 cents in 1935 and 43.2 cents in 1933. The codes set forth under the National Industrial Recovery Act, for example, were instrumental in reducing weekly hours in the men's clothing industry from forty-four to thirty-six, restricting production to one shift, prohibiting home work and child labor, and setting the minimum wage rate at 40 cents per hour. After the codes were abandoned, hours rose substantially in industries where average hourly earnings were below the general average at the time of nullification, but, as pointed out above, they were maintained in clothing and millinery industries through decisions made in the process of collective bargaining. Further effects, though less noticeable, in the 1930's probably flowed from the Walsh-Healey law of 1935 and the Fair Labor Standards Act of 1938.

15 A number of large companies in the mass production industries reportedly granted wage increases in the 1933–34 period. These companies included the big rubber companies, major electrical manufacturing firms, steel and auto companies. Some of these were said to be "unasked for by employee organization" or were associated with the stimulus of the NIRA. Others were credited to the employees' representation plans in vogue at the time, sometimes in the course of threatened organization drives of outside unions. In the spring of 1934, an advance in wages in the automobile industry occurred "when a general strike . . . threatened." Even in this early period it appears difficult to disentangle the effect of government policies and the awakening or threatened stirrings of collective bargaining. Twentieth Century Fund, *How Collective Bargaining Works* (New York: The Fund, 1942), particularly pp. 513, 613–14, 769, 796.

16 Sumner H. Slichter, "Big Unions and Inflation," *American Economic Review*, XLIV (May, 1954), pp. 336–37.

17 These two views were brought out in the President's Labor-Management Conference in 1945. Cf. U.S. Department of Labor, Bureau of

Labor Statistics, *Collective Bargaining Provisions, Union and Management Functions, Rights and Responsibilities,* Bulletin No. 908–12 (Washington: Government Printing Office, 1949).

18 Aeronautics and Mechanics of Burbank Lodge 727, International Association of Machinists, and Lockheed Aircraft Corporation, Vega Airplane Company, 1940.

19 A permanent single arbitrator was to be found in 12 per cent of agreements on file with the U.S. Bureau of Labor Statistics in 1952. These covered 27 per cent of the workers who were covered by arbitration clauses, and included large employers, particularly in the automobile, primary metal, and rubber industries, and the apparel, food, and hotel industries. However, 76 per cent of all agreements provided for either an *ad hoc* board or single arbitrator, chosen when the need arose. This arrangement was common among small companies, and in the chemical, petroleum, coal, lumber, furniture, fabricated metal products, electrical machinery, mining, crude petroleum, natural gas production, communications, electric and gas, and construction industries. "Arbitration Provisions in Collective Agreements," *Monthly Labor Review,* LXXVI (March, 1953), pp. 261–66.

20 *Ibid.* Present-day arbitrators are usually limited to interpretation or application of the agreement and are often not allowed to deal with production, standards, job rates, health, welfare, and pension benefits.

10

Labor and the New Deal in Historical Perspective[1]

SELIG PERLMAN

A HISTORY-CONSCIOUS approach is the closest one can get to the experimental method in dealing with social movements. The individual workman leaves no records, but the labor movement does. The labor leaders who make policy decisions are virtually experimenters, although obliged to operate without "controls." They experiment with the public, which can put them in the "doghouse"; with the employers, who may decide either to crush them or to deal with them; with the politicians, who may further their cause, act neutral or worse; and above all, with the loyalty of their membership, who may show battle fatigue sooner or later. The "laboratory notes," often discontinuous and scattered, bring out the tensions engendered by the changed conditions, especially those of an economic nature resulting in the rise of "bargaining classes." In his shoemaker article,[2] Professor Commons reconstructed, after the manner of the paleontologist, the sequence of industrial stages. But the material is wider than the mere economic data; it is, in fact, the whole stream of American history, notably the ideological factors.

The problem of organizing and of staying organized has continued the paramount problem of the American labor movement. In America, we lacked the rigid class divisions to assist capitalism in producing a made-to-order revolutionary working class or even a labor cohesiveness for mere meliorative purposes. The life of the American labor movement was strictly in its own hands, and the American society, with its horizontal and vertical mobility, was indeed a most difficult environment. The leader was, therefore, forever making decisions upon which the very survival of his organization depended. Should Gompers have heeded the call to mobilize the AFL in aid to the American Railway Union in the deadly grip of the Railway Managers' Association and of Attorney General Richard Olney? Should he have permitted DeLeon to walk off with the AFL? Should he have treated the injunction as merely another one of the devices capitalism will employ to stifle labor, with relief coming when a labor political victory will wipe out all oppression, or should he have invoked the traditional American hatred for "government by usurpation" and have concentrated upon its immediate abolition with the aid of a Bryan or a Woodrow Wilson? Or what position should the AFL have assumed toward the war with Germany in 1917?

These were the questions which life threw at Samuel Gompers, under whose guiding hand American labor first emerged stable in purpose, if not in size. He called his philosophy "voluntarism" and "trade unionism, pure and simple." This students of the labor movement have renamed "job consciousness," but with an undiminished admiration for the author.

Dynamic Job Consciousness

The assailants of America's job conscious unionism, from Daniel DeLeon's day to our own, have consistently viewed it as a phenomenon in labor movement pathology. To this writer, job consciousness is primarily an emphasis on what is *nuclear,* what is the central core of labor's interest which, under the spur of *changing conditions,* is likely to compel a widening of the area of labor interest. At the same time, American labor history teaches us that the job interest must remain the nuclear one if the movement is not to weaken or disintegrate.

The art of building fortifications and their defense offers a good analogy of how change in basic circumstances compels change in strategy, even if the objective remains unaltered. Prior to the airplane, it was enough to fortify a limited area, adequately garrison it, and confidently await the assault. Today, to be impregnable, a fortress must control an area of a radius of many hundreds of miles, even aside from the consideration of the wider strategy of protecting the whole country. The mere "nuclear" interest, the holding of the fortress, has thus compelled the erection of outlying strong points to keep away enemy bombers.

The Gompersian job consciousness had been the product of more than half a century's effort by the American labor movement to attain stability and a real foothold, from the first workingmen's parties in the 1820's to the triumph of the AFL over the Knights of Labor in the

1880's. The struggling unions had to learn to cut the cord that tied them to the farmer and other middle class anti-monopoly movements, with which they had shared an overweening passion for self-employment and a burning faith in salvation through political parties thrust up by the "producing classes," a most unstable conglomerate when tested in action. Labor had to learn to avoid these enthusiasms and "sure" paths to victory and to concentrate on the *job* interest as the only hard reality in the wage earner's life. Labor's historical experimenting also extended to the American community as a whole, the "public," to the employers, and to the government.

It learned that an attack, or even what might be misconstrued as an intended attack, on private property and enterprise as institutions would only be a free gift to its enemies; that employers, if the gods were willing, could be coerced or sometimes cajoled into a joint job administration under a trade agreement; that the structure of political action in the United States doomed a labor party setting up in competition with the "old" parties, but opened a possibility for carrying collective bargaining into politics and even for an infiltration of the old parties; and finally, that the American government with its states' rights, judicial review, and general checks and balances was a very limited instrument for labor's good and often a menace to be warded off (for example, the Sherman Antitrust Act). But if the government of the land was to be handled with caution and fear, labor could still go ahead building up two kinds of unofficial "governments," each around the job interest.

One was a government for the labor movement itself, erected on the principle of exclusive union jurisdiction and setting up the labor movement as a job empire with affiliated job kingdoms, duchies, and baronies and held together through the absolute and pitiless suppression of "dual" or illegitimate unions. The other kind of government, dealing as it did with the conditions of employment, had to reckon with the employers, but under it the unions sought, wherever possible, full possession of the "job territory" through the closed or union shop.

Such was American unionism when the sovereignty of American government was confronted with the apparently stronger sovereignty of American business, when labor believed that the economic system including job opportunities was being kept up and expanded by private enterprise alone. Under those circumstances, labor saw its task clearly as building its union fortifications over the several "job territories," mostly craft, a few covering an industry. Unionism of that period saw little lying outside the immediate economic area that could either improve the conditions of the job or multiply job opportunities.

Yet, as early as 1906, Gompers saw himself compelled to mix his "economism" with forays into politics in order to attempt to influence Congress to curtail the court injunction so restrictive of the unions' economism. That government would ever be eager to lend its strength to unionism and virtually force union recognition upon the biggest employers of the land, as happened in the 1930's, could not then be dreamed even by the most uncontrolled dreamers in the labor movement, and Gompers would have certainly "looked such a gift horse in the mouth."

The New Deal literally opened to unionism the doors to the heretofore barred mass production industries. Unfortunately for the labor movement, the leaders of the AFL managed to couple this windfall with the curse of a civil war in labor ranks. Under Gompers, the AFL had faced the demand of the socialist industrialists for a complete recasting of the structure of the movement, a demand which, if granted, would have undone the internal order obtained with great effort. By contrast the "industrialists" of 1935 were organization-wide, and there was no reason whatsoever why a constitutional crisis in the labor movement should have arisen at this time. At bottom, that crisis was the joint fault of the self-appointed "constitutional lawyers" and pseudo-historians within the high official leadership, and of the leaders of lesser rank, eager for dues and power. As a result of the split, the principle of exclusive union jurisdiction has undergone considerable modification.

As regards the labor program as such, however, no startling change has emerged. The CIO unions, mass production and others, while utterly contemptuous of the crafts' phantom partitions, have largely reproduced the old procedures of job administration, including seniority, job sharing, etc. Even Harry Bridges' Longshoremen's and Warehousemen's Union, of leftist renown, has failed to proclaim the jobs in that occupation free to all comers. The culmination of this "sameness" with the AFL came in 1950 when the CIO abandoned its initial effort to provide a home for all unions regardless of ideology and turned to expelling Communist-controlled unions *en bloc.*

The same community of pattern is found in conjunction with "union-management coöperation," the reward for the farsightedness of both management and union leadership. On the all-important issue of "management prerogatives" again both labor movements have taken a common position. While neither AFL nor CIO is willing to surrender the right of scrutiny of any managerial area, since it might possibly affect the job control and, therefore, warrant the demand of the right of codetermination, neither even questions the necessity of the basic management "mandate" being derived independently of government or labor.

It is this which marks off the American labor movement from most other national movements; it is a labor movement upholding capitalism, not only in practice, but in principle as well.

While labor's views on the social order have thus remained unaltered, the earlier "pure and simple" pattern has shown a definite adaptation to the Roosevelt "revolution" in government, yet not at all in the direction of independent political action through a third or labor party.

The New Deal effected a veritable revolution in American government, comparable to the Jeffersonian and Jacksonian revolutions. Roosevelt's attack on the United States Supreme Court, followed as it was by a counter-reformation in the Court's decisions in 1937, brought together the *disjecta membra* of American government and fashioned them into a powerful instrument. Congress could now abolish regional differentials at the lowest wage level as well as bestow other boons on the weaker groups.

For the bulk of the labor movement this spelled a new political climate, which even raised in some optimistic minds the hope that at long last American labor was coming round to conform to the West European model, with its political class organization. Such glowing expectations might have been checked by a knowledge of American labor history. For decades before the New Deal, unions, such as the railway unions, under conditions where government was a decisive factor in their job control activities, even if their reputation ranked them with the most conservative among their kind, resorted to political pressures, most frequently to arrest adverse interference, without fear of departure from safe labor orthodoxy. Living under one government instead of under forty-nine, and thus finding favorable legislation more attainable, they had in essence become "politicalized" even before World War I—*not because of their defection from job con-*

sciousness, but because of their very fealty to it. This went hand in hand with the conviction that the indirect method, amounting to collective bargaining with a major party, was the only road rather than setting up a political "shop" in competition with the old parties. The support of the independent candidacy of LaFollette in 1924—indeed, not alone by the railway unions but, under Gompers' pressure, also by the AFL—was a move of despair and not labor's first choice. So, it seems, it will continue indefinitely.

With Americans' ingrained aversion to "class" parties and with the labor pattern of action still alien to the majority, especially the over-represented non-metropolitan groups, America can have a government actively favorable to the labor movement only under an exceptionally able leadership. That leadership must itself be free of any "class" label, above all of the "labor" label; it must know how to convince the underprivileged of its deep concern over their woes; and it must be skillful enough, on the one hand, to resolve the mutual antagonisms, material and sentimental, among labor and the middle classes, and on the other hand, to influence its own party managers to permit the nomination of trust-inspiring candidates—perhaps the most difficult assignment of all. And any boastful claims by labor leaders about their importance in the counsels of the party or the administration is almost certain to jeopardize their political partner's success.

On the still more cheerless side for labor is the fact that what political action has given *to* labor under a government free since 1937 of its former constitutional limitations, political action has already begun to take back *from* labor. It is, therefore, not improbable that after some recent frustrating experiences with lobbying and election campaigns, some, if not a majority, of the labor leaders, now that the gates of big industry have been opened to them, may come to hanker for the simpler days of "economism." Yet the very new powers vested in government render it unlikely that its indicator should ever again be permitted to rest on "neutral." Opponents of the Fair Deal may find these powers just as useful as did their recently defeated foes and thus compel labor to stay on political defensive.

The Outlook

Broadly speaking, the American labor movement has so far shown little indication of breaking away from the Gompersian moorings, if these are taken in the sense of the basic social order it favors and of the *method* it employs in its political action. Yet Gompers has been the *bête noire,* not only of intellectuals, but of practical experimenters of his own type, such as Sidney Hillman. With the pride of a member of a more recent ethnic group than the "older" Americans on the AFL's executive council, upon whom Gompers' mantle had fallen, Hillman forever delighted in displaying his superior mastery in shaping new American institutions. Hillman was the anti-Gompers *par excellence,* in his own mind and in the eyes of the public, notably in his molding his own union as a union with a wider awareness than the regular AFL unions, and "industry consciousness"—in effect, forcing the employers toward a superior managerialism under the union's gracious "patronage." As labor's pioneers, however, Gompers and Hillman really did not stand much apart: both excelled in grasping the minds of labor and management and the social topography of America as well. Today, many believe that Walter P. Reuther, of the United Automobile Workers, is in that illustrious line of American labor's great experimenters. He is identified with a new broadening out of labor's horizon to include the consumer interest, having expressly spelled this out during the long General Motors strike. This latter note must have held for those who have had an upbringing like his own, a "muted" socialist appeal, while sounding perhaps as mere keen "public relations" to those not of the "faith."

For the present, the role of experimenter in that great industry seems to have fallen less to Reuther than to the General Motors management, bent on bringing back the welfare capitalism [3] of the twenties, with the sophisticated change of a national union in the place of a company union. In the meantime, something suspiciously akin to the old-fashioned job consciousness has revealed itself in the hot protest of the UAW against the Federal Reserve Board's move to combat inflation by tightening the credit terms in the sales of automobiles.[4]

The American labor program, indicative of its basic philosophy, has shown remarkable steadfastness through times of rapid external change. The objective, as said above, is unaltered from Gompers' day—the methods, even outside the immediate vicinity of the job, showing no more change than could be accounted for by the changing environment. This steadiness of labor's self-integration into the evolving American society is of significance, not only to the labor movement itself and to its theorists, but, even more importantly, for its defense of democracy against totalitarianism. As labor in this country utterly rejects any idea of "class hegemony," it is thus a bulwark for the preservation of the principle of "unity in diversity," upon which western civilization rests.

Notes

1 This chapter is in the nature of an epilogue. With some minor revisions it is an excerpt from "The Basic Philosophy of the American Labor Movement" which appeared in *The Annals of the American Academy of Political and Social Science,* CCLXXIV (March, 1951).

2 John R. Commons, *Labor and Administration* (New York: Macmillan Co., 1913), Chapter XIV.

3 Selig Perlman, *A Theory of the Labor Movement* (New York: Augustus M. Kelly, 1928, 1949), pp. 207–9.

4 *New York Times,* October 22, 1950.

Selected Bibliography *and* Index

Selected Bibliography

Books

Adamic, Louis. *Dynamite: The Story of Class Violence in America*. Rev. ed. New York: Viking Press, 1934.

Alinsky, Saul D. *John L. Lewis: An Unauthorized Biography*. New York: G. P. Putnam's Sons, 1949.

Baldwin, Roger N., and Randall, Clarence B. *Civil Liberties and Industrial Conflict*. Cambridge: Harvard University Press, 1938.

Beard, Charles A. *The Old Deal and the New Deal*. New York: Macmillan Co., 1940.

Bell, Daniel. "The Background and Development of Marxian Socialism in the United States" in *Socialism and American Life*, Vol. I. Edited by Donald Drew Egbert and Stow Persons. Princeton: Princeton University Press, 1952.

Bernstein, Irving. *The New Deal Collective Bargaining Policy*. Berkeley: University of California Press, 1950.

Bow, Frank T. *Independent Labor Organizations and the National Labor Relations Act*. New York: Prentice-Hall, Inc., 1940.

Ching, Cyrus Stuart. *Review and Reflection, a Half-Century of Labor Relations*. New York: Forbes & Sons Publishing Co., 1953.

Congress of Industrial Organizations. *Official Reports on the Expulsion of Communist Dominated Organizations from the CIO*, Publication No. 254, September, 1954.

Cook, Morris L., and Murray, Philip. *Organized Labor and Production*. Rev. ed. New York and London: Harper & Bros., 1946.

Foster, William Z. *Misleaders of Labor*. Chicago: Trade Union Educational League, 1927.

Foster, William Z. *From Bryan to Stalin*. New York: International Publishers, 1937.

Foster, William Z. *American Trade Unionism*. New York: International Publishers, 1947.

Galenson, Walter. *Rival Unionism in the United States.* New York: American Council on Public Affairs, 1940.

Girdler, Tom Mercer, in collaboration with Boyden Sparkes. *Boot Straps, the Autobiography of Tom M. Girdler.* New York: Charles Scribner's Sons, 1943.

Goldbloom, Maurice, *et al. Strikes Under the New Deal.* New York: League for Industrial Democracy, undated.

Golden, Clinton S., and Ruttenberg, Harold J. *Dynamics of Industrial Democracy.* New York: Harper & Bros., 1942.

Gordon, Robert A. *Business Leadership in the Large Corporation.* Washington: Brookings Institution, 1945.

Hall, Reed S. "Changes in Management Policies and Attitudes Toward Unionism and Collective Bargaining in the Automobile Industry, 1929–1941." Unpublished Master's thesis, University of Illinois, 1953.

Harbison, Frederick H. "Labor Relations in the Iron and Steel Industry, 1936 to 1939." Unpublished Ph.D. dissertation, Princeton University, 1940.

Harris, Herbert. *Labor's Civil War.* New York: Alfred A. Knopf, Inc., 1940.

High, Stanley. *Roosevelt—and Then?* New York: Harper & Bros., 1937.

Howe, Irving, and Widick, B. J. *The UAW and Walter Reuther.* New York: Random House, Inc., 1949.

Huberman, Leo. *The Labor Spy Racket.* New York: Modern Age Books, Inc., 1937.

Industrial Relations Research Association. *Proceedings of the Fifth Annual Meeting of the Industrial Relations Research Association.* Madison: The Association, December, 1952.

Jones, Alfred. *Life, Liberty and Property.* New York: J. B. Lippincott Co., 1941.

Josephson, Matthew. *Sidney Hillman: Statesman of American Labor.* Garden City, N. Y.: Doubleday Books, 1952.

Kahn, Eleanor Nora. "Organizations of the Unemployed Workers as a Factor in the American Labor Movement." Unpublished Master's thesis, University of Wisconsin, 1934.

Kampelman, Max M. "The Communist Party and the CIO: A Study in Political Power." Unpublished Ph.D. dissertation, University of Minnesota, 1952.

Kempton, Murray. *Part of Our Time; Some Ruins and Monuments of the Thirties.* New York: Simon and Schuster, 1955.

Kennedy, Thomas. *Effective Labor Arbitration.* Philadelphia: University of Pennsylvania Press, 1948.

Labor Research Association. *Labor Fact Book.* New York: International Publishers, 1931–53 (issued biannually).

Lescohier, Don D., and Brandeis, Elizabeth. *History of Labor in the United*

States, 1896–1932. Vol. III of Commons, John R., and associates, *History of Labor in the United States*. New York: Macmillan Co., 1935.

Litchfield, Paul W. *The President Talks to the Men; A Group of Radio Addresses*. Akron, O.: Goodyear Tire and Rubber Co., 1935.

Lorwin, Lewis L., and Wubnig, Arthur. *Labor Relations Boards: the Regulation of Collective Bargaining under the National Industrial Recovery Act*. (Institute of Economics Publication No. 67) Washington: Brookings Institution, 1935.

Lynd, Robert S., and Lynd, Helen M. *Middletown in Transition*. 1st ed. New York: Harcourt, Brace & Co., 1937.

McPherson, William H. *Labor Relations in the Automobile Industry*. (Institute of Economics Publication No. 80) Washington: Brookings Institution, 1940.

Mariano, John H. *The Wagner Act: A Study*. New York: Hastings House, 1940.

Mariano, John H. *The Employer and His Labor Relations*. New York: National Public and Labor Relations Bureaus, Inc., 1941.

Metcalf, Henry C. (ed.). *Collective Bargaining for Today and Tomorrow*. New York: Harper & Bros., 1937.

Millis, Harry A., and Brown, Emily Clark. *From the Wagner Act to Taft-Hartley*. Chicago: University of Chicago Press, 1950.

Millis, Harry A., and Montgomery, Royal E. *Organized Labor*. (Vol. III of "The Economics of Labor.") New York: McGraw-Hill Book Co., 1945.

Minton, Bruce, and Stuart, John. *Men Who Lead Labor*. New York: Modern Age Books, 1937.

Mitchell, Broadus. *Depression Decade: From New Era Through New Deal, 1929–1941*. (Vol. IX of "The Economic History of the United States.") New York: Rinehart & Co., 1947.

National Industrial Conference Board. *Industrial Relations in Small Plants*. New York: The Board, 1929.

National Industrial Conference Board. *Collective Bargaining Through Employee Representation*. New York: The Board, 1933.

National Industrial Conference Board. *Individual and Collective Bargaining Under the NIRA: A Statistical Study of Present Practice, November, 1933*. New York: The Board, 1933.

National Industrial Conference Board. *What Employers Are Doing for Employees: A Survey of Voluntary Activities for Improvement of Working Conditions in American Business Concerns*. New York: The Board, March, 1936.

National Labor Relations Board. *Characteristics of 60 Company-Dominated Unions*. Research Memo No. 70. Washington: The Board, December, 1939.

Perkins, Frances. *The Roosevelt I Knew*. New York: Viking Press, 1946.

Perlman, Selig. *A Theory of the Labor Movement.* New York: Macmillan Co., 1928.

Perlman, Selig, and Taft, Philip. *History of Labor in the United States, 1896–1932.* New York: Macmillan Co., 1935.

Person, H. S. (ed.). *Scientific Management in American Industry.* New York and London: Harper & Bros., 1947.

Peterson, Florence. *American Labor Unions.* New York: Harper & Bros., 1945, 1952.

Pritchett, C. Herman. *The Roosevelt Court: A Study in Judicial Politics and Values, 1937–1947.* New York: Macmillan Co., 1948.

Quin, Mike. *The Big Strike.* Olema, Calif.: The Olema Publishing Co., 1949.

Richberg, Donald. *The Rainbow.* Garden City, N. Y.: Doubleday Books, 1936.

Robinson, Dwight Edwards. *Collective Bargaining and Market Control in the New York Coat and Suit Industry.* New York: Columbia University Press, 1949.

Saposs, David J. *Left Wing Unionism.* New York: International Publishers, 1926.

Schlesinger, Arthur M. *The New Deal in Action, 1933–1939.* New York: Macmillan Co., 1940.

Slichter, Sumner H. *Union Policies and Industrial Management.* Washington: Brookings Institution, 1941.

Sloan, Alfred Pitchard, in collaboration with Boyden Sparkes. *Adventures of a White-Collar Man.* New York: Doubleday, Doran & Co., Inc., 1941.

Stanford University. *Stanford Industrial Relations Conference.* Papers presented at the annual conference. Vols. I–IV. Stanford University, Calif.: Division of Industrial Relations, Graduate School of Business, 1938, 1939, 1940, 1941.

Stolberg, Benjamin. *The Story of the CIO.* New York: Viking Press, 1938.

Taft, Philip. *The Structure and Government of Labor Unions.* Cambridge: Harvard University Press, 1954.

Twentieth Century Fund. *Labor and the Government.* New York: McGraw-Hill Book Co., 1935.

Twentieth Century Fund. *How Collective Bargaining Works.* New York: The Fund, 1942.

U.S. Bureau of Labor Statistics. *Characteristics of Company Unions, 1935.* Bulletin No. 634. Washington: Government Printing Office, 1938.

U.S. Bureau of Labor Statistics. *Handbook of Labor Statistics.* Washington: Government Printing Office, 1950.

U.S. Bureau of Labor Statistics. *Directory of National and International Labor Unions in the United States, 1955.* Bulletin No. 1185. Washington: Government Printing Office, 1955.

U.S. Senate, Committee on Education and Labor. *Violations of Free Speech and Assembly and Interference with Rights of Labor: Hearings Before a Subcommittee....* Washington: Government Printing Office, 1937–41.

Voorhis, Jerry. *Confessions of a Congressman.* Garden City, N. Y.: Doubleday Books, 1948.

Wecter, Dixon. *The Age of the Great Depression.* New York: Macmillan Co., 1948.

Witte, Edwin E. *The Evolution of Managerial Ideas in Industrial Relations.* Bulletin No. 27. Ithaca, N. Y.: New York State School of Industrial and Labor Relations, November, 1954.

Wolman, Leo. *Ebb and Flow in Trade Unionism.* New York: National Bureau of Economic Research, 1936.

Yellen, Samuel. *American Labor Struggles.* New York: Harcourt, Brace and Co., 1936.

Magazine Articles

Appelbaum, Samuel. "History of the Workers Alliance of America," *Work,* September 24, 1938, pp. 8–9.

Asher, Robert E. "The Jobless Help Themselves: A Lesson from Chicago," *New Republic,* September 28, 1932, pp. 168–69.

Bernstein, Irving. "The Growth of American Unions," *The American Economic Review,* XLIV (June, 1954), 301–18.

High, Stanley. "Who Organized the Unemployed?" *Saturday Evening Post,* December 10, 1938, pp. 9 ff.

Hoeber, Helen S. "Collective Bargaining by the Amalgamated Clothing Workers," *Monthly Labor Review,* XLV (July, 1937), 17–28.

Hoeber, Helen S. "Collective Bargaining with Employers' Associations," *Monthly Labor Review,* XLIX (August, 1939), 302–9.

"Hours and Earnings Before and After N.R.A.," *Monthly Labor Review,* XLIV (January, 1937), 13–14.

"Labor in the American Economy," *Annals of the American Academy of Political and Social Science,* CCXLVII (March, 1951).

Limback, Sarah. "The Tactics of the CPLA," *World Tomorrow,* February 15, 1934, pp. 90–91.

Metcalf, Henry C. "Employee Representation," *Annals of the American Academy of Political and Social Science,* CLXXXIV (March, 1936), 184–91.

Ramuglia, Anthony. "The Unemployed Incorporate," *New Republic,* January 10, 1934, pp. 244–46.

Saposs, David J. "Employee Representation as Labor Organization," *Annals of the American Academy of Political and Social Science,* CLXXXIV (March, 1936), 192–98.

Saposs, David J. "Organizational and Procedural Changes in Employee Representation Plans," *Journal of Political Economy,* XLIV (December, 1936), 803–11.

Seidman, Joel. "Labor Policy of the Communist Party During World War II," *Industrial and Labor Relations Review,* IV (October, 1950), 55–69.

"Types of Employer-Employee Dealing," *Monthly Labor Review,* XLI (December, 1935), 1441–66.

U.S. Bureau of Labor Statistics. "Wage Chronology Series," *Monthly Labor Review,* December, 1948, to date.

Walker, Charles R. "Relief and Revolution," *Forum,* August, 1932, pp. 73–78.

Index

Index

Index

Index